THE CHEROKEE NATION OF INDIANS

 Native American Library

Herman J. Viola, General Editor
Director, National Anthropological Archives
National Museum of Natural History
Smithsonian Institution

THE CHEROKEE NATION OF INDIANS

by
Charles C. Royce

Introduction by
Richard Mack Bettis
President, Tulsa Tsa-La-Gi-Ya
Cherokee Community

A Smithsonian Institution Press Book

Aldine Publishing Company, *Chicago*

All illustrations in this book are from the National Anthropological Archives, Smithsonian Institution.

Copyright © 1975 by Smithsonian Institution Press

All rights reserved. No part of this publication may be reproduced or transmitted in any form or by any means, electronic or mechanical, including photocopy, recording, or any information storage and retrieval system, without permission in writing from the publisher.

First published 1975 by
Aldine Publishing Company
529 South Wabash Avenue
Chicago, Illinois 60605

ISBN: 0-202-01138-0 Clothbound edition
ISBN: 0-202-01139-9 Paperbound edition

Library of Congress Catalog Number 75-20708

Printed in the United States of America

CONTENTS

Preface *by Herman J. Viola*	vii
Introduction *by Richard Mack Bettis*	ix
Introduction	1
Treaty of November 28, 1785	
Material Provisions	5
Historical Data	6
Treaty of July 2, 1791	
Material Provisions	30
Historical Data	32
Treaty of February 17, 1792	
Material Provisions	41
Historical Data	41
Treaty of June 26, 1794	
Material Provisions	43
Historical Data	47
Treaty of October 2, 1798	
Material Provisions	46
Historical Data	47
Treaty of October 24, 1804	
Material Provisions	55
Historical Data	56
Treaties of October 25 and 27, 1805	
Material Provisions	61
Historical Data	62
Treaty of January 7, 1806	
Material Provisions	65

CONTENTS

Treaty of September 11, 1807
    Material Provisions ... 66
    Historical Data ... 67
Treaties of March 22, 1816
    Material Provisions ... 69
    Historical Data ... 71
Treaty of September 14, 1816
    Material Provisions ... 81
    Historical Data ... 82
Treaty of July 8, 1817
    Material Provisions ... 84
    Historical Data ... 86
Treaty of February 27, 1819
    Material Provisions ... 91
    Historical Data ... 93
Treaty of May 6, 1828
    Material Provisions ... 101
    Historical Data ... 103
Treaty of February 14, 1833
    Material Provisions ... 121
    Historical Data ... 123
Treaty of December 29, 1835
    Material Provisions ... 125
    Historical Data ... 130
Treaty of August 6, 1846
    Material Provisions ... 176
    Historical Data ... 178
Treaty of July 19, 1866
    Material Provisions ... 212
Treaty of April 27, 1868
    Material Provisions ... 218
    Historical Data ... 219
General Remarks ... 249
Biographical Notes ... 257
Maps ... 259
Index ... 265
Photo section begins on p. 139

PREFACE

The Bureau of American Ethnology was created in 1879 to collect, record, and document the history and culture of Indian tribes, especially in the United States. Data were published in 200 Bulletins and 81 Annual Reports, which were discontinued when the Bureau was amalgamated with the Department of Anthropology, National Museum of Natural History, Smithsonian Institution, in 1965.

This reorganization affected Archives of the Bureau of American Ethnology, which contained many documents of historic and scientific importance. In 1969, the name was changed to the National Anthropological Archives and activities were expanded. Collections are growing and representatives selected by Indian tribes are assisting in their documentation while receiving guidance in the acquisition, preservation, and use of archival materials.

The Native American Library, in which this book appears, is designed to make old and new data more accessible. It will contain both reprints from Bureau of American Ethnology publications with new introductions by Indians, and original works written or edited by Indians. Requests for reprints are initiated by the governing bodies of native American groups; copies are made available to members of the sponsoring tribe at cost and to other native American groups on a non-profit basis. In this way, we hope to assist in the wider dissemination to and by Indians of information on their heritage, which is also a significant part of the heritage of all other Americans.

Herman J. Viola
Director, National Anthropological Archives

INTRODUCTION

Aside from Charles Royce, the most important historian of the Cherokee was James Mooney, whose contribution was originally published in the Nineteenth Annual Report of the Bureau of American Ethnology. Having prepared an introduction to the reprint of that work, I found myself making comparisons and judgments on the style, accuracy, techniques, and other aspects of the two monographs in preparing this Introduction. Although both men worked at about the same time and dealt with some of the same material, their impact on me was very different. Mooney was easy to write about, but commenting on Royce required deliberate effort. However, when I compared their contributions, expression became easier. This drew my attention from their work to the men themselves. My psychological reaction suggested marked differences between Mooney and Royce, which are reflected in their writing. I felt that Mooney was a warm, personable individual who wrote from experience, whereas Royce was a serious student who consulted books instead of people. He seemed cold and impersonal, an observer rather than a participant. Is this contrast important? After long consideration, I believe that it has value. Since both authors are highly reliable, their different techniques and interests make their work complementary.

Using the old axiom that writing is about "people, places, or things," we can categorize Mooney's work as about "people" and Royce's as about "places and things." While there is some overlap, this characterization seems to fit. Mooney lived with the Cherokee and spoke their language. He became close friends with the people, so much so that he was privy to their innermost thoughts and practices. He wrote, for example, about Swimmer and other leading medicine men, about the sacred formulas, myths, secular songs and dances, medical songs, and many other very personal and sacred topics. Much of his work is biographical in form, dealing with Cherokee friends he consulted. Even today, a traditional Cherokee does not freely discuss these topics with an "outsider." We must conclude that Mooney was accepted by the people with little or no reservations.

Not so Royce. He wrote with an impersonal, academic, very studied approach. His "informant" was an extensive library on the Cherokee. His favorite subjects were treaties and boundary descriptions. He footnotes his work with long trails of writers who have gone before him. He quotes Hayward on tradition, Burke, Beverly, and Adair on history and Pericaut on history and geography, to name only five of literally hundreds of authors whose work he studied to write this book. He expands Mooney's earlier horizon of Cherokee history. Both are needed.

Today, informed Cherokee feel greatly indebted to Royce. Most, however, do not realize his connection with modern tribal activity. His accurate reporting on treaties and boundaries provided the data that enabled Earl Boyd Pierce, General Counsel of the Cherokee Tribe, over many years and with the help of Chief W. W. Keeler, to win legal claims for land that brought more than fourteen million dollars to the tribal treasury from the United States Government. Cases pending may add many times that amount.

The Tulsa *Tribune* of April 16, 1975, ran a full-page feature story on the present status of the Cherokee under the headline: "Cherokee Legal Claims Basis for Rejuvenation of Tribe." The four legal judgments that "provide the basis for the revitalized economy of the Cherokee Nation" emanate from the treaties of May 1828, February 1833, and December 1835, which are included in this reprint. The newspaper summarized the legal decisions as follows:

1. A $14.7 million award in 1961 by the Indian Claims Commission for additional payment for land in the Old Cherokee Outlet west of the Arkansas River.
2. A $4.2 million award in 1972 by the Commission for additional payment for Outlet land east of the Arkansas.
3. A 1970 decision by the U.S. Supreme Court that the Cherokee, along with the Choctaw and Chickasaw, own the Arkansas River bed from Fort Smith to Muskogee. The amount of money this will mean to the Cherokee is uncertain but could total several million dollars.
4. A decision by Cherokee attorneys to press a bill upon Congress for an appropriation of $13.6 million for 545,175 acres the gov-

ernment granted by patent to the tribe in 1838 (pursuant to the 1835 Treaty of New Echota) but never delivered.

The riverbed case, when concluded, will provide gas, oil, sand, gravel, and other mineral rights, plus potential for the development of recreation, hydroelectric power, and other facilities that will bring continuing income to the Tribe. All these pursuits are not empty hopes; they are realities.

Contemporary writings are brought to mind when one reads Royce's chronology of the treaties between Whites and the Cherokee. My first thought was "Trail of Broken Treaties." From the first treaty entered into by the Tribe (in South Carolina in 1721) up through the last, one traces the insidious expansion of White greed and need for territory across each parcel of Cherokee land, east to west. Each treaty begins with euphemisms, such as "Perpetual peace between the United States and the Cherokee Nation," "The Hatchet to be forever buried between the United States and the Cherokees," "The United States gives peace to the Cherokees." Each statement of friendship is followed by a description of what the government is taking from the Tribe.

Actually, not all the treaties were unconscionable in dollars paid, when measured against the market values of farmland or ranchland at the time. Each treaty is unilateral, however, in the sense that the Tribe really had no choice. The Cherokee wanted to remain in their homeland. Even money in excess of commercial worth is not just compensation for a homeland you love and do not want to sell. In this respect, each treaty amounted to confiscation of land. And land is lasting, dollars are not. History shows that if Cherokee land was wanted and the Tribe would not agree to sell or give it up by treaty, the White group involved would simply obtain an agreement signed by some lesser or insignificant chief or leader, or even individual members of the Tribe, and use those signatures as representing the official body of the Tribe. Such practices led to the murder of Doublehead, the Ridges, and Elias Boudinot by tribal loyalists. The Tribe considered the unauthorized treatymakers as traitors who sold them out. No doubt some of these signers were trying to avoid conflicts and bloodshed, knowing that the United States would take the land anyway, maybe without payment or treaty if the Tribe resisted.

The concept of dollars, blankets, and pots in exchange for land was used for several years before land-for-land became the vogue. As Royce points out, the land-for-land concept probably originated at least as early as 1803, when Thomas Jefferson suggested it. He had just acquired the Louisiana Territory and much of it was barren and dry plains, unneeded for settlement and considered worthless.

The description by Royce of the final months of the Cherokee in their homeland makes it clear why they still feel strong resentment toward Andrew Jackson. Originally a friend of the Tribe—in fact, a Cherokee saved his life at the Battle of New Orleans—he gave in to political expediency and ordered the Cherokee driven west into what was called "Indian Territory." Even that name was later eliminated; since 1907, it has been part of Oklahoma. The anti-Jackson sentiment aroused by the removal may explain why many Cherokee have traditionally voted Republican. Jackson was a Democrat, as were the leaders in Congress against the Cherokee. On the other hand, Davy Crockett of Tennessee, Henry Clay, Daniel Webster, and others who sided with the Cherokee were Republicans. Since most children grow up in the religion and politics of their parents, this historical perspective suggests a logical explanation for their political affiliation.

The Tulsa *Tribune* article cited earlier states that "the federal government's arrogant and inconsistent Indian policy in the 19th century is responsible for the money paid the Indians today." It quotes a conversation in 1889 between the U.S. Senate Territory Committee Chairman, Senator Butler, and the Cherokee Chief Joel Mayes concerning the Outlet land owned by the Tribe. The hopeless plight of the Cherokee, who had leased their land to cattlemen for grazing and used the money for government and school financing, is clear:

> THE CHAIRMAN: This $200,000 from the grazing leases is an income to your government.
>
> MR. MAYES: Yes, sir. It is a national revenue—$200,000 and if you should cut us off from that we would suffer for it. That is what would happen. We would have to stop our schools. We do not want to sell you that land now, I can tell you that.
>
> THE CHAIRMAN: Suppose we want to buy it?
>
> MR. MAYES: Well, it takes two to make a bargain. One man cannot make a trade all by himself.
>
> SEN. BUTLER: Unless he does it by force?
>
> MR. MAYES: Well, if it comes to that, of course I shall give up. We are not able to fight you. If we were we would not let you take the land.

Of course, the government did cancel the leases and the Cherokee were not only forced to sell the Outlet land, but to do so for $1.29 per acre when $3.75 per acre was the normal price. This action was judged by the Indian Claims Commission as duress and the price unconscionable in the 1961 and 1972 settlement cases cited above.

INTRODUCTION   xiii

As noted earlier, Royce does not emphasize people in connection with the places and treaties he otherwise so aptly describes and defines. The last part of his article, however, becomes less abstract. He describes personal relationships, events, and political implications surrounding the removal; he also describes conditions in Indian Territory after the removal. And while much of this seems to be second hand (it is heavily footnoted, showing it to be from the work of others), the writing departs from the usual Royce context and style. Certain passages are almost poetic and romantic. For example: "From the summit of their own Blue Ridge they could watch the tiny rivulets on either side of them dashing and bounding over their rocky beds in their eagerness to join and swell the ever increasing volume of waters rolling toward the Atlantic. . . . The bracing and invigorating atmosphere of their mountains was wafted to the valleys and low lands. . . . Their country was a succession of grand mountains clothed with dense forests. . . . The trophies of his skill and valor adorned the sides of his wigwam and furnished the theme for his boastful oratory and song."

The style of these excerpts leads one to wonder if they came from the same pen as the first part of the article. Did Royce have an editor who took liberties with his manuscript where precise dates, places, and quotes were not required?

When coupled with the Mooney monograph, this work brings the Cherokee from the time of European contact to the beginning of the 20th century. Even though approximately seventy-five years have elapsed since the monographs were published, Cherokee conditions are little changed. The small band in North Carolina is on the Qualla reservation and the larger western group are non-reservation Indians, becoming more and more mixed in blood with Whites. Today, most native-born northeastern Oklahomans boast of their Cherokee heritage and, except for immigrants within the last one or two generations, most citizens of the area do have a Cherokee heritage.

Since the Cherokee of Oklahoma are not set off by reservation fences or boundaries, they are not only more mixed racially but also more integrated into the cultural, social, and economic life of the state and region than most tribes. Some are still happy and content with their simple life in log cabins in extremely remote parts of the foothills of the Ozark Mountains that roll over into northeastern Oklahoma, but many have chosen to walk other paths. Will Rogers was one. Another is W. W. Keeler, the present Principal Chief of the Cherokee Nation, who recently retired as Chairman of the Board of Phillips Petroleum Company. Others are leaders in education, industry, or whatever career they have followed.

The money received by the Tribe from the settlements described above has been used to develop a modern and very functional complex of offices, training facilities, industries, motels, and related businesses and people-oriented activities. The tribal complex is three miles south of Tahlequah, Oklahoma, the original national capital of the Nation in Indian Territory. There have been some problems of adjustment, as one would expect, but it is hoped and felt that these are mainly "growing pains." Bilingual programs for students are being established for the first time, in and with the cooperation of schools with high concentrations of Cherokee students. The cultural heritage, native crafts, and the native tongue once again are in widespread evidence. A developing tourist industry in connection with the many tribal facilities and related places of interest is a big operation, visibly expanding each season.

In the summer of 1975, the Tribe voted on a constitution and elected a Chief and governing body. Four years previously, Cherokees went to the polls and chose their own Chief for the first time since Oklahoma statehood; prior to that time, a Chief had been appointed by the President. Self-government, or as it is now more commonly called, "self-determination," is becoming a reality. Community groups elect representatives who meet monthly, and with the Chief as needed, and have direct input into tribal activity.

These recent evidences of tribal growth and renewal are, by and large, made possible by the money from the land settlements. And the settlements can be traced to Cherokee lawyer Earl Boyd Pierce who read this volume by Royce, totaled acres and dollars against those given by the treaties, and came up short on both. There is no question that the government had acted wrongly. In conclusion, today's tribal successes owe much to Royce. Any serious student of treaties, land descriptions, and other data concerning U.S.-Cherokee relations now has this well-documented and accurate information available once again in convenient form.

Richard Mack Bettis
President
Tulsa Tsa-La-Gi-Ya Cherokee Community

THE CHEROKEE NATION OF INDIANS

INTRODUCTORY.

An historical atlas of Indian affairs has for some time past been in course of preparation under the direction of the Bureau of Ethnology, Smithsonian Institution.

The chief aim of this atlas is to show upon a series of State and Territorial maps the boundaries of the various tracts of country which have from time to time been acquired through the medium of treaty stipulation or act of Congress from the several Indian tribes resident within the present territory of the United States from the beginning of the Federal period to the present day.

Accompanying this atlas will be one or more volumes of historical text, wherein will be given with some detail a history of the official relations between the United States and these tribes. This will treat of the various negotiations for peace and for the acquisition of territory, the causes rendering such negotiations necessary, and the methods observed by the Government through its authorized agents in this diplomacy, as well as other matters of public concern growing out of the same.

The following monograph on the history of the Cherokees, with its accompanying maps, is given as an illustration of the character of the work in its treatment of each of the Indian tribes.

The maps are intended to show not only the ancestral but the present home of the Cherokees, and also to indicate the boundaries of the various tracts of territory purchased from them by the Colonial or Federal authorities from time to time since their first contact with the European settlements. A number of purchases made prior to the Federal period by individuals were unauthorized and unrecognized by the Colonial authorities, and their boundaries, though given in the text, are not laid down upon the map, because the same areas of territory were afterwards included within the limits of Colonial purchases.

In the preparation of this article, more particularly in the tracing out of the various boundary lines, much careful attention and research have been given to all available authorities or sources of information. The old manuscript records of the Government, the shelves of the Congressional Library, including its very large collection of American maps, local records, and the knowledge of "old settlers," as well as the accretions of various State historical societies, have been made to pay tribute to the subject.

In the course of these researches the writer has been met in his inquiries with a degree of courtesy and kindly assistance that merits public recognition.

Among others who have shown an earnest desire to promote the object of these investigations are Hon. John M. Lea, vice-president State Historical Society of Tennessee; General Robert N. Hood, Spencer Munson, and R. H. Armstrong, of Knoxville, Tenn. The writer is also deeply indebted to the Hon. Hiram Price, Commissioner of Indian Affairs, and E. L. Stevens, chief clerk, for the readiness with which they afforded him access to the records and files of the Indian Bureau. This permission was earnestly supplemented by the intelligent assistance and encouragement of Mr. C. A. Maxwell, chief of the Land Division, as well as that of R. F. Thompson and Paul Brodie, of the same Bureau, both of whom have taken special and constant pains to aid these researches.

To Captain Adams, of the Bureau of Topographical Engineers, the hearty thanks of the writer are due for many courtesies extended in the examination of the voluminous and valuable collection of maps belonging to that branch of the public service, and equal credit must be given to Mr. G. P. Strum, principal draughtsman of the General Land Office, and his assistants, for their uniform courtesy in affording access to the official plats and records of that Bureau.

The officers of the Congressional Library have also shown a marked degree of courtesy and interest.

The various cessions of land by the Cherokees alluded to in the text are numerically designated upon the accompanying maps, and are as follows:

COLONIAL PERIOD.

No.	Date and designation of Cherokee Treaties.	Description of cession.	Color.
1	Treaty of 1721 with South Carolina	Tract in South Carolina between Santee, Saluda, and Edisto Rivers.	Red.
2	Treaty of Nov. 24, 1755, with South Carolina	Tract in South Carolina between Wateree and Savannah Rivers.	Blue.
3	Treaty of Oct. 14, 1768, with British Superintendent of Indian Affairs.	Tract in Southwestern Virginia	Mauve.
4	Treaty of Oct. 18, 1770, at Lochaber, S. C.	Tract in Virginia, West Virginia, Northeastern Tennessee, and Eastern Kentucky, which is overlapped by No. 7.	Red.
5	Treaty of 1772 with Virginia	Tract in Virginia, West Virginia, and Eastern Kentucky.	Yellow.
6	Treaty of June 1, 1773, with British Superintendent of Indian Affairs.	Tract in Georgia, north of Broad River	Mauve.
7	Treaty of March 17, 1775, with Richard Henderson et al.	Tract in Kentucky, Virginia, and Tennessee (overlaps No. 4).	Blue.
8	Treaty of May 20, 1777, with South Carolina and Georgia.	Tract in Northwestern South Carolina	Red.
9	Treaty of July 20, 1777, with Virginia and North Carolina.	Tract in Western North Carolina and Northeastern Tennessee.	Green.
10	Treaty of May 31, 1783, with Georgia	Tract in Georgia, between Oconee and Tugaloo Rivers.	Green.

INTRODUCTION

FEDERAL PERIOD.

No.	Date and designation of Cherokee Treaties.	Description of cession.	Color.
10a	Treaty of Nov. 28, 1785, with United States	Tract in Western North Carolina	Yellow.
10b	......do......................................	Tract in Southern and Western Kentucky and Northern Tennessee.	Green.
11	Treaty of July 2, 1791, with United States	Tract in Western North Carolina and Eastern Tennessee.	Brown.
12	Treaty of Oct. 2, 1798, with United States	Tract in Tennessee, between Hawkins' Line, Tennessee River, and Chilhowee Mountain.	Red.
13	......do......................................	Tract in North Carolina, between Pickens and Meigs line.	Red.
14	......do......................................	Tract in Tennessee, between Clinch River and Cumberland Mountain.	Red.
15	Treaty of Oct. 24, 1804, with United States	Tract in Georgia, known as Wafford's Settlement.	Red.
16	Treaty of Oct. 25, 1805, with United States	Tract in Kentucky and Tennessee, west of Tennessee River and Cumberland Mountain.	Yellow.
17	Treaty of Oct. 27, 1805, with United States	Tract in Tennessee of one section at Southwest Point.	Green.
18	......do......................................	First island in Tennessee River above the mouth of Clinch River.	Mauve.
19	Treaty of Jan. 7, 1806, with United States	Tract in Tennessee and Alabama, between Tennessee and Duck Rivers.	Red.
20	......do......................................	Long or Great Island in Holston River	Red.
21	Treaty of Mar. 22, 1816, with United States	Tract in northwest corner of South Carolina	Blue.
22	Treaty of Sept. 14, 1816, with United States	Tract in Alabama and Mississippi	Green.
23	Treaty of July 8, 1817, with United States	Tract in Northeastern Georgia	Yellow.
24	......do......................................	Tract in Southern Tennessee	Green.
25	......do......................................	Tract in Northern Alabama, between Cypress and Elk Rivers.	Blue.
26	......do......................................	Tract in Northern Alabama, above mouth of Spring Creek on Tennessee River.	Blue.
27	Treaty of Feb. 27, 1819, with United States	Tract in Northern Alabama and Southern Tennessee.	Yellow.
28	......do......................................	Tract in Southern Tennessee, on Tennessee River.	Red.
29	......do......................................	Tract in Tennessee, North Carolina, and Georgia.	Mauve.
30	......do......................................	Jolly's Island, in Tennessee River	Red.
31	......do......................................	Small tract in Tennessee, at and below the mouth of Clinch River.	Green.
32	......do......................................	Tract of 12 miles square, on Tennessee River, in Alabama.	Mauve.
33	......do......................................	Tract 1 mile square, in Tennessee, at foot of Cumberland Mountain.	Green.
34	......do......................................	Tract of 1 mile square, at Cherokee Talootiske's residence.	Green.
35	......do......................................	Tract of 3 square miles, opposite mouth of Hiwassee River.	Green.
36	Treaty of Dec. 29, 1835, with United States	Tract in Alabama, Georgia and Tennessee, being all remaining lands east of the Mississippi River.	Blue.
37	Treaty of May 6, 1828, with United States	This treaty was with the Cherokees residing west of the Mississippi, and they ceded the lands in Arkansas granted them by treaties of 1817 and 1819, receiving in exchange a tract further west. These latter boundaries were subsequently modified and enlarged by the treaties of Feb. 14, 1833, and Dec. 29, 1835.	Green.
38	Treaty of July 19, 1866, with United States	Tract known as "Neutral Land," in Kansas, ceded in trust to be sold by the United States for the benefit of the Cherokees.	Red.
39	......do......................................	Tract known as "Cherokee Strip," in Kansas, ceded in trust to be sold for the benefit of the Cherokees by the United States.	Yellow.
40	......do......................................	Tract sold to Osages	Green.
41	......do......................................	Tract sold to Kansas or Kaws	Red.
42	......do......................................	Tract sold to Pawnees	Red.
43	......do......................................	Tract sold to Poncas	Red.
44	......do......................................	Tract sold to Nez Percés	Yellow.
45	......do......................................	Tract sold to Otoes and Missourias	Yellow.
46	Present country of the Cherokees east of 96° W. longitude.	This is the country now actually occupied and to be permanently retained by the Cherokees.	Red.
47	Present country of the Cherokees west of 96° W. longitude.	This is the remnant of the country dedicated by the treaty of July 19, 1866, to the location of other friendly tribes. The Cherokees retain their title to and control over it until actual purchase by and location of other tribes thereon.	Blue.

The arrangement of the historical text has seemed to the writer to be that best suited to the object in view. As will be observed, an abstract of the salient provisions of each treaty is given, beginning with the first treaty concluded between the Cherokee Nation and the United States of America. In each instance, immediately following this abstract, will be found the historical data covering the period and the events leading to its negotiation, as well as those of the subsequent period intimately connected with the results of such treaty.

TREATIES WITH THE CHEROKEES.

TREATY CONCLUDED NOVEMBER 28, 1785.[1]

At Hopewell, on the Keowee River, in South Carolina, between Benjamin Hawkins, Andrew Pickens, Joseph Martin, and Lachlane M'Intosh, Commissioners Plenipotentiary of the United States, and the Headmen and Warriors of all the Cherokees.

MATERIAL PROVISIONS.

The United States give peace to the Cherokees and receive them into favor and protection on the following conditions:

1. The Cherokees to restore to liberty all prisoners citizens of the United States or subjects of their allies; also, all negroes and other property taken from citizens during the late war.
2. The United States to restore to the Cherokees all Indian prisoners taken during the late war.
3. The Cherokees to acknowledge themselves under the exclusive protection of the United States.
4. The boundary line between the Cherokees' hunting-ground and the United States to be as follows, viz: Begin at the mouth of Duck River on the Tennessee; thence northeast to the ridge dividing the waters falling into the Cumberland from those falling into the Tennessee; thence eastwardly along said ridge to a northeast line to be run, which shall strike Cumberland River 40 miles above Nashville; thence along said line to the river; thence up the river to the ford where the Kentucky road crosses; thence to Campbell's line near Cumberland Gap; thence to the mouth of Claud's Creek on Holstein; thence to Chimney-Top Mountain; thence to Camp Creek, near the mouth of Big Limestone on Nolichucky; thence southerly six (6) miles to a mountain; thence south to the North Carolina line; thence to the South Carolina Indian boundary, and along the same southwest over the top of Oconee Mountain till it shall strike Tugaloo River; thence a direct line to the top of Currohee Mountain; thence to the head of the south fork of Oconee River.

---

[1] United States Statutes at Large, Vol. VII, p. 18.

5. Citizens of the United States or persons other than Indians who settle or attempt to settle on lands west or south of said boundary and refuse to remove within six months after ratification of this treaty to forfeit the protection of the United States, and the Indians to punish them or not, as they please: *Provided,* That this article shall not extend to the people settled between the fork of French Broad and Holstein Rivers, whose status shall be determined by Congress.

6. The Cherokees to deliver up for punishment all Indian criminals for offenses against citizens of the United States.

7. Citizens of the United States committing crimes against Indians to be punished by the United States in the presence of the Cherokees, to whom due notice of the time and place of such intended punishment shall be given.

8. Retaliation declared unjust and not to be practiced.

9. The United States to have sole right of regulating trade with the Indians and managing their affairs.

10. Traders to have liberty to trade with the Cherokees until Congress shall adopt regulations relative thereto.

11. Cherokees to give notice of any designs formed by other tribes against the peace, trade, or interests of the United States.

12. Cherokees to have the right to send a deputy of their choice to Congress whenever they think fit.

13. The hatchet to be forever buried between the United States and Cherokees.

HISTORICAL DATA.

FERNANDO DE SOTO'S EXPEDITION.

The Cherokee Nation has probably occupied a more prominent place in the affairs and history of what is now the United States of America, since the date of the early European settlements, than any other tribe, nation, or confederacy of Indians, unless it be possible to except the powerful and warlike league of the Iroquois or Six Nations of New York.

It is almost certain that they were visited at a very early period following the discovery of the American continent by that daring and enthusiastic Spaniard, Fernando De Soto.

In determining the exact route pursued by him from his landing in Florida to his death beyond the Mississippi, many insuperable difficulties present themselves, arising not only from an inadequate description on the part of the historian of the courses and distances pursued, but from many statements made by him that are irreconcilable with an accurate knowledge of the topographic detail of the country traversed.

A narrative of the expedition, "by a gentleman of Elvas," was published at Evora in 1557, and translated from the Portuguese by Richard Hakluyt, of London, in 1609. From this narrative it appears that after traveling a long distance in a northeasterly direction from his point of landing on the west coast of Florida, De Soto reached, in the spring of 1540, an Indian town called by the narrator "Cutifachiqui." From the early American maps of De L'Isle and others, upon which is delineated the supposed route of De Soto, this town appears to be located on the Santee River, and, as alleged by the "gentleman of Elvas," on the authority of the inhabitants, was two days' journey from the sea-coast.

The expedition left Cutifachiqui on the 3d of May, 1540, and pursued a northward course for the period of seven days, when it came to a province called Chelaque, "the poorest country of maize that was seen in Florida." It is recorded that the Indians of this province "feed upon roots and herbs, which they seek in the fields, and upon wild beasts, which they kill with their bows and arrows, and are a very gentle people. All of them go naked and are very lean."

That this word "Chalaque" is identical with our modern Cherokee would appear to be almost an assured fact. The distance and route pursued by the expedition are both strongly corroborative of this assumption. The orthography of the name was probably taken by the Spaniards from the Muscogee pronunciation, heard by them among the Creeks, Choctaws, and Chickasaws. It is asserted by William Bartram, in his travels through that region in the eighteenth century, that in the "Muscogulge" language the letter "r" is not sounded in a single word, but that on the contrary it occurs very frequently in the Cherokee tongue.[1]

Through this province of Chalaque De Soto passed, still pursuing his northward course for five days until he reached the province of "Xualla," a name much resembling the modern Cherokee word Qualla. The route from Cutifachiqui to Xualla lay, for the most part, through a hilly country. From the latter province the expedition changed its course to the west, trending a little to the south, and over "very rough and high hills," reaching at the end of five days a town or province which was called "Guaxule," and two days later a town called "Canasagua," an orthography almost identical with the modern Cherokee name of Canasauga, as applied to both a stream and a town within their Georgia limits.

Assuming that these people, whose territory De Soto thus traversed, were the ancestors of the modern Cherokees, it is the first mention made of them by European discoverers and more than a century anterior to the period when they first became known to the pioneers of permanent European occupation and settlement.

Earliest map.—The earliest map upon which I have found "Chalaqua" located is that of "Florida et Apalche" by Cornely Wytfliet, published

---

[1] I am informed by Colonel Bushyhead, principal chief of the Cherokee Nation, that Bartram is mistaken in his latter assumption. The letter "r" was never used except among the Overhill Cherokees, and occurred very infrequently with them.

in 1597.[1] This location is based upon the narrative of De Soto's expedition, and is fixed a short distance east of the Savannah River and immediately south of the Appalachian Mountains. "Xualla" is placed to the west of and near the headwaters of the "Secco" or Savannah River.

EARLY TRADITIONS.

Haywood, in his Natural and Aboriginal History of Tennessee, records many of the traditions concerning the origin and the primal habitat of the Cherokees. He notes the fact that they were firmly established on the Tennessee or Hogohege River before the year 1650, and exercised dominion over all the country on the east side of the Alleghany Mountains, including the headwaters of the Yadkin, Catawba, Broad, and Savannah Rivers, and that from thence westward they claimed the country as far as the Ohio, and thence to the headwaters of the Chattahoochee and Alabama. One tradition which he alleges existed among them asserts their migration from the west to the upper waters of the Ohio, where they erected the mounds on Grave Creek, gradually working eastward across the Alleghany Mountains to the neighborhood of Monticello, Va., and along the Appomattox River.

From this point, it is alleged, they removed to the Tennessee country about 1623, when the Virginians suddenly and unexpectedly fell upon and massacred the Indians throughout the colony. After this massacre, the story goes, they came to New River and made a temporary settlement there as well as one on the head of the Holston; but, owing to the enmity of the northern Indians, they removed in a short time to the Little Tennessee and founded what were known as "Middle Settlements." Another tribe, he alleges, came from the neighborhood of Charleston, South Carolina, and settled lower down the Tennessee. This branch called themselves "Ketawanga," and came last into the country. The tradition as to those who came from Virginia seeks also to establish the idea that the Powhatan Indians were Cherokees. The whole story is of the vaguest character, and if the remainder has no stronger claims to credibility than their alleged identity with the Powhatans, it is scarcely worthy of record except as a matter of curiosity.

In fact the explorations of De Soto leave almost convincing proof that the Cherokees were occupying a large proportion of their more modern territory nearly a century prior to their supposed removal from the Appomattox.

Pickett, in his History of Alabama, improves upon the legend of Haywood by asserting as a well established fact what the latter only presumes to offer as a tradition.

However, as affording a possible confirmation of the legend related by Haywood concerning their early location in Eastern Virginia, it may

---

[1] The full title of this work is "Descriptionis Ptolemaicæ Augmentum; sive Occidentis Notitia, brevi commentario illustrata, studio et opera Cornely Wytfliet, Louaniensis. Lovanii, Typis Iohannis Bogardi, anno Domini MDXCVII."

be worth while to allude to a tradition preserved among the Mohican or Stockbridge tribe. It appears that in 1818 the Delawares, who were then residing on White River, in Indiana, ceded their claim to lands in that region to the United States. This land had been conditionally given by the Miamis many years before to the Delawares, in conjunction with the "Moheokunnuks" (or Stockbridges) and Munsees. Many of the latter two tribes or bands, including a remnant of the Nanticokes, had not yet removed to their western possessions, though they were preparing to remove. When they ascertained that the Delawares had ceded the lands to the United States without their consent, they objected and sought to have the cession annulled.

In connection with a petition presented to Congress by them on the subject in the year 1819, they set forth in detail the tradition alluded to. The story had been handed down to them from their ancestors that "many thousand moons ago" before the white men came over the "great water," the Delawares dwelt along the banks of the river that bears their name. They had enjoyed a long era of peace and prosperity when the Cherokees, Nanticokes, and some other nation whose name had been forgotten, envying their condition, came from the south with a great army and made war upon them. They vanquished the Delawares and drove them to an island in the river. The latter sent for assistance to the Mohicans, who promptly came to their relief, and the invaders were in turn defeated with great slaughter and put to flight. They sued for peace, and it was granted on condition that they should return home and never again make war on the Delawares or their allies. These terms were agreed to and the Cherokees and Nanticokes ever remained faithful to the conditions of the treaty.

The inference to be drawn from this legend, if it can be given any credit whatever, would lead to the belief that the Cherokees and the Nanticokes were at that time neighbors and allies. The original home of the Nanticokes on the Eastern Shore of Maryland is well known, and if the Cherokees (or at least this portion of them) were then resident beyond the Alleghanies, with sundry other powerful tribes occupying the territory between them and the Nanticokes, it is unlikely that any such alliance for offensive operations would have existed between them. Either the tradition is fabulous or at least a portion of the Cherokees were probably at one time residents of the Eastern slope of Virginia.

The Delawares also have a tradition that they came originally from the west, and found a tribe called by them Allegewi or Allegans occupying the eastern portion of the Ohio Valley. With the aid of the Iroquois, with whom they came in contact about the same time, the Delawares succeeded in driving the Allegans out of the Ohio Valley to the southward.

Schoolcraft suggests the identity of the Allegans with the Cherokees, an idea that would seem to be confirmatory of the tradition given by Haywood, in so far as it relates to an early Cherokee occupancy of Ohio.

EARLY CONTACT WITH VIRGINIA COLONISTS.

Whatever the degree of probability attending these legends, it would seem that the settlers of Virginia had an acquaintance with the Cherokees prior to that of the South Carolina immigrants, who for a number of years after their first occupation confined their explorations to a narrow strip of country in the vicinity of the sea-coast, while the Virginians had been gradually extending their settlements far up toward the headwaters of the James River and had early perceived the profits to be derived from the Indian trade.

Sir William Berkeley, governor of Virginia, equipped an expedition, consisting of fourteen Englishmen and an equal number of Virginia Indians, for the exploration of the country to the west of the existing settlements. The party was under the command of Capt. Henry Batt, and in seven days' travel from their point of departure, at Appomattox, they reached the foot of the mountains. The first ridge they crossed is described as not being very high or steep, but the succeeding ones "seemed to touch the clouds," and were so steep that an average day's march did not exceed three miles.

They came upon extensive and fertile valleys, covered with luxuriant grass, and found the forests abounding in all kinds of game, including turkeys, deer, elk, and buffalo. After passing beyond the mountains they entered an extensive level country, through which a stream flowed in a westward course, and after following it for a few days they reached some old fields and recently deserted Indian cabins. Beyond this point their Indian guides refused to proceed, alleging that not far away dwelt a powerful tribe that never suffered strangers who discovered their towns to return alive, and the expedition was therefore compelled to return. According to the historian, Burke, this expedition took place in 1667, while Beverly, not quite so definite, assigns it to the decade between 1666 and 1676.[1] It is believed that the powerful nation of Indians alluded to in the narrative of this expedition was the Cherokees, and, if so, it is apparently the first allusion made to them in the history of the colonial settlements.

That the Virginians were the first to be brought in contact with the Cherokees is further evidenced by the fact that in 1690 an Indian trader from that colony, bearing the name of Daugherty, had taken up his residence among them, which is alleged by the historian[2] to have been several years before any knowledge of the existence of the Cherokees reached the settlers on Ashley River in South Carolina.

EARLY RELATIONS WITH CAROLINA COLONISTS.

The first formal introduction of the Cherokees to the notice of the people of that colony occurred in the year 1693,[3] when twenty Cherokee

---

[1] Campbell's Virginia, p. 268.
[2] Logan's South Carolina, Vol. I, p. 168.
[3] Martin's North Carolina, Vol. I, p. 194.

chiefs visited Charleston, with proposals of friendship, and at the same time solicited the assistance of the governor in their operations against the Esau and Coosaw tribes, who had captured and carried off a number of Cherokees.

The Savannah Indians, it seems, had also been engaged in incursions against them, in the course of which they had captured a number of Cherokees and sold them to the colonial authorities as slaves.

The delegation urgently solicited the governor's protection from the further aggressions of these enemies and the return of their bondaged countrymen. The desired protection was promised them, but as their enslaved brethren had already been shipped to the West Indies and sold into slavery there, it was impossible to return them.

The extreme eastern settlements of the Cherokees at this time were within the limits of the present Chester and Fairfield districts, South Carolina, which lie between the Catawba and Broad Rivers.[1]

MENTION BY VARIOUS EARLY AUTHORS.

We next find an allusion to the Cherokees in the annals of Louisiana by M. Pericaut, who mentions in his chronicle of the events of the year 1702, that " ten leagues from the mouth of this river [Ohio] another falls into it called Kasquinempas [Tennessee]. It takes its source from the neighborhood of the Carolinas and passes through the village of the Cherokees, a populous nation that number some fifty thousand warriors," another example of the enormous overestimates of aboriginal population to which the earlier travelers and writers were so prone.

Again, in 1708, the same author relates that "about this time two Mobilians who had married in the Alibamon nation, and who lived among them with their families, discovered that that nation was inimical to the Mobilians as well as the French, and had made a league with the Cheraquis, the Abeikas, and the Conchaques to wage war against the French and Mobilians and burn their villages around our fort."

On various early maps of North America, and particularly those of De L'Isle, between the years 1700 and 1712, will be found indicated upon the extreme headwaters of the Holston and Clinch Rivers, "gros villages des Cheraqui." These villages correspond in location with the great nation alluded to in the narrative of Sir William Berkeley's expedition.

Upon the same maps will be found designated the sites of sundry other Cherokee villages, several of which are on the extreme headwaters of the "R. des Chaouanons." This river, although indicated on the map as emptying into the Atlantic Ocean to the west of the Santee, from its relation to the other streams in that vicinity, is believed to be intended for the Broad River, which is a principal northwest branch of the Santee. Other towns will also be found on the banks of the Upper Catawba, and they are, as well, quite numerous along the headwaters of the " R. des Caouilas " or Savannah and of the Little Tennessee.

---

[1] Logan's South Carolina, Vol. I, p. 141.

Mention is again found of the Cherokees in the year 1712, when 218 of them accompanied Colonel Barnwell in his expedition against the hostile Tuscaroras and aided in the subjugation of that savage tribe, though along the route of Barnwell's march the settlers were very nearly persuaded that they suffered greater damage to property from the freebooting propensities of their Indian allies than from the open hostilities of their savage enemies.

The old colonial records of South Carolina also contain mention in the following year (1713) of the fact that Peter St. Julien was arraigned on the charge of holding two Cherokee women in slavery.[1]

In 1715 the Yamassees, a powerful and hitherto friendly tribe, occupying the southwesterly portion of the colony of South Carolina and extending to and beyond the Savannah River, declared open hostilities against the settlers. In the desperate struggle that ensued, we find in full alliance with them the Cherokees, as well as the Creeks and Appalachians.

In his historical journal of the establishment of the French in Louisiana, Bernard de la Harpe states that " in January, 1716, some of the Cheraquis Indians, who lived northeast of Mobile, killed MM. de Ramsay and de Longueil. Some time after, the father of the latter gentleman, the King's lieutenant in Canada, engaged the Iroquois to surprise this tribe. They sacked two of their villages and obliged the rest to retreat towards New England."

TERRITORY OF CHEROKEES AT PERIOD OF ENGLISH SETTLEMENT.

At the time of the English settlement of the Carolinas the Cherokees occupied a diversified and well-watered region of country of large extent upon the waters of the Catawba, Broad, Saluda, Keowee, Tugaloo, Savannah, and Coosa Rivers on the east and south, and several of the tributaries of the Tennessee on the north and west. It is impossible at this late day to define with absolute accuracy the original limits of the Cherokee claim. In fact, like all other tribes, they had no definite and concurrent understanding with their surrounding savage neighbors where the possessions of the one left off and those of the other began. The strength of their title to any particular tract of country usually decreased in proportion to the increase of the distance from their villages; and it commonly followed as a result, that a considerable strip of territory between the settlements of two powerful tribes, though claimed by both, was practically considered as neutral ground and the common hunting ground of both.

As has already been stated, the extreme eastern settlements of the Cherokees in South Carolina in 1693 were in the district of country lying between the Catawba and Broad Rivers, and no claim has been found showing the existence at any time of any assertion of territorial right

---

[1] Logan's South Carolina, Vol. I, p. 182.

in their behalf to the east of the former stream. But nevertheless, on Bowen's map of 1752 (obviously copied from earlier maps), there is laid down the name of "Keowee Old Town." The location of this town was on Deep River in the vicinity of the present town of Ashborough, N. C. It was a favorite name of the Cherokees among their towns, and affords a strong evidence of at least a temporary residence of a portion of the tribe in that vicinity. A map executed by John Senex in 1721 defines the Indian boundary in this region as following the Catawba, Wateree, and Santee Rivers as far down as the most westerly bend of the latter stream, in the vicinity of the boundary line between Orangeburg and Charleston districts, whence it pursued a southwesterly course to the Edisto River, which it followed to the sea-coast. The southern portion of this boundary was of course a definition of limits between Carolina and the Creeks, or rather of certain tribes that formed component parts of the Creek confederacy. No evidence has been discovered tending to show an extension of Cherokee limits in a southerly direction beyond the point mentioned above on the Edisto River, which, as near as can be ascertained, was at the junction of the North and South Edisto. Following from thence up the South Edisto to its source the boundary pursued a southwesterly course, striking the Savannah River in the vicinity of the mouth of Stevens Creek, and proceeding thence northwardly along the Savannah.

On the borders of Virginia and North Carolina the ancient limits of the Cherokees seem to be also shrouded in more or less doubt and confusion. In general terms, however, it may be said that after following the Catawba River to its source in the Blue Ridge the course of those mountains was pursued until their intersection with the continuation of the Great Iron Mountain range, near Floyd Court-House, Va., and thence to the waters of the Kanawha or New River, whence their claim continued down that stream to the Ohio. At a later date they also set up a claim to the country extending from the mouth of the Kanawha down the Ohio to the ridge dividing the waters of the Cumberland from those of the Tennessee at the mouths of those streams, and thence following that ridge to a point northeast of the mouth of Duck River; thence to the mouth of Duck River on the Tennessee, and continuing up with the course of the latter river to Bear Creek; up the latter to a point called Flat Rock, and thence to the Ten Islands in Coosa River, &c.

That portion of the country thus covered, comprising a large part of the present States of West Virginia and Kentucky, was also claimed by the Six Nations by right of former conquest, as well as by the Shawnees and Delawares.

Adair, a trader for forty years among the Cherokees, who traveled extensively through their country about the middle of the eighteenth century, thus specifically outlines the boundaries of their country at that period: "The country lies in about 34 degrees north latitude at the distance of 340 computed miles to the northwest of Charlestown,—140 miles west-southwest from the Katahba Nation,—and almost 200 miles to the north of the Muskohge or Creek country. They are settled nearly in an east and west course about 140 miles in length from the lower towns, where Fort-Prince-George stands, to the late unfortunate Fort-Loudon. The natives make two divisions of their country, which they term '*Ayrate*' and '*Otarre*,' the one signifying 'low' and the other 'mountainous.'"

POPULATION.

In point of numbers the Cherokee population now considerably exceeds that first enumerated by the early colonial authorities. As early as 1715 the proprietors of the South Carolina Plantation instructed Governor Robert Johnson to cause a census to be taken of all the Indian tribes within that jurisdiction, and from his report it appears that the Cherokee Nation at that time contained thirty towns and an aggregate population of 11,210, of whom 4,000 were warriors. Adair alleges that in 1735, or thereabouts, according to the computation of the traders, their warriors numbered 6,000, but that in 1738 the ravages of the small-pox reduced their population one-half within one year. Indeed, this disaster, coupled with the losses sustained in their conflicts with the whites and with neighboring tribes, had so far wasted their ranks that a half century after the census taken by Governor Johnson they were estimated by the traders to have but 2,300 warriors.[1] By the last report of the Commissioner of Indian Affairs the total population is estimated to number 22,000.[2] It is true that considerable of this increase is attributable to the fact that several other small tribes or bands, within a few years past, have merged their tribal existence in that of the Cherokees. Independent of this fact, however, they have maintained a slow but steady increase in numbers for many years, with the exception of the severe losses sustained during the disastrous period of the late southern rebellion.

OLD CHEROKEE TOWNS.

It is perhaps impossible to give a complete list of the old Cherokee towns and their location; but in 1755 the authorities of South Carolina, in remodeling the old and prescribing new regulations for the government of the Indian trade, divided the whole Cherokee country into six hunting districts, viz:

1. *Over Hill Towns.*—Great Tellico, Chatugee, Tennessee, Chote, Toqua, Sittiquo, and Talassee.
2. *Valley Towns.*—Euforsee, Conastee, Little Telliquo, Cotocanahut, Nayowee, Tomatly, and Chewohe.
3. *Middle Towns.*—Joree, Watoge, Nuckasee.

---

[1] Adair's American Indians.
[2] Report Commissioner Indian Affairs for 1883, p. 272.

HISTORICAL DATA

4. *Keowee Towns.*—Keowee, Tricentee, Echoee, Torsee, Cowee, Torsalla, Coweeshee, and Elejoy.

5. *Out Towns.*—Tucharechee, Kittowa, Conontoroy, Steecoy, Oustanale, and Tuckasegee.

6. *Lower Towns.*—Tomassee, Oustestee, Cheowie, Estatoie, Tosawa, Keowee, and Oustanalle.

About twenty years later, Bartram,[1] who traversed the country, gives the names of forty-three Cherokee towns and villages then existing and 'nhabited as follows:

No.	Name.	Where situated.
1	Echoe	On the Tanase east of the Jore Mountains.
2	Nucasse	
3	Whatoga	
4	Cowe	
5	Ticoloosa	Inland, on the branches of the Tanase.
6	Jore	
7	Conisca	
8	Nowe	
9	Tomothle	On the Tanase over the Jore Mountains.
10	Noewe	
11	Tellico	
12	Clennuse	
13	Ocunnolufte	
14	Chewe	
15	Quanuse	
16	Tellowe	
17	Tellico	Inland towns on the branches of the Tanase and other waters over the Jore Mountains.
18	Chatuga	
19	Hiwasse	
20	Chewase	
21	Nuanha	
22	Tallase	Overhill towns on the Tanase or Cherokee River.
23	Chelowe	
24	Sette	
25	Chote, great	
26	Joco	
27	Tahasse	
28	Tamahle	
29	Tuskege	
30	— — Big Island	
31	Nilaque	
32	Niowe	
33	Sinica	Lower towns east of the mountains on the Savanna or Keowe River.
34	Keowe	
35	Kulsage	
36	Tugilo	Lower towns east of the mountains on Tugilo River.
37	Estotowe	
38	Qualatche	Lower towns on Flint River.
39	Chote	
40	Estotowe, great	Towns on the waters of other rivers.
41	Allagae	
42	Jore	
43	Naeoche	

Mouzon's map of 1771 gives the names of several Lower Cherokee towns not already mentioned. Among these may be enumerated, on the Tugalco River and its branches, Turruraw, Nayowee, Tetohe, Chagee, Tussee, Chicherohe, Echay, and Takwashnaw; on the Keowee, New Keowee, and Quacoretche; and on the Seneca, Acounee.

In subsequent years, through frequent and long continued conflicts with the ever advancing white settlements and the successive treaties whereby the Cherokees gradually yielded portions of their domain, the

---

[1] Bartram's Travels in North America from 1773 to 1778, p. 371.

location and names of their towns were continually changing until the final removal of the nation west of the Mississippi.¹

EXPULSION OF SHAWNEES BY CHEROKEES AND CHICKASAWS.

In the latter portion of the seventeenth century the Shawnees, or a portion of them, had their villages on the Cumberland, and to some extent, perhaps, on the Tennessee also. They were still occupying that region as late as 1714, when they were visited by M. Charleville, a French trader, but having about this time incurred the hostility of the Cherokees and Chickasaws they were driven from the country. Many years later, in the adjustment of a territorial dispute between the Cherokees and Chickasaws, each nation claimed the sole honor of driving out the Shawnees, and hence, by right of conquest, the title to the territory formerly inhabited by the latter. The Chickasaws evidently had the best of the controversy, though some concessions were made to the Cherokees in the matter when the United States came to negotiate for the purchase of the controverted territory.

TREATY RELATIONS WITH THE COLONIES.

Treaty and purchase of 1721.—The treaty relations between the Cherokees and the whites began in 1721, when jealousy of French territorial encroachments persuaded Governor Nicholson of South Carolina to invite the Cherokees to a general congress, with a view to the conclusion of a treaty of peace and commerce.

The invitation was accepted, and delegates attended from thirty-seven towns, with whom, after smoking the pipe of peace and distributing presents, he agreed upon defined boundaries and appointed an agent to superintend their affairs.²

Treaty of 1730.—Again, in 1730, the authorities of North Carolina commissioned Sir Alexander Cumming to conclude a treaty of alliance with the Cherokees. In April of that year the chiefs and warriors of the nation met him at Requasse, near the sources of the Hiwassee River, acknowledged King George as their sovereign, and sent a delegation of six warriors to carry the crown of the nation (consisting of five eagle tails and four scalps) to England and do homage to the King, where they concluded a treaty of peace and commerce at Dover on the 30th of June.

---

¹ From a distribution roll of Cherokee annuities paid in the year 1799 it appears that there were then 51 Cherokee towns, designated as follows: Oostinawley, Creek Path, Aumoia, Nicojack, Running Water, Ellijay, Cabben, High Tower, Pine Log, High Tower Forks, Tocoah, Coosawaytee, Crowtown, Shoemeck, Aumuchee, Tulloolah, Willstown, Acohee, Cuclon, Duck-town, Ailigulsha, Highwassee, Tennessee, Lookout Mountain, Noyohee, Tusquittee, Coosa, Nantiyallee, Saukee, Keyukee, Red Bank, Nukeza, Cowpens, Telassee, Buffalo Town, Little Tellico, Rabbit Trap, Notley, Turnip Mountain, Sallicoah, Kautika, Tausitu, Watoga, Cowee, Chillhoway, Chestuee, Turkey Town, Toquah, Chota, Big Tellico, and Tusskegee.

² Ramsey's Annals of Tennessee, p. 46.

In this treaty they stipulated:
1. To submit to the sovereignty of the King and his successors.
2. Not to trade with any other nation but the English.
3. Not to permit any but English to build forts or cabins or plant corn among them.
4. To apprehend and deliver runaway negroes.
5. To surrender any Indian killing an Englishman.[1]

Treaty and purchase of 1755.—November 24, 1755, a further treaty was concluded between the Cherokees and Governor Glenn, of South Carolina. By its terms the former ceded to Great Britain a territory which included the limits of the modern districts of Abbeville, Edgefield, Laurens, Union, Spartanburg, Newberry, Chester, Fairfield, Richland, and York, and deeds of conveyance were drawn up and formally executed therefor.[2] This cession included a tract of country between the Broad and Catawba Rivers which was also claimed and generally conceded to belong to the Catawba Nation, the boundary line between the latter and the Cherokees being usually fixed as the Broad River.[3] One of the main objects of this treaty was to prevent an alliance between the Cherokees and the French.

Treaty of 1756.—In the year 1756 Hugh Waddell was commissioned by the authorities of North Carolina to treat with the Cherokees and Catawbas. In pursuance of this authority he concluded a treaty of alliance with both nations.[4] Governor Glenn, also, in the same year erected a chain of military posts on the frontiers of his recent purchase. These consisted of Fort Prince George, on the Savannah, within gunshot of the Indian town of Keowee; Fort Moore, 170 miles farther down the river; and Fort Loudon, on the south bank of Tennessee River, at the highest point of navigation, at the mouth of Tellico River.[5]

Captain Jack's purchase.—A grant signed by Arthur Dobbs, governor of North Carolina, *et al.*, and by The Little Carpenter, half king of the Over-Hill Cherokees, made to Capt. Patrick Jack, of Pennsylvania, is recorded in the register's office of Knox County, Tennessee. It purports to have been made at a council held at Tennessee River, March 1, 1757, consideration $400, and conveys to Captain Jack 15 miles square south of Tennessee River. The grant itself confirmatory of the purchase by Captain Jack is dated at a general council held at Catawba River, May 7, 1762.[6]

Treaty of 1760.—The French finally succeeded in enlisting the active sympathy of the Cherokees in their war with Great Britain. Governor

---

[1] Martin's North Carolina, Vol. II, pp. 3, 9, and 11.
[2] Hewat's History of South Carolina and Georgia, Vol. II, pp. 203, 204.
[3] Broad River was formerly known as Eswaw-Huppedaw or Line River. See Mills' Statistics of South Carolina, p. 555.
[4] Williamson's North Carolina, Vol. II, p. 87.
[5] Martin's North Carolina, Vol. II, p. 87.
[6] Ramsey's Annals of Tennessee, p. 68.

Littleton, of South Carolina, marched against the Indians and defeated them, after which, in 1760, he concluded a treaty of peace with them. By its terms they agreed to kill or imprison every Frenchman who should come into their country during the continuance of the war between France and Great Britain.[1]

Treaty of 1761.—The hostile course of the Cherokees being still continued, the authorities of South Carolina in 1761 dispatched Colonel Grant with a force sufficient to overcome them. After destroying their crops and fifteen towns he compelled a truce, following which Lieutenant Governor Bull concluded a treaty with them at Ashley Ferry, or Charleston.[2] By this instrument the boundaries between the Indians and the settlements were declared to be the sources of the great rivers flowing into the Atlantic Ocean.

In 1767 the legislature of North Carolina made an appropriation and the governor appointed three commissioners for running a dividing-line between the western settlements of that province and the Cherokee hunting grounds.[3]

Treaty and purchase of 1768.—Mr. Stuart, the British superintendent of Indian affairs, on the 14th of October, 1768, concluded a treaty with the Cherokees at Hard Labor, South Carolina. Therein it was agreed that the southwest boundary of Virginia should be a line " extending from the point where the northern line of North Carolina intersects the Cherokee hunting grounds about 36 miles east of Long Island in the Holston River; and thence extending in a direct course north by east to Chiswell's mine on the east bank of the Kenhawa River, and thence down that stream to its junction with the Ohio."[4]

This treaty was made in pursuance of appeals from the Indians to stop further encroachments of settlers upon their lands and to have their boundaries definitely fixed, especially in the region of the north fork of Holston River and the headwaters of the Kanawha.

Treaty and purchase of 1770.—The settlements having encroached beyond the line fixed by the treaty of 1768, a new treaty was concluded on the 18th October, 1770, at Lochabar, South Carolina. A new boundary line was established by this treaty commencing on the south bank of Holston River six miles east of Long Island, and running thence to the mouth of the Great Kanawha.[5]

Treaty and purchase of 1772.—The Virginia authorities in the early part of 1772 concluded a treaty with the Cherokees whereby a boundary line was fixed between them, which was to run west from White Top Mountain in latitude 36° 30'.[6] This boundary left those settlers on

---

[1] Martin's North Carolina, Vol. II, p. 106.
[2] Ib., Vol. II, p. 152.
[3] Ib., Vol. II, p. 226.
[4] Ramsey's Annals of Tennessee, p. 76.
[5] Ib., p. 102.
[6] Ib., p. 109.

the Watauga River within the Indian limits, whereupon, as a measure of temporary relief, they leased for a period of eight years from the Indians in consideration of goods to the value of five or six thousand dollars all the country on the waters of the Watauga. Subsequently in 1775 [March 19] they secured a deed in fee simple therefor upon the further consideration of £2,000.[1] This deed was executed to Charles Robertson as the representative or trustee of the Watauga Settlers' Association, and embraced the following tract of country, viz: All that tract on the waters of the Watauga, Holston, and Great Canaway or New River, beginning on the south or southwest of Holston River six miles above Long Island in that river; thence a direct line in nearly a south course to the ridge dividing the waters of Watauga from the waters of Nonachuckeh and along the ridge in a southeasterly direction to the Blue Ridge or line dividing North Carolina from the Cherokee lands; thence along the Blue Ridge to the Virginia line and west along such line to the Holston River; thence down the Holston River to the beginning, including all the waters of the Watauga, part of the waters of the Holston, and the head branches of New River or Great Canaway, agreeable to the aforesaid boundaries.

Jacob Brown's purchase.—Jacob Brown, in 1772, for a horse load of goods leased from the Cherokees a tract on the Watauga and Nonachucky Rivers.

Three years later (March 25, 1775) for a further consideration of ten shillings he secured from them a deed in fee for the leased tract as well as an additional tract of considerable extent.

The boundary of the first of these bodies of land ran from the mouth of Great Limestone Creek, thence up the same and its main fork to the ridge dividing the Wataugah and Nonachuchy Rivers; thence to the head of Indian Creek, where it joins the Great Iron Mountains, and along those mountains to the Nonachuchy River; across the Nonachuchy River, including its creeks, and down the side of Nonachuchy Mountain against the mouth of Great Limestone Creek and from thence to the place of beginning.

The second purchase comprised a tract lying on the Nonachuchy River below the mouth of Big Limestone on both sides of the river and adjoining the tract just described. Its boundaries were defined as beginning on the south side of the Nonachuchy River below the old fields that lie below the Limestone on the north side of Nonachuchy Mountain at a large rock; thence north 32° west to the mouth of Camp Creek on the south side of the river; thence across the river; thence pursuing a northwesterly course to the dividing ridge between Lick Creek and Watauga or Holston River, thence along the dividing ridge to the rest of Brown's lands; thence down the main fork of Big Limestone to its mouth; thence crossing the Nonachuchy River and pursuing a

---
[1] Ramsey's Annals of Tennessee, p. 119.

straight course to the Nonachuchy Mountains and along such mountains to the beginning.[1]

Treaty and purchase of 1773.—On the 1st of June, 1773, a treaty was concluded jointly with the Creeks and Cherokees by the British superintendent whereby they ceded to Great Britain a tract beginning where the lower Creek path intersects the Ogeechee River, thence along the main channel of that river to the source of the southernmost branch thereof; thence along the ridge between the waters of Broad and Oconee Rivers up to the Buffalo Lick; thence in a straight line to the tree marked by the Cherokees near the head of the branch falling into the Oconee River [on the line between Clarke and Oglethorpe Counties, about 8 miles southeast of Athens]; thence along the said ridge 20 miles above the line already run by the Cherokees, and from thence across to the Savannah River by a line parallel to that formerly marked by them.

Henderson's purchase by the treaty of 1775.—On the 17th of March, 1775, Richard Henderson and eight other private citizens concluded a treaty with the Cherokees at Sycamore Shoals, on Watauga River. By its terms they became the purchasers from the latter (in consideration of £10,000 worth of merchandise) of all the lands lying between Kentucky and Cumberland Rivers, under the name of the Colony of Transylvania in North America. This purchase was contained in two deeds, one of which was commonly known as the "Path Deed," and conveyed the following described tract: "Begin on the Holston River, where the course of Powell's Mountain strikes the same; thence up the river to the crossing of the Virginia line; thence westerly along the line run by Donelson * * * to a point six (6) English miles east of Long Island in Holston River; thence a direct course towards the mouth of the Great Kanawha until it reaches the top of the ridge of Powell's Mountain; thence westerly along said ridge to the beginning."

This tract was located in Northeast Tennessee and the extreme southwestern corner of Virginia.[2] The second deed covered a much larger area of territory and was generally known as the "Great Grant." It comprised the territory " beginning on the Ohio River at the mouth of the Kentucky, Cherokee, or what, by the English, is called Louisa River; thence up said river and the most northwardly fork of the same to the head-spring thereof; thence a southeast course to the ridge of Powell's Mountain; thence westwardly along the ridge of said mountain to a point from which a northwest course will strike the head-

---

[1] Ramsey's Annals of Tennessee, pp. 110, 121.

[2] There seems to be a confused idea in this description as to the identity of Powell's Mountain. This was doubtless occasioned by a lack of definite knowledge concerning the topography of the country. This ridge, as it is commonly known, does not touch the Holston River, but lies between Powell's and Clinch Rivers. The mountains supposed to be alluded to in that portion of the description are a spur of the Clinch Mountains, which close in on the Holston River, near the mouth of Cloud's Creek.

spring of the most southwardly branch of Cumberland River; thence down said river, including all its waters, to the Ohio River; thence up said river as it meanders to the beginning."[1] This tract comprises nearly the whole of Central and Western Kentucky as well as part of Northern Central Tennessee. Although a literal reading of these boundaries would include all the territory watered by the Cumberland River and its branches, the general understanding seems to have been (and it is so specifically stated in the report of the treaty commissioners of 1785) that Henderson's purchase did not extend south of Cumberland River proper.[2] The entire purchase included in both these deeds is shown as one tract on the accompanying map of cessions and numbered 7.

In this connection it is proper to remark that all of these grants to private individuals were regarded as legally inoperative, though in some instances the beneficiaries were permitted to enjoy the benefits of their purchases in a modified degree. All such purchases had been inhibited by royal proclamation of King George III, under date of October 7, 1763,[3] wherein all provincial governors were forbidden to grant lands or issue land warrants locatable upon any territory west of the mountains or of the sources of streams flowing into the Atlantic. All private persons were enjoined from purchasing lands from the Indians. All purchases made of such lands should be for the Crown by the governor or commander-in-chief of the colony at some general council or assembly of the Indians convened for that purpose.

In the particular purchase made by Henderson and his coadjutors, the benefits thereof were afterwards claimed by the authorities of Virginia and North Carolina for those States, as the successors of the royal prerogative within their respective limits. In consideration, however, of Henderson's valuable services on the frontier, and in compensation for his large expenditures of money in negotiating the purchase, the legislature of North Carolina in 1783 granted to him and those interested with him a tract of 200,000 acres,[4] constituting a strip 4 miles in width from old Indian town on Powell's River to the mouth, and thence a strip down the Clinch River for quantity 12 miles in width. The legislature of Virginia also granted them a tract of like extent upon the Ohio River, opposite Evansville, Indiana.[5]

Treaties and purchases of 1777.—In consequence of continued hostilities between the Cherokees and the settlers, General Williamson in 1776 marched an army from South Carolina and destroyed the towns of the former on Keowee and Tugaloo Rivers. General Rutherford marched

---
[1] Mann Butler's Appeal, pp. 26, 27.
[2] American State Papers, Indian Affairs, Vol. I, p. 38.
[3] Martin's North Carolina, Vol. II, p. 339.
[4] Haywood's Tennessee, pp. 16, 17.
[5] Ramsey's Annals of Tennessee, p. 204.

another force from North Carolina and Colonel Christian a third from Virginia, and destroyed most of their principal towns on the Tennessee.[1]

At the conclusion of hostilities with the Cherokees, following these expeditions, a treaty with them was concluded May 20, 1777, at De Witt's or Duett's Corners, South Carolina, by the States of South Carolina and Georgia. By the terms of this treaty the Indians ceded a considerable region of country upon the Savannah and Saluda Rivers,[2] comprising all their lands in South Carolina to the eastward of the Unacaye Mountains.

Two months later (July 20) Commissioners Preston, Christian, and Shelby, on the part of Virginia, and Avery, Sharpe, Winston, and Lanier, for North Carolina, also concluded a treaty with the Cherokees, by which, in the establishment of a boundary between the contracting parties, some parts of "Brown's line," previously mentioned, were agreed upon as a portion of the boundary, and the Indians relinquished their lands as low down on Holston River as the mouth of Cloud's Creek. To this treaty the Chicamauga band of Cherokees refused to give their assent.[3]

The boundaries defined by this treaty are alluded to and described in an act of the North Carolina legislature passed in the following year, wherein it is stipulated that "no person shall enter or survey any lands within the Indian hunting grounds, or without the limits heretofore ceded by them, which limits westward are declared to be as follows: Begin at a point on the dividing line which hath been agreed upon between the Cherokees and the colony of Virginia, where the line between that Commonwealth and this State (hereafter to be extended) shall intersect the same; running thence a right line to the mouth of Cloud's Creek, being the second creek below the Warrior's Ford, at the mouth of Carter's Valley; thence a right line to the highest point of Chimney Top Mountain or High Rock; thence a right line to the mouth of Camp or McNamee's Creek, on south bank of Nolichucky, about ten miles below the mouth of Big Limestone; from the mouth of Camp Creek a southeast course to the top of Great Iron Mountain, being the same which divides the hunting grounds of the Overhill Cherokees from the hunting grounds of the middle settlements; and from the top of Iron Mountain a south course to the dividing ridge between the waters of French Broad, and Nolichucky Rivers; thence a southwesterly course along the ridge to the great ridge of the Appalachian Mountains, which divide the eastern and western waters; thence with said dividing ridge to the line that divides the State of South Carolina from this State."[4]

Emigration of Chicamauga band.—The Cherokees being very much curtailed in their hunting grounds by the loss of the territory wrested

---

[1] Letter of Governor Blount to Secretary of War, January 14, 1793. See American State Papers, Indian Affairs, Vol. I, p. 431.

[2] American State Papers, Indian Affairs, Vol. I, p. 431, and Ramsey's Tenn., p. 172.

[3] Haywood's Tennessee, p. 451.

[4] Scott's Laws of Tennessee and North Carolina, Vol. I, p. 225.

from them by the terms of these two treaties, began a movement further down the Tennessee River, and the most warlike and intractable portion of them, known as the Chicamaugas, settled and built towns on Chicamauga Creek, about one hundred miles below the mouth of the Holston River. Becoming persuaded, however, that this creek was infested with witches they abandoned it in 1782, and built lower down the Tennessee the towns usually called "The Five Lower Towns on the Tennessee." These towns were named respectively Running Water, Nickajack, Long Island Village, Crow Town, and Lookout Mountain Town. From thence marauding parties were wont to issue in their operations against the rapidly encroaching settlements.[1]

Although comparative peace and quiet for a time followed the heroic treatment administered to the Indians by the expeditions of Williamson, Rutherford, Christian, and others, reciprocal outrages between the whites and Indians were of frequent occurrence. The situation was aggravated in 1783 by the action of the assembly of North Carolina in passing an act (without consulting the Indians or making any effort to secure their concurrence) extending the western boundary of that State to the Mississippi River, reserving, however, for the use of the Cherokees as a hunting ground a tract comprised between the point where the Tennessee River first crosses the southern boundary of the State and the head waters of Big Pigeon River.[2]

Treaty and purchase of 1783.—On the 31st of May of this same year, by a treaty concluded at Augusta, Ga., the Cherokee delegates present (together with a few Creeks, who, on the 1st of November succeeding, agreed to the cession) assumed to cede to that State the respective claims of those two nations to the country lying on the west side of the Tugaloo River, extending to and including the Upper Oconee River region.[3] With the provisions of this treaty no large or representative portion of either nation was satisfied, and in connection with the remarkable territorial assertions of the State of North Carolina, together with the constant encroachments of white settlers beyond the Indian boundary line, a spirit of restless discontent and fear was nourished among the Indians that resulted in many acts of ferocious hostility.

Treaties with the State of Franklin.—In 1784, in consequence of the cession by North Carolina to the United States of all her claims to lands west of the mountains (which cession was not, however, accepted by the United States within the two years prescribed by the act) the citizens within the limits of the present State of Tennessee elected delegates to a convention, which formed a State organization under the name of the State of Franklin and which maintained a somewhat precarious po-

---

[1] Letter of Governor Blount to Secretary of War, January 14, 1793. See American State Papers, Indian Affairs, Vol. I, p. 431, also page 263.

[2] Report of Senate Committee March 1, 1797. See American State Papers, Indian Affairs, Vol. I, p. 623. Also Ramsey's Annals of Tennessee, p. 276.

[3] Carpenter and Arthur's History of Georgia, p. 253.

litical existence for about four years. During this interval the authorities of the so called State negotiated two treaties with the Cherokee Nation, the first one being entered into near the mouth of Dumplin Creek, on the north bank of French Broad River, May 31, 1785.[1] This treaty established the ridge dividing the waters of Little River from those of the Tennessee as the dividing line between the possessions of the whites and Indians, the latter ceding all claim to lands south of the French Broad and Holston, lying east of that ridge. The second treaty or conference was held at Chotee Ford and Coytoy, July 31 to August 3, 1786. The Franklin Commissioners at this conference modestly remarked, "We only claim the island in Tennessee at the mouth of Holston and from the head of the island to the dividing ridge between the Holston River, Little River, and Tennessee to the Blue Ridge, and the lands North Carolina sold us on the north side of Tennessee." They urged this claim under threat of extirpating the Cherokees as the penalty of refusal.[2]

TREATY RELATIONS WITH THE UNITED STATES.

This general history of the Cherokee Nation and the treaty relations that had existed with the colonial authorities from the period of their first official contact with each other is given as preliminary to the consideration of the history and provisions of the first treaty negotiated between commissioners on the part of the United States and the said Cherokee Nation, viz, the treaty concluded at Hopewell, on the Keowee River, November 28, 1785, an abstract of the provisions of which is hereinbefore given.[3]

The conclusion of this treaty marked the beginning of a new era in the relations between the whites and Cherokees. The boundaries then fixed were the most favorable it was possible to obtain from the latter without regard to previous purchases and pretended purchases made by private individuals and others. Although the Indians yielded an extensive territory to the United States,[4] yet, on the other hand, the latter conceded to the Cherokees a considerable extent of territory that had already been purchased from them by private individuals or associations, though by methods of more than doubtful legality.

The contentions between the border settlers of Virginia, North Carolina, South Carolina, and Georgia, as well as of the authorities of those States, with the Cherokees and Creeks, concerning boundaries and the constantly recurring mutual depredations and assaults upon each other's lives and property, prompted Congress, though still deriving its powers from the Articles of Confederation, to the active exercise of its treaty-making functions. It was, therefore, determined[5] to appoint commis-

---

[1] Ramsey's Annals of Tennessee, p. 299.
[2] Ib., p. 345.
[3] United States Statutes at Large, Vol. VII, p. 18.
[4] See Nos. 10a and 10b on accompanying map of Cherokee cessions.
[5] By resolution of Congress, March 15, 1785.

sioners who should be empowered under their instructions, subject, of course, to ratification by Congress, to negotiate a treaty with the Cherokees, at which the boundaries of the lands claimed by them should be as accurately ascertained as might be, and the line of division carefully marked between them and the white settlements. This was deemed essential in order that authoritative proclamation might be made of the same, advising and warning settlers against further encroachments upon Indian territory.

PROCEEDINGS AT TREATY OF HOPEWELL.

The commissioners deputed for the performance of this duty were Benjamin Hawkins, Andrew Pickens, Joseph Martin, and Lachlan McIntosh. They convened the Indians in council at Hopewell, S. C., on the 18th of November, 1785.[1] Hopewell is on the Keowee River, 15 miles above the junction of that river with the Tugaloo. The commissioners announced to the Indians the change of sovereignty from Great Britain to Congress that had taken place in the country as a consequence of the successful termination of the Revolution. They further set forth that Congress wanted none of the Indian lands, nor anything else belonging to them, but that if they had any grievances, to state them freely, and Congress would see justice done them. The Indian chiefs drafted a map showing the limits of country claimed by them, which included the greater portion of Kentucky and Tennessee, as well as portions of North Carolina, South Carolina, and Georgia. Being reminded by the commissioners that this claim covered the country purchased by Colonel Henderson, who was now dead, and whose purchase must therefore not be disputed, they consented to relinquish that portion of it. They also consented that the line as finally agreed upon, from the mouth of Duck River to the dividing ridge between the Cumberland and Tennessee Rivers, should be continued up that ridge and from thence to the Cumberland in such a manner as to leave all the white settlers in the Cumberland country outside of the Indian limits.

At the time, it was supposed this could be accomplished by running a northeast line from the ridge so as to strike the Cumberland *forty miles above Nashville*. This portion of the boundary, not having been affected by the treaty of 1791 (as was supposed by the Cherokees), was reiterated in that treaty in a reverse direction. But the language used—whether intentional or accidental—rendered it susceptible of a construction more favorable to the whites. This language read, "Thence down the Cumberland River to a point from which a southwest line will strike the ridge which divides the waters of Cumberland from those of Duck River, 40 miles above Nashville." As this line was not actually surveyed and marked until the fall of 1797,[2] and as the settlements in that

---

[1] Report of Treaty Commissioners, dated Hopewell, December 2, 1785. See American State Papers, Indian Affairs. Vol. I, p. 40.

[2] American State Papers, Indian Affairs, Vol. I, p. 628, and letter of General Winchester to General Robertson, November 9, 1797.

locality had in the meantime materially advanced, it became necessary, in order to exclude the bulk of the settlers from the Indian country, to take advantage of this technicality. The line was consequently so run (from a point on said dividing ridge 40 miles above Nashville) that it struck the Cumberland River about 1 mile above the mouth of Rock Castle River, a distance of perhaps 175 to 200 miles above Nashville. This line was surveyed by General James Winchester, who, under date of November 9, 1797, in a letter to General Robertson, describes a portion of it as running as follows:

> From Walton's road to the Fort Blount road, which it crosses near the two springs at the 32-mile tree; crosses Obey's River about 6 or 7 miles from the mouth; Achmugh about 2 miles above the Salt Lick; the South Fork of Cumberland, or Flute River, 5 or 6 miles from the mouth, and struck Cumberland River about a mile above the mouth of Rock Castle.

He also adds that the total length of the line (from the dividing ridge to Cumberland River above Rock Castle) is $138\frac{11}{16}$ miles.

The Fort Blount here mentioned was on the south side of Cumberland River, about 6 miles in a direct line, southwest of Gainesboro', and the road led from there to Walton's road, which it joined at or near the present site of Cooksville.[1] Walton's or Caney Fork road led from Carthage in an easterly direction, and before the organization of Putnam County formed the boundary line between Overton and White counties, from whence it continued easterly through Anderson's Cross Roads and Montgomery to Wilson's, in Knox County. The "Two Springs," are about 2 or 3 miles northwest of Cooksville.[1]

There is much difficulty in determining the absolute course of the "Winchester line," from the meager description contained in his letter above quoted. Arrowsmith and Lewis, in their Atlas, published in 1805, lay down the line as pursuing a perfectly straight course from its point of departure on the dividing ridge to its termination on the Cumberland above the mouth of Rock Castle River. Their authority for such a definition of the boundary is not given. If such was the true course of the line, the description given in General Winchester's letter would need some explanation. He must have considered Obey's River as emptying into Wolf River in order to bring his crossing of the former stream reasonably near the distance from its mouth specified by him. He must also have been mistaken in his estimate of the distance at which the line crossed above the mouth of the South Fork of the Cumberland. The line of Arrowsmith and Lewis would cross that stream at least 12 miles in a direct line above its mouth, instead of five or six. It is ascertained from correspondence with the officers of the Historical Society of Tennessee, that the line, after crossing the Fort Blount road at the "Two Springs," continued in a northeasterly direction, crossing Roaring Fork near the mouth of a small creek, and, pursuing the same course, passed to the east of the town of Livingston.

---

[1] Letter of Hon. Jno. M. Lea, of Nashville, Tenn., to the author.

"Nettle Carrier," a Cherokee Indian of some local note, lived on the headwaters of Nettle Carrier's Creek, about four or five miles east of Livingston, and the line passed about half-way between his cabin and the present site of that village.[1] Thence it continued to the crossing of Obey's River, and thence to the point of intersection with the Kentucky boundary line, which is ascertained to have been at the northeast corner of Overton County, Tennessee, as originally organized in 1806. From this point the line continued to the crossing of Big South Fork, at the place indicated by General Winchester, and thence on to the Cumberland at the terminal point one mile above the mouth of Rock Castle River. In the interest of clearness a literal following of the line indicated in General Winchester's letter, and also that given by Arrowsmith and Lewis, are shown upon the accompanying map. At the conference preliminary to the signing of the treaty of 1785, the Indians also asserted that within the fork of the French Broad and Holston Rivers were 3,000 white settlers who were there in defiance of their protests. They maintained that they had never ceded that country, and it being a favorite spot with them the settlers must be removed. The commissioners vainly endeavored to secure a cession of the French Broad tract, remarking that the settlers were too numerous to make their removal possible, but could only succeed in securing the insertion of an article in the treaty, providing for the submission of the subject to Congress, the settlers, in the mean time, to remain unmolested.[2]

Protest of North Carolina and Georgia.—During the pendency of negotiations, William Blount, of North Carolina, and John King and Thomas Glasscock, of Georgia, presented their commissions as the agents representing the interests of their respective States. They entered formal protests in the names of those States against the validity of the treaty, as containing several stipulations which infringed and violated the legislative rights thereof. The principal of these was the right, as assumed by the commissioners, of assigning to the Indians, territory which had already been appropriated, by act of the legislature in the case of North Carolina, to the discharge of bounty-land claims of the officers and soldiers of that State who had served in the Continental line during the Revolution.[3]

There were present at this treaty, according to the report of the commissioners, 918 Cherokees, to whom, after the signature and execution thereof, were distributed as presents goods to the value of $1,311$\frac{10}{90}$. The meagerness of the supply was occasioned, as the commissioners explained, by their expectancy of only meeting the chiefs and headmen.[4]

---

[1] Letter of Geo. H. Morgan, of Gainesborough, Tennessee.
[2] Report of Treaty Commissioners. See American State Papers, Indian Affairs, Vol. I, p. 38.
[3] American State Papers, Indian Affairs, Vol. I, p. 44.
[4] Journal of Treaty Commissioners. See American State Papers, Indian Affairs, Vol. I, p. 43.

Location of boundaries.— In the location of the boundary points between the Cherokees and whites, recited in the fourth article of the treaty, it is proper to remark that—

1. The route of the line along the ridge between Cumberland and Tennessee Rivers, and from thence to the Cumberland, at a point 40 miles above Nashville, has already been recited.

2. "The ford where the Kentucky road crosses the river" (Cumberland) is at a point opposite the mouth of Left-Hand Fork, about 12 or 13 miles slightly west of north of Cumberland Gap. From the point "40 miles above Nashville" to this ford, the commissioners adopted, as they declare, the line of Henderson's Purchase; while from the "Kentucky Ford" to the mountain, 6 miles south of the mouth of Camp Creek on Nolichucky, they followed the boundary prescribed by the treaty of July 20, 1777, with Virginia and North Carolina.[1]

3. "Campbell's line" was surveyed in 1777-'78 by General William Campbell, as a commissioner for marking the boundary between Virginia and the Cherokees. It extended from the mouth of Big Creek to the high knob on Poor Valley Ridge, 332 poles S. 70° E. of the summit of the main ridge of Cumberland Mountain, a short distance west of Cumberland Gap.[2] The point at which the treaty line of 1785 struck Campbell's line was at the Kentucky road crossing, about 1½ miles southeast of Cumberland Gap.

4. The treaty line followed Campbell's line until it reached a point due north of the mouth of Cloud's Creek. From this point it ran south to the mouth of that creek, which enters the Holston from the north, 3 miles west of Rogersville.

5. The line from Cloud's Creek pursued a northeasterly direction to Chimney Top Mountain, which it struck at a point about 2 miles to the southward of the Long Island of Holston River.

6. "Camp Creek, near the mouth of Big Limestone, on the Nolichucky" (which is the next point in the boundary line), is a south branch of Nolichucky River in Greene County, Tennessee, between Horse and Cove Creeks, and empties about 6 miles southeast of Greeneville. It was sometimes called McNamee's Creek.

7. The mountain "six miles to the southward of Camp Creek" was in the Great Smoky or Iron Range, not far from the head of that creek.

8. "Thence south to the North Carolina line, thence to the South Carolina Indian boundary." This line was partially surveyed in the winter of 1791, by Joseph Hardin, under the direction of Governor Blount.[3] It ran southeasterly from the mouth of McNamee's or Camp

---

[1] Report of Treaty Commissioners in American State Papers, Indian Affairs, Vol. I, p. 38.

[2] Letter of Return J. Meigs to Secretary of War, May 5, 1803; also, letter of Hon. John M. Lea, Nashville, Tennessee.

[3] Letter of Governor Blount to Secretary of War, December 16, 1792, in American State Papers, Indian Affairs, Vol. I, p. 631.

Creek, a distance, as stated by Governor Blount, of 60 miles to Rutherford's War Trace, although the point at which it struck this "Trace," which is given in Governor Blount's correspondence as being 10 or 12 miles west of the Swannanoa settlement, is only a trifle over 50 miles in a direct line from the mouth of Camp Creek.

The "Rutherford's War Trace" here spoken of was the route pursued by General Griffith Rutherford, who, in the summer of 1776, marched an army of 2,400 men against the Cherokees. He was re-enforced by Colonels Martin and Armstrong at Cathey's Fort; crossed the Blue Ridge at Swannanæ Gap; passed down and over the French Broad at a place yet known as the "War Ford;" continued up the valley of Hominy Creek, leaving Pisgah Mountain to the left and crossing Pigeon River a little below the mouth of East Fork; thence through the mountains to Richland Creek, above the present town of Waynesville; ascended that creek and crossed Tuckaseigee River at an Indian village; continued across Cowee Mountain, and thence to the Middle Cherokee Towns on Tennessee River, to meet General Williamson, from South Carolina, with an army bent on a like mission.[1] The boundary between western North Carolina and South Carolina was not definitely established at the date of the survey of Hardin's line and, as shown by an old map on file in the Office of Indian Affairs, the point at which a prolongation of Hardin's line would have struck the South Carolina Indian boundary was supposed to be on or near the 35th degree of north latitude,[2] whereas it was actually more than 20 miles to the north of that parallel and about 10 miles to the north of the present boundary of South Carolina. The definite establishment of this treaty line of 1785 in this quarter, however, became unnecessary by reason of the ratification in February, 1792, of the Cherokee treaty concluded July 2, 1791,[3] wherein the Indian boundary line was withdrawn a considerable distance to the west.

9. The line along the "South Carolina Indian boundary" ran in a southwesterly direction from the point of contact with the prolongation of Hardin's line, passing over "Ocunna" Mountain a short distance to the northwestwardly of Oconee Station and striking the Tugaloo River at a point about 1 mile above the mouth of Panther Creek.[2]

10. The line from Tugaloo River pursued a west of south course to Currahee Mountain, which is the southern terminus of a spur of the Alleghany Mountains, and is situated 4 miles southwest of "Toccoa Falls" and 16 miles northwest of Carnesville, Georgia.

11. From "Currahee Mountain to the head of the south fork of Oconee River," the line pursued a course south 38° west[2] to the source of that stream, now commonly known as the Appallachee River, and

---

[1] Ramsey's Annals of Tennessee.
[2] Old manuscript map on file in Indian Office, Washington, D. C.
[3] United States Statutes at Large, Vol. VII, p. 39.

was the terminal point of the boundary as defined in this treaty. This line was surveyed in 1798[1] under the direction of Col. Benj. Hawkins.

It is also a pertinent fact in connection with the boundaries defined by this treaty (as already stated in connection with Henderson's treaty), that although a literal reading of the description contained in Henderson's "Great Grant" of 1775 would include all the country watered by the tributaries of the Cumberland, the commissioners who negotiated this treaty of Hopewell in 1785 did not consider Henderson's Purchase as extending south of the Cumberland River proper, except in its course from Powell's Mountain to the head of the most southwardly branch of that river. This branch was considered by these commissioners of 1785 as being the Yellow River, whose source was at best but imperfectly known. They specifically state that they accept the boundaries of Henderson's Purchase in this direction,[2] and as the boundary defined by them between Powell's Mountain and Yellow River was "Campbell's line," they must have considered that line as being the southern limit of Henderson's Great Grant.

TREATY CONCLUDED JULY 2, 1791; PROCLAIMED FEBRUARY 7, 1792.[3]

Held on bank of Holston River, near the mouth of French Broad, between William Blount, governor of the Territory south of Ohio River and superintendent of Indian affairs, representing the President of the United States, on the part and behalf of said States, and the chiefs and warriors of the Cherokee Nation on the part and behalf of said nation.

MATERIAL PROVISIONS.

1. Perpetual peace declared between the United States and the Cherokee Nation.
2. Cherokees to be under sole protection of the United States and to hold no treaty with any State or individuals.
3. Cherokees and the United States to mutually release prisoners captured one from the other.
4. Boundary between the United States and the Cherokees defined as follows: Beginning at the top of Currahee Mountain, where the Creek line passes it; thence a direct line to Tugelo River; thence northeast to Ocunna Mountain and over same along South Carolina Indian boundary

---

[1] See resolution of Georgia legislature, June 16, 1802. It is however stated by Return J. Meigs, in a letter to the Secretary of War dated December 20, 1811, that this line was run by Colonel Hawkins in 1797.

[2] American State Papers, Indian Affairs, Vol. I, p. 38.

[3] United States Statutes at Large, Vol. VII, p. 39.

MATERIAL PROVISIONS

to the North Carolina boundary; thence north to a point from which a line is to be extended to the River Clinch that shall pass the Holston at the ridge dividing waters of Little River from those of Tennessee River; thence up Clinch River to Campbell's line and along the same to the top of Cumberland Mountain; thence a direct line to Cumberland River where the Kentucky road crosses it; thence down Cumberland River to a point from which a southwest line will strike the ridge dividing waters of Cumberland from those of Duck River 40 miles above Nashville; thence down said ridge to a point from which a southwest line will strike the mouth of Duck River.

To prevent future disputes, said boundary to be ascertained and marked by three persons appointed by the United States and three persons appointed by the Cherokees.

To extinguish all claim of Cherokees to lands lying to the right of said line, the United States agree to immediately deliver certain valuable goods to the Cherokees and to pay them $1,000 annually.

5. Citizens of United States to have free use of road from Washington District to Mero District and of navigation of Tennessee River.

6. The United States to have exclusive right of regulating trade with the Cherokees.

7. The United States solemnly guarantee to the Cherokees all their lands not herein ceded.

8. Citizens of the United States or others not Indians settling on Cherokee lands to forfeit protection of the United States and be punished as the Indians see fit.

9. Inhabitants of the United States forbidden to hunt on Cherokee lands, or to pass over the same without a passport from the governor of a State or Territory or other person authorized by the President of the United States to grant the same.

10. Cherokees committing crimes against citizens of the United States to be delivered up and punished by United States laws.

11. Inhabitants of the United States committing crimes or trespass against Cherokees to be tried and punished under United States laws.

12. Retaliation or reprisal forbidden until satisfaction has been refused by the aggressor.

13. Cherokees to give notice of any designs against the peace and interests of the United States.

14. Cherokees to be furnished with useful implements of husbandry. United States to send four persons to reside in Cherokee country to act as interpreters.

15. All animosities to cease and treaty to be faithfully carried out.

16. Treaty to take effect when ratified by the President of the United States by and with the advice and consent of the Senate.

HISTORICAL DATA.

CAUSES OF DISSATISFACTION WITH THE BOUNDARY OF 1785.

The boundary line prescribed by the treaty of November 28, 1785, had been unsatisfactory to both the Cherokees and the whites. On the part of the former the chief cause of complaint was the non-removal of the settlers in the fork of the French Broad and Holston Rivers and their evident disposition to encroach still farther into the Indian country at every opportunity. The whites, on the other hand, were discontented because further curtailment of the Cherokee territory had not been compelled by the commissioners who negotiated the treaty, and the State authorities of North Carolina and Georgia had protested because of the alleged interference by the General Government with the reserved rights of the States.[1] In retaliation for the intrusions of the whites the Indians were continually engaged in pilfering their stock and other property.

The state of affairs resulting from this continual friction rendered some decisive action by Congress necessary. A large portion of the land in Greene and Hawkins Counties, Tennessee, had been entered by the settlers under the laws of North Carolina, whereby she had assumed jurisdiction to the Mississippi River.[2] These lands were south and west of the treaty line of 1785, as were also the lands on the west side of the Clinch upon which settlements had been made. Settlers to the number of several thousand, south of the French Broad and Holston, were also within the Cherokee limits.[3]

It is true that the authorities of the so-called State of Franklin had in the years 1785 and 1786 negotiated two treaties with the Cherokees, obtaining cessions from the latter covering most, if not all, of these lands,[4] but neither the State of North Carolina nor the United States recognized these treaties as of any force or validity.

These trespasses called forth under date of September 1, 1788, a proclamation from Congress forbidding all such unwarrantable intrusions, and enjoining all those who had settled upon the hunting ground of the Cherokees to depart with their families and effects without loss of time.

General Knox, Secretary of War, under date of July 7, 1789, in a communication to the President, remarked that "the disgraceful violation of the treaty of Hopewell with the Cherokees requires the serious consideration of Congress. If so direct and manifest con-

---

[1] American State Papers, Indian Affairs, Vol. I, p. 44.

[2] Protest of Col. William Blount to Treaty Commissioners of 1785. American State Papers, Indian Affairs, Vol. I, p. 44, and Ramsey's Annals of Tenn., p. 549. Also Scott's Laws of Tennessee and North Carolina, Vol. I.

[3] American State Papers, Indian Affairs, Vol. I, p. 38.

[4] Ramsey's Annals of Tennessee, p. 345.

tempt of the authority of the United States be suffered with impunity, it will be in vain to attempt to extend the arm of government to the frontiers. The Indian tribes can have no faith in such imbecile promises, and the lawless whites will ridicule a government which shall, on paper only, make Indian treaties and regulate Indian boundaries."[1]

He recommended the appointment of three commissioners on the part of the United States, who should be invested with full powers to examine into the case of the Cherokees and to renew with them the treaty made at Hopewell in 1785; also to report to the President such measures as should be necessary to protect the Indians in the boundaries secured to them by that treaty, which he suggested would involve the establishment of military posts within the Indian country and the services of at least five hundred troops. President Washington, on the same day, transmitted the report of the Secretary of War, with the accompanying papers, to Congress. He approved of the recommendations of General Knox, and urged upon that body prompt action in the matter.

Congress, however, failed to take any decisive action at that session, and on the 11th of August, 1790, President Washington again brought the subject to the attention of that body. After reciting the substance of his previous communication, he added that, notwithstanding the treaty of Hopewell and the proclamation of Congress, upwards of five hundred families had settled upon the Cherokee lands, exclusive of those between the fork of the French Broad and Holston Rivers.[2] He further added that, as the obstructions to a proper conduct of the matter had been removed since his previous communication, by the accession of North Carolina to the Union and the cession to the United States by her of the lands in question,[3] he should conceive himself bound to exert the powers intrusted to him by the Constitution in order to carry into faithful execution the treaty of Hopewell, unless it should be thought proper to attempt to arrange a new boundary with the Cherokees, embracing the settlements and compensating the Cherokees for the cessions they should make.

United States Senate authorizes a new treaty.—Upon the reception of this message the Senate adopted a resolution advising and consenting that the President should, at his discretion, cause the treaty of Hopewell to be carried into execution or enter into arrangements for such

---

[1] American State Papers, Indian Affairs, Vol. I, p. 53.

[2] Ib., p. 83.

[3] The assembly of North Carolina proceeded in 1789 to mature a plan for the severance of Tennessee, and passed an act for the purpose of ceding to the United States of America certain western lands therein described. In conformity with one of the provisions of the act, Samuel Johnson and Benjamin Hawkins, Senators in Congress from North Carolina, executed a deed to the United States on the 25th of February, 1790. Congress accepted the cession by act of April 2, 1790, and Tennessee ceased to be a part of North Carolina.

further cession of territory from the Cherokees as the tranquillity and interests of the United States should require. A proviso to this resolution limited the compensation to be paid to the Cherokees for such further cession to $1,000 per annum and stipulated that no person who had taken possession of any lands within the limits of the proposed cession should be confirmed therein until he had complied with such terms as Congress should thereafter prescribe.

Accordingly, instructions were issued to William Blount, governor of the Territory south of the Ohio River and *ex officio* superintendent of Indian affairs, to conclude a treaty of cession with the Cherokees.[1]

TENNESSEE COMPANY'S PURCHASE.

In the mean time the troubles between the Indians and the settlers had become aggravated from divers causes. Prominent among these was the fact that Georgia had by act of her legislature disposed of 3,500,000 acres of vacant land lying south of Tennessee River to the Tennessee Company. This association undertook to effect a settlement in the year 1791 at or near the Muscle Shoals.[2] The matter coming to the notice of the Secretary of War was made the subject of a strong protest by him to the President.[3]

The latter issued his proclamation forbidding such settlement. The company persisted in the attempt, and as the President had declared such act would place them without the protection of the United States, the Indians were left free to break up and destroy the settlement, which they did.[4]

DIFFICULTIES IN NEGOTIATING NEW TREATY.

In pursuance of Governor Blount's instructions, he convened the Indians at White's Fort, on the present site of Knoxville, Tenn.; and after a conference lasting seven days, succeeded, with much difficulty and with great reluctance on the part of the Cherokees, in concluding the treaty of July 2, 1791.[5]

In his letter to the Secretary of War,[6] transmitting the treaty, he asserts the greatest difficulty to have been in agreeing on a boundary, and that the one fixed upon might seem singular. The reason for this peculiarity of description was owing to the fact that the Indians in-

---

[1] These instructions were issued in pursuance of the advice and consent of the Senate, under date of August 11, 1790. See American State Papers, Indian Affairs, Vol. I, p. 135.

[2] This act of the Georgia legislature bore date of December 21, 1789. A prior act, bearing date February 7, 1785, had been passed, entitled "An act for laying out a district of land situated on the river Mississippi, within the limits of this State, into a county, to be called Bourbon." See American State Papers, Indian Affairs, Vol. I, p. 114.

[3] January 22, 1791. See American State Papers, Indian Affairs, Vol. I, p. 112.

[4] Ramsey's Annals of Tennessee, pp. 549-556.

[5] United States Statutes at Large, Vol. VII, p. 39.

[6] July 15, 1791. See American State Papers, Indian Affairs, Vol. I, p. 628.

sisted on beginning on the part where they were most tenacious of the land, in preference to the mouth of Duck River, where the Hopewell treaty line began. The land to the right of the line was declared to belong to the United States, because no given point of the compass would describe it. In accordance with his instructions, Governor Blount proposed to the Indians that the ridge dividing the waters of Little River from those of the Tennessee should form a part of the boundary. To this the Indians would not agree, but insisted on the straight line which should cross the Holston where that ridge should strike it. Governor Blount explains that this line is not so limited by the treaty as to the point at which it shall leave the north line or at which it shall strike the Clinch, but that it might be so run as either to include or leave out the settlers south of the ridge; the only stipulations respecting it being that it should cross the Holston at the ridge, and should be run by commissioners appointed by the respective parties.

He urged that the line should be run immediately after the ratification of the treaty, as settlers were already located in the immediate vicinity of it, and more were preparing to follow.

The President transmitted the treaty to the Senate with his message of October 26, 1791,[1] and Senator Hawkins, from the committee to whom it was referred, reported it back to the Senate on the 9th of November following, recommending that the Senate advise and consent to its ratification.[2]

On the 19th of the same month the Secretary of War advised Governor Blount that the treaty had been ratified by the President, by and with the advice and consent of the Senate, and inclosed him 50 printed copies for distribution, although the United States Statutes at Large [Vol. VII, p. 39] give the date of the proclamation of the treaty as February 7, 1792.[3]

SURVEY OF NEW BOUNDARIES.

The Secretary also intrusted the matter of the survey of the new boundary to the discretion of Governor Blount, and suggested the appointment of Judge Campbell, Daniel Smith, and Col. Landon Carter as commissioners to superintend the same. This suggestion was subsequently modified by the appointment of Charles McLung and John McKee in place of Smith and Carter. Governor Blount designated the 1st of May as the date for the survey to commence. Andrew Ellicott was appointed surveyor, he having been previously appointed to survey the line under the Creek treaty of 1790.[4] Before these arrangements could be carried out, the Secretary of War again wrote Governor Blount,[5] remarking that while it was important the line should be run,

---

[1] American State Papers, Indian Affairs, Vol. I, p. 123.
[2] Ib., p. 135.
[3] Ib., p. 629.
[4] Ib., p. 628–630.
[5] January 31, 1792. See American State Papers, Indian Affairs, Vol. I, p. 629.

yet as the United States, in their military operations, might want the assistance of the Cherokees, perhaps it would be better policy to have the lines ascertained and marked after rather than before the campaign then about to commence against the Indians northwest of the Ohio.[1] It was thus determined, in view of numerous individual acts of hostility on the part of the Cherokees and of the desire to soothe them into peace and to engage them as auxiliaries against the northern Indians, to temporarily postpone the running of the line.

After considerable correspondence between Governor Blount and the Cherokee chiefs in council, the 8th of October, 1792, was fixed upon as the date for the meeting of the representatives of both parties at Major Craig's, on Nine-Mile Creek, for the purpose of beginning the survey.[2] In the mean time an increased spirit of hostility had become manifest among the Cherokees and Creeks, the five lower towns of the former having declared war, and an Indian invasion of the frontier seemed imminent. Governor Blount, therefore, in the latter part of September,[2] deemed it wise to call fifteen companies of militia into immediate service, under the command of General Sevier, for the protection of the settlements. Notwithstanding this critical condition of affairs, the boundary line commissioners on the part of the United States assembled at the appointed time and place. After waiting until the following day, the representatives of the Cherokees putting in no appearance, they proceeded to inspect the supposed route of the treaty line. After careful examination they came to the conclusion that the ridge dividing the waters of Tennessee and Little Rivers struck the Holston River at the mouth and at no other point.[4]

They then proceeded to run, but did not mark, a line of experiment from the point of the ridge in a southeast direction to Chilhowee Mountain, a distance of 17½ miles, and also from the point of beginning in a northwest direction to the Clinch River, a distance of 9 miles. From these observations they found that the line, continued to the southeast, would intersect the Tennessee River shortly after it crossed the Chilhowee Mountain, and in consequence would deprive the Indians of all

---

[1] It may not be uninteresting as a historical incident to note the fact that at the time of General Wayne's treaty at Greeneville, in 1795, a band of Cherokees had settled on the head-waters of the Scioto River in Ohio. Not presenting themselves at the conferences preceding that treaty, General Wayne sent them a special message through Captain Long Hair, one of their chiefs, with the information that if they failed to conclude articles of peace with him they would be left unprotected. They sent a delegation to assure General Wayne of their desire for peace, saying that as soon as they gathered their crop of corn they would return to their tribe, which they did.

[2] American State Papers, Indian Affairs, Vol. I, p. 630. According to the original manuscript journal of Col. Benj. Hawkins, Major Craig's house was ¼ mile below the source of Nine-Mile Creek.

[3] September 27, 1792. See American State Papers, Indian Affairs, Vol. I, p. 630.

[4] Report of Boundary Commissioners, November 30, 1792. American State Papers, Indian Affairs, Vol. I, p. 630.

their towns lying on the south side of the Tennessee. This rendered apparent the necessity of changing the direction of the line into a more nearly east and west course, and led the commissioners to express the opinion that the true line should run from the point of the ridge south 60° east to Chilhowee Mountain and north 60° west to the Clinch.

The course thus designated left a number of the settlers on Nine-Mile Creek within the Indian limits.[1]

The records of the War Department having been almost completely destroyed by fire in the month of November, 1800, it is with great difficulty that definite data can be obtained concerning the survey of this and other Indian boundaries prior to that date. It has, however, been ascertained that the above mentioned line was not actually surveyed until the year 1797.

Journal of Col. Benjamin Hawkins.—The manuscript journal of Col. Benjamin Hawkins, now in the possession of the Historical Society of Georgia, shows that instructions were issued by the Secretary of War on the 2d of February, 1797, appointing and directing Col. Benjamin Hawkins, General Andrew Pickens, and General James Winchester as commissioners on the part of the United States to establish and mark the lines between the latter and the Indian nations south of the Ohio. These instructions reached Colonel Hawkins at Fort Fidius, on the Oconee, on the 28th of February. Notice was at once sent to General Pickens at his residence at Hopewell, on the Keowee, and also to General Winchester, through Silas Dinsmoor, at that time temporary agent for the Cherokee Nation, to convene at Tellico, on Tennessee River, on the 1st of April following, for the purpose of determining and marking the Cherokee boundary line pursuant to the treaty of 1791. Colonel Hawkins joined General Pickens at Hopewell, from which point they set out for Tellico on the 23d of March, accompanied by Joseph Whitner, one of their surveyors, as well as by an escort of United States troops, furnished by Lieut. Col. Henry Gaither. Passing Ocunna station, they were joined by their other surveyor, John Clark Kilpatrick. They reached Tellico block-house on the 31st of March, and were joined on the following day by Mr. Dinsmoor, the Cherokee agent. Here they were visited by Hon. David Campbell, who, in conjunction with Charles McLung and John McKee, had been appointed in 1792, as previously set forth, to survey and mark the line. Mr. Campbell informed them that he and his co-commissioners, in pursuance of their instructions, did in part ascertain and establish the boundary and report the same to Governor Blount, and that he would accompany the present commissioners and give them all the information he possessed on the subject. About the same time confidential information was received that General Winchester would not attend the meeting of his co-commissioners, and that this was understood to be in pursuance of a scheme to postpone

---

[1] Report of Boundary Commissioners, November 30, 1792. American State Papers, Indian Affairs, Vol. I, p. 630.

the running of the line in the interest of certain intruders upon Indian land. On the 7th of April the commissioners set out to examine the location and direction of the ridge dividing the waters of Little River from those of Tennessee, at the same time noting that " we received information that the line run between the Indians and white inhabitants by the commissioners, mentioned on the 3d instant by Mr. Campbell, was by order, for the express purpose of ascertaining a line of accommodation for the white settlers, who were then over the treaty line." By arrangement they met a number of the interested settlers at the house of Mr. Bartlett McGee on the 9th, and by them were advised that the ridge between the sources of Nine-Mile, Baker's, Pistol, and Crooked Creeks "is that which divides the waters running into Little River from those running into the Tennessee."

Proceeding with their observations, they set out for the point on this ridge " where the experiment line for fixing the court-house of Blount County passes the ridge between Pistol Creek and Baker's Creek, due east from a point on the Tennessee 13½ miles, and this point on the Tennessee is 1½ miles south from a point from where a line west joins the confluence of the Holston and Tennessee." The point on the ridge here spoken of was 2½ miles north of Bartlett McGee's and 1 mile north of the source of Nine-Mile Creek. The commissioners state that in noting observations they count distances in minutes, at the rate of 60′ to 3 miles. From the foregoing point they proceeded west 8′ to a ridge dividing Pistol and Baker's Creeks; turned south 6′ to the top of a knoll, having on the right the falling grounds of Gallagher's Creek. This knoll they called "Iron Hill." Continuing south 11′, they crossed a small ridge and ascended a hill 4′ SSW., crossing a path from Baker's Creek to the settlements on Holston. From here the ridge bore SSW. 1 mile, SW. by W. 1 mile, SSW. 3 miles, and thence NW., which would make it strike the Holston River near the mouth of that stream. This corresponded with the observations of the previous commissioners who had run the experimental line.

This inspection convinced the commissioners that a considerable number of the white settlers were on the Indian land. The latter were quite anxious that some arrangement should be made for their accommodation in the coming conference with the Indians, but received no encouragement from the commissioners further than an assurance that they should be permitted to gather their crops of small grain and fruit before removal.

Being asked by the commissioners why the line run by Mr. Campbell and his confrères was known by three names, "that of experience, of experiment, and the treaty line with the Indians," they answered that "it was not the treaty line, but a line run to see how the citizens could be covered, as they were then settled on the frontier; that they understood this to be the direction to the commissioners, and that they conformed to it and ran the line as we had noticed in viewing the lands between the two rivers." The settlers also said, "the law, as they were likely to be affected, had been incautiously worded. They understood from it that the line from Clinch to cross the Holston at the ridge would turn thence south to the South Carolina Indian boundary on the North Carolina line. We replied that this understanding of it was erroneous. There was no such course in the treaty, and they should never suppose that the Government would be capable of violating a solemn guarantee; that, although the expression was 'thence south,' yet it must be understood as meaning southeastwardly, to the point next called for, as the point is in that direction and far to the east; that the lands in question had moreover been expressly reserved by the State of North Carolina for the Indians, and the occupants had not, as some others had, even the plea of entry in the land office of that State."

The law referred to above by the settlers and the commissioners was the act of Congress approved May 19, 1796, entitled "An act to regulate trade and intercourse with the Indian tribes and to preserve peace on the frontiers." This act recited the course of the Indian boundary as established by treaty with the various tribes extending from the mouth of Cuyahoga River along the line described in the treaty of 1795 at Greenville, to the Ohio River and down the same to the ridge dividing the Cumberland and Tennessee Rivers; thence up and along said ridge and continuing according to the Cherokee treaty of 1791 to the river Clinch; "thence down said river to a point from which a line shall pass the Holston, at the ridge which divides the waters running into Little River from those running into the Tennessee; thence *south* to the North Carolina boundary," etc.

Owing to fears for their personal safety caused by the hostile tone of the settlers toward them, it was not until the 25th of April that a representative delegation of the Cherokees was convened in council by the commissioners. There were present 147 chiefs and warriors. Commissioners were appointed by them to act on behalf of their nation, in conjuction with those on behalf the United States, to run and mark the boundary line, and an agreement was reached that Messrs. Hawkins and Pickens should have authority to select the necessary sites for the proposed military posts within their country.

During the council a delegation of the intruding settlers presented themselves but were not allowed to attend the deliberations, being advised by the commissioners "that it was not in contemplation to make a new treaty but to carry the treaty of Holston into effect; that we did not expect much light on this subject from the Indians; that we should form our decision from the instrument itself and not from interested reporters on either side; that all who were on the Indian lands could not be relieved by us; * * * that he (Captain Henly) and most of the deputation lived on this side of the line of experiment, and that they had informed us that that line was merely to ascertain how the citizens could be accommodated and *on this side of the true line* intended in the treaty; that to accommodate them a new treaty must be had and a new line agreed on, and, in our opinion, at this time it could not be effected; that the Indians were much alarmed for their situation, and viewed every attempt to acquire land as a violation of the solemn guaranty of the Government; that we need not expect ever to obtain fairly their consent to part with their land, unless our fellow-citizens would pay more respect than we saw they did to their treaties.

Following this conference with the Indians, the commissioners proceeded (examining the country carefully en route) to South West Point, at the mouth of Clinch River, which they reached on the 6th of May, and the journal of Colonel Hawkins concludes with this day's proceedings. It is learned, however, from an old map of the line now on file in the office of Indian Affairs, that the survey was not begun until more than three months after their arrival at South West Point. From another map in the same office it appears that the line as surveyed extended from a point about 1,000 yards above South West Point in a course S. 76° E. to the Great Iron Mountain, and was known as "Hawkins Line."[1] From this point the line continued in the same course until it reached the treaty line of 1785, and was called "Pickens Line." The supposition is that as the commissioners were provided with two surveyors, they separated, Colonel Hawkins with Mr. Whitner as surveyor running the line from Clinch River to the Great Iron Mountains, and General Pickens with Colonel Kilpatrick as surveyor locating the remainder of it. This supposition is verified so far as General Pickens is concerned by his own written statement.[2]

From the point where it struck the Clinch River, the line of cession by this treaty of 1791 followed up the course of that river until it struck Campbell's line at a point 3 or 4 miles southwest of the present town of Sneedville. From this point it became identical with the boundary line prescribed by the treaty of November 28, 1785 at Hopewell.

The tract of country ceded by this treaty comprised the territory within the present limits of Sevier, Cocke, Jefferson, Hamblen, Grainger, and almost the entirety of Knox, as well as portions of Roane, Loudon,

---

[1] See preamble to treaty of 1798; American State Papers, Indian Affairs, Vol. I, pp. 639–641; letters of Indian Bureau, War Department, December 13 and 14, 1828; also, old manuscript maps in Office of Indian Affairs, Nos. 716 and 749. By the former of these maps it appears that the survey of "Hawkins Line" from Clinch River was begun August 13, 1797, and that "the line commences on the Clinch, one-fourth mile above the ferry, in view of South West Point. (The ferry was 600 yards above the point.) From this point the view through the vista or street passing Captain Wade's garden to the right S. 26 W. the same side of the river above N. 47 W. The beginning tree, a Spanish oak, marked U. S. on the north side and C. on the south; on the oak 1797. A wahoo marked U. S. and C. under the U. S. Aug. 13, continues the line 4 cuts 7 strikes to the Cumberland road, here a white oak marked U. S. and C. The mile trees have U. S. and C. marked on them," etc.

[2] Letter of Gen. Andrew Pickens to Hon. Mr. Nott, of South Carolina, January 1, 1800. See American State Papers, Public Lands, Vol. I, p. 104.

Anderson, Union, Hancock, Hawkins, Sullivan, Washington, Greene, and Blount Counties in Tennessee, together with a portion of North Carolina lying principally west of the French Broad River.

TREATY CONCLUDED FEBRUARY 17, 1792; PROCLAIMED FEBRUARY 17, 1792.

Held at Philadelphia, Pennsylvania, between Henry Knox, Secretary of War, on behalf of the United States, and certain chiefs and warriors, in behalf of themselves and the Cherokee Nation.

MATERIAL PROVISIONS.

This treaty was negotiated as, and declared to be, an additional article to the treaty of July 2, 1791, and provided as follows:

1. That the annual sum to be paid to the Cherokees by the United States, in consideration of the relinquishment of lands, made in treaty of 1791, be $1,500 instead of $1,000.

HISTORICAL DATA.

DISCONTENT OF THE CHEROKEES.

As stated in considering the treaty of July 2, 1791, the Secretary of War notified Governor Blount[1] that the President had ratified the same, and inclosed printed copies thereof to him for distribution. This was equivalent to its official promulgation, although the treaty as printed in the United States Statutes at Large gives February 17, 1792, as the date of proclamation.

But, whichever may be the correct date, during the interval elapsing between them, a Cherokee delegation, without the invitation or knowledge of the United States authorities, proceeded to Philadelphia (then the seat of Government), where they arrived on the 28th of December, 1791, bringing with them from Governor Pinckney and General Pickens, of South Carolina, evidence of the authenticity of their mission.[2]

The delegation consisted of six, besides the interpreter, and was headed by Nen-e-too-yah, or the Bloody Fellow. They were kindly received by the President, who directed the Secretary of War to ascertain their business.

Conferences were thereupon held with them, lasting several days, at which the Indians detailed at great length their grievances and made known their wants.

Causes of complaint.—The substance of their communications was to the effect that when they were summoned by Governor Blount to the conference which resulted in the treaty of July 2, 1791, they were una-

---

[1] November 19, 1791. See American State Papers, Indian Affairs, Vol. I, p. 629.
[2] American State Papers, Indian Affairs, Vol. I, p. 203.

ware of any purpose on the part of the Government to secure any further cession of land from them; that they had protested vigorously and consistently for several days against yielding any more territory, but were met with such persistent and threatening demands from Governor Blount on the subject that they were forced to yield; that they had no confidence that the North Carolinians would attach any sacredness to the new boundary, in fact they were already settling beyond it; and that the annuity stipulated in the treaty of 1791, as compensation for the cession, was entirely inadequate. They therefore asked an increase of the annuity from $1,000 to $1,500, and furthermore demanded that the white people who had settled south of the ridge dividing the waters of Little River from those of the Tennessee should be removed, and that such ridge should be the barrier.

President Washington, believing their demand to be a just one, and also desiring that the delegation should carry home a favorable report of the attitude and disposition of the Government toward them, submitted the matter to the Senate[1] and requested the advice of that body as to the propriety of attaching an additional article to the treaty of 1791 which should increase the annuity from $1,000 to $1,500.

Annuity increased.—To this proposition the Senate gave its advice and consent,[2] and what is mentioned in the United States Statutes at Large as a treaty concluded and proclaimed February 17, 1792,[3] became the law of the land.

WAR WITH CHEROKEES.

This concession did not, however, in any large degree heal the differences and antagonisms existing between the Indians and the border settlers, with whom they were brought in constant contact. Even while the treaty of 1792 was being negotiated by the representatives of the Cherokees at the capital of the nation, a portion of their young warriors were consummating arrangements for the precipitation of a general war with the whites, and in September, 1792, a party of upwards of 700 Cherokee and Creek warriors attacked Buchanan's Station, Tenn., within 4 miles of Nashville. They were headed by the Cherokee chief John Watts, who was one of the signers of the treaty of Holston, and had he not been severely wounded early in the attack, it is likely the station would have been destroyed.[4]

A year later, between twelve and fifteen hundred Indians of the same tribes invaded the settlements on the Holston River and destroyed Cavitt's Station, 7 miles below Knoxville.[5] In fact, the intermediate periods between 1791 and 1795 were filled up by the incursions of smaller

---

[1] January 18, 1792.
[2] January 20, 1792.
[3] United States Statutes at Large, Vol. VII, p. 42.
[4] This attack was made about midnight on the 30th of September, 1792. See American State Papers, Indian Affairs, Vol. I, p. 294.
[5] American State Papers, Indian Affairs, Vol. I, p. 463.

war parties, and it was not until the latter year that the frontiers found any repose from Indian depredations.

The general tranquillity enjoyed after that date seems to have been occasioned by the wholesome discipline administered to the tribes northwest of the Ohio by General Wayne, in his victory of August 20, 1794, and as a result of the expedition of Major Ore, with his command of Tennesseeans and Kentuckians, in September of the same year, against the Lower Towns of the Cherokees, wherein two of those towns, Running Water and Nickajack, were destroyed.[1]

TREATY CONCLUDED JUNE 26, 1794; PROCLAIMED JANUARY 21, 1795.[2]

Held at Philadelphia, Pa., between Henry Knox, Secretary of War, on behalf of the United States, and the chiefs and warriors representing the Cherokee Nation of Indians.

MATERIAL PROVISIONS.

The treaty of July 2, 1791, not having been fully carried into effect, by reason of some misunderstanding, this treaty was concluded to adjudicate such differences, and contains the following provisions:

1. The treaty of July 2, 1791, declared to be in full force in respect to the boundaries, as well as in all other respects whatever.

2. The boundaries mentioned in the 4th article of treaty of July 2, 1791, to be ascertained and marked after ninety days' notice shall have been given to the Cherokee Nation of the time and place of commencing the operation by the United States commissioners.

3. The United States agree, in lieu of all former sums, to furnish the Cherokees with $5,000 worth of goods annually, as compensation for all territory ceded by treaties of November 28, 1785, and July 2, 1791.

4. Fifty dollars to be deducted from Cherokee annuity for every horse stolen by Cherokees from whites and not returned within three months.

5. These articles to be considered as additions to treaty of July 2, 1791, as soon as ratified by the President and Senate of the United States.

HISTORICAL DATA.

COMPLAINTS CONCERNING BOUNDARIES.

The destruction of the official records renders it very difficult to ascertain the details of the misunderstandings alleged in the preamble of this

---

[1] Report of Maj. James Ore to Governor Blount, September 24, 1794. He left Nashville September 7, with 550 mounted infantry, crossed the Tennessee on the 12th, about 4 miles below Nickajack, and on the morning of the 13th destroyed Nickajack and Running Water towns, killing upwards of 50 and making a number prisoners. See American State Papers, Indian Affairs, Vol. I, p. 632.

[2] United States Statutes at Large, Vol. VII, p. 43.

treaty of June 26, 1794,[1] to have arisen concerning the provisions of the treaty of 1791. But it is gathered from various sources that the principal cause of complaint was in reference to boundaries.

At the treaty of 1791, Governor Blount, as he alleges, sought, by every means in his power, to have the boundary of the cession follow, so far as might be, the natural barrier formed by the dividing ridge between the waters of Little River and those of the Tennessee,[2] and such in fact was the tenor of his instructions from the Secretary of War; but the Indian chiefs unanimously insisted that the boundary should be a straight line, running from the point where the ridge in question should strike the Holston, and assumed as evidence of the crookedness of Governor Blount's heart the fact that he desired to run a crooked line.[3]

After that treaty was concluded, however, it became evident that there would be difficulty in determining satisfactorily where the ridge came in contact with the Holston, inasmuch as the white settlers in the vicinity could not agree upon it. The Indians also changed their minds in some respect as to the proper course of the line; but, in view of the fact that settlers were encroaching with great persistency upon their territory, they saw the necessity of taking immediate steps to have the boundary officially surveyed and marked. They also revived an old claim to pay for lands yielded by them in the establishment of the treaty line of 1785, for which they had received no compensation.

Increase of annuity.—In the conference preceding the signature of this treaty of 1794 they insisted that for this and other reasons an increase should be made in the annuity provided by the treaty of 1791, as amended by that of 1792. This was agreed to by the United States, and the annuity was increased from $1,500 to $5,000.

Boundary line to be surveyed.—It was also agreed that the treaty line of 1791 should be promptly surveyed and marked after ninety days' notice had been given to the Cherokees of the time when and the place where the survey should begin.

This, as has already been stated in connection with the treaty of 1791, had been so far performed in the fall of 1792 as to run but not mark a preliminary line for a short portion of the distance, but in spite of the additional agreement in this treaty of 1794 the actual and final survey did not take place until 1797,[4] three years after the conclusion of this treaty and more than seven years after it was originally promised to be done.

The treaty of 1794 was concluded by the Secretary of War himself with a delegation of the Cherokees who had visited Philadelphia for

---

[1] United States Statutes at Large, Vol. VII, p. 43.

[2] American State Papers, Indian Affairs, Vol. I, p. 629.

[3] Letter of Governor Blount to Secretary of War, March 2, 1792. See American State Papers, Indian Affairs, Vol. I, p. 629.

[4] American State Papers, Indian Affairs, Vol. I, p. 628.

that purpose. It was communicated by President Washington to the Senate on the 30th of December, 1794.[1]

CHEROKEE HOSTILITIES.

While this treaty was being negotiated, and for some months thereafter, a portion of the Cherokees were engaged in the bitterest hostilities against the white settlements, which were only brought to a close, as has been incidentally remarked in discussing the treaty of 1792, by the expedition of Major Ore against the Lower Cherokee towns in September, 1794.

Peace conference.—Following this expedition the hostile Cherokees sued for peace, and at their request a conference was held with them by Governor Blount, at Tellico Block House, on the 7th and 8th of November of that year.[2]

This council was attended by Col. John Watts, of Willstown, principal leader of the hostiles; Scolacutta, or the Hanging Maw, head chief of the nation, and four hundred other chiefs and warriors. A general disposition seemed to be manifested among them to abandon their habits of depredation and secure for themselves and their families that peace to which they, as well as their white neighbors, had long been strangers. Governor Blount met them in a friendly spirit and sought, by every means in his power, to confirm them in their good disposition.

In reporting the facts of this conference to the Secretary of War he asserted one of the most fruitful causes of friction between the whites and Indians to be the stealing and selling of horses by the latter, for which they could always find a ready and unquestioned market among unscrupulous whites. As measures of frontier protection he suggested the continuance of the three military garrisons of Southwest Point at the mouth of the Clinch, of Fort Granger at the mouth of the Holston, and of Tellico Block House, opposite the remains of old Fort Loudon, and also the erection of a military post, if the Cherokees would permit it, on the north bank of the Tennessee, nearly opposite the mouth of Lookout Mountain Creek. Subsequently[3] he held a further conference with the Cherokees and endeavored to foster hostilities between them and the Creeks by urging the organization of a company of their young warriors to patrol the frontiers of Mero District for its protection against incursions of the Creeks. To this the leading Cherokee chiefs refused assent, not because of any objection to the proposition, but because they desired time for preparation.

INTERCOURSE ACT OF 1796.

Early in the following year[4] President Washington, in an emphatic message, laid before Congress a communication from Governor Blount

---

[1] American State Papers, Indian Affairs, Vol. I, p. 543.
[2] American State Papers, Indian Affairs, Vol. I, p. 536.
[3] January 3, 1795. See American State Papers, Indian Affairs, Vol. I, p. 536.
[4] February 2, 1796. See American State Papers, Indian Affairs, Vol. I, p. 581.

setting forth the determination of a large combination of persons to take possession of certain Indian lands south and southwest of the Cumberland, under the pretended authority of certain acts of the legislature of North Carolina, passed some years previous, for the relief of her officers and soldiers of the Continental line.

In view of the injustice of such intrusions and the mischievous consequences which would of necessity result therefrom, the President recommended that effective provision should be made to prevent them.

This eventuated in the passage of the act of Congress, approved May 19, 1796,[1] providing for the government of intercourse between citizens of the United States and the various Indian tribes.

TREATY CONCLUDED OCTOBER 2, 1798.[2]

Held near Tellico, in the Cherokee Council House between George Walton and Lieut. Col. Thomas Butler, commissioners on behalf of the United States, and the chiefs and warriors of the Cherokee Nation.

MATERIAL PROVISIONS.

Owing to misunderstandings and consequent delay in running the boundary line prescribed by the treaties of 1791 and 1794, and the ignorant encroachment of settlers on the Indian lands within the limits of such boundaries before their survey, it became desirable that the Indians should cede more land. The following treaty was therefore concluded:

1. Peace and friendship are renewed and declared perpetual.
2. Previous treaties acknowledged to be of binding force.
3. Boundaries of the Cherokees to remain the same where not altered by this treaty.
4. The Cherokees cede to the United States all lands within the following points and lines, viz: From a point on the Tennessee River, below Tellico Block House, called the Wild Cat Rock, in a direct line to the Militia Spring near the Maryville road leading from Tellico. From the said spring to the Chill-howie Mountain by a line so to be run as will leave all the farms on Nine Mile Creek to the northward and eastward of it, and to be continued along Chill-howie Mountain until it strikes Hawkins's line. Thence along said line to the Great Iron Mountain, and from the top of which a line to be continued in a southeastwardly course to where the most southwardly branch of Little River crosses the divisional line to Tuggaloe River. From the place of beginning, the Wild Cat Rock, down the northeast margin of the Tennessee River (not including islands) to a point one mile above the junction of that river with

---

[1] United States Statutes at Large, Vol. I, p. 496.
[2] United States Statutes at Large, Vol. VII, p. 62.

the Clinch, and from thence by a line to be drawn in a right angle until it intersects Hawkins's line leading from Clinch. Thence down the said line to the river Clinch; thence up the said river to its junction with Emmery's River; thence up Emmery's River to the foot of Cumberland Mountain. From thence a line to be drawn northeastwardly along the foot of the mountain until it intersects with Campbell's line.

5. Two commissioners to be appointed (one by the United States and one by the Cherokees) to superintend the running and marking of the line, immediately upon signing of the treaty, and three maps to be made after survey for use of the War Department, the State of Tennessee, and the Cherokee Nation respectively.

6. Upon signing the treaty the Cherokees to receive $5,000 cash and an annuity of $1,000, and the United States to guarantee them the remainder of their country forever.

7. The United States to have free use of the Kentucky road running between Cumberland Mountain and river, in consideration of which the Cherokees are permitted to hunt on ceded lands.

8. Notice to be given the Cherokees of the time for delivering annual stipends.

9. Horses stolen by either whites or Indians to be paid for at $60 each (if by a white man, in cash; if by an Indian, to be deducted from annuity). All depredations prior to the beginning of these negotiations to be forgotten.

10. The Cherokees agree that the United States agent shall have sufficient ground for his temporary use while residing among them. This treaty to be binding and carried into effect by both sides when ratified by the Senate and President of the United States.

HISTORICAL DATA.

DISPUTES RESPECTING TERRITORY.

In the year 1797 the legislature of the State of Tennessee addressed a memorial and remonstrance to Congress upon the subject of the Indian title to lands within that State. The burden of this complaint was the assertion that the Indian title was at best nothing greater than a tenancy at will; that the lands they occupied within the limits of the State had been granted by the State of North Carolina, before the admission of Tennessee to the Union, to her officers and soldiers of the Continental line, and for other purposes; that the treaties entered into with the Cherokees by the United States, guaranteeing them the exclusive possession of these lands, were subversive of State as well as individual vested rights, and praying that provision be made by law for the extinguishment of the Indian claim.[1]

This was communicated to Congress by the President. Mr. Pinckney,

---

[1] This address and remonstrance will be found in full in American State Papers, Indian Affairs, Vol. I, page 625.

from the committee of the House of Representatives to which the matter was referred, submitted a report,[1] accompanied by a resolution making an appropriation for the relief of such citizens of the State of Tennessee as had a right to lands within that State, by virtue of the cession out of the State of North Carolina, provided they had made actual settlement thereon and had been deprived of the possession thereof by the operation of the act of May 19, 1796, for regulating intercourse with the Indian tribes. The sum to be appropriated, it was declared, should be subject to the order of the President of the United States, to be expended under his direction, either in extinguishing the Indian claim to the lands in question, by holding a treaty for that purpose, or to be disposed of in such other manner as he should deem best calculated to afford the persons described a temporary relief.

New treaty.—The House of Representatives, on considering the subject, passed a resolution directing the Secretary of War to lay before them such information as he possessed relative to the running of a line of experiment from Clinch River to Chilhowie Mountain by order of Governor Blount, to which the Secretary responded on the 5th of January, 1798.[2]

Following this, on the 8th of the same month, President Adams communicated a message to the Senate, setting forth that the situation of affairs between some of the citizens of the United States and the Cherokees had evinced the propriety of holding a treaty with that nation, to extinguish by purchase their right to certain parcels of land and to adjust and settle other points relative to the safety and convenience of the citizens of the United States. With this view he nominated Fisher Ames, of Massachusetts, Bushrod Washington, of Virginia, and Alfred Moore, of North Carolina, to be commissioners, having authority to hold conferences and conclude a treaty with the Cherokees for the purposes indicated.[3]

The Senate concurred in the advisability of the proposed treaty, but Fisher Ames and Bushrod Washington having declined, George Walton and John Steele were associated with Mr. Moore, and detailed instructions were given for their guidance.[4]

By these instructions they were vested jointly and severally with full powers to negotiate and conclude a treaty with the Cherokees, limited only by the scope of the instructions themselves. The Cherokee agent had already been directed to notify the Indians and the commandant of United States troops in Tennessee to furnish an escort sufficient for the protection of the negotiations.

Further purchase of Cherokee lands proposed.—The commissioners were directed as a primary consideration to secure, if possible, the consent

---

[1] December 20, 1797.
[2] American State Papers, Indian Affairs, Vol. I, p. 629.
[3] American State Papers, Indian Affairs, Vol. I, p. 631.
[4] These instructions were dated March 2, 1798. See American State Papers, Indian Affairs, Vol. I, p. 639

of the Cherokees to the sale of such part of their lands as would give a more convenient form to the State of Tennessee and conduce to the protection of its citizens. Especially was it desirable to obtain their consent to the immediate return of such settlers as had intruded on their lands and in consequence had been removed by the United States troops, such consent to be predicated on the theory that the Cherokees were willing to treat for the sale to the United States of the lands upon which these people had settled. They were directed to renew the unsuccessful effort made by Governor Blount in 1791 to secure the consent of the Cherokees that the boundary should begin at the mouth of Duck River and run up the middle of that stream to its source and thence by a line drawn to the mouth of Clinch River. The following alternative boundary propositions were directed to be submitted for the consideration of the Indians, in their numerical order, viz:

1. A line (represented on an accompanying map by a red dotted line) from a point on the ridge dividing the waters of the Cumberland from the Tennessee River, in a southwest direction, until it should strike the mouth of Duck River; thence from the mouth to the main source of the river; thence by a line over the highest ridges of the Cumberland Mountains to the mouth of Clinch River; thence down the middle of the Tennessee River till it struck the divisional line under the treaties of 1791 and 1794; thence along said line to its crossing of the Cunchee Creek running into Tuckasegee; thence to the Great Iron Mountains; thence a southeasterly course to where the most southerly branch of Little River crossed the divisional line to Tugaloo River.

2. A line (represented on said map by a double red line) beginning at the point 40 miles above Nashville, as ascertained by the commissioners (and laid down on said map); thence due east till it struck the dotted line on Cumberland Mountains; along said mountains to the junction of Clinch and Tennessee Rivers; and down the Tennessee to the extent of the boundary described in the first proposition.

3. A line (dotted blue) beginning at a point 56 miles from the point 40 miles above Nashville, on the northeast divisional line, being $1\frac{1}{2}$ miles south of the road called Walton's or Caney Fork road; thence on a course at the same distance from the said road to where it crosses Clinch River; thence resuming the remaining boundary as described in the first proposition.

4. A line (being a double blue line on the map) beginning at a point one mile south of the junction of the Clinch and Tennessee Rivers; thence westerly along the course of the road $1\frac{1}{2}$ miles south thereof until it entered into Cumberland Mountains; thence a northeasterly course along the ridges of said mountains on the west of Powell's Valley and River to the source of the river next above Clear Fork, and thence down the middle of the same to the northeast divisional line; the Tennessee River and the further line thence, as described in the first proposition, to be the remaining boundary.

In case the Indians should accept the first proposition and cede the tract therein described, or a greater quantity, the commissioners were to solemnly guarantee the Cherokees the remainder of their country and agree to their payment by the United States of either an annuity of $4,000, or to deliver them, on the signing of the treaty, goods to the amount of $5,000 and the further sum of $20,000 in four equal annual installments.

Refusing the first and accepting the second proposition, they were to receive the same guarantee, and an annuity of $3,000, or $5,000 at once in goods and $15,000 in three equal annual installments.

Refusing the first and second and accepting the third proposition, the same guarantee was offered and an annuity of $2,000, or $5,000 in goods on signing the treaty and $10,000 in two equal annual installments.

Accepting the fourth proposition, to the exclusion of the other three, the same guarantee was to be given, together with an annuity of $1,000, or $5,000 in goods on signing the treaty and the same amount during the year 1799.

It was also represented by the Secretary of War that the arts and practices used to obtain Indian land in defiance of treaties and the laws, at the risk of involving the whole country in war, had become so daring, and received such countenance from persons of prominent influence, as to render it necessary that the means to countervail them should be augmented. To this end, as well as to more effectually secure to the United States the advantages of the land which should be obtained by the treaty, the commissioners were instructed to secure the insertion into the treaty of provisions of the following import:

1. That the new line should be run and marked by two commissioners, one of whom should be appointed by the treaty commissioners and the other by the Indians. They should proceed immediately upon the signing of the treaty to the execution of that duty, upon the completion of which three maps thereof should be prepared, one for the use of the Secretary of War, one for the executive of the State of Tennessee, and one for the Cherokees.

2. That the Cherokees should at all times permit the President of the United States to employ military force within their boundaries for the arrest and removal of all persons seeking to make unauthorized negotiations with or to incite their hostility toward the United States or any of its citizens, or toward any foreign nation or Indian nation or tribe within the limits and under the protection of the United States; also, of all persons who should settle on or who should attempt to reside in the Indian country without the written permission of the President.

3. That the treaty should not be construed either to affect the right or title of any ejected settler upon the Indian lands to the tract theretofore occupied by him or in any manner to enlarge his right or claim

thereto; and that all Indian land purchased by the contemplated treaty, which had not been actually occupied as aforesaid, should remain subject to the operation of all the provisions of the proposed as well as any former treaty and of the laws of the United States relative to Indian country, until such time as said lands should be sold by and under the authority of the United States. This provision was intended to prevent any further intrusion on any part of the land ceded by the State of North Carolina to the United States; as also upon the land set apart to the Cherokee Indians by the State of North Carolina, by act of her legislature, passed May 17, 1783, described as follows, viz: "Beginning on the Tennessee, where the southern boundary of this State intersects the same, nearest to the Chicamauga towns; thence up the middle of the Tennessee and Holston to the middle of French Broad; thence up the middle of French Broad River (which lines are not to include any island or islands in the said river) to the mouth of Big Pigeon River; thence up the same to the head thereof; thence along the dividing ridge, between the waters of Pigeon River and Tuckasege River, to the southern boundary of this State."

4. The United States should have the right to establish such military posts and garrisons within the Indian limits for their protection as should be deemed proper. In case it should be found impracticable to obtain Duck River or a line that should include within it the road leading from Southwest Point to Cumberland River for a boundary, the commissioners were to stipulate for certain parcels of land lying on such road at convenient distances from each other for the establishment of houses of entertainment for travelers. Also in case the cession obtained should not include both sides of the ferry on Clinch River, to secure a limitation upon the rates of toll that should be charged by the occupant.

The commissioners repaired to Knoxville, where they ascertained it to be the desire of the Indians that the treaty negotiations should be held at Oostenaula, the Cherokee capital.

To this the commissioners objected, but agreed to meet the Indians at Chota, which they concluded to change to Tuckasege, and, finally, before the date fixed for the meeting, June 25, again changed it to Tellico, where the conference was held.[1]

Tennessee commissioners attend the council.—In the mean time[2] Governor Sevier of Tennessee designated General Robertson, James Stuart, and Lachlan McIntosh as agents to represent the interests of that State at the treaty, and gave them minute instructions covering the following points,[3] viz:

1. To obtain as wide an extinguishment of the Cherokee claim north of the Tennessee River as possible.

---

[1] Ramsey's Annals of Tennessee, pp. 693, 695.
[2] June 20, 1798.
[3] Ramsey's Annals of Tennessee, pp. 693, 695.

2. An unimpeded communication of Holston and Clinch Rivers with the Tennessee and the surrender of the west bank of the Clinch opposite South-West Point.

3. To secure from future molestation the settlements as far as they had progressed on the northern and western borders of the State and the connection of Hamilton and Mero districts, then separated by a space of unextinguished hunting ground 80 miles wide.

4. To examine into the nature and validity of the claim recently set up by the Cherokees to lands north of the Tennessee River; whether it rested upon original right or was derived from treaties; or was founded only upon temporary use or occupancy.

The council opened early in July. The "Bloody Fellow," a Cherokee chief, at the outset delivered a paper which he stated to contain their final resolutions, and which covered a peremptory refusal to sell any land or to permit the ejected settlers to return to their homes. After seeking in vain to shake this determination of the Cherokees, further negotiations were postponed until the ensuing fall, and the commissioners departed.

On the 27th of August, the Secretary of War addressed some additional instructions upon the subject to George Walton and Lieut. Col. Thomas Butler as commissioners (John Steele having resigned and Alfred Moore having returned to his home in North Carolina), authorizing them to renew the negotiations. The original instructions were to form the basis of these negotiations, but if it should be found impracticable to induce the Indians to accede to either of the first three propositions, an abandonment of them was to take place, and resort was to be had to the fourth proposition, which might be altered in any manner as to boundaries calculated to secure the most advantageous results to the United States.[1] The council was resumed at Tellico on the 20th of September, but it was found, during the progress thereof, that there was no possibility of effecting the primary objects of the State agents of Tennessee. General Robertson failed to attend. General White (who had been appointed in the place of Stuart) was there, but Mr. McIntosh resigned and Governor Sevier himself attended in person.

The treaty was finally concluded on the 2d of October, by which a cession was secured covering most of the territory contemplated by the fourth proposition, with something additional. It included most if not all the lands from which settlers had been ejected by the United States troops, and they were permitted to return to their homes.

The road privilege sought to be obtained between East and Middle Tennessee was also realized, except as to the establishment of houses of entertainment for travelers.[2]

---

[1] American State Papers, Indian Affairs, Vol. I, p. 640.

[2] By act of September 27, 1794, the legislature of the territory southwest of the Ohio authorized the raising of a fund for cutting and clearing a wagon road from Southwest Point to Bledsoe's Lick on the Cumberland. The funds for this pur-

HISTORICAL DATA 53

President Adams transmitted the treaty to the Senate,[1] and that body advised and consented to its ratification.

Boundary lines surveyed.—In fulfillment of the provisions of the fifth article of the treaty concerning the survey of boundary lines, the President appointed Captain Butler as a commissioner to run that portion of the line described as extending from Great Iron Mountain in a southeasterly direction to the point where the most southerly branch of Little River crossed the divisional line to Tugaloo River, which trust he executed in the summer of 1799.[2] Owing to the unfortunate destruction of official records by fire, in the year 1800, it is impossible to ascertain all the details concerning this survey, but it was executed on the theory that the "Little River" named in the treaty was one of the northernmost branches of Keowee River.

This survey seems not to have been accepted by the War Department, for on the 3d of June, 1802, instructions were issued by the Secretary of War to Return J. Meigs, as a commissioner, to superintend the execution of the survey of this same portion of the boundary. Mr. Thomas Freeman was appointed surveyor.[3]

From the letter of Commissioner Meigs, transmitting the plat and field notes of survey,[4] it appears that much difference of opinion had existed as to what stream was meant by the "Little River" named in the treaty, there being three streams of that name in that vicinity. Two of these were branches of the French Broad and the other of Keowee River. If the line should be run to the lower one of these two branches of the French Broad, it would leave more than one hundred families of white settlers within the Indian territory. If it were run to the branch of Keowee River, it would leave ten or twelve Indian villages within the State of North Carolina.

It was therefore determined by Commissioner Meigs to accept the upper branch of French Broad as the true intent and meaning of the treaty, and the line was run accordingly, whereby not a single white settlement was cut off or intersected, and but five Indian families were left on the Carolina side of the line.[5]

---

pose were to be raised by a lottery managed by Cols. James White, James Winchester, Stockley Donelson, David Campbell, William Cocke, and Robert Hayes. The Indians not having granted the necessary right of way, its construction was necessarily postponed, but subsequently, by act of the legislature of Tennessee passed November 14, 1801, the Cumberland Road Company was incorporated and required to cut and clear a road from the Indian boundary on the east side of Cumberland Mountain to the fork of the roads leading to Fort Blount and Walton's Ferry.

[1] January 15, 1799.
[2] See letter of General Pickens to Representative Nott, of South Carolina, January 1, 1800. American State Papers, Public Lands, Vol. I, p. 103.
[3] Letter of Secretary of War to Return J. Meigs, in Indian Office records.
[4] Dated October 20, 1802.
[5] Commissioner Meigs mentions that the accompanying plat and field notes of Mr. Freeman, the surveyor, will give more abundant details regarding this survey. After a careful search, however, no trace has been found among the Indian Office records

Status of certain territory.—In this connection it is pertinent to remark that the State of North Carolina claimed for her southern boundary the thirty-fifth degree of north latitude.

The line of this parallel was, however, at that time supposed to run about 12 miles to the north of what was subsequently ascertained to be its true location.

Between this supposed line of 35° north latitude and the northernmost boundary of Georgia, as settled upon by a convention between that State and South Carolina in 1787, there intervened a tract of country of about 12 miles in width, from north to south, and extending from east to west, from the top of the main ridge of mountains which divides the eastern from the western waters to the Mississippi River. This tract remained, as was supposed, within the chartered limits of South Carolina, and in the year 1787 was ceded by that State to the United States, subject to the Indian right of occupancy. When the Indian title to the country therein described was ceded to the United States by the treaty of 1798 with the Cherokees, the eastern portion of this 12-mile tract fell within the limits of such cession.

On its eastern extremity near the head-waters of the French Broad River, immediately at the foot of the main Blue Ridge Mountains, had been located, for a number of years prior to the treaty, a settlement of about fifty families of whites, who by its ratification became occupants of the public domain of the United States, but who were outside the territorial jurisdiction of any State. These settlers petitioned Congress to retrocede the tract of country upon which they resided to South Carolina, in order that they might be brought within the protection of the laws of that State.[1] A resolution was reported in the House of Representatives, from the committee to whom the subject had been referred, favoring such a course,[2] but Congress took no effective action on the subject, and when the State boundaries came to be finally adjusted in that re-

---

and files of the plat and field notes in question. There is much difficulty in ascertaining the exact point of departure of "Meigs Line" from Great Iron Mountains. In the report of the Tennessee and North Carolina boundary commissioners in 1821 it is stated to be 31¼ miles by the course of the mountain ridge in a general southwesterly course from the crossing of Cataluche Turnpike ; 9½ miles in a similar direction from Porter's Gap ; 21¼ miles in a northeasterly direction from the crossing of Equovetley Path, and 33¼ miles in a like course from the crossing of Tennessee River. All of these courses and distances follow the crest of the Great Iron Mountains. It is stated to the author, by General R. N. Hood, of Knoxville, Tenn., that there is a tradition that "Meigs Post" was found some years since about 1¼ miles southwest of Indian Gap. A map of the survey of Qualla Boundary, by M. S. Temple, in 1876, shows a portion of the continuation of "Meigs Line" as passing about 1¼ miles east of Quallatown. Surveyor Temple mentions it as running "S. 50° E. (formerly S. 52¼° E.")

[1] See memorial of Matthew Patterson and others, dated "French Broad, 8th January, 1800," printed in American State Papers, Public Lands, Vol. I, p. 104.

[2] This resolution was reported by Mr. Harper, from the committee to whom it was referred, to the House of Representatives, April 7, 1800, and is printed in American State Papers, Public Lands, Vol. I, p. 103.

gion the tract in question was found to be within the limits of North Carolina.

Yellow Creek settlement.—After that portion of the boundary of the country ceded by the treaty of 1798 which extended along the foot of Cumberland Mountain until it intersected "Campbell's Line" had been surveyed, complaint was made by certain settlers on Yellow Creek that by the action of the surveyors in not prolonging the line to its true point of termination, their homes had been left within the Indian country.

Thereupon the Secretary of War instructed Agent Meigs[1] to go in person and examine the line as surveyed with a view to ascertaining the truth concerning the complaints.

It was ascertained that the "point" of Campbell's Line was not on Cumberland Mountain proper, but on the ridge immediately east thereof, known as Poor Valley Ridge. This ridge is nearly as lofty as the main range, and Colonel Campbell, in approaching it from the east, had mistaken it for that range and established his terminal point accordingly. The surveyors under the treaty of 1798, assuming the correctness of Colonel Campbell's survey, had made the line of their survey close thereon. By such action the Indian boundary in that locality was extended 332 poles further to the east than would have been the case had the true reading of the treaty been followed.

A number of families of settlers on Yellow Creek, together with a tract of about 2,500 acres of land, were thus unfortunately left within the Indian country. All efforts of Agent Meigs to secure a relinquishment of this strip of territory from the Indians were, however, ineffectual.[2]

TREATY CONCLUDED OCTOBER 24, 1804; PROCLAIMED MAY 17, 1824.[3]

Held at "Tellico Block House," Tennessee, between Daniel Smith and Return J. Meigs, commissioners on the part of the United States, and the principal chiefs representing the Cherokee Nation.

MATERIAL PROVISIONS.

It is agreed and stipulated that —

1. The Cherokee Nation relinquish and cede to the United States a tract of land bounding southerly on the boundary line between the State of Georgia and the Cherokee Nation, beginning at a point on the said boundary line northeasterly of the most northeast plantation in the settlement known by the name of Wafford's Settlement, and running at right angles with the said boundary line 4 miles into the Cherokee land, thence at right angles southwesterly and parallel to the first mentioned boundary line so far as that a line to be run at right angles southerly to

---

[1] February 7, 1803. See Indian Office records.

[2] See report of Agent Return J. Meigs to the Secretary of War, May 5, 1803, on file in the Office of Indian Affairs.

[3] United States Statutes at Large, Vol. VII, p. 228.

the said first mentioned boundary line shall include in this cession all the plantations in Wafford's Settlement, so called, as aforesaid.

2. In consideration of this cession the United States agree to pay the Cherokees $5,000, in goods or cash, upon the signing of the treaty, and an annuity of $1,000.

HISTORICAL DATA.

NEW TREATY AUTHORIZED BY CONGRESS.

Congress, under date of February 19, 1799,[1] appropriated $25,000 to defray the expense of negotiating a treaty or treaties with the Indians, and again, on the 13th of May, 1800,[2] appropriated $15,000 to defray the expense of holding a treaty or treaties with the Indian tribes southwest of the Ohio River, with the proviso that nothing in the act should be construed to admit an obligation on the part of the United States to extinguish for the benefit of any State or individual the Indian claim to any lands lying within the limits of the United States.

Pursuant to the authority conferred by these enactments, President Jefferson appointed[3] General James Wilkinson, Wm. R. Davie, and Benj. Hawkins as commissioners, and they were instructed by the Secretary of War to proceed to negotiate treaties with the Cherokees, Creeks, Choctaws, and Chickasaws.

Objects of the treaty.—The objects sought to be attained with the Cherokees were to secure their consent, 1st. To cede to the United States all that portion of their territory lying to the northward of a direct line to be run from a point mentioned in treaty of October 2, 1798, on Tennessee River, 1 mile above its junction with the Clinch, to the point at or near the head of the West Fork of Stone's River, on the ridge dividing the waters of the Cumberland and Duck Rivers which is struck by a southwest line from the point where the Kentucky road crosses Cumberland River, as described in the treaty of Holston.

2. That the Tennessee River should be the boundary from its mouth to the mouth of Duck River; that Duck River should be the boundary thence to the mouth of Rock Creek; and that a direct line should be run for a continuation of the boundary from the mouth of Rock Creek to the point on the ridge that divides the waters of Cumberland from Duck River.

3. That a road should be opened from the boundary line to a circular tract on Tennessee River at the mouth of Bear River, reserved to the United States by treaty of 1786 with the Chickasaws. From this point the road should continue until it reached the Choctaw territory, where it was to connect with a road through the country of the latter to

---

[1] United States Statutes at Large, Vol. I, p. 618.

[2] United States Statutes at Large, Vol. II, p. 82.

[3] The President's appointment of these commissioners bore date of June 18, 1801.

Natchez. The entire line of this road must be open to the free use of citizens of the United States.

4. In case the Indians should refuse to cede any of the lands designated, the commissioners were instructed to obtain, if possible, a cession of all the land lying northward of the road leading from Knoxville to the Nashville settlements, run conformably to the treaty of 1791. If they should be unwilling to grant this, then to ask for a strip of land from 1 to 5 miles in width, to include the said road in its whole extent across their lands. Whether success or failure should attend the first or second objects of their mission, the commissioners were to seek the consummation of the third proposition for a road to the Bear Creek reservation, which would otherwise be of no practical value to the United States.

If consent was obtained to the first three proposals or to the alternative marked 4th, an annuity of $1,000 was authorized and an immediate sum not exceeding $5,000 in cash or goods. If, as had been represented to the War Department, the Cherokees and Chickasaws both claimed the land on either side of Tennessee River for a considerable distance, the commissioners were instructed that they must obtain the assent of both tribes to the opening of the road.

Six days after the issuance of these instructions, a delegation of Cherokees, headed by Chief "Glass," arrived in Washington, and obtained an interview with the Secretary of War.[1] They represented that the promise had been made them, at the treaty of 1798, that they would never be asked to cede any more land. Now they learned that the United States was about to hold another treaty with them to secure further cessions. They also desired to know whether the United States or the settlers got the land theretofore ceded, and why they had not been furnished with the map showing the boundary lines by the treaty of 1798, as had been promised them. In his reply,[2] after seeing the President, the Secretary of war informed them that no desire existed to purchase any more land from them unless they were anxious to sell; that the map should be at once furnished them; that the States of Kentucky and Tennessee had been formed out of the lands already purchased from them, and the main object of the proposed treaty with their nation was to secure the right of way for roads through their country in order to maintain communication between detached white settlements.

The delegation strenuously objected to the proposed "Georgia" road and were informed that the matter would not be pressed, but that the road to Bear River and Natchez was a necessity.

As a result of the visit of this delegation, the instructions to Messrs. Wilkinson, Davie, and Hawkins were modified,[2] it being stated by the

---

[1] This interview occurred, as shown by the Indian Office records, on the 30th of June, 1801, and was adjourned to meet again on the 3d of July.

[2] July 3, 1801. See Indian Office records.

Secretary of War that he had been mistaken as to part of the line between the United States and the Cherokees. He therefore directed that the second object of their instructions should be suspended as regarded both the Cherokees and the Chickasaws. Commissioner Davie having declined his appointment, General Andrew Pickens was substituted in his stead.[1]

Failure of negotiations.—It is only necessary to observe that the commissioners failed in the accomplishment of any of their designs with the Cherokees.

WAFFORD'S SETTLEMENT.

Prior to the survey and marking of the boundary line near Currahee Mountain in Georgia, provided for by the Cherokee treaty of 1785 and the Creek treaty of 1790, which survey did not occur until 1798, one Colonel Wafford, in company with sundry other persons, had formed a settlement in that vicinity, which proved to be within the limits of the Indian country.

Inasmuch as it was supposed these parties had ignorantly placed themselves within the Indian line and had made considerable and valuable improvements, the Government was indisposed to use harsh or forcible means for their ejection, but rather approved of the urgent appeals from Colonel Wafford and his neighbors to make an effort to secure the relinquishment from the Indians of a tract sufficient to embrace their settlement.

The Government had been laboring under the impression that these lands belonged to the Creeks, but the delegation of the Cherokees, headed by "The Glass," who visited Washington in the summer of 1801, claimed them as Cherokee territory, and asked for the removal of the settlers. Commissioners Wilkinson, Hawkins, and Pickens had been instructed[2] to negotiate with the Creeks for the purchase of this tract, but they having reported, upon examination, that the title was undoubtedly in the Cherokees, were directed[3] to report upon the expediency of applying to the Cherokees for a cession of the same.

Such an application having at this time been unfavorably received by the Cherokees, nothing further was done in the matter until the winter of 1803,[4] when the Secretary of War directed a conference to be held with them for the double purpose of securing a cession or a lease for seven years of the "Wafford Settlement" tract and the Indian consent to a right of way for a road through their country from Southwest Point or Tellico Factory to Athens, Ga., with the establishment of the necessary houses of entertainment for travelers along such route. For this latter concession he was authorized to offer them the sum of $500. The

---
[1] July 16, 1801. See Indian Office records.
[2] July 17, 1801. See Indian Office records.
[3] June 10, 1802. See Indian Office records.
[4] February 19, 1803. See Indian Office records.

Cherokees having refused both these propositions, Agent Meigs was directed[1] to secure the granting of the road privilege, if possible, by offering Vann[2] and other men of influence among them a proper inducement to enlist their active co-operation in the matter. This latter method seems to have been effective, for later in the season[3] the Secretary of War transmitted to the governors of Georgia and Tennessee an extract from an agreement entered into with the Cherokees providing for an opening of the desired road, stating that, as the United States had no funds applicable to the laying out and construction of such a road, it would be proper for the legislatures of those States to make the necessary provision therefor.

The clamor for more land by the constant tide of immigration that was flowing into Kentucky, Tennessee, and Georgia from the North and East became more and more importunate. The desire to settle on Indian land was as potent and insatiable with the average border settler then as it is now.

FURTHER NEGOTIATIONS AUTHORIZED.

Notwithstanding the recent and oft-repeated refusals of the Cherokees to part with more land, a new commission, consisting of Return J. Meigs and Daniel Smith, was appointed and instructed[4] by the Secretary of War to negotiate a treaty for the cession of lands in Kentucky, Tennessee, or Georgia, and particularly of the tract near the Currahee Mountain, including the Wafford settlement.

They were authorized to pay for the first cession a sum not exceeding $14,000, coupled with an annuity of $3,000, and for the "Wafford tract" not exceeding $5,000, together with an annuity of $1,000, and were directed to give "Vann," a Cherokee chief, $200 or $300 to secure his influence in favor of the proposed purchase.

Purchase of Wafford settlement tract.—In pursuance of these instructions a conference was held with the Cherokees at Tellico, Tenn.,[5] at which they concluded the arrangements for the cession of the Wafford tract, but failed in their further objects. The treaty was signed on the 24th of October, and transmitted to the Secretary of War a week later,[6] two persons having been appointed to designate and run the

---

[1] May 30, 1803.

[2] "Vann" was a half-breed of considerable ability and shrewdness, and was at this time perhaps the most influential chief among the Cherokees. His home was on the route of the proposed Georgia road, and when the road was constructed he opened a store and house of entertainment for travelers, from which he derived a considerable income.

[3] Letter of Secretary of War to governors of Georgia and Tennessee, dated November 21, 1803.

[4] April 4, 1804.

[5] October 10, 1804. See letter of Daniel Smith to Secretary of War, October 31, 1804.

[6] October 31, 1804.

lines of the ceded tract, which was found to be 23 miles and 64 chains in length and 4 miles in width.[1]

Singular disappearance of treaty.—No action having been taken looking toward the ratification of this treaty for several years ensuing, Return J. Meigs, in the winter of 1811,[2] addressed a letter to the Secretary of War calling attention to it, setting forth the fact that its consideration had theretofore been postponed on account of a misunderstanding in relation to the limits of the ceded tract, but that the Cherokees had now of their own motion, and at their own expense, had a survey made of 10 miles and 12 chains in length in addition to the original survey, which would make the tract ceded 33 miles and 76 chains in length, and which would include the plantation of every settler who could make the shadow of a claim to settlement prior to the survey of the general boundary line run in 1797[3] by Colonel Hawkins. He therefore concluded that there could be no reason for further postponing the ratification of the treaty, and urged that it be done without delay.

Notwithstanding this letter of Agent Meigs no further notice seems to have been taken of the treaty, and it had been entirely lost sight of until attention was again called to it by a Cherokee delegation visiting Washington early in 1824, nearly twenty years after its conclusion.[4]

After diligent search among the records of the War Department, Secretary Calhoun reported[5] that no such treaty could be found and no evidence that any such treaty had ever been concluded. Whereupon the Cherokee delegation produced their duplicate copy of the treaty together with other papers relating to it. The Secretary of War, after receiving a reply[6] to a letter addressed by him to Colonel McKee, of the House of Representatives (who was one of the subscribing witnesses to the treaty), became satisfied of its authenticity, and the President thereupon[7] transmitted the Cherokee duplicate to the Senate, which body advised and consented to its ratification. It was duly proclaimed by the President on the 17th of May, 1824.[8]

---

[1] Commissioner Smith in his letter of October 31, 1804, to the Secretary of War, states that two persons on the part of the United States, to be accompanied by two Cherokee chiefs, had been designated to run the boundaries of this cession. The propriety was then urged on the Cherokees by the commissioners of making a cession of the lands lying between East and West Tennessee. Several days were consumed in urging this proposal, and a majority of the chiefs were probably in favor of it, but Commissioner Smith remarks that a majority, unless it amounts almost to unanimity, is not considered with them sufficient to determine in matters of great interest, particularly in making cessions of lands.

[2] December 20, 1811.

[3] It is stated in a resolution of the Georgia legislature, passed June 16, 1802, that this line was surveyed by Colonel Hawkins in 1798.

[4] The letter of the Cherokee delegation calling attention to this matter is dated January 19, 1824.

[5] February 6, 1824.

[6] April 15, 1824.

[7] April 30, 1824.

[8] United States Statutes at Large, Vol. VII, p. 228.

TREATY CONCLUDED OCTOBER 25, 1805; PROCLAIMED APRIL 24, 1806.[1]

Held at Tellico, Tenn., between Return J. Meigs and Daniel Smith, commissioners on behalf of the United States, and certain chiefs and headmen of the Cherokees, representing that nation.

MATERIAL PROVISIONS.

1. All former treaties providing for peace and prevention of crimes are continued in force.

2. The Cherokees cede to the United States all the land which they have heretofore claimed lying to the north of the following boundary line: Beginning at the mouth of Duck River; thence up the main stream of the same to the junction of the fork at the head of which Fort Nash stood, with the main south fork; thence a direct course to a point on the Tennessee River bank opposite the mouth of Hiwassa River. If the line from Hiwassa should leave out Field's settlement, it is to be marked around his improvement and then continued the straight course; thence up the middle of the Tennessee River (but leaving all the islands to the Cherokees) to the mouth of Clinch River; thence up the Clinch River to the former boundary line agreed upon with the said Cherokees, reserving at the same time to the use of the Cherokees a small tract lying at and below the mouth of Clinch River; from the mouth extending thence down the Tennessee River from the mouth of Clinch to a notable rock on the north bank of the Tennessee in view from Southwest Point; thence a course at right angles with the river to the Cumberland road; thence eastwardly along the same to the bank of Clinch River, so as to secure the ferry landing to the Cherokees up to the first hill and down the same to the mouth thereof, together with two other sections of one square mile each, one of which is at the foot of Cumberland Mountain, at and near the place where the turnpike gate now stands, the other on the north bank of the Tennessee River where the Cherokee Talootiske now lives. And whereas from the present cession made by the Cherokees, and other circumstances, the sites of the garrisons at Southwest Point and Tellico are become not the most convenient and suitable places for the accommodation of the said Indians, it may become expedient to remove the said garrisons and factory to some more suitable place; three other square miles are reserved for the particular disposal of the United States on the north bank of the Tennessee opposite to and below the mouth of Hiwassa.

3. In consideration of the foregoing cession the United States agree to pay $3,000 at once in merchandise, $11,000 in 90 days, and an annuity of $3,000.

4. The United States to have the use of two roads through the Cherokee country, one from the head of Stone's River to Georgia road, and

---

[1] United States Statutes at Large, Vol. VII, p. 93.

the other from Franklin to the Tombigbee settlements, crossing the Tennessee River at Muscle Shoals.

5. Treaty to take effect upon ratification by the President by and with the advice and consent of the Senate.

TREATY CONCLUDED OCTOBER 27, 1805; PROCLAIMED JUNE 10, 1806.[1]

Held at Tellico, Tenn., between Return J. Meigs and Daniel Smith, commissioners on behalf of the United States, and certain chiefs and headmen of the Cherokees, representing that nation.

MATERIAL PROVISIONS.

1. The Cherokees cede the section of land at Southwest Point, extending to Kingston, reserving the ferries and the first island in Tennessee River above the mouth of Clinch River.

2. The Cherokees consent to the free and unmolested use by the United States of the mail road from Tellico to Tombigbee so far as it passes through their country.

3. In consideration of the foregoing the United States agree to pay the Cherokees $1,600 within 90 days.

4. Treaty to be obligatory on ratification by the President by and with the advice and consent of the Senate.

HISTORICAL DATA RESPECTING BOTH TREATIES.

CONTINUED NEGOTIATIONS AUTHORIZED.

The commissioners (Return J. Meigs and Daniel Smith) who were appointed and instructed under date of April 4, 1804, and who negotiated the treaty of October 24, 1804, with the Cherokees, it will be remembered, failed in the object of their instructions, except as to the single matter of securing the cession of a tract covering the settlement of Colonel Wafford and others near Currahee Mountain. They were, however, directed to continue their negotiations from time to time until the full measure of their original instructions should be secured.

Treaties of October 25 and 27, 1805, considered together.—This course was pursued, and after several fruitless conferences the commissioners succeeded in concluding the treaties of October 25, 1805, and October 27, 1805. Inasmuch as these two treaties were negotiated by the same commissioners, acting under the same instructions and at the same conference, they will be considered together. The treaties were upon their conclusion transmitted to the Secretary of War,[2] and, upon submission to the Senate, that body duly advised and consented to their ratification. They were ratified and proclaimed by the President on the 24th of April and 10th of June, 1806, respectively.[3]

---

[1] United States Statutes at Large, Vol. VII, p. 95.
[2] November 2, 1805. See letter of transmittal of Return J. Meigs and Daniel Smith.
[3] United States Statutes at Large, Vol. VII, pp. 93 and 95.

Secret agreement with Doublehead.—Following the transmission of the treaties to the Secretary of War by the commissioners, the latter addressed[1] an explanatory communication to him, in which they set forth that by the terms of the treaty of October 25, 1805, there were reserved three square miles of land, "for the particular disposal of the United States, on the north bank of the Tennessee, opposite and below the mouth of Hiwassa." This reservation, they affirmed, was predicated ostensibly on the supposition that the garrison at Southwest Point and the United States factory at Tellico would be placed thereon during the pleasure of the United States, but that they had stipulated with "Doublehead," a Cherokee chief, that whenever the United States should find this land unnecessary for the purposes mentioned it was to revert to him (Doublehead), provided that he should retain one of the square miles to his own use, but should relinquish his right and claim to the other two sections in favor of John D. Chisholm and John Riley in equal shares.

Purchase of site for State capital.—The cession by the treaty of October 27, 1805, of the section of land at Southwest Point was secured upon the theory that the State of Tennessee would find Kingston a convenient and desirable place for the establishment of the State capital. A subsequent change of circumstances and public sentiment, however, caused it to be located seven years later at Nashville.

Boundaries surveyed.—On the 11th of July, 1806, the Secretary of War notified Return J. Meigs of his appointment as commissioner to superintend the running and marking of the line "from the junction of the fork at the head of which Fort Nash stood with the main south fork of Duck River to a point on the Tennessee River bank opposite the mouth of Hiwassee River." He was also to superintend the survey of the lines of the reserved tracts agreeably to the treaty of October 25, 1805.

He was directed to appoint a surveyor, but before running the line from Duck to Tennessee Rivers above described, to have him survey and mark the lines of the 3-mile tract reserved opposite to and below the mouth of Hiwassee, and also, when completed, to designate the most suitable site for the military post, factory, and agency, each site to be 300 feet square and 40 rods distant from the others.

Commissioner Meigs followed the letter of his instructions and caused the lines to be surveyed in accordance therewith. The line from Duck River to the mouth of Hiwassee was begun on the 9th and finished on the 26th of October, 1806. The point of departure at the west end of the boundary line was a red elm tree, trimmed and topped, standing on the extreme point of land formed by the confluence of that branch of Duck River at the head of which Fort Nash stood, with the main south fork of the river. The eastern terminus of the line was a mulberry tree

---

[1] January 10, 1806.

on the north bank of Tennessee River opposite the mouth of Hiwassee River, 73 miles and 166 poles from the beginning.[1]

CONTROVERSY CONCERNING "DOUBLEHEAD" TRACT.

Colonel Martin, who was employed by Commissioner Meigs, also surveyed under the latter's direction during the same month the four small reserved tracts described in the treaty of October 25, 1805.[1] One of these afterwards produced much controversy. The language of the treaty called for three square miles on the north bank of Tennessee River, *opposite to and below* the mouth of Hiwassee River. Colonel Meigs, who was one of the commissioners who negotiated the treaty and was therefore entirely familiar with its intent, caused this tract to be surveyed adjoining the main line of cession, extending from Duck River to the mouth of Hiwassee and north of that line, which placed the tract opposite to and *above* the mouth of Hiwassee, instead of "opposite to and below" the mouth of that river.[2]

As above stated, while this reserve was ostensibly for the location of a military post and factory or trading establishment, it was really intended for the Cherokee chief Doublehead and other influential persons, as the price of their influence in securing from the Cherokees the extensive cession of land granted by the treaty.

This was sought to be secured by means of a secret article attached to the treaty. This article was reported to the War Department by the treaty commissioners[3] and made a matter of record, but it was never sent to the State Department nor to the Senate for the advice and consent of that body. After Agent Meigs had erected the Hiwassee garrison buildings on the tract, suit was brought in 1809 by Colonel McLung against the agent for the recovery of the land and mesne profits, basing his claim to title upon a grant from the State of North Carolina, of date long prior to the treaty of 1805. The suit was decided in the plaintiff's favor by the Tennessee courts. Subsequently, in 1838, John Riley made application to the Government for compensation for the loss of his one-third interest in this tract. The question was submitted to the Attorney General of the United States for his opinion. He decided that the secret article, not having been submitted to the Senate for approval, was not to be considered as any part of the treaty; but that, if the commissioners had any authority for making such an agreement, the defective execution of their powers ought not to prejudice parties acting in good faith and relying on their authority; nevertheless, no relief could be had except through the action of Congress.

This secret article was also applicable to the small tract at and below the mouth of Clinch River, to the 1 mile square at the foot of Cumber-

---

[1] See field notes of Colonel Martin on file in office of Indian Affairs.
[2] Letter of R. J. Meigs to Secretary of War, March 4, 1811.
[3] Letter of Meigs and Smith to Secretary of War, January 10, 1806.

land Mountain, and to the 1 mile square on the north bank of the Tennessee River, where Cherokee Talootiske lived. The first mentioned tract was also intended for the benefit of Doublehead, who leased it February 19, 1806, to Thomas H. Clark for twenty years. Before the expiration of the lease Doublehead was killed by some of his own people. December 10, 1820, the State of Tennessee assumed to grant the tract to Clark.[1]

The other two tracts alluded to of one square mile each were intended for Cherokee Talootiske. May 31, 1808, Talootiske perpetually leased his interest in the Cumberland Mountain tract to Thomas H. Clark. September 17, 1816, Clark purchased the interest of Robert Bell in the same tract, the latter deriving his alleged title under a grant from North Carolina to A. McCoy in July, 1793. This tract was also included in a grant from North Carolina to J. W. Lackey and Starkey Donaldson, dated January 4, 1795. The tract on Tennessee River, Talootiske sold to Robert King, whose assigns also claimed the title under the aforesaid grant from North Carolina to Lackey and Donaldson.[1]

From the phraseology of the treaty in making these several reservations, it was concluded advisable in subsequent negotiations to secure a relinquishment of the tribal title thereto, which was done by the treaty of July 18, 1817.

TREATY CONCLUDED JANUARY 7, 1806; PROCLAIMED MAY 23, 1807.[2]

Held at Washington City, D. C., between Henry Dearborn, Secretary of War, specially authorized thereto by the President of the United States, and certain chiefs and headmen of the Cherokee Nation, duly authorized and empowered by said nation.

MATERIAL PROVISIONS.

1. The Cherokees relinquish to the United States all claim to "all that tract of country which lies to the northward of the river Tennessee and westward of a line to be run from the upper part of Chickasaw Old Fields, at the upper point of an island called Chickasaw Island on said river, to the most easterly head-waters of that branch of said Tennessee River called Duck River, excepting the two following described tracts, viz: one tract bounded southerly on the said Tennessee River, at a place called the Muscle Shoals; westerly, by a creek called Te Kee, ta, no-eh, or Cyprus Creek, and easterly, by Chu, wa, lee, or Elk River or Creek, and northerly by a line to be drawn from a point on said Elk River, ten miles on a direct line from its mouth * * * to a point on the said Cyprus Creek, ten miles on a direct line from its junction with

---

[1] See report of Commissioner Indian Affairs to Secretary of War, December 9, 1834.
[2] United States Statutes at Large, Vol. VII, p. 101.

the Tennessee River. The other tract is to be two miles in width on the north side of Tennessee River, and to extend northerly from that river three miles, and bounded as follows, viz: Beginning at the mouth of Spring Creek and running up said creek three miles on a straight line; thence westerly two miles at right angles with the general course of said creek; thence southerly on a line parallel with the general course of said creek to the Tennessee River; thence up said river by its waters to the beginning, which first reserved tract is to be considered the common property of the Cherokees who now live on the same, including John D. Chesholm, Au, tow, we, and Cheh Chuh, and the other reserved tract, on which Moses Melton now lives, is to be considered the property of said Melton and of Charles Hicks, in equal shares. * * * Also relinquish * * * all right or claim * * * to the Long Island in Holston River."

2. The United States agree to pay, in consideration of the foregoing cession, $2,000 in money upon the ratification of the treaty; $8,000 in four equal annual installments; to erect a grist-mill within one year in the Cherokee country; to furnish a machine for cleaning cotton; and to pay the Cherokee chief, Black Fox, $100 annually during his life.

3. The United States agree to urge upon the Chickasaws to consent to the following boundary between that nation and the Cherokees south of Tennessee River, viz: Beginning at the mouth of Caney Creek near the lower part of Muscle Shoals, and run up said creek to its head, and in a direct line from thence to the Flat Stone, or Rock, the old corner boundary.

4. The United States agree that the claims of the Chickasaws to the two tracts reserved by article 1 of this treaty, on north side of the Tennessee River, shall be settled by the United States in such manner as will secure the title to the Cherokees.

TREATY CONCLUDED SEPTEMBER 11, 1807; PROCLAIMED APRIL 22, 1808.[1]

Held at upper end of Chickasaw Island, in Tennessee River, between James Robertson and Return J. Meigs, acting under authority of the Executive of the United States, and a delegation of Cherokee chiefs representing said nation.

MATERIAL PROVISIONS.

This treaty is simply an elucidation of the first article of the treaty of January 7, 1806, and declares that the eastern limits of the tract ceded by the latter treaty "shall be bounded by a line so to be run from the upper end of the Chickasaw Old Fields, a little above the upper point of an island, called Chickasaw Island, as will most directly intersect the first waters of Elk River; thence carried to the great Cumberland

---

[1] United States Statutes at Large, Vol. VII, p. 103.

Mountain, in which the waters of Elk River have their source; then along the margin of said mountain, until it shall intersect the lands heretofore ceded to the United States at the said Tennessee ridge."

In consideration of this concession, the United States agree to pay to the Cherokees $2,000 and to permit the latter to hunt upon the tract ceded until the increase of settlements renders it improper.

HISTORICAL DATA.

CONTROVERSY CONCERNING BOUNDARIES.

Shortly after the conclusion of the treaties of October 25 and 27, 1805, a delegation of Cherokee chiefs and headmen visited Washington. Messrs. Return J. Meigs and Daniel Smith, the commissioners who had negotiated those treaties, accompanied them.

The Secretary of War, Hon. Henry Dearborn, was specially deputized by the President to conduct negotiations with them for the purchase of such portions of their country as they might feel willing to sell, but more especially to extinguish their claim to the region of territory lying to the north and east of Tennessee River and west of the head waters of Duck River.

The negotiations were concluded and the treaty was signed on the 7th of January, 1806,[1] and the President transmitted the same to the Senate on the 24th of the same month ; but that body did not consent to its ratification for more than a year afterwards.[2]

At the time of the conclusion of this treaty, it was supposed by all the parties thereto that the eastern limit of the cession therein defined would include all of the waters of Elk River, the impression being that the headwaters of Duck River had their source farther to the east than those of the Elk.[3]

The region of country in question had for many years been claimed by both the Cherokees and the Chickasaws, and the Government of the United States, not desiring to incur the animosity of either of these Indian nations, had preferred rather to extinguish by purchase the claim of each. With this end in view, a treaty had already been concluded with the Chickasaws, under date of July 23, 1805,[4] resulting in their relinquishment of all claim to the land north of Duck River lying east of the Tennessee and to a tract lying between Duck and Tennessee Rivers, on the north and south, and east of the Columbian Highway, so as to include all the waters of Elk River. It had been the intention that the eastern boundary of the cession made by both these nations should be

---

[1] United States Statutes at Large, Vol. VII, p. 101.

[2] May, 1807.

[3] Message of President Jefferson to U. S. Senate, March 29, 1808, and letter of R. J. Meigs, September 28, 1807. American State Papers, Indian Affairs, Vol. I, p. 753.

[4] United States Statutes at Large, Vol. VII.

coincident from the head of Chickasaw Island northward, but when the country came to be examined with a view to running the line, it was found that a strict adherence to the text of the Cherokee cession would leave about two hundred families of settlers on the headwaters of Elk River still within the Indian country.[1] In the mean time the Chickasaws, having learned that the United States had purchased of the Cherokees their supposed claim to the territory as far west as the Tennessee River, including a large region of country to the westward of the limits of the cession of 1805 by the former, construed that fact as a recognition of the sole and absolute title of the Cherokees thereto, and became in consequence very much excited and angered. They were only pacified by an official letter of assurance from the Secretary of War, addressed to Maj. George Colbert, their principal chief,[2] wherein he stated that in purchasing the Cherokee right to the tract in question the United States did not intend to destroy or impair the right of the Chickasaw Nation to the same; but that, being persuaded no actual boundary had ever been agreed on between the Chickasaws and Cherokees and that the Cherokees had some claim to a portion of the lands, it was thought advisable to purchase that claim, so that whenever the Chickasaws should be disposed to convey their title there should be no dispute with the Cherokees about it.

The Cherokees by this treaty also relinquished all claim they might have to the Long Island or Great Island, as it was sometimes called, of Holston River. This island was in reality outside the limits of the country assigned the Cherokees by the first treaty between them and the United States, at Hopewell, in 1785, but they had always since maintained that no cession had ever been made of it by them, and it was deemed wise to insert a specific clause in the treaty under consideration to that effect.[3]

Boundaries to be surveyed.—Early in 1807[4] the Secretary of War notified Agent Meigs that Mr. Thomas Freeman had been appointed to survey and mark the boundary line conformably to both the treaty of 1805 with the Chickasaws and of 1806 with the Cherokees, as well as to survey the land ceded between the south line of Tennessee and the Tennessee River, lying west of the line from about the Chickasaw Old Fields to the most eastern source of Duck River. He was also advised that General Robertson and himself had been designated to attend and superintend the running of such boundary lines. Furthermore, that it

[1] President Jefferson to U. S. Senate, March 29, 1808. American State Papers, Indian Affairs, Vol. I, p. 753.

[2] February 21, 1806. Indian Office records.

[3] On the return home of the Cherokee delegation that visited Washington in 1801, "The Glass," a noted Cherokee chief, represented to his people that the Secretary of War had said, "One Joseph Martin has a claim on the Long Island of Holston River." This the Secretary of War denied, in a letter dated November 20, 1801, to Col. R. J. Meigs.

[4] April 1. Indian Office records.

was desirable that the eastern line of both cessions should be one and the same, for although by the Chickasaw treaty the whole waters of Elk River were included, it was evident their claim to any lands east of the line agreed upon by the Cherokees was more than doubtful; that, therefore, the United States ought not to insist on such a line as would go to the eastward of the one defined in the Cherokee treaty, unless the latter could be prevailed upon to extend the same, in which event they were authorized to offer the Cherokees a moderate compensation therefor.

EXPLANATORY TREATY NEGOTIATED.

This led, upon the assembly of the commissioners and surveyor at Chickasaw Old Fields, in the fall of 1807 (for the purpose of surveying and marking the boundary lines in question), to the negotiation of an explanatory treaty with certain of the Cherokee chiefs, on the 11th of September, 1807,[1] whereby it was agreed that the Cherokee cession line should be extended so far to the eastward as to include all the waters of Elk River and thereby be made coincident and uniform with the Chickasaw line.

Secret article.—The ostensible consideration paid for this concession, as shown by the treaty, was $2,000; but it was secretly agreed that $1,000 and two rifles should be given to the chiefs with whom the treaty was negotiated.[2]

President Jefferson transmitted this latter treaty to the Senate on the 29th of March, 1808, and having received the consent of that body to its ratification, it was proclaimed by the President on the 22d of April following.

TREATY CONCLUDED MARCH 22, 1816; RATIFIED APRIL 8, 1816.[3]

Held at Washington City, D. C., between George Graham, specially authorized as commissioner therefor by the President of the United States, and certain chiefs and headmen duly authorized and empowered by the Cherokee Nation.

MATERIAL PROVISIONS.

1. The Cherokees cede to the State of South Carolina the following tract: Beginning on the east bank of Chattuga River, where the boundary line of the Cherokee Nation crosses the same, running thence with the said boundary line to a rock on the Blue Ridge, where the boundary line crosses the same, and which rock has been lately estab-

---

[1] United States Statutes at Large, Vol. VII, p. 103.

[2] Letter of Return J. Meigs to Secretary of War, September 28, 1807, in which he says: "With respect to the chiefs who have transacted the business with us, they will have their hands full to satisfy the ignorant, the obstinate, and the cunning of some of their own people, for which they well deserve this *silent* consideration."

[3] United States Statutes at Large, Vol. VII, p. 138.

lished as a corner to the States of North and South Carolina; running thence south sixty-eight and a quarter degrees west, twenty miles and thirty-two chains, to a rock on the Chattuga River at the thirty-fifth degree of north latitude, another corner of the boundaries agreed upon by the States of North and South Carolina; thence down and with the Chattuga to the beginning.

2. The United States promise that the State of South Carolina shall pay to the Cherokee Nation, in consideration of the above cession, $5,000, within ninety days after the ratification of the treaty by the President and Senate, provided the Cherokee Nation and the State of South Carolina shall also ratify the same.

TREATY CONCLUDED MARCH 22, 1816;[1] RATIFIED APRIL 8, 1816.[2]

Held at Washington City, D. C., between George Graham, specially authorized as commissioner therefor by the President of the United States, and certain chiefs and headmen duly authorized and empowered by the Cherokee Nation.

MATERIAL PROVISIONS.

1. The north boundary of the lands ceded by the Creek treaty of 1814, as between such cession and the Cherokees, is declared to extend from a point on the west bank of Coosa River opposite the lower end of the Ten Islands and above Fort Strother, in a direct line, to the Flat Rock or Stone on Bear Creek, a branch of the Tennessee, which line shall constitute the south boundary of the Cherokee country lying west of Coosa River and south of Tennessee River.

2. The Cherokees concede to the United States the right to lay off, open, and have the free use of all roads through their country north of said line necessary to convenient intercourse between the States of Tennessee, Georgia, and Mississippi Territory; also the free navigation of all rivers within the Cherokee territory. The Cherokees agree to establish and maintain on the aforementioned roads the necessary ferries and public houses.

3. In order to prevent future disputes concerning the boundary above recited, the Cherokees agree to appoint two commissioners to accompany the United States commissioners appointed to run said line.

4. When the United States appoint a commissioner to lay off a road as provided for above, the Cherokees shall also appoint one to accompany him, who will be paid by the United States.

5. The United States agree to reimburse individual Cherokees for losses sustained by them in consequence of the marching of militia and United States troops through their territory, amounting to $25,000.

---

[1] Two treaties appear of the same date and negotiated by the same parties. It is to be noted that the first controls a cession to the State of South Carolina and the second defines certain other concessions to the United States.

[2] United States Statutes at Large, Vol. VII, p. 139.

HISTORICAL DATA.

Subsequent to the ratification of the treaty of September 11, 1807, with the Cherokees, no other treaty receiving the final sanction of the Senate and President was concluded with them until March 22, 1816;[1] but in the interval sundry negotiations and matters of official importance were conducted with them, which it will be proper to summarize.

COLONEL EARLE'S NEGOTIATIONS FOR THE PURCHASE OF IRON-ORE TRACT.

In the early part of the year 1807, Col. Elias Earle, of South Carolina, proposed to the Secretary of War the establishment of iron works, with suitable shops, in the Cherokee Nation, on substantially the following conditions, viz: That a suitable place should be looked out and selected where sufficient quantities of good iron ore could be found, in the vicinity of proper water privileges, for such an establishment; that the Indians should be induced to make a cession of a tract of land, not less than 6 miles square, which should embrace the ore bed and water privilege; that so much of the land so ceded as the President of the United States should deem proper should be conveyed to him (Earle), including the ore and water facilities, whereon he should be authorized to erect iron works, smith shops, and so forth. Earle, on his part, engaged to erect such iron works and shops as to enable him to furnish such quantities of iron and implements of husbandry as should be sufficient for the use of the various Indian tribes in that part of the country, including those on the west side of the Ohio and Mississippi Rivers; also to deliver annually to the order of the Government of the United States such quantities of iron and implements as should be needed for the Indian service, and on such reasonable terms as should be mutually agreed upon.

The Secretary of War referred the propositions of Colonel Earle to the President of the United States, who gave them his sanction, and accordingly Agent Meigs, of the Cherokees, was instructed[2] to endeavor to procure from the Cherokees such a cession as was proposed, so soon as Colonel Earle should have explored the country and selected a suitable place for the proposed establishment. Colonel Earle made the necessary explorations, and found a place at the mouth of Chickamauga Creek which seemed to meet the requirements of the case.

Thereupon Agent Meigs convened the Indians in council at Highwassee, Tennessee, at which Colonel Earle was present, and concluded a treaty[3] with them. By its terms, in consideration of the sum of $5,000 and 1,000 bushels of corn, the Cherokees ceded a tract of country 6

---

[1] United States Statutes at Large, Vol. VII, pp. 138 and 139.
[2] February 28, 1807.
[3] December 2, 1807. See American State Papers, Indian Affairs, Vol. I, p. 753.

miles square at the mouth of Chickamauga Creek, on the south side of Tennessee River, to be laid off in square form so as to include the creek to the best advantage for such site. The treaty also contained a proviso that in case the ore supply should fail at this point, the United States should have full liberty to procure it within the Cherokee territory at the most suitable and convenient place. Twenty-five hundred dollars of the consideration was at once paid in cash to the Indians and 1,000 bushels of corn agreed to be delivered to them the following spring. Colonel Earle carried the treaty to Washington at the next session of Congress for ratification.[1]

President Jefferson transmitted it to the Senate with a favorable message,[2] but before any action was taken by that body it was ascertained that the tract selected and ceded was within the limits of the State of Tennessee.

The matter of ratification was therefore postponed, with the hope that the State of Tennessee would consent to relinquish her claim to the land. In this the President was disappointed. No further action was taken for several years, until, it having become evident that no concession would be made in the matter by the legislature of Tennessee, the United States Senate[3] unanimously rejected the treaty. In consequence of this action, Colonel Earle made claim[4] against the Government either for the value of his time and expenses incurred in exploring the Cherokee country, selecting the site, and procuring the conclusion of the treaty, or, as an alternative, that the consent of the Cherokees should be secured to the cession of another tract of similar area and character.

The latter proposition was accepted, and Agent Meigs was advised[5] that Mr. Earle had been granted permission to select some other site suitable for his iron works, and instructed that in case he did so, negotiations should again be opened with the Cherokees for an exchange of the tract covered by the cession of 1807 for the one newly selected.

Success, however, does not seem to have attended this second attempt, and Agent Meigs was advised[6] by the Secretary of War that $985 had been paid Colonel Earle for damages sustained by him in the Cherokee country while detained there by the Indians, which amount must be deducted from the Cherokee annuity.

A third attempt of a similar character was made in 1815, when[7] Colonel Earle was appointed to negotiate, in conjunction with the Indian agent, a treaty with the Cherokees or Chickasaws for the purchase of a

---

[1] Letter of Return J. Meigs to Secretary of War, December 3, 1807.
[2] March 10, 1808. See American State Papers, Indian Affairs, Vol. I, p. 752.
[3] January 10, 1812.
[4] In March, 1812.
[5] May 14, 1812.
[6] March 24, 1814.
[7] February 3, 1815.

6-mile square tract for the erection of his proposed iron works. Like the previous efforts, it was without results.¹

TENNESSEE FAILS TO CONCLUDE A TREATY WITH THE CHEROKEES.

Congress on the 18th of April, 1806,² had passed an act entitled "An act to authorize the State of Tennessee to issue grants and perfect titles to certain lands therein described, and to settle claims to the vacant and unappropriated lands within the same."

This act, for the purpose of defining the limits of the vacant and unappropriated lands in the State of Tennessee, thereafter to be subject to the sole control and disposition of the United States, established the following described line, viz: Beginning at the place where the eastern or main branch of Elk River intersects the southern boundary of Tennessee; running thence due north until such line shall intersect the northern or main branch of Duck River; thence down the waters of Duck River to the military boundary line established by North Carolina in 1783; thence with the military line west to the place where it intersects Tennessee River; thence down the waters of Tennessee River to where it intersects the northern line of Tennessee. The act further provided that upon the execution by the State of Tennessee (through her Senators and Representatives in Congress, duly authorized thereto) of a deed of relinquishment to the United States of all the claim of that State to lands lying south and west of the described line, the United States should thereupon cede and convey to the State of Tennessee all claim to the land north and east of the line, with certain conditions and limitations therein prescribed, and with the proviso that nothing contained in the act should be construed to affect the Indian title.

Predicated upon this act of Congress, the legislature of Tennessee passed an act, on the 3d of December, 1807,³ appropriating $20,000 for the purpose of holding a treaty or treaties with the Cherokees (when authorized so to do by the Federal Government) for the purpose of extinguishing their claim to all or any part of the lands within the territorial limits of Tennessee lying to the north and east of the line described in the act of Congress just mentioned.

Congress having assented to the request of Tennessee, the Secretary of War appointed⁴ Return J. Meigs a commissioner to superintend the negotiations with the Cherokees about to be held with them by the two commissioners appointed on the part of that State. Mr. Meigs was advised that all the expenses incident to the holding of the treaty, as well as any consideration that should be agreed upon in case of a cession by

---

¹ A full history of Colonel Earle's attempt to secure a site for the erection of iron works will be found among the records and files of the Office of Indian Affairs.

² United States Statutes at Large, Vol. II, p. 381. See also amendment to this act by act of February 18, 1841, United States Statutes at Large, Vol. V, p. 412.

³ Scott's Laws of North Carolina and Tennessee.

⁴ March 26, 1808.

the Indians, should be borne by the State of Tennessee, and that the only lands the commission were authorized to treat for was that portion of the territory described in the act of April 18, 1806, as being ceded to Tennessee which should be found to lie east of the line established by Robertson and Meigs, running from the upper part of Chickasaw Old Fields northwardly so as to include all the waters of Elk River. The jealousy with which the Cherokees regarded a proposition for the sale of more land, and their especial aversion toward the people and government of Tennessee, prevented success from attending these negotiations in any degree.

REMOVAL OF CHEROKEES TO THE WEST OF THE MISSISSIPPI PROPOSED.

It had been the policy of the Federal Government, from the beginning of its official relations with the Indian tribes, to encourage and assist the individuals of those tribes in grasping and accepting the pursuits and habits of civilized life, with a view to their preparation for the condition in which the rapidly encroaching white settlements would in a few years inevitably place them.

With the disappearance of game the hunter must become a tiller of the soil or a herdsman, with the alternative of starvation. This humane policy, begun systematically in the first administration of Washington,[1] took the form of a considerable annual expenditure in the purchase for the Indians of hoes, plows, rakes, and other agricultural implements, as well as looms, cards, and spinning wheels. Among the northwestern tribes these efforts at industrial civilization were productive of trifling results. The southern tribes, however, and more especially the Creeks and Cherokees, had, in considerable numbers, manifested a partial though gradually increasing tendency toward self-support. Many of them, in addition to raising the necessaries of life, were producers in a limited degree of cotton, from which their women had learned to make a coarse article of cloth; others owned considerable herds of cattle and hogs, and altogether these tribes had made a degree of progress which was alike commendable to themselves and encouraging to the Government.

However, the persistent and unremitting demands of the border settlers for more land, backed by the thorough sympathy and influence of the State governments of Tennessee, North Carolina, and Georgia, as well as by their Senators and Representatives in Congress, acted as a powerful lever for moving the Congress and Executive of the United States to seek the complete possession of the Creek, Cherokee, Choctaw, and Chickasaw lands.

As early as 1803[2] President Jefferson had suggested the desirability

---

[1] See report of General Knox, Secretary of War, to President Washington, July 7, 1789; Creek treaty of 1790; Cherokee treaty of 1791, etc.

[2] Confidential message of President Jefferson to Congress, January 18, 1803.

of the removal of these tribes beyond the Mississippi River, although the first official action taken in this direction was contained in the fifth section of an act of Congress approved March 26, 1804, erecting Louisiana into two Territories. This act appropriated $15,000 to enable the President to effect the desired object. This was supplemented in 1808,[1] when the Secretary of War, in a letter to Agent Meigs giving permission for a delegation of Cherokees to visit Washington, instructed him to improve every opportunity of securing the consent of the Cherokees to an exchange of their lands for a tract west of the Mississippi.

The delegation here spoken of (composed of what were known as Upper Cherokees) visited Washington about the 1st of May, 1808, and, in the course of a discussion of the subject with the Secretary of War, took occasion to complain of an unequal distribution of annuities between the Upper and Lower Cherokees, and advanced a proposition that a dividing line be run between the territory of these two branches of the tribe, inasmuch as the former were cultivators of the soil, and desired to divide their lands in severalty and become citizens of the United States, while the latter were addicted to the hunter life and were indisposed to adopt civilized habits.[2] This proposition met with the personal approval of the Secretary of War. He instructed the agent[3] to ascertain the sentiments of the nation upon such a proposition, to the end that, if possible, those who adhered to aboriginal habits could be induced to accept a country in the newly acquired Territory of Louisiana, in lieu of their proportionate share of the country then occupied by the Cherokee Nation. In pursuance of this plan, the agent lost no opportunity of impressing upon the Cherokees the importance of the approaching crisis in their tribal affairs, and the necessity that some practical method should be adopted to solve the problem of subsistence involved in the rapid diminution of game. Many of the Lower or "hunter" Cherokees became persuaded of the necessity of looking out a new home, and early in January, 1809,[4] President Jefferson addressed a "talk" to them, approving their project and promising facilities for the transportation of a delegation to visit the Arkansas and White River countries, where, in case they found a suitable location, the United States would assign them a sufficient area of territory for their occupation in exchange for their share of the Cherokee domain east of the Mississippi.

Based upon this proposition, a pioneer delegation of the Indians visited that country in the year 1809, and upon their report large numbers (about 2,000, as reported by Agent Meigs) of the nation signified their intention of removal as early as the autumn of that year. The

---

[1] March 25.
[2] See letter of Secretary of War to Col. R. J. Meigs, May 5, 1808.
[3] May 5, 1808.
[4] January 9, 1809

United States authorities were not as yet prepared to defray the pecuniary expense of so large a migration. The agent was therefore directed to discourage for the present anything except the removal of individual families.[1] The situation remained unchanged until the spring of 1811,[2] when the Secretary of War informed Agent Meigs that time and circumstances had rendered it expedient to revive the subject of a general removal and exchange of lands. The latter was advised that it was very desirable to secure a cession of the Cherokee lands lying within the States of Tennessee and South Carolina, and that in case the whole nation could be brought to agree to the proposition of ceding these tracts, as the proportionate share of the "emigrant party," in exchange for lands to be assigned such party on White and Arkansas Rivers, he would be authorized and directed to negotiate a treaty with the Cherokee Nation for that purpose. From this time the subject remained *in statu quo* for several years, except that small parties of Cherokees, consisting of a few individuals or families, continued to emigrate to the "promised land." It is perhaps interesting to state, in connection with this emigration movement of the Cherokees, that it was primarily inaugurated shortly after the treaty of 1785, at Hopewell, when a few of those dissatisfied with the terms of that instrument embarked in pirogues, and, descending the Tennessee, Ohio, and Mississippi Rivers, reached and ascended the Saint Francis, then in the Spanish province of Louisiana, where they formed a settlement, from whence in a few years they removed to a more satisfactory location on White River. Here they were joined from time to time by their dissatisfied eastern brethren, in families and small parties, until they numbered, prior to the treaty of 1817, between two and three thousand souls.

EFFORTS OF SOUTH CAROLINA TO EXTINGUISH CHEROKEE TITLE.

On the 31st of December, 1810, the governor of South Carolina transmitted to the President a resolution of the legislature of that State urging an extinguishment of the Cherokee Indian title to lands within her State limits.[3] The Secretary of War, in his letter of acknowledgment,[4] assured the governor that measures would soon be taken to bring about the desired cession if possible. Nothing of importance seems, however, to have been done until the winter of 1814, when Agent Meigs was appointed[5] a commissioner for the purpose of negotiating a treaty with this end in view. He was instructed that the State of South Carolina would have an agent present, authorized to defray the expenses of the treaty and to adjust the compensation that should be agreed upon in consideration of the proposed cession, agreeably to the

---
[1] Letter of Secretary of War to Col. R. J. Meigs, November 1, 1809.
[2] March 27, 1811.
[3] Indian Office files.
[4] March 28, 1811.
[5] December 26.

provisions of the twelfth section of an act of Congress approved March 30, 1802, for regulating trade and intercourse with the Indian tribes.

These negotiations not having proved successful, the Secretary of War authorized Agent Meigs[1] to bring a delegation of the Cherokees to Washington for this and other purposes of negotiation.

This delegation arrived early in the spring of 1816, and the Hon. George Graham, being specially authorized by the President, concluded a treaty on the 22d of March of that year.[2] Therein, in consideration of the sum of $5,000, to be paid by the State of South Carolina within ninety days from the date of its ratification by the President and Senate, subject also to ratification by the Cherokee national council and by the governor of South Carolina, the Cherokees ceded to that State all claim to territory within her boundaries.

This treaty was transmitted[3] to the Senate by President Madison, and ratified and proclaimed, as set forth in the abstract of its provisions hereinbefore given, on the 8th of April, 1816.

BOUNDARY BETWEEN CHEROKEES, CREEKS, CHOCTAWS, AND CHICKASAWS.

The lines of demarkation between the respective possessions of the Cherokee, Creek, Choctaw, and Chickasaw Nations had long been a subject of dispute between them. People living in a state of barbarism and principally dependent upon the chase for a livelihood, necessarily roam over a vast amount of territory within which no permanent habitations have been established by themselves. An accurate definition of the boundaries between them and their nearest neighbors pursuing a similar mode of life is unnecessary so long as no disturbing factor is brought into the case. But contact with an ever-encroaching tide of civilization renders essential an accurate definition of limits. The United States, in several of its numerous treaties for the acquisition of territory from these four tribes, had been met with conflicting claims as to its ownership. In order that future disputes and embarrassments of this character should be avoided, the authorities of the United States entertained the idea of causing a boundary line to be run and marked between the adjoining territory of these tribes. The Indian agents were advised by the Secretary of War[4] that the subject was under consideration, the plan being to constitute a commission, consisting of two representatives selected by each tribe and of the United States agents for those tribes, who should, after full examination of the country and the subject, agree upon and fix their respective boundaries. Owing, however, to the complicated state of our foreign relations and the feverish condition of mind manifested by the border tribes, soon followed by war with England and with the

---
[1] November 22, 1815.
[2] United States Statutes at Large, Vol. VII, p. 138.
[3] March 26, 1816.
[4] May 8, 1811.

Creek Indians, it became necessary to drop further negotiations on the subject, and the matter was not again revived in this form.

After the treaty of 1814 with the Creeks, however, whereby General Jackson exacted from them, as indemnity for the expenses of the war, the cession of an immense tract of country in Alabama and Georgia,[1] the question of the proper limits of this cession on the north and west became a subject of controversy between the United States and the Cherokees, Choctaws, and Chickasaws.

The United States authorities at Washington were anxious that nothing should occur in the adjustment of these boundaries which should cause a feeling of irritation among those tribes. Commissioners had been appointed in the summer of 1815 to survey and mark the boundaries of this Creek cession, and in August of that year we find the Secretary of War giving instructions to Agent Meigs, of the Cherokees, to meet the boundary commissioners, with a few of the principal Cherokee chiefs, at the point on Coosa River where the south boundary of the Cherokee Nation crossed the same, in order that the Cherokees should be satisfied that the commissioners began at the proper point. Several additional reminders were given the agent, during the progress of the survey, that the matter of boundary was a question of fact to be ascertained and determined from the best attainable evidence, and that care must be taken that no injustice should be done the Cherokees.[2] In the following spring[3] a delegation of Cherokees was brought to Washington, by direction of the War Department, and, pending the completion of treaty negotiations with them, the boundary commissioners were instructed not to mark the line between the Cherokees and the Creek cession until further orders.

These negotiations resulted in a second treaty of March 22, 1816[4] (the one for the cession of the tract in South Carolina bears the same date), wherein it was declared that the northern boundary line of the Creek cession of 1814 should be established by the running of a line from a point on the west bank of Coosa River opposite to the lower end of the Ten Islands, above Fort Strother, directly to the Flat Rock or Stone on Bear Creek, said Flat Rock being the southwest corner of the Cherokee possessions, as defined by the treaty with them concluded January 7, 1806.

This boundary brought forth a vigorous though unavailing protest from General Jackson, who argued that the Cherokees never had any right to territory south of the Tennessee and west of Coosa River, but that it belonged to the Creeks and was properly within the limits of their cession of 1814.[5]

---

[1] United States Statutes at Large, Vol. VII, p. 120.
[2] Letter of Secretary of War to Agent Meigs, November 22, 1815.
[3] March, 1816.
[4] United States Statutes at Large, Vol. VII, p. 139.
[5] Letter from General Jackson to Secretary of War, June 10, 1816.

All efforts were fruitless in securing any further cession of lands, either north or south of the Tennessee.[1]

Previous to the visit of the Cherokee delegation to Washington and to the instructions given, as referred to above, to the boundary commissioners to suspend the running of the boundary line between the Creek cession and the Cherokees pending negotiations with the latter, General Coffee had been engaged in surveying the line from Coosa River to the Tennessee River.[2] As a result of the negotiations with the Cherokees, additional instructions were given the boundary commissioners[3] (accompanying which was a copy of the Cherokee treaty concluded on the 22d of March preceding) to run and mark the boundary line therein agreed upon from the lower end of the Ten Islands, on Coosa River, to the Flat Rock, on Bear Creek. They were advised that the surveys already made by General Coffee might be of advantage to them, though from an examination of his report it did not appear he had taken any notice of the point at which this line was to terminate, notwithstanding he seemed to have had in view the treaty made with the Cherokees in the year 1806, which proposed Caney Creek and a line from its source to the Flat Rock as the boundary between the Cherokees and Chickasaws. Coffee's line had already excited the jealousy and opposition of the Chickasaws, and on the same day final instructions were given the commissioners to run the line from Coosa River to Flat Rock, Major Cocke, the Chickasaw agent, was directed to advise the Chickasaws that in agreeing upon this line with the Cherokees the United States had in no degree interfered with the conflicting claims of the Chickasaws south of that line and east of Coffee's line; that from an examination of the treaties with the Chickasaws and Cherokees, and especially that of 1786 with the former tribe, it appeared that a point called the Flat Rock was considered a corner of the lands belonging to them, and had since been considered as the corner to the Cherokee, Creek, and Chickasaw hunting grounds. It is proper to state in this connection that for many years an uncertainty had existed in the minds of both the Indians and the United States authorities as to the exact location of this Flat Rock,[4] and whether it was on Bear Creek or on the headwaters of the Long Leaf Pine, a branch of the Black Warrior River. The line as finally run by the commissioners from Flat Rock, on Bear Creek, to Ten Islands, pursued a course bearing S. 67° 56′ 27″ E. 118 miles and 40 perches.[5] It may be interesting also to quote from a letter[6] from Will-

---

[1] Letter from Secretary of War to United States Senators from Tennessee, April 4, 1816.

[2] See letter of Secretary of War to Barnett, Hawkins, and Gaines, April 16, 1816.

[3] April 16, 1816. These boundary commissioners were William Barnett, Col. Benjamin Hawkins, and Maj. E. P. Gaines.

[4] Letter of General Jackson to Secretary of War, June 10, 1816; also from Commissioner Barnett, June 7, 1816.

[5] Old map on file in General Land Office.

[6] June 7, 1816.

iam Barnett, one of the United States boundary commissioners, to his co-commissioner, General Coffee, in which he states that he has just returned from the council at Turkeytown, at which the Cherokees, Choctaws, Chickasaws, and Creeks were represented, and that the principal purpose of the council was to agree upon and adjust their several boundaries. He notes the fact that the Creeks and Cherokees had agreed to make a joint stock of their lands, with a privilege to each nation to settle where they pleased. The Creeks and Choctaws had fixed on the ridge dividing the waters of the Black Warrior and the Cahawba as their former boundary. The Chickasaws and Cherokees could come to no understanding as to their divisional line, the former alleging that they had no knowledge of any lands held by the latter on the south side of the Tennessee River adjoining them; that they always considered the lands so claimed by the Cherokees as belonging to the Creeks, and in support of this they had exhibited to him a number of affidavits in proof that their line ran from the mouth of a small creek emptying into the Tennessee near Ditto's Landing (opposite Chickasaw Island), up the same to its source, thence to the head of the Sipsey Fork of the Black Warrior, and down the same to the Flat Rock, where the Black Warrior is 200 yards wide; that they had no knowledge of any place on Bear Creek known as Flat Rock, and that running the line to the last mentioned place would be taking from them a considerable tract of country, to which they could by no means consent.[1]

ROADS THROUGH THE CHEROKEE COUNTRY.

In order to secure a proper system of communication between the Tennessee and the Lower Alabama and Mississippi settlements, the United States had long desired the establishment of sufficient roads through the Indian country between those points. The Indians, however, were shrewd enough to perceive that the granting of such a permission would be but an entering wedge for splitting their country in twain, and afford excuse for the encroachments of white settlers.

---

[1] From a letter of Agent Meigs bearing date December 26, 1804, it seems that he was just in receipt of a communication from the Chickasaw chiefs relative to their claim to lands on the north side of Tennessee River. The chiefs assert that part of their people formerly lived at a place called Chickasaw Old Fields, on the Tennessee, about 20 miles above the mouth of Elk River; that while living there they had a war with the Cherokees, when, finding themselves too much separated from their principal settlements, they removed back thereto. Afterwards, on making peace with the Cherokees, their boundaries were agreed on as they are defined in the instrument given them by President Washington in 1794.

They further state that they had a war with the Shawnees and drove them from all the waters of the Tennessee and Duck Rivers, as well as conflicts with the Cherokees, Choctaws, and Creeks, in which they defeated all attempts of their enemies to dispossess them of their country.

Agent Meigs remarks that he is convinced the claim of the Chickasaws is the best founded; that until recently the Cherokees had always alluded to the country in controversy as the hunting ground of the four nations, and that their few settlements within this region were of recent date.

The establishment of new thoroughfares had therefore been regarded with extreme jealousy and had never been yielded to by them except after a persistency of urging that bordered on force.

In the spring of 1811[1] Agent Meigs was advised by the Secretary of War of the expediency of having a road opened without delay from the Tennessee to the Tombigbee, and also one from Tellico. Both these propositions would require the consent of the Creeks, and for the purpose of securing the most advantageous routes it was contemplated that Captain Gaines should make a journey of exploration and survey of the country between the Alabama and Coosa Rivers on the south and Tennessee and Hiwassee Rivers on the north. The fruition of these plans was also postponed on account of the ensuing war with the Creeks, and the subject was not again broached until after their subjugation. In the spring of 1814 the legislature of Tennessee transmitted two memorials to Congress on the subject, and, by direction of the Secretary of War, Agent Meigs was again instructed[2] to ascertain the bent of the Indian mind in relation thereto. The result was the conclusion, with the approval of the President, of two agreements between the Cherokees and the agents of certain road companies for the opening of two roads through the country of the latter from Tennessee to Georgia. But when the treaty of March 22, 1816, came to be negotiated at Washington, the United States authorities, after much persuasion, procured the insertion therein of an article conceding to the United States a practically free and unrestrained permission for the construction of any and all roads through the Cherokee country necessary to convenient intercourse between the northern and southern settlements.

TREATY CONCLUDED SEPTEMBER 14, 1816; PROCLAIMED DECEMBER 30, 1816.[3]

Held at Chickasaw Council House, between Maj. Gen. Andrew Jackson, General David Merriwether, and Jesse Franklin, commissioners plenipotentiary on the part of the United States, and the delegates representing the Cherokee Nation.

MATERIAL PROVISIONS.

To perpetuate peace and friendship between the United States and the Cherokees and to remove all future dissensions concerning boundaries it is agreed:

1. Peace and friendship are established between the United States and Cherokees.
2. The Cherokee Nation acknowledge the following as their western boundary: South of the Tennessee River, commencing at Camp Coffee,

---

[1] May 25.
[2] April 7.
[3] United States Statutes at Large, Vol. VII, p. 148.

on the south side of the Tennessee River, which is opposite the Chickasaw Island; running from thence a due south course to the top of the dividing ridge between the waters of the Tennessee and Tombigby Rivers; thence eastwardly along said ridge, leaving the headwaters of the Black Warrior to the right hand until opposed by the west branch of Wells' Creek; down the east bank of said creek to the Coosa River, and down said river.

3. The Cherokees cede all claim to land south and west of the above line. In consideration for such cession the United States agree to pay an annuity of $6,000 for ten years and the sum of $5,000 within sixty days after ratification of the treaty.

4. The boundary line above described, after due notice given to the Cherokees, shall be ascertained and marked by commissioners appointed by the President, accompanied by two representatives of the Cherokee Nation.

5. The Cherokee Nation agree to meet the United States treaty commissioners at Turkeytown, on Coosa River, September 28, 1816, to confirm or reject said treaty; a failure to so meet the commissioners to be equivalent to ratification.

Ratified at Turkeytown by the whole Cherokee Nation, October 4, 1816.

HISTORICAL DATA.

FURTHER PURCHASE OF CHEROKEE LANDS.

On the 27th of May, 1816, the Secretary of War instructed Agent Meigs to endeavor, at the next session of the national council of the Cherokees, to obtain a cession of the Cherokee claim north of Tennessee River within the State of Tennessee. For this proposed cession he was authorized to pay $20,000, in one or more payments, and $5,000 in presents; also to give Colonel Lowry, an influential chief among them, a sum equal to the value of his improvements.[1]

He was further instructed to make an effort to secure the cession of the lands which they had declined to sell the previous winter and which lay to the west of a line drawn due south from that point of the Tennessee River intersected by the eastern boundary of Madison County, Alabama.

The necessity for these cessions, and especially that of the former tract, had been urged upon the Government of the United States by the legislature and by the citizens of Tennessee, many of whom had been purchasers of land within its limits, from the State of North Carolina, a quarter of a century previous, and who had been restrained from possession and occupancy of the same by the United States authorities so long as the Indian title remained unextinguished. In the event that the national council of the Cherokees should decline to

---

[1] See Indian Office records.

accede to the desired cessions, Agent Meigs was to urge that the Cherokee delegation appointed to meet the boundary commissioners at the Chickasaw Council House on the 1st of September following should be invested with full authority for the conclusion of such adjustment of boundaries as might be determined on at that place. This authority was conditionally granted by the council,[1] and when the delegation came to meet the United States commissioners at the Chickasaw Council House, in the month of September, an agreement was made as to boundaries as set forth in the second article of the treaty of September 14, 1816. By this agreement the Cherokees ceded all claim west of a line from Camp Coffee to the Coosa River and south of a line from the latter point to Flat Rock, on Bear Creek.[2] The treaty was ratified by the nation in general council, at Turkeytown, on the 4th of October following.[3]

Alabama alleges error in survey.—When the due-south line from Camp Coffee provided for in the treaty was surveyed, the surveyor, through an error in running it, deflected somewhat to the west. When the adjacent country came to be surveyed and opened up to settlement much complaint was made, and the legislature of Alabama[4] passed a joint resolution reciting the fact that through this erroneous survey much valuable land had been left within the Cherokee limits which had properly been ceded to the United States and instructing Alabama's delegation in Congress to take measures for having the line correctly run. The matter having been by Congress referred to the Secretary of War for investigation and report, the Commissioner of the General Land Office, at his request, reported[5] that when the public surveys were made in that section it was found that neither the line due south from Camp Coffee nor from the head of Caney Creek had been surveyed on a true meridian. Inasmuch, however, as they had been run and marked by commissioners appointed by the United States, the surveyors necessarily made the public surveys in conformity to them. By this deviation from the true meridian the United States and the State of Alabama had gained more land from the manner in which the Caney Creek or Chickasaw boundary line had been run than had been lost by the deviation in the Cherokee or Camp Coffee line, and the quantity in either case did not perhaps exceed six or eight thousand acres.

---

[1] Letter of Return J. Meigs to the Secretary of War, dated August 19, 1816. American State Papers, Indian Affairs, Vol. II, p. 113.

[2] Report of Commissioners Jackson, Merriwether, and Franklin to Secretary of War, dated Chickasaw Council House, September 20, 1816. American State Papers, Indian Affairs, Vol. II, p. 104.

[3] Report of Commissioners Jackson and Merriwether to Secretary of War, October 4, 1816.

[4] January 7, 1828.

[5] February 25, 1828.

TREATY CONCLUDED JULY 8, 1817; PROCLAIMED DECEMBER 26, 1817.[1]

Held at Cherokee Agency, in the Cherokee Nation, between Maj. Gen. Andrew Jackson, Joseph McMinn, governor of Tennessee, and General David Merriwether, commissioners plenipotentiary of the United States, and the chiefs, headmen, and warriors of the Cherokee Nation east of the Mississippi River, and those on the Arkansas River, by their deputies, John D. Chisholm and James Rogers, duly authorized by written power of attorney.

MATERIAL PROVISIONS.

1. The whole Cherokee Nation cede to the United States all the lands lying north and east of the following boundaries, viz: Beginning at the High Shoals of the Appalachy River, and running thence along the boundary line between the Creek and Cherokee Nations westwardly to the Chatahouchy River; thence up the Chatahouchy River to the mouth of Souque Creek; thence continuing with the general course of the river until it reaches the Indian boundary line; and should it strike the Turrurar River, thence with its meanders down said river to its mouth, in part of the proportion of land in the Cherokee Nation east of the Mississippi to which those now on the Arkansas and those about to remove there are justly entitled.

2. The whole Cherokee Nation do also cede to the United States all the lands lying north and west of the following boundary lines, viz: Beginning at the Indian boundary line that runs from the north bank of the Tennessee River opposite to the mouth of Hywassee River, at a point on the top of Walden's Ridge where it divides the waters of the Tennessee River from those of the Sequatchie River; thence along said ridge southwardly to the bank of the Tennessee River at a point near to a place called the Negro Sugar Camp, opposite to the upper end of the first island above Running Water Town; thence westwardly a straight line to the mouth of Little Sequatchie River; thence up said river to its main fork; thence up its northermost fork to its source; and thence due west to the Indian boundary line.

3. A census to be taken of the whole Cherokee Nation during June, 1818. The enumeration of those east of the Mississippi River to be made by a commissioner appointed by the President of the United States and a commissioner appointed by the Cherokees residing on the Arkansas. That of those on the Arkansas by a United States commissioner and one appointed by the Cherokees east of the Mississippi.

4. The annuities for 1818 and thereafter to be divided upon the basis of said census between Cherokees east of the Mississippi and those on the Arkansas. The lands east of the Mississippi also to be divided, and the proportion of those moved and agreeing to remove to the Arkansas to be surrendered to the United States.

---

[1] United States Statutes at Large, Vol. VII, p. 156.

5. The United States agree to give to the removing Cherokees a tract of land on the Arkansas and White Rivers equal in area to the quantity ceded the United States by first and second articles hereof. Said tract to begin on north side of the Arkansas River, at mouth of Point Remove, or Budwell's Old Place; thence northwardly by a straight line to strike Chataunga Mountain, the first hill above Shield's Ferry, on White River, and running up and between said rivers for quantity. Said boundary from point of beginning to be surveyed, and all citizens of the United States except Mrs. P. Lovely to be removed therefrom. All previous treaties to remain in full force and to be binding on both parts of the Cherokee Nation. The United States reserves the right to establish factories, a military post, and roads within the boundaries last above defined.

6. The United States agree to give all poor warriors who remove a rifle, ammunition, blanket, and brass kettle or beaver trap each, as full compensation for improvements left by them; to those whose improvements add real value to the land, the full value thereof, as ascertained by appraisal, shall be paid. The United States to furnish flat-bottomed boats and provisions on the Tennessee River for transportation of those removing.

7. All valuable improvements made by Cherokees within the limits ceded to the United States by first and second articles hereof shall be paid for by the United States or others of equal value left by removing Cherokees given in lieu thereof. Improvements left by emigrant Cherokees not so exchanged shall be rented to the Indians, for the benefit of the poor and decrepit of the Eastern Cherokees.

8. Each head of a Cherokee family residing on lands herein or hereafter ceded to the United States who elects to become a citizen of the United States shall receive a reservation of 640 acres, to include his or her improvements, for life, with reversion in fee simple to children, subject to widow's dower. On removal of reservees their reservations shall revert to the United States. Lands reserved under this provision shall be deducted from the quantity ceded by first and second articles.

9. All parties to the treaty shall have free navigation of all waters herein mentioned.

10. The Cherokee Nation cedes to the United States all claim to reservations made to Doublehead and others by treaty of January 7, 1806.

11. Boundary lines of lands ceded to the United States by first and second articles, and by the United States to the Cherokees in fifth article hereof, to be run and marked by a United States commissioner, to be accompanied by commissioners appointed by the Cherokees.

12. Citizens of the United States are forbidden to enter upon lands herein ceded by the Cherokees until ratification and proclamation of this treaty.

13. Treaty to be binding upon the assent and ratification of the Senate and President of the United States.

TREATY OF JULY 8, 1817

HISTORICAL DATA.

POLICY OF REMOVING INDIAN TRIBES TO THE WEST OF THE MISSISSIPPI RIVER.

In the settlement and colonization by civilized people of a country theretofore a wilderness, and inhabited only by savage tribes, many important and controlling reasons exist why the occupation of such a country should be accomplished by regular and gradual advances and in a more or less connected and compact manner. It was expedient that a united front should be presented by the earlier settlers of this continent, in order that the hostile raids and demonstrations of the Indian warriors might be successfully resisted and repulsed. Therefore, the settlements were, as a rule, extended from the coast line toward the interior by regular steps, without the intermission of long distances of unoccupied territory. This seemed to be the policy anterior to the Revolution, and was announced in the proclamation of King George in 1763 wherein he prohibited settlements being made on Indian lands or the purchase of the same by unauthorized persons.

The first ordinances of Congress under the Articles of Confederation for disposing of the public lands were predicated upon the same theory. But after the close of the war for independence, circumstances arising out of the treaty of 1783 with Great Britain and the acquisition of Louisiana from France imposed the necessity for a departure from the old system. Within the limits of the territory thus acquired sundry settlements had been made by the French people at points widely separated from one another and with many hundreds of miles of wilderness intervening between them and the English settlements on the Atlantic slope. The evils and inconveniences resulting from this irregular form of frontier were manifest.

Settlements thus widely separated, or projecting in long, narrow column far into the Indian country, manifestly increased in large ratio the causes of savage jealousy and hostility. At the same time the means of defense were rendered less certain and the expense and difficulty of adequately protecting such a frontier were largely enhanced.

Such, however, was the condition and shape of our frontier settlements during the earlier years of the present century. Settlements on the Tennessee and Cumberland were cut off from communication with those of Georgia, Lower Alabama, and Mississippi by long stretches of territory inhabited or roamed over by the Cherokees, Creeks, Choctaws, and Chickasaws.

The French communities of Kaskaskia, Vincennes, and Detroit were similarly separated from the people of Virginia, Pennsylvania, and newly settled Ohio by the territory of the hostile Shawnees, Miamis, Wyandots, Pottawatomies, Ottawas, Kickapoos, *et al.*

A cure for all this inconvenience and expense had been sought and given much consideration by the Government authorities.

President Jefferson (as has been previously stated) had, as early as 1803,[1] suggested the propriety of an exchange of lands by those tribes east of the Mississippi for an equal or greater area of territory within the newly acquired Louisiana purchase, and in 1809 had authorized a delegation of Cherokees to proceed to that country with a view to selecting a suitable tract to which they might remove, and to which many of them did remove in the course of the years immediately succeeding.[2]

The matter of a general exchange of lands, however, became the subject of Congressional consideration, and the Committee on Public Lands of the United States Senate reported[3] a resolution for an appropriation to enable the President to negotiate treaties with the Indian tribes which should have for their object an exchange of territory owned by any tribe residing east of the Mississippi for other land west of that river.

The committee expressed the opinion that the proposition contained in the foregoing resolution would be better calculated to remedy the inconvenience and remove the evils arising out of the existing condition of the frontier settlements than any other within the power of the Government. It was admitted, however, that this object could not be attained except by the voluntary consent of the several tribes interested, made manifest through duly negotiated treaties with them.

The Senate was favorable to this proposition, but the House of Representatives interposed a negative upon the action taken by the former body.[4]

Removal of Cherokees encouraged.—The subject had long been under consideration by the Cherokees, and no opportunity had been lost on the part of the executive authorities of the United States to encourage a sentiment among them favorable to the removal scheme. Many individuals of the tribe had already emigrated, and on the 18th of October, 1816, General Andrew Jackson, in addressing the Secretary of War upon the subject of the recent Cherokee and Chickasaw treaties, suggested his belief that the Cherokees would shortly make a tender of their whole territory to the United States in exchange for lands on the Arkansas River. He further remarked that a council would soon be held by them at Willstown to select a proper delegation who should visit the country west of the Mississippi and examine and report upon its character and adaptability for their needs. In case this report should prove favorable, a Cherokee delegation would thereupon wait upon the President, with authority to agree upon satisfactory terms of exchange. To this the Secretary of War replied that whenever the

---

[1] Confidential message of President Jefferson to Congress, January 18, 1803.

[2] The letter of President Jefferson authorizing a delegation of Cherokees to visit the Arkansas and White River country was dated January 9, 1809, and will be found in the American State Papers, Indian Affairs, Vol. II, p. 125, as well as among the records of the Indian Office.

[3] January 9, 1817.

[4] Letter of Secretary of War to General Jackson, May 14, 1817.

Cherokee Nation should be disposed to enter into an arrangement for an exchange of the lands occupied by them for lands on the west side of the Mississippi River and should appoint delegates clothed with full authority to negotiate a treaty for such exchange they would be received by the President and treated with on the most liberal terms.

This state of feeling among the Cherokees had been considerably increased by the fact that those of their people who had already settled upon the Arkansas and White Rivers had become involved in territorial disputes of a most serious character with the Osages and Quapaws. The latter tribes claimed ownership of the lands upon which the former were settled Upon the Arkansas Cherokees laying their complaints before the United States authorities, they were informed that nothing could be done for their relief until the main body of the nation should take some definite action, in accordance with previous understanding, toward relinquishing a portion of their territory equal in area to the tract upon which the emigrant party had located.[1]

FURTHER CESSION OF TERRITORY BY THE CHEROKEES.

With a view to reaching a full understanding on this subject, the Secretary of War notified[2] General Andrew Jackson, Governor McMinn. of Tennessee, and General David Merriwether that they had been appointed commissioners for the purpose of holding a treaty with the Cherokees on or about the 20th of June, 1817.[3] In pursuance of these instructions a conference was called and held at the Cherokee Agency, which resulted in the treaty of July 8, 1817.[4] By this treaty the Cherokees ceded two large tracts of country[5] in exchange for one of equal area on the Arkansas and White Rivers adjoining the territory of the

---

[1] In a letter to Return J. Meigs, under date of September 18, 1816, the Secretary of War says that "the difficulties which have arisen between the Cherokees and the Osages, on the north of the Arkansas, and with the Quapaws, on the south, cannot be finally settled until the line of the cession shall be run and the rights of the Quapaws shall be ascertained. Commissioners appointed by the President are now sitting at Saint Louis for the adjustment of those differences; but should the line of the Osage treaty prove that they are settled upon the Osage lands, nothing can be done for the Cherokees. It is known to you and to that nation that the condition upon which the emigration was permitted by the President was that a cession of Cherokee lands should be made equal to the proportion which the emigrants should bear to the whole nation. This condition has never been complied with on the part of the nation, and of course all obligation on the part of the United States to secure the emigrants in their new possessions has ceased. When the subject was mentioned to the Cherokee deputation last winter, so far were they from acknowledging its force, that they declared the emigrants should be compelled to return."

[2] May 14, 1817.

[3] On the 17th of May, 1817, these commissioners were advised that the lands proposed to be given the Cherokees on the west of the Mississippi River, in exchange for those then occupied by them, were the lands on the Arkansas and immediately adjoining the Osage boundary line.

[4] United States Statutes at Large, Vol. VII, p. 156.

[5] These tracts are designated on the accompanying map as Nos. 23 and 24.

Osages. The Cherokees also ceded two small reservations made by the treaty of January 7, 1806.[1]

The large cession by the first article of the treaty of 1817, though partially in Georgia, was at the time supposed to cover all the territory claimed by the Cherokees within the limits of North Carolina,[2] and was secured in deference to the urgent importunities of the legislature and people of that State. It was subsequently ascertained that this supposition was incorrect.

Majority of Cherokees averse to removal.—During the conference, but before the negotiations had reached any definite result, a memorial was presented to the United States commissioners, signed by sixty-seven of the chiefs and headmen of the nation, setting forth that the delegation of their nation who in 1809 visited Washington and discussed with President Jefferson the proposition for an exchange of lands had acted without any delegated authority on the subject. The memorialists claimed to represent the prevailing feeling of the nation and were desirous of remaining upon and retaining the country of their nativity. They were distressed with the alternative proposals to remove to the Arkansas country or remain and become citizens of the United States. While they had not attained a sufficient degree of civilization to fit them for the duties of citizenship, they yet deprecated a return to the same savage state and surroundings which had characterized their mode of life when first brought in contact with the whites. They therefore requested that the subject should not be further pressed, but that they might be enabled to remain in peaceable possession of the land of their fathers.[3]

The commissioners, however, proceeded with their negotiations, and concluded the treaty as previously set forth, which was finally signed by twenty-two of the chiefs and headmen whose names appeared attached to the memorial, as well as six others, on behalf of the eastern portion of the nation, and by fifteen chiefs representing those on the Arkansas.[4] The treaty was submitted to the Senate, for its advice and consent, at the ensuing session of Congress, and although it encountered the hostility of those Senators who were opposed to the general policy of an exchange of lands with the Indians, and of some who argued, because of the few chiefs who had signed it, that it did not represent the full and free expression of their national assent,[5] that body approved its provisions, and the President ratified and proclaimed it on the 26th of December, 1817.

---

[1] These tracts are designated on the accompanying map as Nos. 25 and 26.

[2] August 1, 1817, the Secretary of War advised the governor of North Carolina that a treaty with the Cherokees had been concluded, by which the Indian claim was relinquished to a tract of country including the whole of the land claimed by them in North Carolina.

[3] This memorial bore date of July 2, 1817.

[4] United States Statutes at Large, Vol. VII, p. 156.

[5] Letter of Secretary of War to Treaty Commissioners August 1, 1817.

A portion of the Cherokees emigrate west.—Immediately upon the signing of the treaty, the United States authorities, presuming upon its final ratification, took measures for carrying into effect the scheme of emigration. Within a month Agent Meigs reported that over 700 Cherokees had already enrolled themselves for removal the ensuing fall.

The Secretary of War entered into a contract for 60 boats, to be delivered by 1st of November at points between the mouths of the Little Tennessee and Sequatchie Rivers, together with rifles, ammunition, blankets, and provisions;[1] and, under the control and directions of Governor McMinn, of Tennessee, the stream of emigration began to flow, increasing in volume until within the next year over 3,000 had emigrated to their new homes, which numbers had during the year 1819 increased to 6,000.[2]

Persecution of those favorable to emigration.—There can be no question that a very large portion, and probably a majority, of the Cherokee Nation residing east of the Mississippi had been and still continued bitterly opposed to the terms of the treaty of 1817. They viewed with jealous and aching hearts all attempts to drive them from the homes of their ancestors, for they could not but consider the constant and urgent importunities of the Federal authorities in the light of an imperative demand for the cession of more territory. They felt that they were, as a nation, being slowly but surely compressed within the contracting coils of the giant anaconda of civilization; yet they held to the vain hope that a spirit of justice and mercy would be born of their helpless condition which would finally prevail in their favor. Their traditions furnished them no guide by which to judge of the results certain to follow such a conflict as that in which they were engaged.

This difference of sentiment in the nation upon a subject so vital to their welfare was productive of much bitterness and violent animosities. Those who had favored the emigration scheme and had been induced, either through personal preference or by the subsidizing influences of the Government agents, to favor the conclusion of the treaty, became the object of scorn and hatred to the remainder of the nation. They were made the subjects of a persecution so relentless, while they remained in the eastern country, that it was never forgotten, and when,

---

[1] Letters of Secretary of War to General Jackson and Colonel Meigs, August 9, 1817.

[2] Letter of Governor McMinn to Secretary of War, November 29, 1818, and subsequent correspondence during 1819. Governor McMinn's letter of November 29, 1818, states that 718 families had enrolled for emigration since December 20, 1817, and 146 families had taken reservations, which made in all, including those who had already emigrated, about one-half of the Cherokee Nation as committed to the support of the policy involved in the treaty of 1817.

February 17, 1819, a Cherokee delegation advised the Secretary of War that, while Governor McMinn's enrollment showed the number of Cherokees who had removed or enrolled to go prior to November 15, 1818, to be 5,291, by their calculation the number did not exceed 3,500, and that they estimated the number of Cherokees remaining east of the Mississippi at about 12,544.

in the natural course of events, the remainder of the nation were forced to remove to the Arkansas country and join the earlier emigrants, the old hatreds and dissensions broke out afresh, and to this day they find lodgment in some degree in the breasts of their descendants.

Dissatisfaction with the treaty of 1817.—The dissatisfaction with the treaty of 1817 took shape in the assemblage of a council at Amoha, in the Cherokee Nation, in September of the same year, at which six of the principal men were selected as a deputation to visit the President at Washington and present to him in person a detailed statement of the grievances and indignities to which they had been subjected in greater or less degree for many years and to ask relief and redress.

They were to present, with special particularity, to the President's notice a statement of the improper methods and influences that had been used to secure the apparent consent of the nation to the treaty of 1817. They were authorized to enter into a new treaty with the United States, in lieu of the recent one, in which an alteration might be made in certain articles of it, and some additional article inserted relative to the mode of payment of their annuity as between the Eastern and Arkansas Cherokees.[1]

The delegation was received and interviews were accorded them by the President and Secretary of War, but they secured nothing but general expressions of good will and promises of protection in their rights and property.

TREATY CONCLUDED FEBRUARY 27, 1819; PROCLAIMED MARCH 10, 1819.[2]

Held at Washington City, D. C., between John C. Calhoun, Secretary of War, specially authorized therefor by the President of the United States, and the chiefs and headmen of the Cherokee Nation of Indians.

MATERIAL PROVISIONS.

1. The Cherokee Nation cedes to the United States all of their lands lying north and east of the following line, viz: Beginning on the Tennessee River at the point where the Cherokee boundary with Madison County, in the Alabama Territory, joins the same; thence along the main channel of said river to the mouth of the Highwassee; thence along its main channel to the first hill which closes in on said river, about two miles above Highwassee Old Town; thence along the ridge which divides the waters of the Highwassee and Little Tellico to the Tennessee River at Talassee; thence along the main channel to the junction of the Cowee and Nanteyalee; thence along the ridge in the

---

[1] The instructions of the Amoha council to the delegation of six bear date of Fortville, Cherokee Nation, September 19, 1817.
[2] United States Statutes at Large, Vol. VII, p. 195.

fork of said river to the top of the Blue Ridge; thence along the Blue Ridge to the Unicoy Turnpike Road; thence by straight line to the nearest main source of the Chestatee; thence along its main channel to the Chattahouchee; and thence to the Creek boundary; it being understood that all the islands in the Chestatee, and the parts of the Tennessee and Highwassee (with the exception of Jolly's Island, in the Tennessee, near the mouth of the Highwassee) which constitute a portion of the present boundary, belong to the Cherokee Nation; and it is also understood that the reservations contained in the second article of the treaty of Tellico, signed the twenty-fifth October, eighteen hundred and five, and a tract equal to twelve miles square, to be located by commencing at the point formed by the intersection of the boundary line of Madison County already mentioned and the north bank of the Tennessee River, thence along the said line and up the said river twelve miles, are ceded to the United States, in trust for the Cherokee Nation, as a school fund, to be sold by the United States, and the proceeds vested as is hereafter provided in the fourth article of this treaty; and also that the rights vested in the Unicoy Turnpike Company by the Cherokee Nation * * * are not to be affected by this treaty.

The foregoing cessions are understood and declared to be in full satisfaction of all claims of the United States upon the Cherokees on account of the cession to a part of their nation who have emigrated or who may emigrate to the Arkansas and as a final adjustment of the treaty of July 8, 1817.

2. The United States agree to pay, according to the treaty of July 8, 1817, for all valuable improvements on land within the country ceded by the Cherokees, and to allow a reservation of 640 acres to each head of a family (not enrolled for removal to Arkansas) who elects to become a citizen of the United States.

3. Each person named in a list accompanying the treaty shall have a reserve of 640 acres in fee simple, to include his improvements, upon giving notice within six months to the agent of his intention to reside permanently thereon. Various other reservations in fee simple are made to persons therein named.

4. The reservations and 12-mile tract reserved for a school fund in the first article are to be sold by the United States and the proceeds invested in good stocks, the interest of which shall be expended in educational benefits for the Cherokees east of the Mississippi.

5. The boundary lines of the land ceded by the first article shall be established by commissioners appointed by the United States and the Cherokees. Leases made under the treaty of 1817 of land within the Cherokee country shall be void. All white people intruding upon the lands reserved by the Cherokees shall be removed by the United States, under the act of March 30, 1802.

6. Annuities shall be distributed in the proportion of two-thirds to those east to one-third to those west of the Mississippi. Should the

latter object within one year to this proportion, a census shall be taken of both portions of the nation to adjust the matter.

7. The United States shall prevent intrusion on the ceded lands prior to January 1, 1820.

8. The treaty shall be binding upon its ratification.

HISTORICAL DATA.

CHEROKEES WEST OF THE MISSISSIPPI — THEIR WANTS AND CONDITION.

Early in 1818 a representative delegation from that portion of the Cherokees who had removed to the Arkansas visited Washington with the view of reaching a more satisfactory understanding concerning the location and extent of their newly acquired homes in that region. As early as January 14 of that year, they had addressed a memorial to the Secretary of War asking, among other things, that the United States should recognize them as a separate and distinct people, clothed with the power to frame and administer their own laws, after the manner of their brethren east of the Mississippi.

Long and patient hearings were accorded to this delegation by the authorities of the Government, and, predicated upon their requests, instructions were issued[1] to Governor William Clark, superintendent of Indian affairs at Saint Louis, among other things, to secure a cessation of hostilities then raging between the Arkansas Cherokees and the Osages; furthermore, to induce, if possible, the Shawnees and Delawares then residing in the neighborhood of Cape Girardeau to relinquish their land and join the Western Cherokees, or, in the event of a favorable termination of the Quapaw treaty then pending, that they might be located on lands acquired from them.

During the year the Arkansas Cherokees had also learned that the Oneidas of New York were desirous of obtaining a home in the West, and had made overtures for their settlement among them.[2] The main object of the Cherokees in desiring to secure these originally eastern Indians for close neighbors is to be found in the increased strength they would be able to muster in sustaining their quarrel with their native western neighbors.

It may be interesting in this connection to note the fact that in 1825 the Cherokees sent a delegation to Wapakoneta, Ohio, accompanied by certain Western Shawnees, whose mission was to induce the Shawnees at that point to join them in the West. Governor Lewis Cass, under instructions from the War Department, held a council at Wapakoneta, lasting nine days,[3] having in view the accomplishment of this end, but it was unsuccessful.

Governor Clark was also advised by his instructions of the desire of

---

[1] May 8, 1818.
[2] Secretary of War to Reuben Lewis, United States Indian agent, May 16, 1818.
[3] May 16 to 24, inclusive.

the Cherokees to secure an indefinite outlet west, in order that they should not in the future, by the encroachments of the whites and the diminution of game, be deprived of uninterrupted access to the more remote haunts of the buffalo and other large game animals. He was instructed to do everything consistent with justice in the matter to favor the Cherokees by securing from the Osages the concession of such a privilege, it being the object of the President that every favorable inducement should be held out to the Cherokees east of the Mississippi to remove and join their western brethren. This extension of their territory to the west was promised them by the President in the near future, and in the summer of 1819[1] the Secretary of War instructed Reuben Lewis, United States Indian agent, to assure the Cherokees that the President, through the recent accession of territory from the Osages, was ready and willing to fulfill his promise.

Survey of east boundary of Cherokees in Arkansas.—Provision having been made in the treaty of 1817[2] for a definition of the east line of the tract assigned the Cherokees on the Arkansas, Mr. Reuben Lewis, the Indian agent in that section, was designated, in the fall of 1818,[3] to run and mark the line, and upon its completion to cause to be removed, without delay, all white settlers living west thereof, with the single exception mentioned in the treaty.

These instructions to Mr. Lewis miscarried in the mails and did not reach him until the following summer. The line had in the mean time been run by General William Rector, under the authority of the Commissioner of the General Land Office, which survey Mr. Lewis was authorized to accept as the correct boundary provided the Cherokees were satisfied therewith.[4] The field notes of this survey were certified by General Rector April 14, 1819, and show the length of the line from Point Remove to White River to have been 71 miles 55 chains and the course N. 53° E.[5]

Treaty between Cherokees and Osages.—During this interval[6] Governor Clark had succeeded in securing the presence at Saint Louis of representative delegations of both the Osage and Western Cherokee tribes, between whom, after protracted negotiations, he succeeded in establishing the most peaceful and harmonious relations, which were evidenced by all the usual formalities of a treaty.

DISPUTES AMONG CHEROKEES CONCERNING EMIGRATION.

The unhappy differences of mind among the Cherokees east of the Mississippi on the subject of removal, which had been fast approaching

---

[1] July 22.
[2] United States Statutes at Large, Vol. VII, p. 156.
[3] Letter of Secretary of War to Capt. William Bradford, September 9, 1818.
[4] Secretary of War to Agent Lewis, July 22, 1819.
[5] Field notes and diagram on file in Indian Office.
[6] October 6, 1818.

a climax as a consequence of the treaty of 1817, had been rather stimulated than otherwise by the frequent departure of parties for their new western home, and the constant importunities of the United States and State officials (frequently bearing the semblance of threats) having in view the removal of the entire tribe. The many and open acts of violence practiced by the "home" as against the "emigration" party at length called forth[1] a vigorous letter of denunciation from the Secretary of War to Governor McMinn, the emigration superintendent. After detailing at much length the many advantages that would accrue to the Cherokee Nation by a removal beyond the contaminating influences always attendant upon the contact of a rude and barbarous people with a higher type of civilization, the unselfish and fatherly interest the Government of the United States had always manifested and still felt in the comfort and progress of the Cherokee people, and the great degree of liberality that had characterized its action in securing for the Cherokees in their new homes an indefinite outlet to the bountiful hunting grounds of the West, the Secretary concluded by an expression of the determination on the part of the United States to protect at all hazards from insult and injury to person or property every Cherokee who should express an opinion or take action favorable to the scheme of emigration. He also instructed Governor McMinn to lose no opportunity of impressing upon the minds of the Cherokees that the practical effect of a complete execution of the treaty of 1817 would be, as had been the intention of the Government when it was negotiated, to compel them either to remove to the Arkansas or to accept individual reservations and become citizens of the States within whose limits they respectively resided.

PUBLIC SENTIMENT IN TENNESSEE AND GEORGIA CONCERNING CHEROKEE REMOVAL.

Governor McMinn, being the executive of the State of Tennessee, could hardly be supposed to present the views of the Secretary of War to the Cherokees on the subject of their removal in milder terms or manner than they had been communicated to him. The public officer in that State who should have neglected such an opportunity of compelling the Cherokees to appreciate the benefits of a wholesale emigration to the West would have fared but ill at the polls in a contest for re-election. The people of both Tennessee and Georgia were unalterably determined that the Indians should be removed from their States, and no compromise or temporary expedient of delay would satisfy their demands.

Millions of acres of valuable lands, rich in all the elements that combine to satisfy the necessities and the desires of the husbandman — mountain, valley, and plain — comprising every variety of soil, fertilized by innumerable running streams and clothed with heavy forests of the finest timber, were yet in the possession of the native tribes of this re-

---

[1] July 29, 1818.

gion. Other lands in great quantities, available for white settlement and occupation, both in Kentucky and the adjoining States, were, it is true, lying idle. In point of soil, water, and timber they were doubtless equal if not superior to the Indian possessions. But the idea was all-prevalent then as it is now in border communities, that, however attractive may be the surrounding districts of public lands open to the inclination of anybody who desires to settle thereon, the prohibited domain of a neighboring Indian reservation must of necessity surpass it, and no application of the principles of reason, philosophy, or justice will serve to lessen the desire for its possession. Governor McMinn convened[1] a council of the Cherokees, at which he presented to them in the strongest light the benefits that would accrue to their nation in the increasing happiness, prosperity, and population such as would attend their removal to the Arkansas, while, on the other hand, nothing but evil could follow their continued residence east of the Mississippi. Their lands would be constantly encroached upon by white settlers; border desperadoes would steal their stock, corrupt their women, and besot their warriors. However anxious the Government might be to protect them in the uninterrupted enjoyment of their present possessions, it would, from the circumstances of the case, be utterly unable to do so. He therefore proposed to them that they should, as a unit, agree to remove west of the Mississippi, and that the United States should pay them for their lands the sum of $100,000, in addition to all expenses of removal; which amount, upon their prompt and indignant refusal, he at once offered to double, but with as small measure of success.

The treaty of 1817 had made provision for the taking of a census of the whole Cherokee people during the month of June of the following year. The census was to form the basis for an equitable distribution of the annuities and other benefits of which the Cherokee Nation was in receipt, between the portion who continued to abide in their eastern homes and those who had removed to the Arkansas country, in proportion to their respective numbers. Pending this enumeration no annuities had been paid them, which produced much annoyance and dissatisfaction among both parties.

In consequence of the hostile and vindictive attitude manifested toward the emigrant party by the remainder of the nation and the many obstacles sought to be thrown in the path of removal, the authorities of the United States had hitherto refused to comply with the census provision of the treaty of 1817. Governor McMinn, after the rejection of both his purchase and his removal propositions, then proposed (in answer to the demand of the Cherokee council that he should cause the census to be taken in the manner provided) that if they would pass a formal vote of censure upon such of their officers as he should name as having violated the treaty by the use of intimidating measures against the Arkansas emigrants, he would cause the work of taking

---

[1] November 13, 1818.

the census to be at once begun. The council also declined to do this, admitting that if such conduct had characterized any of their officers it was deserving of censure but denying that any proof of the charges had been submitted. They at last, however, as an evidence of their good disposition toward the United States, consented to the removal of one of the offensive officers named from his position as a member of the council, and the Secretary of War authorized[1] the taking of the census to be proceeded with. Governor McMinn, in summing up the results of this council,[2] assumes that about one-half of the nation had already committed themselves to the policy outlined in the treaty of 1817, by the fact that since December 28 of that year 718 families had enrolled themselves for removal (aggregating, with those already removed, 5,291 individuals), besides 146 families who had elected to take reservations in severalty. The lack of tangible results following this council was promptly reported to the Secretary of War by both Governor McMinn and Agent Meigs. The latter advised the authorities[3] that a fully authorized and representative delegation of the Cherokee Nation would shortly proceed to Washington, and that, in his judgment, the nation was rapidly becoming satisfied of their inability to long postpone what to every impartial observer must appear as inevitable—an exchange of their country for a location west of the Mississippi River.

This delegation in due time[4] arrived at the capital, and a series of councils or interviews was at once entered upon between themselves and the Secretary of War, as representing the President. Many and just were the causes of complaint presented to the Secretary by the delegation. The recital of their wrongs, the deep affection manifested for their native hills and streams, and the superstitious dread with which they looked upon removal to a new country as being the decisive step in their dispersion and destruction as a people were calculated to excite the sympathy of an unprejudiced mind. It had long been evident, however, that the simple minded barbarian was unable to cope with the intelligent and persistent demands of civilization, and that, with or without his consent, the advancing host of white settlers would ere many years be in full enjoyment of his present possessions.

TREATY CONCLUDED FOR FURTHER CESSION OF LAND.

After several preliminary discussions concerning the best method of adjusting their difficulties, the Secretary of War submitted to them,[5] in writing, a statement of the basis upon which the United States would enter into a treaty with them, urging prompt action thereon, in order that the Senate might have time to exercise its constitutional functions upon the same prior to its approaching adjournment.

---

[1] December 29, 1818.
[2] November 29, 1818.
[3] December 19, 1818.
[4] February, 1819.
[5] February 11, 1819.

The salient points of this proposition were that the Cherokees should make a cession of land in proportion to the estimated number of their nation who had already removed or enrolled themselves for removal to the Arkansas; that the United States preferred the cession to be made in Tennessee and Georgia, and that in the latter State it should be as near and convenient to the existing white settlements as was possible; that the reservation which the Cherokees had expressed a desire to make for the benefit of a proposed school fund should be located within the limits of Alabama Territory, inasmuch as the cession to be made in Georgia would, under the provisions of the act of Congress of 1802, belong to that State, and the lands covering the proposed cession in Tennessee would be subject to location by North Carolina military land warrants. Neither was such school reservation to constitute any portion of the land which the Cherokees were to cede in conformity to the principle of exchange embodied in the first paragraph. The United States would continue to extend its protection to both branches of the Cherokee people, but those remaining east of the Mississippi, having expressed a desire that the lands retained by them should be absolutely guaranteed from any danger of future cession, were informed that in order to secure such guarantee it was indispensable that the cessions they were about to make should be ample, and that the portion of territory reserved by them should not be larger than was essential to their wants and convenience. The Secretary reminded them that should a larger quantity be retained it would not be possible, by any stipulation in the treaty, to prevent future cessions; that so long as they retained more land than was necessary or convenient for themselves they would feel inclined to sell and the United States to purchase. He commented on the fact that they were rapidly becoming like the white people, and could not longer live by hunting, but must work for their subsistence. In their new condition of life far less land would be essential to their happiness. Their great object should be to hold their land by severalty titles and to gradually adopt the manners and laws of life which prevailed among their white neighbors. It was only thus that they could be prosperous and happy, and neglect to accept and profit by the situation would inevitably result in their removal or extinction.

The question as to the area of territory that should be ceded as the equitable proportion of the Arkansas Cherokees formed the subject of much dispute. The Eastern Cherokees denied the accuracy of the emigration roll of Governor McMinn, and asserted that, instead of 5,291 emigrants, as stated by him, there had actually been not exceeding 3,500, while the non-emigrant portion of the nation they gave as numbering 12,544, or more than three-fourths of the entire community.[1]

It being impossible to reconcile these radical differences of estimate and the Indians becoming wearied and discouraged with the persistent importunities of the United States officials, they consented to the

---

[1] Cherokee delegation to Secretary of War, February 17, 1819.

cession of those tracts of country naively described in the treaty of February 27, 1819,[1] as "*at least as extensive*" as that to which the United States was entitled under the principles and provisions of the treaty of 1817. These cessions were made, as recited in the preamble to the treaty, as the commencement of those measures necessary to the civilization and preservation of their nation, and in order that the treaty of July 8, 1817, might, without further delay or the trouble or expense of taking the census therein provided for, be finally adjusted. It was also agreed that the distribution of annuities should be made in the proportion of two to one in favor of the Eastern Cherokees (it being assumed that about one-third of the nation had gone west), with the proviso that if the Arkansas Cherokees should offer formal objection to this ratio within one year after the ratification of the treaty, then a census, solely for the purpose of making a fair distribution of the annuity, should be taken at such time and in such manner as the President of the United States should designate. All leases of any portion of the territory reserved to the Cherokees were declared void, and the removal of all intruders upon their lands was promised, to which latter end an order was issued requiring such removal to take place on or before July 1, 1819.

Thus was concluded the treaty of February 27, 1819, which was promptly and favorably acted upon by the Senate and ratified and proclaimed by the President on the 10th of March following. The gist of such provisions of importance as are not detailed in these historical notes will be found by reference to the abstract preceding them.

Immediately upon the approval of the treaty by the Senate, the Secretary of War notified Governor McMinn[2] of the fact, directing him to give no further encouragement to emigration to the Arkansas, but to proceed at once to wind up the business under the treaty of 1817.

Survey of boundaries.—Preparations were at once made for surveying and marking the lines of the cessions. Hon. Wilson Lumpkin, who was engaged in running the line between East Florida and the State of Georgia, was directed[3] to suspend that work, and designated to survey the line of cession, commencing at the point where the Unicoi Turnpike crossed the Blue Ridge, and thence to the nearest main source of the Chestatee, and also to lay off the individual reservations that should be selected within the State of Georgia.

The following day[4] Robert Houston was appointed to run the line of the cession within the State of Tennessee, commencing on the Highwassee River about 2 miles above Highwassee Old Town, as well as to survey the individual reservations within that State, and also the tracts reserved in North Carolina and Alabama Territory.

Mr. Houston performed his services as a surveyor to the satisfaction

---

[1] United States Statutes at Large, Vol. VII, p. 195.
[2] March 6, 1819.
[3] March 11, 1819.
[4] March 12, 1819.

of all parties;[1] but in running the line from the Unicoi Turnpike crossing of the Blue Ridge to the nearest main source of the Chestatee, a dispute arose between Mr. Lumpkin and the Cherokees as to which was the nearest main source of that river, the Frogtown or the Tessentee Fork. The surveyor ran the line to the source of the first named fork, while the Indians insisted that the latter was the proper stream, and demanded a re-examination of the survey. Agent Meigs having, however, reported[2] in favor of the correctness of the survey, it was allowed to stand.[3]

STATUS OF CERTAIN CHEROKEES.

Early in the year 1820[4] complaints began to arise as to the status of those Cherokees who had made their election to remove to the Arkansas country but had subsequently concluded to remain east. These, it was stated, numbered 817, and they found themselves placed in rather an anomalous situation. Their proportion of the Cherokee national domain had been ceded to the United States by the treaties of 1817 and 1819 Their share of annuities was being paid, under the treaty of 1819, to the Cherokees of the Arkansas. Their right to individual reservations under either treaty was denied, and they were not even allowed to vote, hold office, or participate in any of the affairs of the nation.

In this condition they soon became an element of much irritation in the body politic of the tribe. The Cherokee authorities urged that they should be furnished with rations and transportation to their brethren in the West, whither they were now willing to remove, but the Secretary of War instructed Agent Meigs[5] that emigration to the Arkansas under the patronage of the Government had ceased, and that those Cherokees who had enrolled themselves for removal but had not yet gone, as well as all others thereafter determining to go, must do so at their own expense.

---

[1] Mr. Houston began his survey at the point where the first hill closes in on Hiwassee River, which he found to be 2½ miles above Hiwassee Old Town. He also states in his report that he found no ridge dividing the waters of Hiwassee from those of Little River. This line from the Hiwassee River to the Tennessee River at Talassee was 46 miles and 300 poles in length. It was begun May 28 and completed June 12, 1819. The line from the junction of Cowee and Nauteyalee Rivers to the Blue Ridge was begun June 12 and completed June 18, 1819, and was 36 miles long. His report, with accompanying map, was communicated to the Secretary of War with letter dated July 30, 1819. A copy of the field notes may be found in American State Papers, Indian Affairs, Vo¹. II, pp. 192 and 193.

[2] July 24, 1820.

[3] Secretary of War to Agent Meigs, August 14, 1820.

[4] February 9. See letter of Return J. Meigs to Secretary of War.

[5] June 15, 1820.

TREATY CONCLUDED MAY 6, 1828.—PROCLAIMED MAY 28, 1828.[1]

Held at Washington City, D. C., between James Barbour, Secretary of War, specially authorized therefor by the President of the United States, and the chiefs and headmen of the Cherokee Nation west of the Mississippi.

MATERIAL PROVISIONS.

The preamble recites the desire of the United States to secure to the Cherokees, both east and west of the Mississippi, a permanent home, "that shall never in all future time be embarrassed by having extended around it the lines or placed over it the jurisdiction of a Territory or State, nor be pressed upon by the extension in any way of any of the limits of any existing Territory or State."

It also assumes that their actual surroundings, both east and west of such river, were unadapted to the accomplishment of such a purpose, and therefore the following articles of agreement were made:

1. The western boundary of Arkansas shall be * * * viz: A line shall be run commencing on Red River at the point where the Eastern Choctaw line strikes said river, and run due north with said line to the river Arkansas; thence in a direct line to the southwest corner of Missouri.

2. The United States agree to possess the Cherokees, and to guarantee it to them forever, * * * of seven million of acres of land, to be bounded as follows, viz: Commencing at that point on Arkansas River where the eastern Choctaw boundary lines strikes said river, and running thence with the western line of Arkansas, as defined in the foregoing article, to the southwest corner of Missouri, and thence with the western boundary line of Missouri till it crosses the waters of Neasho, generally called Grand River; thence due west to a point from which a due-south course will strike the present northwest corner of Arkansas Territory; thence continuing due south on and with the present western boundary line of the Territory to the main branch of Arkansas River; thence down said river to its junction with the Canadian River, and thence up and between the said rivers Arkansas and Canadian to a point at which a line running north and south from river to river will give the aforesaid seven million of acres.

In addition to the seven millions of acres thus provided for and bounded, the United States guarantee to the Cherokee Nation a perpetual outlet west, and a free and unmolested use of all the country lying west of the western boundary of the above described limits and as far west as the sovereignty of the United States and their right of soil extend.

3. The United States agree to survey the lines of the above cession

---

[1] United States Statutes at Large, Vol. VII, p. 311.

without delay, and to remove all white settlers and other objectionable people living to the west of the east boundary of the Cherokee tract.

4. The United States agree to appraise and pay the value of all Cherokee improvements abandoned by the latter in their removal; also to sell the property and improvements connected with the agency, for the erection of a grist and saw mill in their new home.

5. The United States agree to pay the Cherokees $50,000 as the difference in value between their old and their new lands; also an annuity for three years of $2,000 to repay cost and trouble of going after and recovering stray stock; also $8,760 in full for spoliations committed on them by the Osages or citizens of the United States; also $1,200 for losses sustained by Thomas Graves, a Cherokee chief; also $500 to George Guess, the discoverer of the Cherokee alphabet, as well as the right to occupy a saline; also an annuity of $2,000 for ten years to be expended in the education of Cherokee children; also $1,000 for the purchase of printing press and type; also, the benevolent society engaged in instructing Cherokee children to be allowed the amount expended by it in erection of buildings and improvements; also, the United States to release the indebtedness of the Cherokees to the United States factory to an amount not exceeding $3,500.

6. The United States agree to furnish the Cherokees, when they desire it, a system of plain laws and to survey their lands for individual allotment.

7. The Cherokees agree within fourteen months to leave the lands in Arkansas assigned them by treaties of January 8, 1817, and February 27, 1819.

8. Each head of a Cherokee family east of the Mississippi desiring to remove to the country described in the second article hereof to be furnished by the United States with a good rifle, a blanket, a kettle, five pounds of tobacco, and compensated for all improvements he may abandon; also a blanket to each member of his family. The United States to pay expenses of removal and to furnish subsistence for one year thereafter. Each head of family taking with him four persons to receive $50.

9. The United States to have a reservation 2 by 6 miles at Fort Gibson, with the right to construct a road leading to and from the same.

10. Capt. James Rogers to have $500 for property lost and services rendered to the United States.

11. Treaty to be binding when ratified.

NOTE.—The Senate consented to the ratification of this treaty with the proviso that the "western outlet" should not extend north of 36°, nor to interfere with lands assigned or to be assigned to the Creeks; neither should anything in the treaty be construed to assign to the Cherokees any lands previously assigned to any other tribe.

HISTORICAL DATA.

RETURN J. MEIGS AND THE CHEROKEES.

Return J. Meigs had for nearly twenty years[1] occupied the position of United States agent for the Cherokee Nation. As a soldier of the Revolutionary war he had marched with Arnold through the forests of Maine and Canada to the attack on Quebec in 1775.[2]

He had also, by his faithful, intelligent, and honest administration of the duties of his office as Indian agent, secured the perfect confidence of his official superiors through all the mutations of administration. He had acquired a knowledge of and familiarity with the habits, character, and wants of the Cherokees such as was perhaps possessed by few, if indeed by any other man.

Any suggestions, therefore, that he might make concerning the solution of the Cherokee problem were deserving of grave consideration. His views were submitted in detail upon the condition, prospects, and requirements of the Cherokee Nation in a communication to the Secretary of War.[3] To his mind the time had arrived when a radical change in the policy of managing their affairs had become essential. Ever since the treaty of 1791 the United States, in pursuance of a policy therein outlined for leading the Cherokees toward the attainment of a higher degree of civilization, in becoming herdsmen and cultivators instead of hunters, had been furnishing each year a supply of implements for husbandry and domestic use. In consequence a respectable proportion of that nation had become familiarized with the use of the plow, spade, and hoe. Many of their women had learned the art of spinning

---

[1] Meigs was appointed, May 15, 1801, superintendent of Indian affairs for the Cherokee Nation and agent for the War Department in the State of Tennessee.

[2] Letter of Meigs to General Wilkinson, dated Marietta, Ohio, February 10, 1801. This letter is in reply to one received from General Wilkinson, in which the latter, among other things, inquires if he can in any way serve the former. Meigs replies: "I will answer these kind inquiries truly. In the first place, I enjoy excellent health; in the next place, I am doing what I can at farming business, endeavoring to maintain a credible existence by industry. I have been for more than two years one of the Territorial legislators; this, though credible, is not profitable. My principal dependence for living is on the labor of my own hands. I am confident, sir, you *can serve* me, as you are conversant with every department of the Government and may know what places can be had and whether I am capable of being usefully employed. I don't care what it is, whether civil or military or where situated, provided it be an object which you shall think proper for me. I don't know Mr. Jefferson; have always revered his character as a great and good man. I am personally acquainted with Colonel Burr. He ascended the river Kennebeck as a volunteer in the year 1775 and was with me in the Mess a great part of that march to Canada. I think I have his friendship, but he is not yet, perhaps, in a situation to assist me." Colonel Meigs was also a member of the court-martial convened for the trial of General Arthur St. Clair for the evacuation of Ticonderoga. He died at his post of duty in February, 1823, as shown by a letter to the Secretary of War from ex-Governor McMinn, dated the 22d of that month.

[3] May 30, 1820.

and weaving, and in individual instances considerable progress had been made in the accumulation of property. Agent Meigs now thought that the point had been reached where the Cherokee people should begin to fight their own battles of life, and that any further contributions to their support, either in the shape of provisions or tools, would have only a tendency to render them more dependent upon the Government and less competent to take care of themselves. Those who were already advanced in the arts of civilized life should be the tutors of the more ignorant. They possessed a territory of perhaps 10,000,000 acres of land, principally in the States of Georgia, North Carolina, and Tennessee, for the occupation of which they could enumerate little more than 10,000 souls or 2,000 families. If they were to become an agricultural and pastoral people, an assignment of 640 acres of land to each family would be all and more than they could occupy with advantage to themselves. Such an allotment would consume but 1,280,000 acres, leaving more than 8,000,000 acres of surplus land which might and ought to be sold for their benefit, and the proceeds (which he estimated at $300,000, to be paid in fifty annual installments) applied to their needs in the erection of houses, fences, and the clearing and breaking up of their land for cultivation. The authority and laws of the several States within whose limits they resided should become operative upon them, and they should be vested with the rights, privileges, and immunities of citizens of those States. These views met with the concurrence of the administration, and would possibly have been carried into effect but for the intense hostility thereto of not only the unprogressive element among the Cherokees themselves but of the officials and people of the States most interested, who could not view with complacency the permanent occupation of a single acre of land within their limits by the aboriginal owners.

TENNESSEE DENIES THE VALIDITY OF CHEROKEE RESERVATIONS.

About this time trouble arose between the authorities of the State of Tennessee and the surveyor (Robert Houston) who had been intrusted with the duty of laying off such individual reservations as should be taken under the provisions of the treaties of 1817 and 1819. Mr. Houston reported to the Secretary of War that the legislature of Tennessee had refused to confirm all such reservations taken in virtue of the provisions of those treaties subsequent to the 1st of July, 1818, or, in other words, after the time provided for taking the Cherokee census had expired, and desired the opinion and instructions of the Department thereon. The question involved in this dispute was deemed of sufficient importance to secure an official opinion from the Attorney-General prior to directing any further action.[1] An opinion was rendered[2] by Attorney-General Wirt, the substance of which was that the right of taking these reservations having been in the first instance given by

---

[1] Letter of Secretary of War to Attorney-General, July, 26, 1820.
[2] August 12, 1820.

the treaty of 1817 until the census should be taken, and the time for taking the census having been, by the acquiescence of both parties to the treaty, kept open until the conclusion of the treaty of February 27, 1819, all the reservations taken prior to this latter date were legal, more especially as they had been ratified by the recognition of them contained in the treaty of 1819. Furthermore, the second article of that treaty, taken in connection with the seventh article, continued the period for taking reservations until the 1st of January, 1820. Mr. Houston was instructed[1] to proceed to lay off the reservations in consonance with this opinion, notwithstanding which the authorities of Tennessee took issue therewith and passed a law providing for the sale of the disputed reserves, whereupon the War Department instructed[2] Agent Meigs to cause one or two test cases to be prepared for trial in the courts.

While on the subject of these reservations it is pertinent to remark that by act of March 3, 1823, Congress appropriated $50,000 to be expended in extinguishing the Indian title to such individual fee simple reservations as were made within the limits of Georgia by the Cherokee treaties of 1817 and 1819 and by the Creek treaties of 1814 and 1821. James Merriwether and Duncan G. Campbell were appointed as commissioners to carry the same into effect. Twenty-two thousand dollars were also appropriated May 9, 1828, to reimburse the State of North Carolina for the amount expended by her authorities in extinguishing Cherokee reservation titles in that State under the treaties of 1817 and 1819.

UNITED STATES AGREE TO EXTINGUISH INDIAN TITLE IN GEORGIA.

By an agreement between the United States and the State of Georgia bearing date April 24, 1802,[3] Georgia ceded to the United States all the lands lying south of Tennessee and west of Chattahoochee River and a line drawn from the mouth of Uchee Creek direct to Nickojack, on the Tennessee River. In consideration of this cession the United States agreed to pay Georgia $1,250,000, and to extinguish the Indian title whenever the same could be done on peaceable and reasonable terms; also to assume the burden of what were known as the Yazoo claims.

Georgia charges the United States with bad faith.—Ever since the date of this agreement the utmost impatience had been manifested by the Government and the people of the State of Georgia at the deliberate and careful course which had characterized the action of the General Government in securing relinquishment of their lands in that State from the Creeks and Cherokees. Charges of bad faith on the part of the United States, coupled with threats of taking the matter into their own

---

[1] August 14, 1820.
[2] March 7, 1821.
[3] American State Papers, Public Lands, Vol. I, p. 125.

hands, had been published in great profusion by the Georgians. These served only to enhance the difficulties of the situation and to excite a stubborn resistance in the minds of the Indians against any further cessions of territory.

Report of Congressional committee.—The subject was brought to the attention of Congress through the action of the governor and legislature of Georgia. A select committee was appointed by the House of Representatives, at the first session of the Seventeenth Congress, to take the matter into consideration and to report whether the said articles of agreement between that State and the United States had so far been executed according to the terms thereof, and what were the best means of completing the execution of the same. This committee submitted a report to the House,[1] wherein, after reciting the terms of the agreement, allusion is made to the Creek treaty of 1814, and the opinion expressed that the agreement might have been more satisfactorily complied with by demanding the cession at that treaty of the Creek lands within Georgia's limits, instead of accepting in large measure those within the Territory of Alabama. The Indians were by this action forced, in the opinion of the committee, within the limits of Georgia, instead of being withdrawn therefrom.

Respecting the Cherokee treaty of July 8, 1817, the committee say that some time previous to its conclusion the Cherokees had represented to the President that their upper and lower towns wished to separate; that the Upper Cherokees desired to be confined to a smaller section of country and to engage in the pursuits of agriculture and civilized life; that the Lower Cherokees preferred continuing the hunter's life, and, owing to the scarcity of game in their own country, proposed to exchange it for land on the west of the Mississippi River; that to carry into effect these wishes of the Indians the treaty of 1817 was held, and the United States then had it in their power to have so far complied with their contract with Georgia as to have extinguished the title of the Cherokees to most of their lands within the limits of that State; that this could readily have been done, for the reason that the Upper Cherokees resided beyond the boundaries of Georgia, and had expressed a desire to retain lands on the Hiwassee River, in Tennessee, whilst the Lower Cherokees, who were desirous of emigrating west, mostly resided in the former State. But, in spite of this opportunity, the United States had purchased an inconsiderable tract of country in Georgia and a very considerable one in Tennessee, apparently in opposition to the wishes of the Indians, the interests of Georgia, and of good faith in themselves. By this treaty the United States had also granted a reservation of 640 acres to each head of an Indian family who should elect to remain on the eastern side of the Mississippi. This the committee viewed as an attempt on the part of the United States to grant lands in fee simple within the limits of Georgia in direct

---

[1] January 7, 1822.

violation of the rights of that State. The provision permitting Cherokees to become citizens of the United States was also characterized as an unwarrantable disregard of the rights of Congress. It was further asserted that by the treaty of 1819 the United States had shown a disposition and determination to permanently fix the Cherokee Indians upon the soil of Georgia, and thereby render it impossible to comply with their contract with that State. Yet another feature of this treaty too objectionable to be overlooked was the agreement of the United States that 12 miles square of land ceded by the Indians should be disposed of and the proceeds invested for the establishment of a school fund for those Indians. In conclusion the committee suggested that in order to a proper execution of the agreement with Georgia it would be necessary for the United States to relinquish the policy they had apparently adopted with regard to civilizing the Indians and keeping them permanently on their lands, at least in respect to the Creeks and Cherokees, and that appropriations should be made from time to time sufficiently large to enable the Government to hold treaties with those Indians for the extinguishment of their title.

Commissioners appointed to negotiate a new treaty.—Stimulated by the sentiments so strongly expressed in this report of a committee of the House of Representatives, the executive authorities determined to make another effort to secure a further cession of territory from the Cherokees.

Accordingly the President appointed[1] General John Floyd, Maj. Freeman Walker, and Hon. J. A. Cuthbert, all of Georgia, commissioners to negotiate a treaty with that nation, and advised them of his earnest desire that a cession should be secured from the Indians such as would prove satisfactory to that State. Messrs. Walker and Cuthbert declined their appointments, and Duncan G. Campbell and General David Merriwether were appointed[2] in their places. General Merriwether dying shortly after, was succeeded by Maj. James Merriwether, whom it had been the original intention to appoint, but for whose name that of General Merriwether had been inserted in the primary appointment through mistake. Before any active steps had been taken toward the performance of the duties assigned the commission, General Floyd resigned,[3] and the President determined to allow the remaining two members to constitute the full commission. Their appointment was submitted to and approved[4] by the Senate, and in the transmission of their new commissions by the Secretary of War perseverance and judicious management were enjoined upon them as essential to success in their negotiations. It would seem that all their perseverance was needed, for the commissioners were unable to secure even an interview with the Cherokee authorities until a date and place had been designated for the fourth time.

---

[1] June 15, 1822.
[2] August 24, 1822.
[3] November 19, 1822.
[4] March 17, 1823.

Death of Agent Meigs.—About this time[1] Agent Meigs, who since 1801 had represented the Government with the Cherokees, died, and ex-Governor McMinn, of Tennessee, was appointed[2] to succeed him.

Failure to conclude proposed treaty.—The treaty commissioners finally met the council of the Cherokee Nation at Newtown, their capital, on the 4th of October, 1823.[3] They were also accompanied by Johnson Wellborn and James Blair, who had been appointed by the governor of Georgia as commissioners to advance the interests and protect the rights of that State. The negotiations were all conducted in writing, and form an interesting chapter in the history of the methods used throughout a long series of years to secure from the Cherokees, by "voluntary, peaceful, and reasonable means," the relinquishment of their ancestral territory. The commissioners set forth their desire to procure the cession of a tract of country comprising all to which the Cherokees laid claim lying north and east of a line to begin at a marked corner at the head of Chestatee River, thence along the ridge to the mouth of Long Swamp Creek, thence down the Etowah River to the line to be run between Alabama and Georgia, thence with that line to the dividing line between the Creeks and Cherokees, and thence with the latter line to the Chattahoochee. In consideration of this proposed cession, the commissioners agreed that the United States should pay the sum of $200,000 and also indemnify the nation against the Georgia depredation claims, as well as the further sum of $10,000 to be paid immediately upon the signing of the treaty.

To this proposition, in spite of the threatening language used by the commissioners, the Indians invariably and repeatedly returned the answer, "We beg leave to present this communication as a positive and unchangeable refusal to dispose of one foot more of land."[4]

The commissioners, seeing the futility of further negotiations, adjourned *sine die*,[5] and a report of their proceedings was made by Commissioner Campbell thirty days later, Major Merriwether having in the mean time resigned.

Cherokees ask protection against Georgia's demands.—Shortly following these attempted negotiations, which had produced in the minds of the Indians a feeling of grave uneasiness and uncertainty, a delegation of Cherokees repaired to Washington for a conference with the President touching the situation. Upon receiving their credentials, the Secretary of War sounded the key-note of the Government's purpose by asking if they had come authorized by their nation to treat for a further relinquishment of territory. To this pointed inquiry the delegation returned a respectful and earnest memorial,[6] urging that their nation

---

[1] February, 1823.

[2] March 17, 1823.

[3] Report of commissioners on file in Office Indian Affairs.

[4] See correspondence between commissioners and Cherokee council. American State Papers, Indian Affairs, Vol. II, pp. 465-473.

[5] October 28, 1823.

[6] January 19, 1824. This memorial is signed by John Ross, George Lowrey, Major Ridge, and Elijah Hicks, as the Cherokee delegation.

labored under a peculiar inconvenience from the repeated appropriations made by Congress for the purpose of holding treaties with them having in view the further purchase of lands. Such action had resulted in much injury to the improvement of the nation in the arts of civilized life by unsettling the minds and prospects of its citizens. Their nation had reached the decisive and unalterable conclusion to cede no more lands, the limits preserved to them by the treaty of 1819 being not more than adequate to their comfort and convenience. It was represented as a gratifying truth that the Cherokees were rapidly increasing in number, rendering it a duty incumbent upon the nation to preserve, unimpaired to posterity, the lands of their ancestors. They therefore implored the interposition of the President with Congress in behalf of their nation, so that provision might be made by law to authorize an adjustment between the United States and the State of Georgia, releasing the former from its compact with the latter so far as it respected the extinguishment of the Cherokee title to land within the chartered limits of that State.

The response [1] of the Secretary of War to this memorial was a reiteration of the terms of the compact with Georgia and of the zealous desire of the President to carry out in full measure the obligations of that compact. The manifest benefits and many happy results that would inure to the Cherokee Nation from an exchange of their country for one beyond the limits of any State and far removed from the annoying encroachments of civilization were pictured in the most attractive colors, but all to no purpose, the Cherokees only maintaining with more marked emphasis their original determination to part with no more land. Seeing the futility of further negotiations, the Secretary of War addressed [2] a communication to the governor of Georgia advising him of the earnest efforts that had been made to secure further concessions from the Cherokees and of the discouraging results, and inviting an expression of opinion from him upon the subject.

Governor Troup's threatening demands.—Governor Troup lost no time in responding to this invitation by submitting [3] a declaration of views on behalf of the government and people of the State of Georgia, the vigorously aggressive tone of which in some measure perhaps compensated for its lack of logical force. After censuring the General Government for the tardiness and weakness that had characterized its action on this subject throughout a series of years and denying that the Indians were anything but mere tenants at will, he laid down the proposition that Georgia was determined at all hazards to become possessed of the Cherokee domain; that if the Indians persisted in their refusal to yield, the consequences would be that the United States must either assist the Georgians in occupying the country which is their own and

---

[1] January 30, 1824.
[2] February 17, 1824.
[3] February 28, 1824.

which is unjustly withheld from them, or, in resisting the occupation, to make war upon and shed the blood of brothers and friends. He further declared that the proposition to permit the Cherokees to reserve a portion of their land within that State for their future home could not be legitimately entertained by the General Government except with the consent of Georgia; that such consent would never be given; and, further that the suggestion of the incorporation of the Indians into the body politic of that State as citizens was neither desirable nor practicable. The conclusion of this remarkable state paper is characterized by a broadly implied threat that Georgia's fealty to the Union would be proportioned to the vigor and alertness with which measures were adopted and carried into effect by the United States for the extinguishment of the Cherokee title.

Response of President Monroe.—These criticisms by the executive of Georgia, which were sanctioned and in large measure reiterated by the legislature and by the Congressional delegation of that State,[1] called forth[2] from President Monroe a message to Congress upon the subject in defense of the course that had been pursued by the executive authorities of the United States. Accompanying this message was a report[3] from John C. Calhoun, Secretary of War, wherein it is alleged that at the date of the compact of 1802 between the United States and Georgia the two Indian nations living within the limits of that State (the Creeks and the Cherokees) were respectively in possession of 19,578,890 and 7,152,110 acres of territory. At the date of such compact, treaties existed between the United States and those tribes defining the limits of their territories. In fulfillment of the stipulation with Georgia, seven treaties had been held with them, five of which were with the Creeks and two with the Cherokees. The lands thus acquired from the former in Georgia amounted to 14,449,480 acres and from the latter to 995,310 acres. In acquiring these cessions for the State of Georgia the United States had expended $958,945.90, to which should be added the value of the 995,310 acres given by the Cherokees in exchange for lands west of the Mississippi, the estimated value of which, at the minimum price of public lands, would amount to $1,244,137.50. The United States had also (in addition to $1,250,000 paid to Georgia as a part of the original consideration) paid to the Yazoo claimants, under the same compact, $4,282,151.12, making in the aggregate $7,735,243.52, which sum did not include any portion of the expense of the Creek war, whereby upwards of 7,000,000 acres were acquired for the State of Georgia.[4]

---

[1] Letter of Georgia delegation to Congress, March 10, 1824. Memorial of Georgia legislature to Congress, December 18, 1823.

[2] March 30, 1824.

[3] March 29, 1824.

[4] This Creek war was in large measure, if not wholly, superinduced by the unlawful and unjust aggressions by citizens of that State upon the rights and territory of the Creeks. Foreign emissaries, however, it is true, encouraged and inflamed the just indignation of the Creeks against the Georgians to the point of armed resistance.

The President expressed it as his opinion that the Indian title was not in the slightest degree affected by the compact with Georgia, and that there was no obligation resting on the United States to remove the Indians by force, in the face of the stipulation that it should be done *peaceably* and on *reasonable* conditions. The compact gave a claim to the State which ought to be executed in all its conditions with good faith. In doing this, however, it was the duty of the United States to regard its strict import, and to make no sacrifice of their interest not called for by the compact, nor to commit any breach of right or humanity toward the Indians repugnant to the judgment and revolting to the feelings of the whole American people. The Cherokee agent, Ex-Governor McMinn, was shortly afterward ordered,[1] " without delay and in the most effectual manner, forthwith to expel white intruders from Cherokee lands."

Alarm of the Cherokees and indignation of Georgia.—The views expressed by the governor and legislature of Georgia upon this subject were the cause of much alarm among the Cherokees, who, through their delegation, appealed[2] to the magnanimity of the American Congress for justice and for the protection of the rights, liberties, and lives of the Cherokee people. On the other hand, the doctrines enunciated in President Monroe's special message, quoted above, again aroused the indignation of the governor of Georgia, who, in a communication[3] to the President, commented with much severity upon the bad faith that for twenty years had characterized the conduct of the executive officers of the United States in their treatment of the matter in dispute.

Message of President John Quincy Adams.—Every day but added acrimonious intensity to the feelings of the officials and people of Georgia. Their determination to at once possess both the Creek and the Cherokee territory within her chartered limits would admit of no delay or compromise. Following the Creek treaty of 1826, her surveyors were promptly and forcibly introduced into the ceded country, in spite of an express provision of the treaty forbidding such action prior to the 1st of January, 1827. So critical was the state of affairs considered to be that President John Quincy Adams invited the attention of Congress to the subject in a special message.[4] Therein the President declared that it ought not to be disguised that the act of the legislature of Georgia, under the construction given to it by the governor of that State, and the surveys made or attempted by his authority beyond the boundary secured by the treaty of 1826 to the Creek Indians, were in direct violation of the supreme law of the land, set forth in a treaty which had received all the sanctions provided by the Constitution; that happily distributed as the sovereign powers of the people of this Union had been between their general and State governments, their history had already too often presented collisions between these divided author-

---

[1] May 3, 1824.
[2] April 16, 1824.
[3] April 24, 1824.
[4] February 5, 1827.

ities with regard to the extent of their respective powers. No other case had, however, happened in which the application of military force by the Government of the Union had been suggested for the enforcement of a law the violation of which had within any single State been prescribed by a legislative act of that State. In the present instance it was his duty to say that if the legislative and executive authorities of the State of Georgia should persevere in acts of encroachment upon the territories secured by a solemn treaty to the Indians and the laws of the Union remained unaltered, a superadded obligation, even higher than that of human authority, would compel the Executive of the United States to enforce the laws and fulfill the duties of the nation by all the force committed for that purpose to his charge.

CHEROKEE PROGRESS IN CIVILIZATION.

Notwithstanding the many difficulties that had beset their paths and the condition of uncertainty and suspense which had surrounded their affairs for years, the Cherokees seem to have continued steadily in their progress toward civilization.

The Rev. David Brown, who in the fall of 1825 made an extended tour of observation through their nation, submitted, in December[1] of that year, for the information of the War Department, an extended and detailed report of his examination, from which it appeared that numberless herds of cattle grazed upon their extensive plains; horses were numerous; many and extensive flocks of sheep, goats, and swine covered the hills and valleys; the climate was delicious and healthy and the winters were mild; the soil of the valleys and plains was rich, and was utilized in the production of corn, tobacco, cotton, wheat, oats, indigo, and potatoes; considerable trade was carried on with the neighboring States, much cotton being exported in boats of their own to New Orleans; apple and peach orchards were quite common; much attention was paid to the cultivation of gardens; butter and cheese of their own manufacture were seen upon many of their tables; public roads were numerous in the nation and supplied at convenient distances with houses of entertainment kept by the natives; many and flourishing villages dotted the country; cotton and woolen cloths were manufactured by the women and home-made blankets were very common; almost every family grew sufficient cotton for its own consumption; industry and commercial enterprise were extending themselves throughout the nation; nearly all the merchants were native Cherokees; the population was rapidly increasing, a census just taken showing 13,563 native citizens, 147 white men and 73 white women who had intermarried with the Cherokees, and 1,277 slaves; schools were increasing every year, and indolence was strongly discountenanced; the nation had no debt, and the revenue was in a flourishing condition; a printing press was soon to be established, and a national library and museum were in contemplation.

---

[1] Letter of Rev. David Brown to Thomas L. McKenney, December 13, 1825.

HISTORICAL DATA 113

FAILURE OF NEGOTIATIONS FOR FURTHER CESSION OF LANDS.

On the 2d of March, 1827,[1] Congress passed an act authorizing the President to open negotiations with the Cherokees for the extinguishment of their title to such lands as were claimed by them within the limits of the State of North Carolina, and also for such quantity of land as should be necessary in the building of a canal to connect the Hiwassee and Canasauga Rivers.

Ten thousand dollars were appropriated to defray the expenses of such negotiations, and Generals John Cocke, G. L. Davidson, and Alexander Grey were[2] appointed commissioners to conduct the same. Their negotiations were barren of results, as were also those of Maj. F. W. Armstrong, who in the following year[3] was dispatched on a similar mission.

THE CHEROKEE NATION ADOPTS A CONSTITUTION.

At a general convention of delegates, "duly authorized for that purpose," held at New Echota, in the Cherokee Nation, July 26, 1827, a constitution was adopted for the nation, predicated upon their assumed sovereignty and independence as one of the distinct nations of the earth. Such an instrument could not fail of exciting to the highest pitch the feelings and animosity of the authorities and people of Georgia.

Georgia's opinion of the Indian title.—Governor Forsyth inclosed[4] a copy of the "presumptuous" document to the President, at the same time desiring to know what the United States proposed to do about the "erection of a separate government within the limits of a sovereign State."

He also inclosed the report of a committee and the resolutions of the legislature of Georgia predicated thereon as exhibiting the sentiments of that body on the subject. This committee, in reporting to the legislature the results of their investigations, assert that anterior to the Revolutionary war the Cherokee lands in Georgia belonged to Great Britain, and that the right as to both domain and empire was complete and perfect in that nation. The possession by the Indians was permissive. They were under the protection of Great Britain. Their title was temporary, being mere tenants at will, and such tenancy might have been determined at any moment either by force or by negotiation, at the pleasure of that power. Upon the close of the Revolution, Georgia assumed all the rights and powers in relation to the lands and Indians in question previously belonging to Great Britain, and had not since divested herself of any right or power in relation to such lands, further than she had in respect of all the balance of her territory. She was now at full liberty and had the power and the right to possess herself, by any means she might choose, of the lands in dispute, and to extend over them her au-

---
[1] United States Statutes at Large, Vol. IV . 217.
[2] March 13, 1827.
[3] June 4, 1828.
[4] January 26, 1828.

thority and laws. Although possessing this right, she was averse to exercising it until all other means of redress had failed. She now made one other and last appeal to the General Government to open negotiations with the Cherokees on this subject. If no such negotiation should be opened, or if, being opened, it should result unsuccessfully, it was recommended to the next legislature of Georgia to take immediate possession of the disputed territory and to extend her jurisdiction and laws over the same. In a spirit of liberality, however, it was suggested that, in any treaty the United States might make with the Cherokees, Georgia would agree to allow reserves to be made to individual Indians not exceeding in the aggregate one-sixth part of the entire territory in dispute. Should the Indians still refuse to negotiate, they were solemnly warned of the unfortunate consequences likely to follow, as the lands *belonged* to Georgia, and that she *must* and *would* have them.

A resolution of the House of Representatives of the United States, in the month of March following, calling upon the President for information upon the subject, brought forth[1] copies of all the correspondence relative to the matter, and the distinct avowal that the records of the United States failed to show any act of executive recognition of the new form of Cherokee government, but that, on the contrary, their status toward the United States was regarded as not in the slightest degree changed.

CHEROKEE AFFAIRS WEST OF THE MISSISSIPPI.

Whilst all these events having a bearing upon the condition and prospective welfare of that portion of the Cherokee people who had remained in their old homes east of the Mississippi River were happening, those who had taken up their abode in the Arkansas country were likewise having their troubles.

Difficulties with the Osages.—Their disagreements with the Osages, which had, with slight intermission, existed for years, broke out afresh when in February, 1820, a party of Osages robbed and killed three Cherokees. The latter determined upon the prosecution of a general war against the aggressors, and were only persuaded to pause at the earnest solicitation[2] of Governor Miller, of Arkansas Territory, until he could visit the villages of the Osages and demand the surrender of the murderers. In company with four of the Cherokee chiefs, he proceeded to the principal Osage village, where they were kindly received by the Osages, who repudiated the action of the murderers and agreed conditionally to surrender them. They, however, produced the treaty concluded in 1818, under the superintendence of Governor Clark, between themselves and the Cherokees, Shawnees, and Delawares, wherein it was agreed that a permanent peace should thenceforth exist between them, and that the Cherokees were to meet them at Fort Smith the

---

[1] March 20, 1828.   [2] April 20, 1820.

following spring and surrender all Osage prisoners, which the former had neglected to do and still retained a number of Osage captives. The Cherokee chiefs admitted that this was true, whereupon Governor Miller advised them that before the Osage murderers could be surrendered, the Cherokees must comply with their agreement by surrendering all prisoners in their hands. An arrangement was made to meet at Fort Smith in October following and effect the exchange,[1] which was done. Notwithstanding this adjustment, the feeling of hostility between the two tribes remained. Active warfare broke out again in the summer of 1821,[2] and was not suppressed by the most strenuous efforts of the United States authorities until the fall of the following year.[3]

Boundaries and area.—Governor Miller reported, in connection with this subject, that the Arkansas Cherokees were very restless and dissatisfied. They complained much in that, as they said, no part of the treaty of 1819 had been complied with by the United States and in that they had received no annuity money since their removal to the west of the Mississippi River. Furthermore, their boundaries had not been established, and they still awaited the fulfillment of the promise made them for an extension of their line to the west as far as the Osage line. To this latter scheme the Osages were much opposed, preferring rather to have the country occupied by whites. The adjustment of this boundary question would seem to have been very desirable, inasmuch as nearly one-half of the Cherokees had taken up their abode south of the Arkansas River,[4] which was clearly outside of their proper limits. It formed the subject of much correspondence and complaint throughout several years, and was the occasion of a number of visits of representative delegations from the Arkansas Cherokees to Washington. The eastern boundary had, as already stated, been run by General Rector in 1818-'19, but the difficulty in fixing the western line arose from the fact that the quantity of land to which the Cherokees were entitled was to be measured by the area already ceded by them to the United States by the treaties of 1817 and 1819. The ascertainment of this latter quantity with exactness could not be made in advance of the completion of the surveys thereof by the States of North Carolina, Tennessee, and Georgia. From such reports and estimates as the United States were able to secure from the several State authorities, it was estimated, early in 1823,[5] that the quantity to which the Cherokees were entitled was about 3,285,710 acres, and they were informed that measures would at once be taken to have the western boundary established. This was performed

---

[1] Letter of Governor Miller, of Arkansas, to Secretary of War, June 20, 1820.
[2] Letter of Secretary of War to Maj. William Bradford, July 21, 1821.
[3] Letter of Secretary of War to Governor Miller, of Arkansas, November 6, 1822.
[4] October 8, 1821, Governor Miller was instructed by the Secretary of War to remove the Cherokees from lands south of the Arkansas, but its execution was deferred several years pending the establishment of the Cherokee boundaries.
[5] Secretary of War to Arkansas Cherokee delegation in Washington, February 12, 1823.

under direction of Governor Miller, in compliance with instructions given him for that purpose on the 4th of March, 1823. A year later[1] a delegation of the Indians visited Washington to complain that the boundary had been run without notice to them and in such a manner as to be highly prejudicial to their interests. It was also urged that the quantity of land included was largely less than the quantity ceded by the Cherokees east of the Mississippi.

It would seem that in the survey of this western boundary Governor Miller, through a misconception of his instructions, had caused the line to be run due north and south, instead of in a direction parallel with that of the east line, as was the evident intention of the treaty of 1817.[2] The effect of this action was to largely curtail the Cherokee frontage on Arkansas River, where the lands were rich and capable of remunerative cultivation, and to extend their frontier on the Upper White River, toward the rough and comparatively valueless region of the Ozark Mountains. It was also admitted by the Secretary of War that the quantity of land within these boundaries was probably less than that to which the Cherokees were entitled.[3] Inquiries were accordingly again made of the several State authorities as to the area of territory acquired by them through the treaties of 1817 and 1819, the replies to which, though partially estimated, aggregated 4,282,216 acres.[4] Directions were therefore given to Agent Duval[5] to propose to the Indians the running of a provisional line, subject to such future alterations as the official returns of the quantity ceded in the States should render necessary and proper. It seems, however, from a report of Agent Duval, that the Cherokees in council had expressed to him a preference to adopt for their western boundary what was known as the "upper" or Governor Miller line, and to run thence down and between the Arkansas and White Rivers for quantity, ignoring the line run under the treaty of 1817 by General Rector, the effect of which would be to give them an extension of territory to the east instead of toward the west. This proposition called forth directions from the Secretary of War to Governor Izard, in the spring of 1825, to open negotiations with the Cherokees upon the subject of an exchange of territory with them for an equal quantity of land lying to the west of Arkansas and Missouri, and for their removal thereto, but that the matter must not be pressed to the point of irritation. If, through the aversion of the Indians to entertain such a proposition, it should be dropped, then, if the same should be satisfactory to the citizens of Arkansas, the proposal

---

[1] March 3, 1824.

[2] Indian Office to Cherokee delegation of Arkansas, March 13, 1824, and Secretary of War to Governor Crittenden, of Arkansas, April 28, 1824.

[3] Secretary of War to Governor Crittenden, of Arkansas, April 28, 1824.

[4] Indian Office to Agent E. W. Duval, Little Rock, Arkansas, July 8, 1824.

[5] July 8, 1824.

contained in the report of Agent Duval would meet the views of the Government.[1]

The Indians were brought to no definite agreement to either of these propositions. In the meantime their provisional western boundary was established and run, in January and February, 1825.[2] The line began at the upper end of Table Rock Bluff, on the Arkansas River, and ran north 1 mile and 70 chains, crossing Skin Bayou at a distance of 66 chains from the beginning; thence it ran north 53° east 132 miles and 31 chains, to White River, which it struck at a point opposite the mouth of Little North Fork.

As a matter of fact, so strong was the prejudice of the Cherokees against any concession of territory that their council passed[3] what they denominated a "perpetual law" denouncing the death penalty against any of their nation who should propose the sale or exchange of their lands.

Lovely's purchase.—In the mean time the legislature of Arkansas, through Acting Governor Crittenden, had forwarded to the President in the summer of 1824, a memorial urging that the tract of country known as "Lovely's purchase" be thrown open to white settlement by a revocation of the prohibitory order of December 15, 1818. This the President declined to do until a final adjustment should be made of the west boundary of the Cherokees and the east boundary of the Choctaws. A history of "Lovely's purchase" is to be found in a letter dated January 30, 1818, from Major Long, of the Topographical Engineers, to General Thomas A. Smith. From this it seems that by a treaty then recently made (but without any authority) with the Osages, "by Mr. Lovely, late Indian agent,"[4] that tribe had ceded to the United States the country between the Arkansas and Red Rivers, and also a tract on the north of the Arkansas situated between the Verdigris River and the boundary established by the Osage treaty of 1808. It appears, however, that it was not the intention of the Osages to cede to the United States so large a tract on the north of the Arkansas, but, as

---

[1] Secretary of War to Governor Izard, of Arkansas, April 16, 1825.
[2] See map on file in Indian Office.
[3] May, 1825.
[4] In a letter from Agent Meigs to the Secretary of War, dated June 2, 1817, Major Lovely is spoken of as having been agent residing with the Cherokees on the Arkansas. He had been an officer of the Virginia line throughout the Revolution and participated in the capture of Burgoyne. He had lived some time in the family of President Madison's father, and went to Tennessee at an early day, whence (after living many years among the Cherokees) he removed with the emigrant party to the Arkansas. In a letter to the Hon. John Cocke from the Secretary of War, December 15, 1826, it is, however, stated that Major Lovely was a factor or trader in the Arkansas country, who took an active part in the preliminary negotiations that led finally to the conclusion of the treaty with the Osages of September 25, 1818. It also appears from the same letter that the estimated area of Lovely's purchase was 7,392,000 acres, and that when the west boundary line of the Cherokees was run, in 1825, it was found that 200 square miles of Lovely's purchase were included within its limits.

afterwards alleged by their chiefs, they only desired to surrender the country lying south of a line commencing at the Falls of the Verdigris and running due east to the treaty line of 1808, and east of another line beginning at the same place and running due south as far as their possessions should extend, and thence east again to the 1808 boundary, excepting and reserving therefrom the point of land between the Verdigris and Six Bulls or Grand River. The Osages, never having been informed that the treaty was not duly authorized and had not been confirmed, still considered the country described therein as belonging to the United States, and had repeatedly solicited whites to settle on it, alleging that the main object of the cession on their part was to secure the convenient approach of civilized neighbors, who should instruct the men how to cultivate the ground and the women to spin and weave, that they might be able to live when the forests should afford no further supplies of game. They were therefore much irritated when they found civilized settlements prohibited, in order to protect the introduction and establishment adjoining or upon this territory of their inveterate enemies, the Cherokees.

Western outlet.—The indefinite outlet to the west which had been promised the Cherokees by the President in 1818 formed the subject of much complaint by them from time to time. In the spring of 1823[1] they were advised that until their western boundary was established it would be improper to make any decision upon the "outlet" question. Two years earlier[2] it had been declared to them that in removing settlers from "Lovely's Purchase," for the purpose of giving them their western outlet, it must always be understood that they thereby acquired no right to the soil, and that the Government reserved to itself the right of making such disposition as it might think proper of all salt springs therein. But this troublous question was definitively disposed of when the treaty of 1828 came to be negotiated.

By the provisions of an act of Congress approved April 5, 1826,[3] the land districts of the Territory of Arkansas were extended so as to include all the country within the limits of that Territory as then existing (the limits having been extended 40 miles to the west by act of Congress of May 26, 1824),[4] with the proviso, however, that nothing in the act should be so construed as to authorize any survey or interference whatever upon any lands the right whereof resided in any Indian tribes. Notwithstanding this proviso, reports became current that surveys had been begun of "Lovely's Purchase," causing much irritation and ill feeling among the Cherokees and eliciting an order[5] from the Secretary of War forbidding any further surveys until it should be

---

[1] Secretary of War to Arkansas Cherokee delegation in Washington, February 12, 1823.

[2] Secretary of War to Arkansas Cherokee delegation in Washington, October 8, 1821.

[3] United States Statutes at Large, Vol. IV, p. 153.

[4] United States Statutes at Large, Vol. IV, p. 40.

[5] April 3, 1827.

finally ascertained how much land the Cherokees were entitled to receive from the United States in pursuance of the treaties of 1817 and 1819.

Negotiation and conclusion of treaty of 1828.—Matters remained thus *in statu quo* until the spring of 1828, when a delegation of the Western Cherokees arrived in Washington, clothed with authority to present to the attention of the President their numerous grievances and to adjust all matters in dispute for their people. The burden of their complaints had relation to the delays that had occurred in fixing their boundaries; to the failure to secure to them the promised " western outlet;" to the adjustment of the hostilities that continued to exist between themselves and the Osages; and to the irregularity in the receipt of their annuities, as well as to the encroachments of white settlers.[1]

The delegation were not clothed with authority to negotiate for any cession or exchange of territory, the "perpetual law" against entertaining such a proposition being still in force among them. Notwithstanding this fact, a communication was addressed to them from the War Department[2] desiring to be advised if they had any objection to opening negotiations upon a basis of an exchange of land for territory west of the west boundary of Arkansas, provided that boundary should be removed a distance of 40 miles to the east, so as to run from Fort Smith to the southwest corner of the State of Missouri, and also that the Creeks should be removed from their location above the Falls of Verdigris River to territory within the forks of the Canadian and Arkansas Rivers. To this proposal the delegation returned a polite but determined refusal, and demanded that the actual number of acres to which they were entitled in Arkansas be ascertained and laid off with exact definiteness. The whole subject of an exchange of lands was thereupon submitted by the Secretary of War to the President for his direction, and it was announced[3] to the visiting delegation that the President had concluded to order a permanent western line to be run, within which should be embraced the full quantity of land to which they were entitled, and which was found to be, as nearly as possible, as follows:[4]

	Acres.
In lieu of quantity ceded in Georgia (actual survey)	824,384
In lieu of quantity ceded in Alabama (actual survey)	738,560
In lieu of quantity ceded in Tennessee (actual survey)	1,024,000
In lieu of quantity ceded in North Carolina (survey 70,000, estimate 630,000)	700,000
	3,286,944
Less 12 miles square, school reservation in Alabama	92,160
	3,194,784

[1] Letter of T. L. McKenney to Secretary of War, March 18, 1828.
[2] March 27, 1828.
[3] April 11, 1828.
[4] The areas here given by the State authorities were largely below the quantity actually contained within the limits of the cessions within the States of Georgia, North Carolina, and Tennessee, as will be seen by a glance at the table of such areas on page 378.

As to their promised "western outlet," the President was unprepared to say anything definite, inasmuch as that matter was then in the hands of Congress.

From this showing it was made evident to the delegation, and no opportunity was lost to impress the fact strongly upon them, that if they insisted upon refusing to arrange for an exchange of lands, instead of being entitled to a large additional tract beyond their provisional western boundary, they would, in fact, be entitled to several hundred thousand acres less than had already been placed in their possession. In addition to this it was more than doubtful, from the temper of the President and Congress, whether their long anticipated "western outlet" would ever crystallize into anything more tangible than a promise. With these facts staring them in the face, with the alluring offers held out to them of double the quantity of land possessed by them in Arkansas in exchange, with liberal promises of assistance in their proposed new homes, and with the persistent importunities of their agent and other United States officials, they yielded, and the treaty of May 6, 1828,[1] an abstract of which has been already given, was the result. It was promptly ratified and proclaimed on the 28th of the same month.

So nervous were the members of the delegation, after the treaty had been concluded and signed, as to the reception that would greet them on their return home, that the Secretary of War felt the necessity of giving them a letter of explanation to their people. In this letter the Cherokees were advised of the integrity, good conduct, and earnest zeal for the welfare of their nation that had invariably characterized the actions of their delegation at Washington. The nation was assured that their representatives had done the best thing possible for them to do in the late treaty.[2]

Notwithstanding this testimonial, the delegation met with an angry reception on their return home. Their lives and property were unsafe; the national council pronounced them guilty of fraud and deception, declared the treaty to be null and void, as having been made without any authority, and expressed an earnest desire to send a delegation to Washington clothed with power to arrange all differences.[3]

In the mean time Agent Duval had been advised[4] of the ratification of the treaty, and Messrs. R. Ellis and A. Finney had been appointed, in conjunction with him, as commissioners to value all improvements and property abandoned by the Cherokees, and to sell the agency property as a means of raising funds for the erection of mills in their new country.

Survey of new boundaries.—The eastern line of this new Cherokee

---

[1] United States Statutes at Large, Vol. VII, p. 311.
[2] Letter of Secretary of War to Western Cherokee delegation, May 17, 1828
[3] Letter of Sub-Agent Brearly to Secretary of War, September 27, 1828.
[4] May 28, 1828.

country, dividing it from Arkansas, was surveyed in 1829,[1] but it was not until April 13, 1831, that instructions were given to Isaac McCoy to survey the remaining boundaries.

The fourth article of the treaty of 1828 contained a provision requiring the United States to sell the property and improvements connected with the agency for the erection of a grist and saw mill for the use of the Indians in their new home. In lieu of this grist and saw mill the United States furnished them with patent corn-mills to the amount of the appraised value of the improvements. A tract in townships 7 and 8 of range 21, including these agency improvements, was surveyed separately in 1829, and was commonly known as the "Cherokee Agency Reservation." In after years the Cherokees claimed that they had never been compensated for this so-called reserve and asserted that it still belonged to them. After a dispute continuing through many years, it was finally decided by the Secretary of the Interior, on the 28th of June, 1878, that the reserve did not belong to the Cherokees, but that, through the operation of the treaty with them, it became a part of the public domain.

TREATY CONCLUDED FEBRUARY 14, 1833.—PROCLAIMED APRIL 12, 1834.[2]

Held at Fort Gibson, on the Arkansas River, between Montfort Stokes, Henry L. Ellsworth, and John F. Schermerhorn, commissioners on the part of the United States, and the chiefs and headmen of the Cherokee Nation of Indians west of the Mississippi.

MATERIAL PROVISIONS.

It having been ascertained that the territory assigned to the Cherokees by the treaty of May 6, 1828, conflicted with a portion of the territory selected by the Creek Nation in conformity with the provisions of the Creek treaty of January 24, 1826, and the representative men of those two nations having met each other in council and adjusted all disputes as to boundaries, the United States, in order to confirm this adjustment, concluded the following articles of treaty and agreement with the Cherokees:

1. The United States agree to possess the Cherokees, and to guarantee it to them forever, * * * of seven millions of acres of land, to be bounded as follows, viz: Beginning at a point on the old western Territorial line of Arkansas Territory, being twenty-five miles north from the point where the Territorial line crosses Arkansas River; thence running from said north point south on the said Territorial line to the place where said Territorial line crosses the Verdigris River; thence

---

[1] Letter of T. L. McKenney to Secretary of War, January 21, 1830.
[2] United States Statutes at Large, Vol. VII, p. 414.

down said Verdigris River to the Arkansas River; thence down said Arkansas River to a point where a stone is placed opposite to the east or lower bank of Grand River at its junction with the Arkansas; thence running south forty-four degrees west one mile; thence in a straight line to a point four miles northerly from the mouth of the North Fork of the Canadian; thence along the said four miles line to the Canadian; thence down the Canadian to the Arkansas; thence down the Arkansas to that point on the Arkansas where the eastern Choctaw boundary strikes said river, and running thence with the western line of Arkansas Territory, as now defined, to the southwest corner of Missouri; thence along the western Missouri line to the land assigned to the Senecas; thence on the south line of the Senecas to Grand River; thence up said Grand River as far as the south line of the Osage Reservation, extended if necessary; thence up and between said south Osage line, extended west if necessary, and a line drawn due west from the point of beginning, to a certain distance west at which a line running north and south from said Osage line to said due-west line will make seven millions of acres within the whole described boundaries.

In addition to the seven millions of acres of land thus provided for and bounded, the United States further guarantee to the Cherokee Nation a perpetual outlet west, and a free and unmolested use of all the country lying west of the western boundary of said seven millions of acres, as far as the sovereignty of the United States and their right of soil extend: *Provided, however*, That if the saline or salt plain on the great western prairie shall fall within said limits prescribed for said outlet, the right is reserved to the United States to permit other tribes of red men to get salt on said plain in common with the Cherokees. And letters patent shall be issued by the United States as soon as practicable for the land hereby guaranteed.

2. The Cherokees relinquish to the United States all claim to all land ceded or claimed to have been ceded to them by treaty of May 6, 1828, not embraced within the limits fixed in this present supplementary treaty.

3. The United States agree to cancel, at the request of the Cherokees, the sixth article of the treaty of May 6, 1828.

4. The United States agree to furnish the Cherokees, during the pleasure of the President, four blacksmith's shops, one wagon-maker's shop, one wheelwright's shop, and necessary tools, implements, and material for the same; also four blacksmiths, one wagon-maker, and one wheel wright; also eight patent railway corn mills, in lieu of those agreed to be furnished by article 4 of the treaty of May 6, 1828.

5. These articles are supplementary to the treaty of May 6, 1828.

6. One mile square to be set apart for the accommodation of the Cherokee Agency, to be selected jointly by the Cherokee Nation and United States agent.

7. This treaty to be obligatory after ratification by the President and Senate.

HISTORICAL DATA.

CONFLICTING LAND CLAIMS OF CREEKS AND CHEROKEES WEST OF THE MISSISSIPPI.

The treaty of January 24, 1826,[1] with the Creek Indians had provided for the removal of that tribe west of the Mississippi. In accordance with its provisions, a delegation consisting of five representative men of the tribe proceeded to the western country and selected the territory designed for their future occupancy. The year following this selection a party of Creeks removed to and settled thereon. The country thus selected and occupied lay along and between the Verdigris, Arkansas, and Canadian Rivers.[2]

Subsequently, on the 6th day of May, 1828,[3] a treaty was concluded with the Cherokee Nation west of the Mississippi, by the terms of which they ceded all their lands within the present limits of Arkansas and accepted a tract of 7,000,000 acres within the present limits of Indian Territory, in addition to a perpetual outlet extending as far west as the western limits of the United States at that time, being the one hundredth meridian of longitude west from Greenwich.

This new assignment of territory to the Cherokees, it was soon found, included a considerable portion of the lands selected by and already in the possession of the Creeks.

The discovery of this fact produced much excitement and ill feeling in the minds of the people of both tribes, and led to many acts of injustice and violence during the course of several years.

Territorial difficulties adjusted.—In the year 1832 a commission was constituted, consisting of Montfort Stokes, Henry L. Ellsworth, and John F. Schermerhorn, with instructions to visit the country west of the Mississippi and to report fully all information relating to the country assigned as a permanent home to the aborigines. Among the formidable difficulties presented for and earnestly urged upon their attention and consideration were these conflicting territorial claims of the Creeks and the Cherokees. Both parties claimed several million acres of the same land under treaty stipulations; both were equally persuaded of the justice of their respective claims, and at first were unyielding in their dispositions.

After a protracted public council, however, in which a careful examination and exposition of the various treaties was made, the commissioners succeeded in inducing the Creeks to accept other lands to the southward of their upper settlements on Verdigris River,[4] and concluded treaties with both the Creeks and the Cherokees modifying their respective boundaries.

---

[1] United States Statutes at Large, Vol. VII, p. 286.

[2] See Creek treaty of 1833, United States Statutes at Large, Vol. VII, p. 417.

[3] United States Statutes at Large, Vol. VII, p. 311.

[4] See preamble to Creek treaty of February 14, 1833, United States Statutes at Large, Vol. VII, p. 417.

This treaty of February 14, 1833, with the latter tribe occasioned a material change in the boundaries previously assigned them.

Instead of following the western line of Arkansas and Missouri as far north as the point where the Grand or Neosho River crosses the boundary of the latter State, and running from thence due west to a point due north of the old western boundary line of Arkansas Territory, and thence south to the Arkansas River, the new line followed the present western boundary of Arkansas and Missouri as far north as the south line of the territory then recently assigned to the Senecas; thence west along the south line of the Senecas to Grand River, and following up Grand River to the south boundary of the Osage reservation, which was parallel with the present southern boundary of Kansas, and on the average about two miles to the north of it; thence west for quantity.

PURCHASE OF OSAGE HALF-BREED RESERVES.

Prior[1] to the conclusion of this treaty of 1833, a delegation of the Western Cherokees had visited Washington to insist upon a literal fulfillment of the treaty of 1828 and especially to demand that they be possessed of all lands and improvements within the outboundaries of their country as defined by the last named treaty. The lands and improvements alluded to were seven reservations of one section each on the Neosho River assigned to certain half-breed Osage Indians by the terms of the treaty of 1825[2] with that tribe.

Although the treaty of 1833 failed to make provision for the extinguishment of these Osage half-breed titles, the desired object was attained by the terms of the fourth article of the treaty of December 29, 1835, wherein $15,000 were appropriated for the purchase.[3]

PRESIDENT JACKSON REFUSES TO APPROVE THE TREATY OF 1834.

On the 10th of February, 1834, George Vashon, agent for the Western Cherokees, negotiated a treaty with them[4] having in view an adjustment of certain differences between themselves and their eastern brethren, whereby the feelings of the latter should be more favorably affected toward an emigration to the western country. The treaty provided for a readjustment of the tribal annuities proportioned to the respective numbers of the Cherokees east and west, the basis of division to be ascertained by an accurate census. The country provided for the Cherokees by the treaty of 1833 was to be enlarged so that it should equal in quantity, acre for acre, the country ceded by the Cherokees east in 1817 and 1819, as well as the proportional quantity of those who should agree to emigrate to the West under the provisions of this treaty. It was also agreed that all Cherokees should possess equal

---

[1] In March, 1832.

[2] United States Statutes at Large, Vol. VII, p. 240.

[3] United States Statutes at Large, Vol. VII, p. 478.

[4] See Indian Office files.

rights in the new country, and that an asylum should be established for the maintenance of the orphan children of the tribe. The negotiations thus entered into were, however, barren of results, inasmuch as President Jackson refused to recommend the treaty to the Senate for the advice and consent of that body.[1]

TREATY CONCLUDED DECEMBER 29, 1835; PROCLAIMED MAY 23, 1836.

Held at New Echota, Georgia, between General William Carroll and John F. Schermerhorn, commissioners on the part of the United States, and the chiefs, headmen, and people of the Cherokee tribe of Indians.[2]

MATERIAL PROVISIONS.

The preamble recites at considerable length the reasons for the negotiation of the treaty and the preliminary steps taken, following which the provisions of the treaty as concluded are given.

1. The Cherokee Nation cedes to the United States all the land claimed by said Nation east of the Mississippi River, and hereby releases all claims on the United States for spoliations of every kind for and in consideration of $5,000,000. In case the United States Senate should decide that this sum does not include spoliation claims, then $300,000 additional should be allowed for that purpose.

2. The description of the 7,000,000 acres of land guaranteed to the Cherokees west of the Mississippi by the treaties of 1828 and 1833 is repeated, and in addition thereto the further guaranty is made to the Cherokee Nation of a perpetual outlet west, and a free and unmolested use of all the country west of the western boundary of said 7,000,000 acres, as far west as the sovereignty of the United States and their right of soil extend, provided that if the salt plain shall fall within the limits of said outlet the right is reserved to the United States to permit other tribes of Indians to procure salt thereon. "And letters patent shall be issued by the United States as soon as practicable for the land hereby guaranteed."

It being apprehended that the above would afford insufficient land for the Cherokees, the United States, in consideration of $500,000, agree to patent to them in fee simple the following additional tract, viz: Beginning at the southeast corner of the Osage Reservation, and running north along the east line of the Osage lands 50 miles to the northeast corner thereof, thence east to the west line of the State of Missouri, thence with said line south 50 miles, thence west to the place of beginning, estimated to contain 800,000 acres, it being understood that if any of the Quapaw lands should fall within these limits they should be excepted.

3. All the foregoing described lands to be included in one patent, under the provisions of the act of May 28, 1830; the United States to

---

[1] See Indian Office records.
[2] United States Statutes at Large, Vol. VII, p. 478.

retain possession of the Fort Gibson military reservation until abandoned, when it shall revert to the Cherokees. The United States reserve the right to establish post and military roads and forts in any part of the Cherokee country.

4. The United States agree to extinguish for the Cherokees the Osage half-breed titles to reservations under the treaty of 1825 for the sum of $15,000. The United States agree to pay to the American Board of Commissioners for Foreign Missions the appraised value of their improvements at Union and Harmony missions.

5. The United States agree that the land herein guaranteed to the Cherokees shall never, without their consent, be included within the limits or jurisdiction of any State or Territory. The United States also agree to secure them the right to make and carry into effect such laws as they deem necessary, provided they shall not be inconsistent with the Constitution of the United States and such acts of Congress as provide for the regulation of trade and intercourse with the Indian tribes; and provided also they shall not affect such citizens and army of the United States as may travel or reside in the Indian country by permission granted under the laws or regulations thereof.

6. Perpetual peace shall exist between the United States and the Cherokees. The United States shall protect the Cherokees from domestic strife, foreign enemies, and from war with other tribes, as well as from the unlawful intrusion of citizens of the United States. The Cherokees shall endeavor to maintain peace among themselves and with their neighbors.

7. The Cherokees shall be entitled to a delegate in the United States House of Representatives whenever Congress shall make provision for the same.

8. The United States agree to remove the Cherokees to their new home and to provide them with one year's subsistence thereafter. Those desiring to remove themselves shall be allowed a commutation of $20 per head therefor, and, if they prefer it, a commutation of $33⅓ per head in lieu of the one year's promised subsistence. Cherokees residing outside the limits of the nation who shall remove within two years to the new Cherokee country shall be entitled to the same allowances as others.

9. The United States agree to make an appraisement of the value of all Cherokee improvements and ferries. The just debts of the Indians shall be paid out of any moneys due them for improvements and claims. The Indians shall be furnished with sufficient funds for their removal, and the balance of their dues shall be paid them at the Cherokee Agency west of the Mississippi. Missionary establishments shall be appraised and the value paid to the treasurers of the societies by whom they were established.

10. The President of the United States shall invest in good interest-paying stocks the following sums for the benefit of the Cherokee people, the interest thereon only to be expended: $200,000, in addition to

their present annuities, for a general national fund; $50,000 for an orphans' fund; $150,000, in addition to existing school fund, for a permanent national school fund: the disbursement of the interest on the foregoing funds to be subject to examination and any misapplications thereof to be corrected by the President of the United States.

On two years' notice the Cherokee council may withdraw their funds, by the consent of the President and the United States Senate, and invest them in such manner as they deem proper. The United States agree to appropriate $60,000 to pay the just debts and claims against the Cherokee Nation held by citizens of the same, and also claims of citizens of the United States for services rendered the nation. Three hundred thousand dollars is appropriated by the United States to liquidate Cherokee claims against the United States for spoliations of every kind.

11. The Cherokees agree to commute their existing permanent annuity of $10,000 for the sum of $214,000, the same to be invested by the President as a part of the general fund of the nation. Their present school fund shall also constitute a portion of the permanent national school fund.

12. Such Cherokees as are averse to removal west of the Mississippi and desire to become citizens of the States where they reside, if qualified to take care of themselves and their property, shall receive their proportion of all the personal benefits accruing under this treaty for claims, improvements, and per capita.

Such heads of Cherokee families as desire to reside within the States of North Carolina, Tennessee, and Alabama, subject to the laws thereof and qualified to become useful citizens, shall be entitled to a pre-emption right of 160 acres at the minimum Congress price, to include their improvements. John Ross and eleven others named are designated as a committee on the part of the Cherokees to recommend persons entitled to take pre-emption rights, to select the missionaries who shall be removed with the nation, and to transact all business that may arise with the United States in carrying the treaty into effect. One hundred thousand dollars shall be expended by the United States for the benefit of such of the poorer classes of Cherokees as shall remove west.

13. All Cherokees and their heirs to whom reservations had been made by any previous treaty, and who had not sold or disposed of the same, such reservations being subsequently sold by the United States should be entitled to receive the present value thereof from the United States as unimproved lands. All such reservations not sold were to be confirmed to the reservees or their heirs. All persons entitled to reservations under treaty of 1817, whose reservations, as selected, were included by the treaty of 1819 in the unceded lands of the Cherokee Nation, shall be entitled to a grant for the same. All reservees who were obliged by the laws of the States in which their reservations were situated to abandon the same or purchase them from the States, shall be deemed to have a just claim against the United States for the value

thereof or for the amount paid therefor, with interest. The amount allowed for reservations under this article is to be paid independently, and not out of the consideration allowed to the Cherokees for spoliation claims and their cession of lands.

14. Cherokee warriors wounded in the service of the United States during the late war with Great Britain and the southern tribes of Indians shall be allowed such pensions as Congress shall provide.

15. The balance of the consideration herein stated, after deducting the amount actually expended for improvements, ferries, claims, spoliations, removal, subsistence, debts, and claims upon the Cherokee Nation, additional quantity of lands, goods for the poorer class of Cherokees, and the several sums to be invested for the general national funds, shall be divided equally among all the people belonging to the Cherokee Nation east, according to the census just completed. Certain Cherokees who had removed west since June, 1833, were to be paid for their improvements.

16. The Cherokees stipulate to remove west within two years from the ratification of this treaty, during which time the United States shall protect them in the possession and enjoyment of their property, and in case of failure to do so shall pay all losses and damages sustained by them in consequence thereof.

The United States and the several States interested in the Cherokee lands shall immediately proceed to survey the lands ceded by this treaty, but the agency buildings and tract of land surveyed and laid off for the use of Col. R. J. Meigs, Indian agent, shall continue subject to the control of the United States or such agent as may be specially engaged in superintending the removal of the tribe.

17. All claims arising under or provided for in this treaty shall be examined and adjudicated by General William Carroll and John F. Schermerhorn, or by such commissioners as shall be appointed by the President of the United States for that purpose, and their decision shall be final, and the several claimants shall be paid on their certificate by the United States. All stipulations of former treaties not superseded or annulled by this treaty shall continue in force.

18. The annuities of the nation which may accrue during the next two years preceding their removal shall, on account of the failure of crops, be expended in provision and clothing for the benefit of the poorer classes of the nation as soon after the ratification of this treaty as an appropriation shall be made. No interference is, however, intended with that part of the annuities due the Cherokees west under the treaty of 1819.

19. This treaty is to be obligatory after ratification.

20. The United States guarantee the payment of all unpaid just claims upon the Indians, without expense to them, out of the proper funds of the United States for the settlement of which a cession or cessions of land has or have been heretofore made by the Indians in

Georgia, provided the United States or State of Georgia has derived benefit therefrom without having made payment therefor.

This article was inserted by unanimous request of the Cherokee committee after the signing of the treaty, it being understood that its rejection by the Senate of the United States should not impair any other article of the treaty.

On the 31st of December, 1835, James Rogers and John Smith, as delegates from the Western Cherokees, signed an agreement which is attached to the treaty wherein they agreed to its provisions on behalf of the Western Cherokees, with the proviso that it should not affect any claims of the latter against the United States.

SUPPLEMENTARY ARTICLES TO FOREGOING TREATY, CONCLUDED MARCH 1, 1836; PROCLAIMED MAY 23, 1836.[1]

Agreed on between John F. Schermerhorn, commissioner on the part of the United States, and the committee duly authorized at a general council held at New Echota, Georgia, to act for and on behalf of the Cherokee people.

MATERIAL PROVISIONS.

These articles were concluded as supplementary to the treaty of December 29, 1835, and were ratified at the same time and as a part of that treaty. They were rendered necessary by the determination of President Jackson not to allow any pre-emptions or reservations, his desire being that the whole Cherokee people should remove together to the country west of the Mississippi.

1. All pre-emption rights and reservations provided for in articles 12 and 13 are declared void.

2. The Cherokees having supposed that the sum of $5,000,000, fixed as the value of Cherokee lands, did not include the amount required to remove them, nor the value of certain claims held by them against citizens of the United States, and the President being willing that the subject should be referred to the Senate of the United States for any further provision that body should deem just,

3. It is agreed, should it receive the concurrence of that body, to allow the Cherokees the sum of $600,000, to include the expenses of removal and all claims against the United States not otherwise specifically provided for, and to be in lieu of the aforesaid reservations and pre-emptions and of the $300,000 for spoliations provided in article 1 of the original treaty to which this is supplementary. This sum of $600,000 shall be applied and distributed agreeably to the provisions of said treaty, the surplus, if any, to belong to the education fund.

4. The provision of article 16 concerning the agency reservations is not intended to interfere with the occupant right of any Cherokees whose improvements may fall within the same.

---

[1] United States Statutes at Large, Vol. VII, p. 488.

The $100,000 appropriated in article 12 for the poorer class of Cherokees, and intended as a set-off to the pre-emption rights, shall now be added to the general national fund of $400,000.

5. The expenses of negotiating the treaty and supplement and of such persons of the Cherokee delegation as may sign the same shall be defrayed by the United States.

NOTE.—The following amendments were made by the United States Senate: In article 17 strike out the words " by General William Carroll and John F. Schermerhorn, or;" also, in the same article, after the word " States," insert " by and with the advice and consent of the Senate of the United States;" and strike out the 20th article, which appears as a supplemental article.

HISTORICAL DATA.

ZEALOUS MEASURES FOR REMOVAL OF EASTERN CHEROKEES.

While the events connected with the negotiation and the execution of the treaty of 1828 with the Western Cherokees were occurring those Cherokees who yet remained in their old homes east of the Mississippi River were burdened with a continually increasing catalogue of distressing troubles. So soon as the treaty of 1828 was concluded it was made known to them that inducements were therein held out for a continuance of the emigration to the Arkansas country. Agent Montgomery was instructed[1] to use every means in his power to facilitate this scheme of removal, and especially among those Cherokees who resided within the chartered limits of Georgia.

Secret agents were appointed and $2,000 were authorized by the Secretary of War to be expended in purchasing the influence of the chiefs in favor of the project.[2] A. R. S. Hunter and J. S. Bridges were appointed[3] commissioners to value the improvements of the Cherokees who should elect to remove.

After nearly a year of zealous work in the cause, Agent Montgomery was only able to report the emigration of four hundred and thirty-one Indians and seventy-nine slaves, comparatively few of whom were from Georgia.[4] Nine months later three hundred and forty-six persons had emigrated from within the limits of that State.[5] The hostility manifested by the larger proportion of the Cherokees toward those who gave favorable consideration to the plan of removal was so great as to require the establishment of a garrison of United States troops within the nation for their protection.[4]

President Jackson's advice to the Cherokees.—Early in 1829,[6] a delegation from the nation proceeded to Washington to lay their grievances before

---

[1] May 27, 1828.

[2] Letter of War Department to Hugh Montgomery, Cherokee agent, May 27, 1828, and to General William Carroll, May 30, 1829.

[3] December 18, 1828.

[4] Letter of T. L. McKenney to Secretary of War, November, 17, 1829.

[5] Letter of T. L. McKenney to Hugh Montgomery, Cherokee agent, August 6, 1830

[6] Letter of Cherokee delegation (East) to Secretary of War, January 21, 1829.

HISTORICAL DATA

President Jackson, but they found the Executive entertaining opinions about their rights very different from those which had been held by his predecessors. They were advised[1] that the answer to their claim of being an independent nation was to be found in the fact that during the Revolutionary war the Cherokees were the allies of Great Britain, a power claiming entire sovereignty of the thirteen colonies, which sovereignty, by virtue of the Declaration of Independence and the subsequent treaty of 1783, became vested respectively in the thirteen original States, including North Carolina and Georgia. If they had since been permitted to abide on their lands, it was by permission, a circumstance giving no right to deny the sovereignty of those States. Under the treaty of 1785 the United States "give peace to all the Cherokees and receive them into favor and protection." Subsequently they had made war on the United States, and peace was not concluded until 1791. No guarantee, however, was given by the United States adverse to the sovereignty of Georgia, and none could be given. Their course in establishing an independent government within the limits of Georgia, adverse to her will, had been the cause of inducing her to depart from the forbearance she had so long practiced, and to provoke the passage of the recent[2] act of her legislature, extending her laws and jurisdiction over their country. The arms of the United States, the President remarked, would never be employed to stay any State of the Union from the exercise of the legitimate powers belonging to her in her sovereign capacity. No remedy for them could be perceived except removal west of the Mississippi River, where alone peace and protection could be afforded them. To continue where they were could promise nothing but interruption and disquietude. Beyond the Mississippi the United States, possessing the sole sovereignty, could say to them that the land should be theirs while trees grow and water runs.

The delegation were much cast down by these expressions of the President, but they abated nothing of their demand for protection in what they considered to be the just rights of their people. They returned to their country more embittered than before against the Georgians, and lost no opportunity, by appeals to the patriotism as well as to the baser passions of their countrymen, to excite them to a determination to protect their country at all hazards against Georgian encroachment and occupation.[3]

GENERAL CARROLL'S REPORT ON THE CONDITION OF THE CHEROKEES.

About this time[4] General William Carroll was designated by the President to make a tour through the Cherokee and Creek Nations,

---

[1] Letter of Secretary of War to Cherokee delegation, April 18, 1829.
[2] December 20, 1828.
[3] Agent Montgomery to the Secretary of War, July 11, 1829.
[4] Secretary of War to General William Carroll, May 27, 1829.

with both of which he was supposed to possess much influence. His mission was to urge upon them, and especially upon the former, the expediency of their removal west of the Mississippi under the inducements held out by the treaty of 1828. A month later[1] Col. E. F. Tatnall and on the 8th of July General John Coffee were appointed to cooperate with General Carroll in the accomplishment of his mission. The results of this tour were communicated[2] to the War Department by General Carroll in a report in which he remarked that nothing could be done with the Cherokees by secret methods; they were too intelligent and too well posted on the current news of the day to be long kept in ignorance of the methods and motives of those who came among them. He had met their leading men at Newtown and had submitted a proposal for their removal which was peremptorily rejected. The advancement the Cherokees had made in religion, morality, general information, and agriculture had astonished him beyond measure. They had regular preachers in their churches, the use of spirituous liquors was in great degree prohibited, their farms were worked much after the manner of white people, and were generally in good order. Many families possessed all the comforts and some of the luxuries of life. Cattle, sheep, hogs, and fowl of every kind were found in great abundance. The Cherokees had been induced by Eastern papers to believe the President was not sustained by the people in his views of their proposed removal. Eastern members of Congress had given their delegation to understand while in Washington the preceding spring that the memorial left by them protesting against the extension of the laws of Georgia and Alabama over Cherokee territory would be sustained by Congress, and that until that memorial had been definitely acted on by that body all propositions to them looking toward removal would be worse than useless.

Cherokees refuse to cede lands in North Carolina.—In the early summer of 1829[3] a commission had also been appointed, consisting of Humphrey Posey and a Mr. Saunders, having in view the purchase from the Cherokees of that portion of their country within the limits of North Carolina, but it, too, failed wholly of accomplishing its purpose.

Coercive measures of the United States and Georgia.—Sundry expedients were resorted to, both by the General Government and by the authorities of Georgia, to compel the acquiescence of the Indians in the demands for their emigration.

The act of the Georgia legislature of December 20, 1828, already alluded to, was an act "to add the territory within this State and occupied by the Cherokee Indians to the counties of De Kalb *et al.*, and to extend the laws of this State over the same." This was followed[4] by

---

[1] June 25, 1829.
[2] November 19, 1829.
[3] June 23, 1829.
[4] December 19, 1829.

the passage of an act reasserting the territorial jurisdiction of Georgia and annulling all laws made by the Cherokee Indians. It further declared that in any controversy arising between white persons and Indians the latter should be disqualified as witnesses. Supplementary legislation of a similar character followed in quick succession, and the proclamation of the governor of the State was issued on the 3d of June, 1830, declaring the arrival of the date fixed by the aforesaid acts and the consequent subjection of the Cherokee territory to the State laws and jurisdiction.[1]

The President of the United States about the same time gave directions[2] to suspend the enrollment and removal of Cherokees to the west in small parties, accompanied by the remark that if they (the Cherokees) thought it for their interest to remain, they must take the consequences, but that the Executive of the United States had no power to interfere with the exercise of the sovereignty of any State over and upon all within its limits. The President also directed[3] that the previous practice of paying their annuities to the treasurer of the Cherokee Nation should be discontinued, and that they be thereafter distributed among the individual members of the tribe. Orders were shortly after[4] given to the commandant of troops in the Cherokee country to prevent *all persons*, including members of the tribe, from opening up or working any mineral deposits within their limits. All these additional annoyances and restrictions placed upon the free exercise of their supposed rights, so far from securing compliance with the wishes of the Government, had a tendency to harden the Cherokee heart.

---

[1] Among other legislation on this subject enacted by Georgia may be enumerated the following, viz:

1. A penalty of forfeiture of all right to his land and improvements was denounced against any Cherokee who should employ any white man, or the slave of any white man, as a tenant-cropper, or assistant in agriculture, or as a miller or millwright.

2. Any Indian who should enroll for emigration and afterwards refuse to emigrate should forfeit all right to any future occupancy within the State.

3. No Indian should be allowed the use of more than 160 acres of land, including his dwelling house.

4. Grants were to be issued for all lots drawn in the late land and gold lottery, though they might lie within the improvements of an Indian who had by any previous Cherokee treaty received a reservation either in Georgia or elsewhere.

5. No contract between a white man and an Indian, either verbal or written, should be binding unless established by the testimony of two white witnesses.

6. Any Indian forcibly obstructing the occupancy by the drawer of any lot drawn in the land and gold lottery should be subject to imprisonment in the discretion of the court.

[2] Letter of War Department to Hugh Montgomery, Cherokee agent, June 9, 1830.

[3] Letter of Acting Secretary of War to H. Montgomery, Cherokee Agent, June 18, 1830.

[4] Letter of Acting Secretary of War to H. Montgomery, Cherokee Agent, June 26, 1830.

FAILURE OF COLONEL LOWRY'S MISSION.

In this situation of affairs Col. John Lowry was appointed[1] a special commissioner to visit the Cherokee Nation and again lay before them a formal proposition for their removal west. The substance of Mr. Lowry's proposal as communicated by him to their national council[2] was: (1) To give to the Cherokees a country west of the Mississippi, equal in value to the country they would leave; (2) each warrior and widow living within the limits of Alabama or Tennessee was to be permitted, if so desiring, to select a reservation of 200 acres, which, if subsequently abandoned, was to be sold for the reservee's benefit; (3) each Indian desiring to become a citizen of the United States was to have a reservation in fee-simple; (4) all emigrants were to be removed and fed one year at the expense of the United States, and to be compensated for all property, except horses, they should leave behind them, and, (5) the nation was to be provided with a liberal school fund.

Again the result was an emphatic refusal[3] on the part of the Cherokees to enter into negotiations on the subject. Other special commissioners and emissaries, of whom several were appointed in the next few months, met with the same reception.

DECISION OF THE SUPREME COURT IN CHEROKEE NATION VS. GEORGIA.

Determined to test the constitutionality of the hostile legislation of Georgia, application was made at the January term, 1831, of the Supreme Court of the United States, by John Ross, as principal chief, in the name of the Cherokee Nation, for an injunction against the State of Georgia. The application was based on the theory that the Cherokee Nation was a sovereign and independent power in the sense of the language of the second section of the third article of the Constitution of the United States providing for judicial jurisdiction of cases arising between a State, or the citizens thereof, and foreign states, citizens, or subjects. The majority of the court declared that the Cherokee Nation was not a foreign nation in the sense stated in the Constitution, and dismissed the suit for want of jurisdiction. From this decision, however, Justices Thompson and Story dissented.[4]

FAILURE OF MR. CHESTER'S MISSION.

No further formal attempt was made to secure a compliance with the wishes of the Government until the winter and spring of 1831–'32. A delegation of Cherokees had visited Washington in the interests of their people, and though nothing was accomplished through them, the language used by some members of the delegation had led the Govern-

---

[1] September 1, 1830.
[2] October 20, 1830.
[3] Action of Cherokee national council, October 22, 1830.
[4] Cherokee Nation *vs.* State of Georgia, Peters's United States Supreme Court Reports, Vol. V, p. 1.

ment authorities to hope that a change of sentiment on the subject of removal was rapidly taking place in their minds. In pursuance of this impression the Secretary of War, in the spring of 1832,[1] intrusted Mr. E. W. Chester with a mission to the Cherokees, and with instructions to offer them as a basis for the negotiation of a treaty the following terms:

1. The United States to provide them with a country west of Arkansas sufficiently large for their accommodation.

2. This country to be conveyed to them by patent under the act of Congress of May 28, 1830, and to be forever outside the limits of any State or Territory.

3. The Cherokees to retain and possess all the powers of self-government consistent with a supervisory authority of Congress.

4. To have an agent resident in Washington to represent their interest, who should be paid by the United States.

5. With the consent of Congress they should be organized as a Territory and be represented by a delegate in that body.

6. All white persons should be excluded from their country.

7. The United States to remove them to their new country and to pay the expenses of such removal, which might be conducted in either of three ways, viz:

(a) By a commutation in money, to be allowed either individuals or families.

(b) By persons to be appointed and paid by the United States.

(c) By arrangement among themselves, through which some competent person should remove them at a fixed rate.

8. The United States to provide them with subsistence for one year after removal.

9. An annuity to be secured to them proportioned to the value of the cession of territory they should make.

10. The United States to pay for all Indian improvements upon the ceded land.

11. Provision to be made for the support of schools, teachers, blacksmiths and their supplies, mills, school-houses, churches, council-houses, and houses for the principal chiefs.

12. A rifle to be presented to each adult male, and blankets, axes, plows, hoes, spinning-wheels, cards, and looms to each family.

13. Indian live stock to be valued and paid for by the United States.

14. Annuities under former treaties to be paid to them upon their arrival west of the Mississippi.

15. Provision to be made by the United States for Cherokee orphan children.

16. Protection to be guaranteed to the Cherokees against hostile Indians.

---

[1] April 17, 1832.

17. A few individual reservations to be permitted east of the Mississippi, but only on condition that the reservees shall become citizens of the State in which they reside, and that all reservations between them and the United States, founded upon their previous circumstances as Indians, must cease.

Cherokees contemplate removal to Columbia River.—In the discussion of these propositions the fact was developed that a project had been canvassed, and had received much favorable consideration among the Cherokees themselves (in view of the difficulties and harrassing circumstances surrounding their situation), to abandon their eastern home and to remove to the country adjacent to the mouth of the Columbia River, on the Pacific coast. This proposition having reached the ears of the Secretary of War, he made haste, in a letter to Mr. Chester,[1] to discourage all idea of such a removal, predicated upon the theory that they would be surrounded by tribes of hostile savages, and would be too remote from the frontier and military posts of the United States to enable the latter to extend to them the arm of protection and support.

Nothing was accomplished by the negotiations of Mr. Chester, and in the autumn[2] of the same year Governor Lumpkin, of Georgia, was requested to attend the Cherokee council in October and renew the proposition upon the same basis. A similar fate attended this attempt.

DECISION OF SUPREME COURT IN WORCESTER VS. GEORGIA.

Among other laws passed by the State of Georgia was one that went into effect on the 1st of February, 1831, which prohibited the Cherokees from holding councils, or assembling for any purpose; provided for a distribution of their lands among her citizens; required all whites residing in the Cherokee Nation within her chartered limits to take an oath of allegiance to the State, and made it an offense punishable by four years' imprisonment in the penitentiary to refuse to do so. Under this law two missionaries, Messrs. Worcester and Butler, were indicted in the superior court of Gwinnett County for residing without license in that part of the Cherokee country attached to Georgia by her laws and in violation of the act of her legislature approved December 22, 1830. In the trial of Mr. Worcester's case, which was subsequently made the test case in the Supreme Court of the United States, he pleaded that he was a citizen of Vermont and entered the Cherokee country as a missionary with the permission of the President of the United States and the approval of the Cherokee Nation; that Georgia ought not to maintain the prosecution inasmuch as several treaties had been entered into by the United States with the Cherokee Nation, by which the latter were acknowledged as a sovereign nation, and by which the territory occupied by them had been guaranteed to them by the

---

[1] July 18, 1832.
[2] September 4, 1832.

United States. The superior court overruled this plea, and Mr. Worcester was tried, convicted, and sentenced to four years in the penitentiary.

The case was carried up on a writ of error to the Supreme Court of the United States, and that court asserted its jurisdiction. In rendering its decision the court remarks that the principle that discovery of parts of the continent of America gave title to the government by whose subjects or by whose authority it was made against all other European governments, which title might be consummated by possession, was acknowledged by all Europeans because it was the interest of all to acknowledge it, and because it gave to the nation making the discovery, as its inevitable consequence, the sole right of acquiring the soil and of making settlements on it. It was an exclusive principle which shut out the right of competition among those who had agreed to it, but not one which could annul the rights of those who had not agreed to it. It regulated the rights of the discoverers among themselves, but could not affect the rights of those already in possession as aboriginal occupants. It gave the exclusive right of purchase, but did not found it on a denial of the right of the possessor to sell. The United States succeeded to all the claims of Great Britain, both territorial and political. Soon after Great Britain had determined on planting colonies in America the King granted sundry charters to his subjects. They purport generally to convey the soil from the Atlantic to the South Sea. The soil was occupied by numerous warlike nations, willing and able to defend their possessions. The absurd idea that feeble settlements made on the sea-coast acquired legitimate power to govern the people or occupy the lands from sea to sea did not then enter the mind of any man. These charters simply conferred the right of purchasing such lands as the natives were willing to sell. The acknowledgment of dependence made in the various Cherokee treaties with Great Britain and the United States merely bound them as a dependent ally claiming the protection of a powerful friend and neighbor and receiving the advantages of that protection, without involving a surrender of their national character. Neither the Government nor the Cherokees ever understood it otherwise. Protection did not imply the destruction of the protected.

Georgia herself had furnished conclusive evidence that her former opinions on the subject of the Indians concurred with those entertained by her sister States and by the Government of the United States. Various acts of her legislature had been cited in the argument of the case, including the contract of cession made in 1802, all tending to prove her acquiescence in the universal conviction that the Cherokee Nation possessed a full right to the lands they occupied, until that right should be extinguished by the United States with their consent; that their territory was separated from that of any State within whose chartered limits they might reside, by a boundary line established by treaties; that within their boundary they possessed rights with which no State could interfere, and that the whole power of regulating the intercourse with them was vested in the United States. The legislation of Georgia on this subject was therefore unconstitutional and void.[1]

Georgia refuses to submit to the decision of the Supreme Court.—Georgia refused to submit to the decision and alleged that the court possessed no right to pronounce it, she being by the Constitution of the United States a sovereign and independent State, and no new State could be formed within her limits without her consent.

President Jackson's dilemma.—The President was thus placed between two fires, Georgia demanding the force of his authority to protect her constitutional rights by refusing to enforce the decision of the court, and the Cherokees demanding the maintenance of their rights as guaranteed them under the treaty of 1791 and sustained by the decision of the Supreme Court.

It was manifest the request of both could not be complied with. If he assented to the desire of the Cherokees a civil war was likely to ensue with the State of Georgia. If he did not enforce the decision and protect the Cherokees, the faith of the nation would be violated.[2] In this dilemma a treaty was looked upon as the only alternative, by which the Cherokees should relinquish to the United States all their interest in lands east of the Mississippi and remove to the west of that river, and more earnest, urgent, and persistent pressure than before was applied from this time forward to compel their acquiescence in such a scheme.

DISPUTED BOUNDARIES BETWEEN CHEROKEES AND CREEKS.

Mention has already been made in discussing the terms of the treaty of September 22, 1816, of the complications arising out of the question of disputed boundaries between the Cherokees, Creeks, Choctaws, and Chickasaws. These disputes related chiefly to an adjustment of boundaries within the Territory of Alabama, rendered necessary for the definite ascertainment of the limits of the Creek cession of 1814. But as a result of the Cherokee cession of 1817 and the Creek cessions of 1818, 1821, 1826, and 1827, the true boundary between the territories of these two latter nations became not only a matter of dispute, but one that for years lent additional bitterness to the contest between the people of Georgia and the Indians, especially the Cherokees. Prior to the Revolution, the latter had claimed to own the territory within the limits of Georgia, as far south as the waters of Broad River, and extending from the headwaters of that river westward. Some of this territory

---

[1] Worcester *vs.* State of Georgia, Peters's United States Supreme Court Reports, Vol. VI, p. 515.

[2] According to the statement of Hon. Geo. N. Briggs, a member of Congress from Massachusetts, President Jackson remarked, after the case of Worcester *vs.* State of Georgia was decided, "Well, John Marshall has made his decision, now let him enforce it."

Views of the Cherokee Country of North Carolina. Photographs by James Mooney of the Bureau of American Ethnology, 1888.

Cherokee Terrain, Eastern Cherokee Reservation, North Carolina. Photograph by W. H. Gilbert, 1932.

Scene on Oconaluftee River, Qualla Reservation, Swain and Jackson Counties, North Carolina. Photograph by James Mooney of the Bureau of American Ethnology, 1888.

William P. Ross

Ex-chief of the Cherokee Nation. Photographer not recorded, 1875.

Typical mountain scenes on Qualla Reservation, North Carolina. Photographs by James Mooney of the Bureau of American Ethnology, 1888.

Some of the signatures on the Treaty with the Western Cherokee or Sequoya's Treaty of 1828. Sequoya's signature is the fourth down. He was also known as George Gist, Guest, or Guess. The signature on the treaty reads "Geo: Guess". Photographed by DeLancey Gill of the Bureau of American Ethnology, Washington, D.C., 1908, from the original manuscript. The original manuscript is not in the National Anthropological Archives.

Delegation as follows (left to right): John Rollin Ridge, Saladin Watie (son of Stand Watie), Richard Fields, Col. E. C. Boudinot (son of Elias Boudinot or Buck Watie), Col. William Penn Adair. Photograph by Alexander Gardner, Washington, D.C., 1866. (A Cherokee treaty was concluded at Washington, July 19, 1866; this photograph was presumably made at that time.)

was also claimed by the Creeks, and the British Government had therefore in purchasing it accepted a cession from those tribes jointly.[1]

At the beginning of the Federal relations with the Cherokees, a definition of their boundaries had been made by treaty of November 28, 1785, extending on the south as far west as the headwaters of the Appalachee River. Beyond that point to the west no declaration as to the limits of the Cherokee territory was made, because, for the purposes of the Federal Government, none was at that time necessary. But when in course of time other cessions came to be made, both by the Cherokees and Creeks, it began to be essential to have an exact definition of the line of limits between them. Especially was this the case when, as by the terms of the Creek treaty of February 12, 1825,[2] they ceded all the territory to which they laid claim within the limits of Georgia, and although this treaty was afterwards declared void by the United States, because of alleged fraud, Georgia always maintained the propriety and validity of its negotiation.

As early as June 10, 1802, a delegation of Cherokees interviewed Colonel Hawkins and General Pickens, and after demanding the removal of certain settlers claimed to be on their lands, asserted the boundary of their nation in the direction of the Creeks to be the path running from Colonel Easley's, at High Shoals of the Appalachee, to Etowah River. This they had agreed upon in council with the Creeks. A delegation of the Creeks, whom they brought with them from the council, were then interrogated on the subject by Messrs. Hawkins and Pickens, and they replied that the statement of the Cherokees was correct.

In the spring of 1814 (May 15) Agent Meigs had written the Secretary of War that the Cherokees were sensible that the Creeks ought to cede to the United States sufficient land to fully compensate the latter for the expenses incurred in prosecuting the Creek war. However, they (the Cherokees) were incidentally interested in the arrangements, and hoped that the United States would not permit the Creeks to point out the specific boundaries of their cession until the division line between the two nations had been definitely determined. In the following year, in a discussion of the subject with Colonel Hawkins, the Creek agent, Colonel Meigs declares that the Cherokees repel the idea entertained by the Creeks that the Cherokee or Tennessee River was ever their southern boundary. On the contrary, the dividing line between the territories of the two nations should begin at Vann's Old Store, on the Ocmulgee River, thence pursuing such a course as would strike the Coosa River below the Ten Islands. This claim was predicated upon the assertion that the Cherokees had in the course of three successive wars with the Creeks driven them more than a degree of latitude below the point last

---

[1] Treaty June 1, 1773, between the British superintendent of Indian affairs and the Creeks and Cherokees.

[2] United States Statutes at Large, Vol. VII, p. 237.

named. Another Cherokee version was to the effect that at a joint council of the two nations, held prior to the Revolutionary War, the boundary question was a subject of discussion, when it was agreed to allow the oldest man in the Creek Nation to determine the point. This man was James McQueen, a soldier who had deserted from Oglethorpe's command soon after the settlement of Savannah. McQueen decided that the boundary should be a line drawn across the headwaters of Hatchet and Elk Creeks, the former being a branch of the Coosa and the latter a tributary of the Tallapoosa. This decision was predicated upon the fact that the Cherokees had driven the Creeks below this line, and it had been mutually agreed that it should constitute the boundary.

In contradiction of this it was asserted by the Creeks that in the year 1818 it had been admitted at a public meeting of the Creeks by "Sour Mush," a Cherokee chief, that the Creeks owned all the land up to the head of Coosa River, including all of its waters; that the Tennessee was the Cherokee River, and the territories of the two nations joined on the dividing ridge between those rivers. In former times, on the Chattahoochee, the Cherokees had claimed the country as low down as a branch of that river called Choky (Soquee) River. Subsequently they were told by the Coweta king, that they might live as low down as the Currahee Mountain, but that their young men had now extended their claim to Hog Mountain, without however any shadow of right or authority.[1]

With a view to an amicable adjustment of their respective rights a council was held between the chiefs and headmen of the two nations at the residence of General William McIntosh, in the Creek country, at which a treaty was concluded between themselves on the 11th of December, 1820. In the first article of this treaty the boundary line between the two nations was fixed as running from the Buzzard's Roost, on the Chattahoochee, in a direct line to the Coosa River, at a point opposite the mouth of Wills Town Creek, and thence down the Coosa River to a point opposite Fort Strother. This boundary was reaffirmed by them in a subsequent treaty concluded October 30, 1822.[2]

The Cherokee treaty of 1817 had assumed to cede a tract of country "Beginning at the high shoals of the Appalachy River and running thence along the boundary line between the Creek and Cherokee Nations westwardly to the Chatahouchy River," etc.

The Creek treaty of 1818[3] in turn ceded a tract the northern boundary of which extended from Suwanee Old Town, on the Chattahoochee, to the head of Appalachee River, and which overlapped a considerable portion of the Cherokee cession of 1817.

The Creek treaty of 1821[4] ceded a tract running as far north as the Shallow Ford of the Chattahoochee, which also included a portion of

---

[1] Letter of D. B. Mitchell, Creek agent, to Secretary of War.
[2] See Indian Office files for these two treaties.
[3] United States Statutes at Large, Vol. VII, p. 171.
[4] Ib., p. 215.

the territory within the limits of the Cherokee domain, as claimed by the latter.

By the treaty of 1825[1] with the Creeks they ceded all their remaining territory in Georgia. Complaint being made that this treaty had been entered into by only a small non-representative faction of that nation, an investigation was entered upon by the United States authorities, and as the result it was determined to declare the treaty void and to negotiate a new treaty with them, which was done on the 24th of January, 1826.[2]

By this last treaty as amended the Creeks ceded all their land east of the Chattahoochee River, as well as a tract north and west of that river. In the cession of this latter tract it was assumed that a point on Chattahoochee River known as the Buzzard's Roost was the northern limit of the Creek supremacy.

The authorities of Georgia strongly insisted that not only had the treaty of 1825 been legitimately concluded, whereby they were entitled to come into possession of all the Creek domain within her limits, but also that the true line of the Creek limits toward the north had been much higher up than would seem to have been the understanding of the parties to the treaty of 1826.

In the following year the Creeks ceded all remaining territory they might have within the limits of Georgia.[3] This left the only question to be decided between the State of Georgia and the Cherokees the one of just boundaries between the latter and the country recently acquired from the Creeks.

The War Department had been of the impression that the proper boundary between the two nations was a line to be run directly from the High Shoals of the Appalachee to the Ten Islands, or Turkeytown, on the Coosa River.[4] On this hypothesis Agent Mitchell, of the Creeks, had been instructed, if he could do so, "without exciting their sensibilities," to establish it as the northern line of the Creek Nation.

Georgia, on the contrary, claimed that the proper boundary extended from Suwanee Old Town, on the Chattahoochee, to Sixes Old Town, on the Etowah River; from thence to the junction of the Etowah and Oostanaula Rivers, and following the Creek path from that point to Tennessee River. In pursuance of this claim Governor Forsyth instructed[5] Mr. Samuel A. Wales as the surveyor for that State to proceed to establish the line of limits in accordance therewith. Mr. Wales, upon commencing operations, was met with a protest from Colonel Montgomery, the Cherokee agent,[6] notwithstanding which he continued his operations in conformity with his original instructions.

---

[1] United States Statutes at Large, Vol. VII, p. 237.
[2] Ib., p. 289.
[3] Ib., p. 307; Creek treaty of November 15, 1827.
[4] Letter of Secretary of War to D. B. Mitchell, Creek agent.
[5] Letter of Governor Forsyth, of Georgia, to Samuel A. Wales, May 5, 1829.
[6] Letter of Montgomery to Wales, May 13, 1829.

This action of the surveyor having produced a feeling of great excitement and hostility within the Cherokee Nation, rendering the danger of collision and bloodshed imminent, the United States authorities took the matter in hand, and, by direction of the President, General John Coffee was appointed and instructed[1] to proceed to the Cherokee Nation, and from the most reliable information and testimony attainable to report what, in his judgment, should in justice and fairness to all parties concerned be declared to be the true line of limits between Georgia, as the successor of the Creeks, and the Cherokee Nation.

General Coffee proceeded to the performance of the duty thus assigned him. A large mass of testimony and tradition on the subject was evoked, in summing up which General Coffee reported[2] to the Secretary of War that the line of demarkation between the two nations should begin at the lower Shallow Ford of the Chattahoochee, which was about 15 miles below the Suwanee Old Town. From thence the line should run westwardly in a direction to strike the ridge dividing the waters running into Little River (a branch of the Hightower or Etowah) from those running into Sweet Water Creek (a branch of the Chattahoochee emptying about 2 miles below Buzzard's Roost). From this point such ridge should be followed westwardly, leaving all the waters falling into Hightower and Coosa Rivers to the right and all the waters that run southwardly into Chattahoochee and Tallapoosa Rivers to the left, until such ridge should intersect the line (which had been previously as per agreement of 1821 between the Creeks and Cherokees themselves) run and marked from Buzzard Roost to Wills Creek, and thence with this line to the Coosa River opposite the mouth of Wills Creek.

Two weeks later[3] General Coffee, in a communication to the Secretary of War, alludes to the dissatisfaction of Georgia with the line as determined by him, and her claim to an additional tract of territory by remarking that "I have thought it right to give this statement for your own and the eye of the President only, that you may the better appreciate the character of the active agents and partisans of the Georgia claim, for really I cannot see any reasonable or plausible evidence on which she rests her claim."

The President, after a careful examination of the testimony and much solicitude upon the subject, decided to approve General Coffee's recommendation. The Cherokee agent was therefore directed[4] to notify all white settlers living north of Coffee's line to remove at once. The governor of Georgia was also notified of the President's decision, and, though strongly and persistently protesting against it, the President

---

[1] October 10, 1829.
[2] December 30, 1829.
[3] January 15, 1830.
[4] March 14, 1830.

firmly refused to revoke his action.[1] The Cherokees were equally dissatisfied with the decision, because the line was not fixed as far south as Buzzard's Roost, in accordance with the agreement of 1821 between themselves and the Creeks.[2]

---

[1] Secretary of War to Governor Gilmer, of Georgia, June 1, 1830.

[2] The following paper, which is on file in the Office of Indian Affairs, is interesting in connection with the subject matter of this boundary:
Extract from treaties and other documents relative to the Cherokee lines in contact with the Creeks and Chickasaws west of Coosa River:

"*June* 10, 1786.—In the treaty of this date with the Chickasaws the lands allotted them eastwardly 'shall be the lands allotted to the Choctaws and Cherokees to live and hunt on.' In the conference which took place between the commissioners of the United States and the Chickasaws and Cherokees, it was apparent that their claims conflicted with each other on the ridge dividing the waters of Cumberland from those of Duck River and around to the Chickasaw Oldtown Creek on Tennessee, thence southwardly, leaving the mountains above the Muscle Shoals on the south side of the river, and to a large stone or flat rock, where the Choctaw line joined with the Chickasaws. The journal of occurrences at the time were lodged with the papers of the old Congress, and probably were transferred to the office of Secretary of State. On the 7th of January, 1806, in a convention between the United States and Cherokees, on the part of the former by Mr. Dearborn, the United States engaged to use their best endeavors to fix a boundary between the Cherokees and Chickasaws, 'beginning at the mouth of Caney Creek, near the lower part of the Muscle Shoals, and to run up the said creek to its head, and in a direct line from thence to the flat stone or rock, the old corner boundary,' the line between the Creeks and Cherokees east of Coosau River.

"In 1802, at the treaty of Fort Wilkinson, it was agreed between the parties that the line was 'from the High Shoals on Apalatche, the old path, leaving Stone Mountain to the Creeks, to the shallow ford on the Chatahoochee.'

"This agreement was in presence of the commissioners of the United States and witnessed by General Pickens and Colonel Hawkins. On the 10th October, 1809, a letter was sent from the Cherokees to the Creeks and received in February in the public square at Tookaubatche, stating the line agreed upon at Fort Wilkinson, and that 'all the waters of Etowah down to the ten islands below Turkeytown these lands were given up to the Cherokees at a talk at Chestoe in presence of the Little Prince, and Tustunnuggee Thlucco Chulioah, of Turkeystown, was the interpreter.'

"In August, 1814, at the treaty of Fort Jackson, the Creeks and Cherokees were invited to settle their claims, and Colonel Meigs was engaged for three or four days in aiding them to do so. The result was they could not agree, but would at some convenient period agree. This was signed by General Jackson, Colonel Hawkins, and Colonel Meigs.

"At the convention with the Creeks, in September, 1815, the Cherokees manifested a sincere desire to settle their boundaries with the Creeks, but the latter first declined and then refused. Tustunnuggee Thlucco, being asked where their boundary was west of Coosau, said there never was any boundary fixed and known as such between the parties, and after making Tennessee the boundary from tradition, and that the Cherokees obtained leave of them to cross it, the policy of the Creeks receiving all destroyed red people in their confederacy, the Cherokees were permitted to come over and settle as low down on the west of Coosau as Hauluthee Hatchee, from thence on the west side of Coosau on all its waters to its source. He has never heard, and he has examined all his people who can have any knowledge on the subject, that the Cherokees had any pretensions lower down Coosau on that side. He does not believe, and he has never heard, there was any boundary agreed upon between them. Being asked by Colonel Hawkins his opinion where the boundary should be, he says it

CHEROKEES PLEAD WITH CONGRESS AND THE PRESIDENT FOR JUSTICE.

A delegation of the Cherokees, with John Ross at their head, was quartered in Washington during the greater part of the winter of 1832-'33, bringing to bear in behalf of their nation every possible influence upon both Congress and the Executive. A voluminous correspondence was conducted between them and the War Department upon the subject of their proposed removal. In a communication on the 28th of January, 1833, they ask leave to say that, notwithstanding the various perplexities which the Cherokee people had experienced under the course of policy pursued toward them, they were yet unshaken in their objections to a removal west of the Mississippi River. On the question of their rights and the justice of their cause, their minds were equally unchangeable. They were, however, fully sensible that justice and weakness could not control the array of oppressive power, and that in the calamitous effects of such power, already witnessed, they could not fail to foresee with equal clearness that a removal to the west would be followed in a few years by consequences no less fatal.

They therefore suggested for the consideration of the President, whether it would not be practicable for the Government to satisfy the claims of Georgia by granting to those of her citizens who had in the lotteries of that State drawn lots of land within Cherokee limits other

---

should go up Hauluthee Hatchee, passing a level of good land between two mountains, to the head of Itchau Hatchee, and down the same to Tennessee, about 8 or 9 miles above Nickajack. In the year 1798 the Cherokees had a settlement at the Muscle Shoals, Doublehead and Katagiskee were the chiefs, and the Creeks had a small settlement above the Creek path on Tennessee. The Cherokee settlement extended southwardly from the shoal probably a mile and a half. The principal temporary agent for Indian affairs south of the Ohio was early instructed in 1777 to ascertain the boundary line of the four nations, and instructions were given accordingly by him to Mr. Dinsmore and Mr. Mitchell to aid in doing it. Several attempts were made, but all proved abortive, owing to the policy of the Creeks, which was to unite the four nations in one confederacy and the national affairs of all to be in a convention to be held annually among the Creeks, where the speaker for the Creeks should preside.

"At every attempt made among the Creeks when these conventions met, the answer was, 'We have no dividing lines, nor never had, between us. We have lines only between us and the white people, our neighbors.' At times, when the subject was discussed in the convention of the Creeks, they claimed Tombigby, called by them Choctaw River (Choctau Hatchee), the boundary line between them and the Choctaws. Tustunneggee Hopoie, brother of the old Efau Hajo (mad dog), who died at ninety-six years of age, and retained strength of memory and intelligence to this great age, reported publicly to the agent, 'When he was a boy his father's hunting camp was at Puttauchau Hatchee (Black Warrior).' His father had long been at the head of the Creeks, and always told him 'Choctaw River was their boundary with the Choctaws.' He never saw a Choctaw hunting camp on this side the Black Warrior.

"A true copy from the original.

"PHIL. HAWKINS, JR.,
"*Ast. A. I. A.*"

lands of the United States lying within the Territories and States of the Union, or in some other way.

The President urges their assent to removal.—The Secretary of War, in replying for the President (February 2, 1833), was unable to see that any practicable plan could be adopted by which the reversionary rights held under the State of Georgia could be purchased upon such terms as would justify the Government in entering into a stipulation to that effect. Nor would it at all remove the difficulties and embarrassments of their condition. They would still be subject to the laws of Georgia, surrounded by white settlements and exposed to all those evils which had always attended the Indian race when placed in immediate contact with the white population. It was only by removing from these surroundings that they could expect to avoid the fate which had already swept away so many Indian tribes.

Reply of John Ross.—Ross retorted, in a communication couched in diplomatic language, that it was with great diffidence and deep regret he felt constrained to say, that in this scheme of Indian removal he could see more of expediency and policy to get rid of the Cherokees than to perpetuate their race upon any permanent, fundamental principle. If the doctrine that Indian tribes could not exist contiguous to a white population should prevail, and they should be compelled to remove west of the States and Territories of this republic, what was to prevent a similar removal of them from there for the same reason?

Without securing any promises of relief, and without reaching any definite understanding with the executive authorities of the Government, the delegation left for their homes in March, 1833. They agreed, however, to lay before their national council in the ensuing May a proposition made to them by the President, offering to pay them $2,500,000 in goods for their lands, with the proviso that they should remove themselves at their own expense.[1] This proposition, it is hardly necessary to remark, was not favorably considered by the council, though the Secretary of War designated[2] Mr. Benjamin F. Curry to attend the meeting and urge its acceptance.

Alleged attempted bribery of John Ross.—In this connection a story having been given currency that the Government had offered Chief Ross a bribe, provided he would secure the conclusion of a treaty of cession and removal, the Commissioner of Indian Affairs denied it as being "utterly without foundation, and one of those vile expedients that unprincipled men sometimes practice to accomplish an evil purpose," and as being "too incredible to do much injury."[3] While this story was perhaps without solid foundation in fact, its improbability would possibly have been more evident but for the fact that only five years earlier the Secretary of War had appointed secret agents and

---

[1] Letter of Secretary of War to Governor Lumpkin, of Georgia, March 12, 1833.
[2] March 21, 1833.
[3] Commissioner of Indian Affairs to Agent Montgomery, April 22, 1833.

authorized them to expend $2,000 in bribing the chiefs for this very purpose, and had made his action in this respect a matter of public record.

CHEROKEES PROPOSE AN ADJUSTMENT.

In January, 1834, a few weeks after the assembling of Congress, the Cherokee delegation again arrived in Washington.[1] Sundry interviews and considerable correspondence with the War Department seemed barren of results or even hope. The delegation submitted[2] a proposition for adjustment in another form. Remarking upon their feeble numbers, and surrounded as they were by a nation so powerful as the United States, they could not but clearly see, they said, that their existence and permanent welfare as a people must depend upon that relation which should eventually lead to an amalgamation with the people of the United States. As the prospects of securing this object collectively, in their present location in the character of a territorial or State government, seemed to be seriously opposed and threatened by the States interested in their own aggrandizement, and as the Cherokees had refused, and would never voluntarily consent, to remove west of the Mississippi, the question was propounded whether the Government would enter into an arrangement on the basis of the Cherokees becoming prospectively citizens of the United States, provided the former would cede to the United States a portion of their territory for the use of Georgia; and whether the United States would agree to have the laws and treaties executed and enforced for the effectual protection of the Cherokees on the remainder of their territory for a definite period, with the understanding that upon the expiration of that period the Cherokees were to be subjected to the laws of the States within whose limits they might be, and to take an individual standing as citizens thereof, the same as other free citizens of the United States, with liberty to dispose of their surplus lands in such manner as might be agreed upon.

Cherokee proposals declined.—The reply[3] to this proposition was that the President did not see the slightest hope of a termination to the embarrassments under which the Cherokees labored except in their removal to the country west of the Mississippi.

Proposal of Andrew Ross.—In the mean time[4] Andrew Ross, who was a member of the Cherokee delegation, suggested to the Commissioner of Indian Affairs that if he were authorized so to do he would proceed to the Cherokee country and bring a few chiefs or respectable individuals of the nation to Washington, with whom a treaty could be effected for the cession of the whole or part of the Cherokee territory. His plan

---

[1] Secretary of War to Governor Lumpkin, of Georgia, January 28, 1834.
[2] March 28, 1834.
[3] May 1, 1834.
[4] March 3, 1834.

was approved, with the understanding that if a treaty should be concluded the expenses of the delegation would be paid by the United States. Ross succeeded in assembling some fifteen or twenty Cherokees at the Cherokee agency, all of whom were favorable to the scheme of emigration. Under the self-styled appellation of a committee, they proceeded to appoint a chief and assistant chief in the persons of William Hicks and John McIntosh, and selected eight of their own number as the remainder of the delegation to visit Washington.[1]

Protest of John Ross and thirteen thousand Cherokees.—Upon their arrival Hon. J. H. Eaton was designated[2] to conduct the negotiations with them. During the pendency of the negotiations Mr. Eaton advised John Ross of the purpose in view and solicited his co-operation in the scheme. Mr. Ross refused[3] this proposal with much warmth, and took occasion to add in behalf of the Cherokee Nation that "in the face of Heaven and earth, before God and man, I most solemnly protest against any treaty whatever being entered into with those of whom you say one is in progress so as to affect the rights and interests of the Cherokee Nation east of the Mississippi River."

Chief Ross also presented a protest, alleged to have been signed by more than thirteen thousand Cherokees, against the negotiation of such a treaty.

Preliminary treaty concluded with Andrew Ross et al.—Disregarding the protest of Chief Ross and distrusting the verity of that purporting to have been so numerously signed in the nation, the negotiations proceeded, and a treaty or agreement was concluded on the 19th day of June, 1834. The treaty provided for the opening of emigrant enrolling books, with a memorandum heading declaring the assent of the subscriber to a treaty yet to be concluded with the United States based upon the terms previously offered by the President, covering a cession and removal, and with the proviso that if no such subsequent treaty should be concluded within the next few months then the subscribers would cede to the United States all their right and interest in the Cherokee lands east of the Mississippi. In consideration of this they were to be removed and subsisted for one year at the expense of the United States, to receive the ascertained value of their improvements, and to be entitled to all such stipulations as should thereafter be made in favor of those who should not then remove.

The treaty, however, failed of ratification, though the enrolling books were opened[4] and a few of the Cherokees entered their names for emgration.

CHEROKEES MEMORIALIZE CONGRESS.

While the negotiations leading up to the conclusion of this treaty were in progress John Ross and his delegation, finding no disposition

---

[1] Letter of John Ross and others to Secretary of War, inclosing protest, May 24, 1834.
[2] Letter of Hon. J. H. Eaton to John Ross, May 26, 1834.
[3] May 29, 1834.
[4] Secretary of War to governor of Georgia, July 8, 1834.

on the part of the executive authority to enter into a discussion of Cherokee affairs predicated upon any other basis than an abandonment by them of their homes and country east of the Mississippi, presented[1] a memorial to Congress complaining of the injuries done them and praying for redress. Without affecting to pass judgment on the merits of the controversy, the writer thinks this memorial well deserving of reproduction here as evidencing the devoted and pathetic attachment with which the Cherokees clung to the land of their fathers, and, remembering the wrongs and humiliations of the past, refused to be convinced that justice, prosperity, and happiness awaited them beyond the Mississippi.

The memorial of the Cherokee Nation respectfully showeth, that they approach your honorable bodies as the representatives of the people of the United States, intrusted by them under the Constitution with the exercise of their sovereign power, to ask for protection of the rights of your memorialists and redress of their grievances.

They respectfully represent that their rights, being stipulated by numerous solemn treaties, which guaranteed to them protection, and guarded as they supposed by laws enacted by Congress, they had hoped that the approach of danger would be prevented by the interposition of the power of the Executive charged with the execution of treaties and laws; and that when their rights should come in question they would be finally and authoritatively decided by the judiciary, whose decrees it would be the duty of the Executive to see carried into effect. For many years these their just hopes were not disappointed.

The public faith of the United States, solemnly pledged to them, was duly kept in form and substance. Happy under the parental guardianship of the United States, they applied themselves assiduously and successfully to learn the lessons of civilization and peace, which, in the prosecution of a humane and Christian policy, the United States caused to be taught them. Of the advances they have made under the influence of this benevolent system, they might a few years ago have been tempted to speak with pride and satisfaction and with grateful hearts to those who have been their instructors. They could have pointed with pleasure to the houses they had built, the improvements they had made, the fields they were cultivating; they could have exhibited their domestic establishments, and shown how from wandering in the forests many of them had become the heads of families, with fixed habitations, each the center of a domestic circle like that which forms the happiness of civilized man. They could have shown, too, how the arts of industry, human knowledge, and letters had been introduced amongst them, and how the highest of all the knowledge had come to bless them, teaching them to know and to worship the Christian's God, bowing down to Him at the same seasons and in the same spirit with millions of His creatures who inhabit Christendom, and with them embracing the hopes and promises of the Gospel.

But now each of these blessings has been made to them an instrument of the keenest torture. Cupidity has fastened its eye upon their lands and their homes, and is seeking by force and by every variety of oppression and wrong to expel them from their lands and their homes and to tear them from all that has become endeared to them. Of what they have already suffered it is impossible for them to give the details, as they would make a history. Of what they are menaced with by unlawful power, every citizen of the United States who reads the public journals is aware. In this their distress they have appealed to the judiciary of the United States, where their rights have been solemnly established. They have appealed to the Executive of the United States to protect these rights according to the obligations of treaties and the injunctions of the laws. But this appeal to the Executive has been made in vain.

---

[1] May 17, 1834.

In the hope that by yielding something of their clear rights they might succeed in obtaining security for the remainder, they have lately opened a correspondence with the Executive, offering to make a considerable cession from what had been reserved to them by solemn treaties, only upon condition that they might be protected in the part not ceded. But their earnest supplication has been unheeded, and the only answer they can get, informs them, in substance, that they must be left to their fate, or renounce the whole. What that fate is to be unhappily is too plain.

The State of Georgia has assumed jurisdiction over them, has invaded their territory, has claimed the right to dispose of their lands, and has actually proceeded to dispose of them, reserving only a small portion to individuals, and even these portions are threatened and will no doubt, soon be taken from them. Thus the nation is stripped of its territory and individuals of their property without the least color of right, and in open violation of the guarantee of treaties. At the same time the Cherokees, deprived of the protection of their own government and laws, are left without the protection of any other laws, outlawed as it were and exposed to indignities, imprisonment, persecution, and even to death, though they have committed no offense whatever, save and except that of seeking to enjoy what belongs to them, and refusing to yield it up to those who have no pretense of title to it. Of the acts of the legislature of Georgia your memorialists will endeavor to furnish copies to your honorable bodies, and of the doings of individuals they will furnish evidence if required. And your memorialists further respectfully represent that the Executive of the United States has not only refused to protect your memorialists against the wrongs they have suffered and are still suffering at the hands of unjust cupidity, but has done much more. It is but too plain that, for several years past, the power of the Executive has been exerted on the side of their oppressors and is co-operating with them in the work of destruction. Of two particulars in the conduct of the Executive your memorialists would make mention, not merely as matters of evidence but as specific subjects of complaint in addition to the more general ones already stated.

The first of these is the mode adopted to oppress and injure your memorialists under color of enrollments for emigration. Unfit persons are introduced as agents, acts are practiced by them that are unjust, unworthy, and demoralizing, and have no object but to force your memorialists to yield and abandon their rights by making their lives intolerably wretched. They forbear to go into particulars, which nevertheless they are prepared, at a proper time, to exhibit.

The other is calculated also to weaken and distress your memorialists, and is essentially unjust. Heretofore, until within the last four years, the money appropriated by Congress for annuities has been paid to the nation, by whom it was distributed and used for the benefit of the nation. And this method of payment was not only sanctioned by the usage of the Government of the United States, but was acceptable to the Cherokees. Yet, without any cause known to your memorialists, and contrary to their just expectations, the payment has been withheld for the period just mentioned, on the ground, then for the first time assumed, that the annuities were to be paid, not as hitherto, to the nation, but to the individual Cherokees, each his own small fraction, dividing the whole according to the numbers of the nation. The fact is, that for the last four years the annuities have not been paid at all.

The distribution in this new way was impracticable, if the Cherokees had been willing thus to receive it, but they were not willing; they have refused and the annuities have remained unpaid. Your memorialists forbear to advert to the motives of such conduct, leaving them to be considered and appreciated by Congress. All they will say is, that it has coincided with other measures adopted to reduce them to poverty and despair and to extort from their wretchedness a concession of their guaranteed rights. Having failed in their efforts to obtain relief elsewhere, your memorialists now appeal to Congress, and respectfully pray that your honorable bodies will look into their whole case, and that such measures may be adopted as will give them redress and security.

TREATY NEGOTIATIONS RESUMED.

Rival delegations headed by Ross and Ridge.—But little else was done and practically nothing was accomplished until the following winter. Early in February, 1835, two rival delegations, each claiming to represent the Cherokee Nation, arrived in Washington. One was headed by John Ross, who had long been the principal chief and who was the most intelligent and influential man in the nation. The rival delegation was led by John Ridge, who had been a subchief and a man of some considerable influence among his people.[1] The Ross delegation had been consistently and bitterly opposed to any negotiations having in view the surrender of their territory and a removal west of the Mississippi. Ridge and his delegation, though formerly of the same mind with Ross, had begun to perceive the futility of further opposition to the demands of the State and national authorities. Feeling the certainty that the approaching crisis in Cherokee affairs could have but one result, and perceiving an opportunity to enhance his own importance and to secure the discomfiture of his hitherto more powerful rival, Ridge caused it to be intimated to the United States authorities that he and his delegation were prepared to treat with them upon the basis previously laid down by President Jackson of a cession of their territory and a removal west.

Rev. J. F. Schermerhorn was therefore appointed,[2] and instructions were prepared authorizing him to meet Ridge and his party and to ascertain on what terms an amicable and satisfactory arrangement could be made. After the instructions had been delivered to Mr. Schermerhorn, but before he had commenced the negotiation, Ross and his party requested to be allowed to make a proposal to be submitted to the President for his approval. He was assured that his proposal would be considered, and in the mean time Mr. Schermerhorn was requested to suspend his operations. So much time, however, elapsed before anything more was heard from Ross and his party that the negotiations with the Ridge party were proceeded with. They terminated in a general understanding respecting the basis of an arrangement, leaving, however, many of the details to be filled up. The total amount of the various stipulations provided for, as a full consideration for the cession of their lands, was $3,250,000, besides the sum of $150,000 for depredation claims. In addition, a tract of 800,000 acres of land west of the Mississippi was to be added to the territory already promised them, amounting in the aggregate, including the western outlet, to about 13,800,000 acres.[3]

---

[1] The Ross delegation was composed of John Ross, R. Taylor, Daniel McCoy, Samuel Gunter, and William Rogers. The Ridge delegation consisted of John Ridge, William A. Davis, Elias Boudinot, A. Smith, S. W. Bell, and J. West.

[2] February 11, 1835.

[3] Memorandum delivered by Secretary of War to Senator King, of Georgia, February 28, 1835.

Proposition of John Ross.—On the 25th of February, Ross and his delegation, finding that the negotiations with Ridge were proceeding, submitted a proposition for removal based upon an allowance of $20,000,000 for the cession of the territory and the payment of a class of claims of uncertain number and value. This was considered so unreasonable as to render the seriousness of his proposition doubtful at the time, but it was finally modified by an assertion of his willingness to accept such sum as the Senate of the United States should declare to be just and proper.[1] Thereupon a statement of all the facts was placed in the hands of Senator King, of Georgia, who submitted the same to the Senate Committee on Indian Affairs on the 2d of March. It was not contemplated that any arrangement made with these Cherokee delegations at this time should be definitive, but that the Cherokee people should be assembled for the purpose of considering the subject, and their assent asked to such propositions as they might deem satisfactory.

Resolution of United States Senate on John Ross's proposition.—The Senate gave the matter prompt consideration, and on the 6th of March the Secretary of War advised Mr. Ross that by a resolution they had stated their opinion that "a sum not exceeding $5,000,000 should be paid to the Cherokee Indians for all their lands and possessions east of the Mississippi River," and he was invited to enter into negotiations upon that basis, but declined to do so.

Preliminary treaty concluded with the Ridge party.—The treaty between Schermerhorn and the Ridge party was thereupon completed with some modifications and duly signed on the 14th of March, but with the express stipulation that it should receive the approval of the Cherokee people in full council assembled before being considered of any binding force. The consideration was changed to read $4,500,000 and 800,000 acres of additional land, but in the main its provisions differed but little in the important objects sought to be secured from those contained in the treaty as finally concluded, December 29, 1835.

Schermerhorn and Carroll appointed to complete the treaty.—In the mean time,[2] two days after the conclusion of the preliminary Ridge treaty, President Jackson issued an address to the Cherokees, inviting them to a calm consideration of their condition and prospects, and urging upon them the benefits certain to inure to their nation by the ratification of the treaty just concluded and their removal to the western country. This address was intrusted to Rev. J. F. Schermerhorn and General William Carroll, whom the President had appointed on the 2d of April as commissioners to complete in the Cherokee country the negotiation of the treaty.

General Carroll being unable on account of ill-health to proceed from Nashville to the Cherokee Nation, Mr. Schermerhorn was compelled to assume the responsibilities of the negotiation alone. The entire sum-

---

[1] Memorandum delivered by Secretary of War to Senator King, of Georgia, February 28, 1835.
[2] March 16, 1835.

mer and fall were spent in endeavors to reconcile differences of opinion, to adjust feuds among the different factions of the tribe, and to secure some definitive and consolidated action. Meeting with no substantial encouragement, he suggested, in a communication to the Secretary of War,[1] two alternative propositions, by either of which a treaty might be secured.

These propositions were: (1) That the appraising agents of the Government should ascertain from influential Cherokees their own opinion of the value of their improvements, and promise them the amount, if this estimate should be in any degree reasonable, and if they would take a decided stand in favor of the treaty and conclude the same. (2) To conclude the treaty with a portion of the nation only, should one with the whole be found impracticable, and compel the acquiescence of the remainder in its provisions.

He was at once[2] advised of the opposition of the President to any such action. If a treaty could not be concluded upon fair and open terms, he must abandon the effort and leave the nation to the consequences of its own stubbornness. He must make no particular promise to any individual, high or low, to gain his co-operation. The interest of the whole must not be sacrificed to the cupidity of a few, and if a treaty was concluded at all it must be one that would stand the test of the most rigid scrutiny.

The Ridge treaty rejected.—The Cherokee people in full council at Red Clay, in the following October, rejected the Ridge treaty. Mr. John Ridge and Elias Boudinot, who had been the main stay and support of Mr. Schermerhorn in the preceding negotiations, at this council, through fear or duplicity and unexpectedly to him, abandoned their support of his measures and coincided with the preponderance of Cherokee sentiment on the subject. In his report of this failure to bring the negotiations to a successful termination Commissioner Schermerhorn says: "I have pressed Ross so hard by the course I have adopted that although he got the general council to pass a resolution declaring that they would not treat on the basis of the $5,000,000, yet he has been forced to bring the nation to agree to a treaty, here or at Washington. They have used every effort to get by me and get to Washington again this winter. They dare not yet do it. You will perceive Ridge and his friends have taken apparently a strange course. I believe he began to be discouraged in contending with the power of Ross; and perhaps also considerations of personal safety have had their influence, but the Lord is able to overrule all things for good."[3]

Council at New Echota.—During the session of this council notice was given to the Cherokees to meet the United States commissioners on the third Monday in December following, at New Echota, for the pur-

---

[1] September 10, 1835.

[2] September 26, 1835.

[3] Senate Document 120, Twenty-fifth Congress, second session, p. 124.

pose of negotiating and agreeing upon the terms of a treaty. The notice was also printed in Cherokee and circulated throughout the nation, informing the Indians that those who did not attend would be counted as assenting to any treaty that might be made.[1] In the mean time the Ross delegation, authorized by the Red Clay council to conclude a treaty either there or at Washington, finding that Schermerhorn had no authority to treat on any other basis than the one rejected by the nation, proceeded, according to their people's instructions, to Washington. Previous to their departure, John Ross was arrested. This took place immediately upon the breaking up of the council. He was detained some time under the surveillance of a strong guard, without any charge against him, and ultimately released without any apology or explanation. At this arrest all his papers were seized, including as well all his private correspondence and the proceedings of the Cherokee council.[2] In accordance with the call for a council at New Echota the Indians assembled at the appointed time and place, to the number of only three to five hundred, as reported[3] by Mr. Schermerhorn himself, who could hardly be accused of any tendency to underestimate the gathering. That gentleman opened the council December 22, 1835, in the absence of Governor Carroll, whose health was still such as to prevent his attendance. The objects of the council were fully explained, the small attendance being attributed to the influence of John Ross. It was also suggested by those unfriendly to the proposed treaty as a good reason for the absence of so large a proportion of the nation, that the right to convene a national council was vested in the principal chief, and they were unaware that that officer's authority had been delegated to Mr. Schermerhorn.[2]

Those present resolved on the 23d to enter into negotiations and appointed a committee of twenty to arrange the details with the Commissioner and to report the result to the whole council.

The following five days were occuqied by the commissioner and the committee in discussing and agreeing upon the details of the treaty, one point of difference being as to whether the $5,000,000 consideration for their lands as mentioned in the resolution of the Senate was meant to include the damages to individual property sustained at the hands of white trespassers.

The Indians insisted that $300,000 additional should be allowed for that purpose, but it was finally agreed that the treaty should not be presented to the Senate without the consent of their delegation until they were satisfied the Senate had not included these claims in the sum named in the resolution of that body. It was also insisted by the Cherokee committee that reservations should be made to such of their people

---

[1] See proceedings of council.
[2] National Intelligencer, May 22, 1838.
[3] Schermerhorn to Commissioner of Indian Affairs, December 31, 1835.

as desired to remain in their homes and become citizens of the United States.

As a compromise of this demand, it was agreed by the United States commissioner to allow pre-emptions of 160 acres each, not exceeding 400 in number, in the States of North Carolina, Tennessee, and Alabama, to such heads of Cherokee families only as were qualified to become useful members of society. None were to be entitled to this privilege unless their applications were recommended by a committee of their own people (a majority of which committee should be composed of those members of the tribe who were themselves enrolled for removal) and approved by the United States commissioners. The latter also proposed to make the reservations dependent upon the approval of the legislatures of the States within which they might be respectively located, but to this proposition a strenuous objection was offered by the Indians.

The articles as agreed upon were reported by the Cherokee committee to their people, and were approved, transcribed, and signed on the 29th.

The council adjourned on the 30th, after designating a committee to proceed to Washington and urge the ratification of the treaty, clothed with power to assent to any alterations made necessary by the action of the President or Senate.[1]

Commissioner Schermerhorn reports conclusion of a treaty.—Immediately following the adjournment of the council, Commissioner Schemerhorn wrote the Secretary of War, saying: "I have the extreme pleasure to announce to you that yesterday I concluded a treaty. * * * Ross after this treaty is prostrate. The power of the nation is taken from him, as well as the money, and the treaty will give general satisfaction."[2]

Supplemental treaty concluded.—Several provisions of the treaty met with the disapproval of the President, in order to meet which supplementary articles of agreement were concluded under date of March 1, 1836,[3] wherein it was stipulated that all pre-emption rights provided for should be declared void; also that, in lieu of the same and to cover expenses of removal and payment of claims against citizens of the United States, the sum of $600,000 should be allowed them in addition to the five millions allowed for cession of territory. And, furthermore, that the $100,000 stipulated to be expended for the poorer class of Cherokees who should remove west should be placed to the credit of the general national fund.[4]

Opposition of the Ross party.—Whilst these events were happening, and strenuous efforts were being made to encourage among Senators a

---

[1] See report of proceedings of council.
[2] National Intelligencer, May 22, 1838.
[3] United States Statutes at Large, Vol. VII, p. 488.
[4] In addition to these sums, an appropriation of $1,047,067 was made by the act of June 13, 1838, in full of all objects specified in the third supplemental article and for the one year's subistence provided for in the treaty.

sentiment favorable to the ratification of the treaty, John Ross was manifesting his usual zeal and activity in the opposite direction. Early in the spring of 1836 he made his appearance in Washington, accompanied by a delegation, and presented two protests against the ratification of the treaty, one purporting to have been signed by Cherokees residing within the limits of North Carolina to the number of 3,250, and the other representing the alleged sentiments of 12,714 persons residing within the main body of the nation. Mr. Ross also demanded the payment of the long withheld annuities to himself as the duly authorized representative of the nation, which was declined unless special direction to that effect should be given by an authentic vote of the tribe from year to year. He was further assured that the President had ceased to recognize any existing government among the Eastern Cherokees.[1]

Treaty ratified by United States Senate.—In spite of the opposition of Mr. Ross and his party, the treaty was assented to by the Senate by one more than the necessary two-thirds majority,[2] and was ratified and proclaimed by the President on the 23d of May, 1836.[3] By its terms two years were allowed within which the nation must remove west of the Mississippi.

Measures for execution of the treaty.— Preparatory steps were promptly taken for carrying the treaty into execution. On the 7th of June Gov. Wilson Lumpkin, of Georgia, and Gov. William Carroll, of Tennessee, were designated as commissioners under the 17th article, and vested with general supervisory authority over the execution of the treaty. The selection and general supervision (under the foregoing commissioners) of the agents to appraise the value of Cherokee improvements was placed in charge of Benjamin F. Curry, to whom detailed instructions were given[4] for his guidance. General John E. Wool was placed in command of the United States troops within the Cherokee Nation, but with instructions[5] that military force should only be applied in the event of hostilities being commenced by the Cherokees.

The Ross party refuse to acquiesce.—John Ross and his delegation, having returned home, at once proceeded to enter upon a vigorous campaign of opposition to the execution of the treaty. He used every means to incite the animosity of his people against Ridge and his friends, who had been instrumental in bringing it about and who were favorable to removal. Councils were held and resolutions were adopted denouncing in the severest terms the motives and action of the United States authorities and declaring the treaty in all its provisions abso-

---

[1] Commissioner of Indian Affairs to John Ross, March 9, 1836.

[2] Hon. P. M. Butler, in a confidential letter to the Commissioner of Indian Affairs, March 4, 1842, says: "The treaty, as the Department is aware, was sustained by the Senate of the United States by a majority of one vote."

[3] United States Statutes at Large, Vol. VII, p. 478 *et seq.*

[4] July 25, 1836.

[5] July 30, 1836.

lutely null and void.¹ A copy of these resolutions having been transmitted to the Secretary of War by General Wool, the former was directed² by the President to express his astonishment that an officer of the Army should have received or transmitted a paper so disrespectful to the Executive, to the Senate, and through them to the people of the United States. To prevent any misapprehension on the subject of the treaty the Secretary was instructed to repeat in the most explicit terms the settled determination of the President that it should be executed without modification and with all the dispatch consistent with propriety and justice. Furthermore, that after delivering a copy of this letter to Mr. Ross no further communication should be held with him either orally or in writing in regard to the treaty.

To give a clearer idea of the actual state of feeling that pervaded the Cherokee Nation on the subject of removal, as well as the character of the methods that distinguished the negotiators on the part of the United States, a few quotations from the letters and reports of those in a position to observe the passing events may not be inappropriate.

REPORT OF MAJOR DAVIS.

Maj. William M. Davis had been appointed an agent by the Secretary of War for the enrollment of Cherokees desirous of removal to the West and for the appraisement of the value of their improvements. He had gone among the Cherokees for this specific purpose. He held his appointment by the grace and permission of the President. It was natural that his desire should be strongly in the line of securing the Executive approval of his labors.

Strong, however, as was that desire he was unable to bring himself to the support of the methods that were being pursued in the negotiation of the proposed treaty. On the 5th of March following the conclusion of the treaty of 1835, he wrote the Secretary of War thus:

> I conceive that my duty to the President, to yourself, and to my country, reluctantly compels me to make a statement of facts in relation to a meeting of a small number of Cherokees at New Echota last December, who were met by Mr. Schermerhorn and articles of a general treaty entered into between them for the whole Cherokee Nation.
>
> * * * I should not interpose in the matter at all but I discover that you do not receive impartial information on the subject; that you have to depend upon the *ex parte*, partial, and interested reports of a person who will not give you the truth. I will not be silent when I see that you are about to be imposed on by a gross and base betrayal of the high trust reposed in Rev. J. F. Schermerhorn by you. His conduct and course of policy was a series of blunders from first to last. * * * It has been wholly of a partisan character.

---

[1] The Secretary of War, October 12, 1836, directed General Wool to inform Mr. Ross that the President regarded the proceedings of himself and associates in council as in direct contravention of the plighted faith of their people, and a repetition of them would be considered as indicative of a design to prevent the execution of the treaty even at the hazard of actual hostilities, and they would be promptly repressed.

[2] October 17, 1836.

Sir, that paper * * * called a treaty is no treaty at all, because not sanctioned by the great body of the Cherokees and made without their participation or assent. I solemnly declare to you that upon its reference to the Cherokee people it would be instantly rejected by nine-tenths of them and I believe by nineteen-twentieths of them. There were not present at the conclusion of the treaty more than one hundred Cherokee voters, and not more than three hundred, including women and children, although the weather was everything that could be desired. The Indians had long been notified of the meeting, and blankets were promised to all who would come and vote for the treaty. The most cunning and artful means were resorted to to conceal the paucity of numbers present at the treaty. No enumeration of them was made by Schermerhorn. The business of making the treaty was transacted with a committee appointed by the Indians present, so as not to expose their numbers. The power of attorney under which the committee acted was signed only by the president and secretary of the meeting, so as not to disclose their weakness. * * * Mr. Schermerhorn's apparent design was to conceal the real number present and to impose on the public and the Government upon this point. The delegation taken to Washington by Mr. Schermerhorn had no more authority to make a treaty than any other dozen Cherokees accidentally picked up for that purpose. I now warn you and the President that if this paper of Schermerhorn's called a treaty is sent to the Senate and ratified you will bring trouble upon the Government and eventually destroy this (the Cherokee) nation. The Cherokees are a peaceable, harmless people, but you may drive them to desperation, and this treaty cannot be carried into effect except by the strong arm of force.[1]

ELIAS BOUDINOT'S VIEWS.

About this time there also appeared, in justification of the treaty and of his own action in signing it, a pamphlet address issued by Elias Boudinot of the Cherokee Nation. Mr. Boudinot was one of the ablest and most cultured of his people, and had long been the editor and publisher of a newspaper in the nation, printed both in English and Cherokee. The substance of his argument in vindication of the treaty may have been creditable from the standpoint of policy and a regard for the future welfare of his people, but in the abstract it is a dangerous doctrine. He said:

We cannot conceive of the acts of a minority to be so reprehensible and unjust as are represented by Mr. Ross. If one hundred persons are ignorant of their true situation and are so completely blinded as not to see the destruction that awaits them, we can see strong reasons to justify the action of a minority of fifty persons to do what the majority would do if they understood their condition, to save a nation from political thralldom and moral degradation.[2]

SPEECH OF GENERAL R. G. DUNLAP.

It having been extensively rumored, during the few months immediately succeeding the conclusion of the treaty, that John Ross and other evil disposed persons were seeking to incite the Cherokees to outbreak and bloodshed, the militia of the surrounding States were called into service for the protection of life and property from the supposed existing dangers. Brig. Gen. R. G. Dunlap commanded the East

---

[1] Senate confidential document, April 12, 1836, p. 200.
[2] National Intelligencer, May 22, 1838.

Tennessee volunteers. In a speech to his brigade at their disbandment in September, 1836, he used the following language:

> I forthwith visited all the posts within the first three States and gave the Cherokees (the whites needed none) all the protection in my power. * * * My course has excited the hatred of a few of the lawless rabble in Georgia, who have long played the part of unfeeling petty tyrants, and that to the disgrace of the proud character of gallant soldiers and good citizens. I had determined that I would never dishonor the Tennessee arms in a servile service by aiding to carry into execution at the point of the bayonet a treaty made by a lean minority against the will and authority of the Cherokee people. * * * I soon discovered that the Indians had not the most distant thought of war with the United States, notwithstanding the common rights of humanity and justice had been denied them.[1]

REPORT OF GENERAL JOHN E. WOOL.

Again, February 18, 1837, General John E. Wool, of the United States Army, who had been ordered to the command of the troops that were being concentrated in the Cherokee country " to look down opposition" to the enforcement of the treaty, wrote Adjutant-General Jones, at Washington, thus:

> I called them (the Cherokees) together and made a short speech. It is, however, vain to talk to a people almost universally opposed to the treaty and who maintain that they never made such a treaty. So determined are they in their opposition that not one of all those who were present and voted at the council held but a day or two since, however poor or destitute, would receive either rations or clothing from the United States lest they might compromise themselves in regard to the treaty. These same people, as well as those in the mountains of North Carolina, during the summer past, preferred living upon the roots and sap of trees rather than receive provisions from the United States, and thousands, as I have been informed, had no other food for weeks."

Four months later,[2] General Wool again, in the course of a letter to the Secretary of War concerning the death of Major Curry, who had been a prominent factor in promoting the conclusion of the treaty of 1835, said that—

> Had Curry lived he would assuredly have been killed by the Indians. It is a truth that you have not a single agent, high or low, that has the slightest moral control over the Indians. It would be wise if persons appointed to civil stations in the nation could be taken from among those who have had nothing to do with making the late treaty.

REPORT OF JOHN MASON, JR.

In further testimony concerning the situation of affairs in the Cherokee Nation at this period, may be cited the report of John Mason, jr., who was in the summer of 1837[3] sent as the confidential agent of the War Department to make observations and report. In the autumn[4] of that year he reported that—

> The chiefs and better informed part of the nation are convinced that they cannot retain the country. But the opposition to the treaty is unanimous and irreconcilable.

---

[1] National Intelligencer, May 22, 1838.
[2] June 3, 1837.
[3] July 15, 1837.
[4] September 25, 1837.

They say it cannot bind them because they did not make it; that it was made by a few unauthorized individuals; that the nation is not a party to it. * * * They retain the forms of their government in their proceedings among themselves, though they have had no election since 1830; the chiefs and headmen then in power having been authorized to act until their government shall again be regularly constituted. Under this arrangement John Ross retains the post of principal chief. * * * The influence of this chief is unbounded and unquestioned. The whole nation of eighteen thousand persons is with him, the few, about three hundred, who made the treaty having left the country. It is evident, therefore, that Ross and his party are in fact the Cherokee Nation. * * * Many who were opposed to the treaty have emigrated to secure the rations, or because of fear of an outbreak. * * * The officers say that, with all his power, Ross cannot, if he would, change the course he has heretofore pursued and to which he is held by the fixed determination of his people. He dislikes being seen in conversation with white men, and particularly with agents of the Government. Were he, as matters now stand, to advise the Indians to acknowledge the treaty, he would at once forfeit their confidence and probably his life. Yet though unwavering in his opposition to the treaty, Ross's influence has constantly been exerted to preserve the peace of the country, and Colonel Lindsay says that he (Ross) alone stands at this time between the whites and bloodshed. The opposition to the treaty on the part of the Indians is unanimous and sincere, and it is not a mere political game played by Ross for the maintenance of his ascendancy in the tribe.

HENRY CLAY'S SYMPATHY WITH THE CHEROKEES.

It is interesting in this connection, as indicating the strong and widespread public feeling manifested in the Cherokee question, to note that it became in some sense a test question among leaders of the two great political parties. The Democrats strenuously upheld the conduct of President Jackson on the subject, and the Whigs assailed him with extreme bitterness. The great Whig leader, Henry Clay, in replying[1] to a letter received by him from John Gunter, a Cherokee, took occasion to express his sympathy with the Cherokee people for the wrongs and sufferings experienced by them. He regretted them not only because of their injustice, but because they inflicted a deep wound on the character of the American Republic. He supposed that the principles which had uniformly governed our relations with the Indian nations had been too long and too firmly established to be disturbed. They had been proclaimed in the negotiation with Great Britain by the commissioners who concluded the treaty of peace, of whom he was one, and any violation of them by the United States he felt with sensibility. By those principles the Cherokee Nation had a right to establish its own form of government, to alter and amend it at pleasure, to live under its own laws, to be exempt from the United States laws or the laws of any individual State, and to claim the protection of the United States. He considered that the Chief Magistrate and his subordinates had acted in direct hostility to those principles and had thereby encouraged Georgia to usurp powers of legislation over the Cherokee Nation which she did not of right possess.

---

[1] September 30, 1836.

POLICY OF THE PRESIDENT CRITICISED—SPEECH OF COL. DAVID CROCKETT.

Among many men of note who denounced in most vigorous terms the policy of the Administration toward the Cherokees were Daniel Webster and Edward Everett, of Massachusetts; Theodore Frelinghuysen, of New Jersey; Peleg Sprague, of Maine; Henry R. Storrs, of New York; Henry A. Wise, of Virginia; and David Crockett, of Tennessee. The latter, in a speech in the House of Representatives, denounced the treatment to which the Indians had been subjected at the hands of the Government as unjust, dishonest, cruel, and short-sighted in the extreme. He alluded to the fact that he represented a district which bordered on the domain of the southern tribes, and that his constituents were perhaps as immediately interested in the removal of the Indians as those of any other member of the House. His voice would perhaps not be seconded by that of a single fellow member living within 500 miles of his home. He had been threatened that if he did not support the policy of forcible removal his public career would be summarily cut off. But while he was perhaps as desirous of pleasing his constituents and of coinciding with the wishes of his colleagues as any man in Congress, he could not permit himself to do so at the expense of his honor and conscience in the support of such a measure. He believed the American people could be relied on to approve their Representatives for daring, in the face of all opposition, to perform their conscientious duty, but if not, the approval of his own conscience was dearer to him than all else.

Governor Lumpkin, immediately upon his appointment as commissioner, had repaired to the Cherokee country, but Governor Carroll, owing to some pending negotiations with the Choctaws and subsequently to ill health, was unable to assume the duties assigned him. He was succeeded[1] by John Kennedy. To this commission a third member was added in the summer of 1837[2] in the person of Colonel Guild, who was found to be ineligible, however, by reason of being a member of the Tennessee legislature. His place was supplied by the appointment[3] of James W. Gwin, of North Carolina.

On the 22d of December James Liddell was also appointed, vice Governor Lumpkin resigned.[4]

---

[1] October 25, 1836.

[2] Secretary of War to Andrew Jackson, August 21, 1837.

[3] October 16, 1837.

[4] The amounts adjudicated and paid by this commission, as shown by the records of the Indian Office (see Commissioner of Indian Affairs' letter of March 7, 1844), were as follows:

1. For improvements	$1,683,192 77½
2. Spoliations	416,306 82½
3. National debts due to Cherokees	19,058 14
4. National debts due to citizens of the United States	51,642 87
5. Reservations	159,324 87
Total	2,329,524 86

(The figures as given here are correctly copied from the commissioner's letter, but there is an obvious error either in the footing or in the items.)

Superintendent Currey having died, General Nathan Smith was appointed[1] to succeed him as superintendent of emigration.

Census of Cherokee Nation.—It appears from a statement about this time,[2] made by the Commissioner of Indian Affairs, that from a census of the Cherokees, taken in the year 1835, the number residing in the States of Georgia, North Carolina, Alabama, and Tennessee was 16,542, exclusive of slaves and of whites intermarried with Cherokees.[3]

In May, 1837,[4] General Wool was relieved from command at his own request, and his successor, Col. William Lindsay, was instructed to arrest John Ross and turn him over to the civil authorities in case he did anything further calculated to excite a spirit of hostility among the Cherokees on the subject of removal. This threat, however, seemed to have little effect, for we find Mr. Ross presiding over a general council, convened at his instigation, on the 31st of July, to attend which the Government hastily dispatched Mr. John Mason, jr., with instructions to traverse and correct any misstatements of the position of the United States authorities that might be set forth by Ross and his followers. An extract from Mr. Mason's report has already been given.

Cherokee memorial in Congress.—Again, in the spring of 1838 Ross laid before Congress a protest and memorial for the redress of grievances, which, in the Senate, was laid upon the table[5] by a vote of 36 to 10, and a memorial from citizens of New York involving an inquiry into the validity of the treaty of 1835 shared a similar fate in the House of Representatives two days later by a vote of 102 to 75.

Speech of Henry A. Wise.—The discussion of these memorials in Congress took a wide range and excited the warmest interest, not only in that body, but throughout the country. The speeches were characterized by a depth and bitterness of feeling such as had never been exceeded even on the slavery question. Hon. Henry A. Wise, of Virginia, who was then a member of the House of Representatives from that State, was especially earnest in his denunciation of the treaty of 1835 and of the administration that had concluded it. He looked

---

[1] January 3, 1837.

[2] December 1, 1836.

[3] This census showed a distribution of the Cherokee population, according to State boundaries, as follows:

States.	Cherokees.	Slaves.	Whites intermarried with Cherokees.
In Georgia	8,946	776	68
In North Carolina	3,644	37	22
In Tennessee	2,528	480	79
In Alabama	1,424	299	32
Total	16,542	1,592	201

[4] Secretary of War to Col. William Lindsay, May 8, 1837.

[5] March 26, 1838.

upon it as null and void. In order to make treaties binding the assent of both parties must be obtained, and he would assert without fear of contradiction that there was not one man in that House or out of it who had read the proceedings in the case who would say that there had ever been any assent given to that treaty by the Cherokee Nation. If this were the proper time he could go further and show that Georgia had done her part, too, in this oppression. He could show this by proving the policy of that State in relation to the Indians and the institutions of the General Government. That was the only State in the Union that had ever actually nullified, and she now tells you that if the United States should undertake to naturalize any portion of the Indian tribes within her limits as citizens of the United States she would do so again. He had not disparaged the surrounding people of Georgia, far from it—"but" (said he) "there are proofs around us in this city of the high advancement in civilization which characterizes the Cherokees." He would tell the gentleman from Georgia (Mr. Halsey) that a statesman of his own State, who occupied a high and honorable post in this Government, would not gain greatly by a comparison, either in civilization or morals, with a Cherokee chief whom he could name. He would fearlessly institute such a comparison between John Ross and John Forsyth.[1]

Speech of Daniel Webster.—Mr. Webster, of Massachusetts, also took occasion[2] to remark in the Senate that "there is a strong and growing feeling in the country that great wrong has been done to the Cherokees by the treaty of New Echota."

President Van Buren proffers a compromise.—Public feeling became so deeply stirred on the subject that, in the interests of a compromise, President Van Buren, in May, 1838, formulated a proposition to allow the Cherokees two years further time in which to remove, subject to the approval of Congress and the executives of the States interested.

Georgia hostile to the compromise.—To the communication addressed to Governor Gilmer, of Georgia, on the subject, he responded:

* * * I can give it no sanction whatever. The proposal could not be carried into effect but in violation of the rights of this State. * * * It is necessary that I should know whether the President intends by the instructions to General Scott to require that the Indians shall be maintained in their occupancy by an armed force in opposition to the rights of the owners of the soil. If such be the intention, a direct collision between the authorities of the State and the General Government must ensue. My duty will require that I shall prevent any interference whatever by the troops with the rights of the State and its citizens. I shall not fail to perform it.

This called forth a hurried explanation from the Secretary of War that the instructions to General Scott were not intended to bear the construction placed upon them by the executive of Georgia, but, on the contrary, it was the desire and the determination of the President to

---

[1] Speech in reply to Mr. Halsey, of Georgia, January 2, 1838.
[2] May 22, 1838.

secure the removal of the Cherokees at the earliest day practicable, and he made no doubt it could be effected the present season.[1]

GENERAL SCOTT ORDERED TO COMMAND TROOPS IN THE CHEROKEE COUNTRY.

The executive machinery under the treaty had in the mean time been placed in operation, and at the beginning of the year 1838, 2,103 Cherokees had been removed, of whom 1,282 had been permitted to remove themselves.[2]

Intelligence having reached the President, however, causing apprehension that the mass of the nation did not intend to remove as required by the treaty General Winfield Scott was ordered[3] to assume command of the troops already in the nation, and to collect an increased force, comprising a regiment of artillery, a regiment of infantry, and six companies of dragoons. He was further authorized, if deemed necessary, to call upon the governors of Tennessee, North Carolina, Georgia, and Alabama for militia and volunteers, not exceeding four thousand in number, and to put the Indians in motion for the West at the earliest moment possible, following the expiration of the two years specified in the treaty.

Proclamation of General Scott.—On reaching the scene of operations General Scott issued[4] a proclamation to the Cherokees in which he announced that —

The President of the United States has sent me with a powerful army to cause you, in obedience to the treaty of 1835, to join that part of your people who are already established in prosperity on the other side of the Mississippi. Unhappily the two years * * * allowed for that purpose you have suffered to pass away * * * without making any preparation to follow, and now * * * the emigration must be commenced in haste. * * * The full moon of May is already on the wane, and before another shall have passed away every Cherokee, man, woman, and child * * * must be in motion to join their brethren in the far West. * * * This is no sudden determination on the part of the President. * * * I have come to carry out that determination. My troops already occupy many positions, * * * and thousands and thousands are approaching from every quarter to render resistance and escape alike hopeless. * * * Will you then by resistance compel us to resort to arms? * * * Or will you by flight seek to hide yourselves in mountains and forests and thus oblige us to hunt you down? Remember that in pursuit it may be impossible to avoid conflicts. The blood of the white man or the blood of the red man may be spilt, and if spilt, however accidentally, it may be impossible for the discreet and humane among you, or among us, to prevent a general war and carnage.

JOHN ROSS PROPOSES A NEW TREATY.

John Ross, finding no sign of wavering in the determination of the President to promptly execute the treaty, then submitted[5] a project for the negotiation of a new treaty as a substitute for that of 1835, and differing

---

[1] National Intelligencer, June 8, 1838.
[2] Secretary of War to James K. Polk, Speaker of the House of Representatives, January 8, 1838.
[3] General Macomb to General Scott, April 6, 1838.
[4] May 10, 1838.
[5] May, 18, 1838.

but little from it in its proposed provisions, except in the idea of securing a somewhat larger consideration, as well as some minor advantages. He was assured in reply that while the United States were willing to extend every liberality of construction to the terms of the treaty of 1835 and to secure the Cherokee title to the western country by patent, they could not entertain the idea of a new treaty.

As soon as it became absolutely apparent, not only that the Cherokees must go but that no unnecessary delay would be tolerated beyond the limit fixed by the treaty, a more submissive spirit began to be manifested among them. During the summer of 1838 several parties of emigrants were dispatched under the direction of officers of the Army. The number thus removed aggregated about 6,000.[1]

CHEROKEES PERMITTED TO REMOVE THEMSELVES.

Later in the season John Ross and others, by virtue of a resolution of the national council, submitted a proposition to General Scott that the remainder of the business of emigration should be confided to the nation, and should take place in the following September and October, after the close of the sickly season, the estimated cost of such removal to be fixed at $65.88 per head. To this proposal assent was given,[2] and the last party of Cherokee emigrants began their march for the West on the 4th of December, 1838.[3] Scattered through the mountains of North Carolina and Tennessee, however, were many who had fled to avoid removal, and who, nearly a year later, were represented to number 1,046,[4] and Mr. James Murray was, in the spring of 1840, appointed[5] a commissioner to ascertain and enroll for removal those entitled to the benefits of the treaty of 1835.

DISSENSIONS AMONG CHEROKEES IN THEIR NEW HOME.

The removal of the Cherokees having at last been accomplished, the next important object of the Government was to insure their internal tranquillity, with a view to the increase and encouragement of those habits of industry, thrift, and respect for lawfully constituted authority which had made so much progress among them in their eastern home.

---

[1] Annual report of Commissioner of Indian Affairs, November 25, 1838.

[2] Proposal was accepted July 25; emigration to begin September 1 and end before October 20, 1838.

[3] The number, according to the rolls of John Ross, who removed under his direction, was 13,149. According to the rolls of Captain Stevenson, the agent who received them on their arrival West, there were only 11,504, and, according to Captain Page, the disbursing officer, there were 11,721. Mr. Ross received on his settlement with Captain Page subsequent to the removal, $486,939.50¼, which made a total payment to Ross by the Government on account of Cherokee removals of $1,263,338.38. (Letter of Commissioner Indian Affairs, June 15, 1842). See, also, Commissioner of Indian Affairs to Commissioner of Land Office, January 9, 1839.

[4] Commissioner of Indian Affairs to Secretary of War, September 12, 1839.

[5] April 21, 1840.

But this was an undertaking of much difficulty. The instrumentalities used by the Government in securing the conclusion and approval of not only the treaty of 1835 but also those of 1817 and 1819 had caused much division and bitterness in their ranks, which had on many occasions in the past cropped out in acts of injustice and even violence.

Upon the coming together of the body of the nation in their new country west of the Mississippi, they found themselves torn and distracted by party dissensions and bitterness almost beyond hope of reconciliation. The parties were respectively denominated:

1. The "Old Settler" party, composed of those Cherokees who had prior to the treaty of 1835 voluntarily removed west of the Mississippi, and who were living under a regularly established form of government of their own.

2. The "Treaty" or "Ridge" party, being that portion of the nation led by John Ridge, and who encouraged and approved the negotiation of the treaty of 1835.

3. The "Government" or "Ross" party, comprising numerically a large majority of the nation, who followed in the lead of John Ross, for many years the principal chief of the nation, and who had been consistently and bitterly hostile to the treaty of 1835 and to any surrender of their territorial rights east of the Mississippi.

Upon the arrival of the emigrants in their new homes, the Ross party insisted upon the adoption of a new system of government and a code of laws for the whole nation. To this the Old Settler party objected, and were supported by the Ridge party, claiming that the government and laws already adopted and in force among the Old Settlers should continue to be binding until the general election should take place in the following October, when the newly elected legislature could enact such changes as wisdom and good policy should dictate.[1] A general council of the whole nation was, however, called to meet at the new council-house at Takuttokah, having in view a unification of interests and the pacification of all animosities. The council lasted from the 10th to the 22d of June, but resulted in no agreement. Some six thousand Cherokees were present. A second council was called by John Ross for a similar purpose, to meet at the Illinois camp-ground on the 1st of July, 1839.[2]

Murder of Boudinot and the Ridges.—Immediately following the adjournment of the Takuttokah council three of the leaders of the Treaty party, John Ridge, Major Ridge his father, and Elias Boudinot were murdered[3] in the most brutal and atrocious manner. The excitement throughout the nation became intense. Boudinot was murdered within 300 yards of his house, and only 2 miles distant from the residence of John Ross. The friends of the murdered men were persuaded that the

---

[1] Report of Commissioner of Indian Affairs for 1839.
[2] Letter of John Ross to General Arbuckle, June 24, 1839.
[3] June 22, 1839.

crimes had been committed at the instigation of Ross, as it was well known that the murderers were among his followers. Ross's friends, however, at once rallied to his protection and a volunteer guard of six hundred patrolled the country in the vicinity of his residence.[1]

A number of the chiefs and prominent men of the Old Settler and Ridge parties fled to Fort Gibson for safety. From there on the 28th of June, John Brown, John Looney, John Rogers, and John Smith, signing themselves as the executive council of the Western Cherokees, addressed a proposition to John Ross to send a delegation of the chiefs and principal men of his party with authority to meet an equal number of their own at Fort Gibson, with a view to reach an amicable agreement between the different factions. Ross responded[2] by inviting them to meet at the council convened upon his call on the 1st of July, which was declined. A memorial was thereupon[3] addressed to the authorities of the United States by Brown, Looney, and Rogers as chiefs of the Western Cherokees, demanding protection in the territory and government guaranteed to them by treaty. Against this appeal the Ross convention or council in session at Illinois camp-ground filed a protest.[4] Between the dates of the appeal and the protest a part of the Old Settlers, acting in concert with Ross and his adherents, passed resolutions[5] declaratory of their disapproval of the conduct of Brown and Rogers, and proclaimed their deposition from office as chiefs. Looney escaped deposition by transferring his fealty to the Ross party.

Unification of Eastern and Western Cherokees.—It is proper to remark in this connection that on the 12th of July the Ross council adopted resolutions uniting the Eastern and the Western Cherokees "into one body politic under the style and title of the Cherokee Nation." This paper, without mentioning or referring to the treaty of 1835, speaks of the late emigration as constrained by the force of circumstances. The council also passed[6] a decree, wherein after reciting the murders of the Ridges and Boudinot, and that they in conjunction with others had by their conduct rendered themselves liable to the penalties of outlawry, extended to the survivors a full amnesty for past offenses upon sundry very stringent and humiliating conditions. They also passed[7] a decree condoning the crime of the murderers, securing them from any prosecution or punishment by reason thereof, and declaring them fully restored to the confidence and favor of the community.

Treaty of 1835 declared void.—At a council held at Aquohee Camp a decree was passed on the 1st of August, declaring the treaty of 1835

---

[1] Agent Stokes to Secretary of War, June 24, 1839.
[2] July 5, 1839.
[3] August 9, 1839.
[4] August 27, 1839.
[5] August 23, 1839.
[6] July 7, 1839.
[7] July 10, 1839.

void, and reasserting the Cherokee title to their old country east of the Mississippi. Later in the same month a decree was passed,[1] citing the appearance before them, under penalty of outlawry, of the signers of the treaty of 1835, to answer for their conduct. This act called forth[2] a vigorous protest from General Arbuckle, commanding Fort Gibson, and was supplemented by instructions[3] to him from the Secretary of War to cause the arrest and trial of Ross as accessory to the murder of the Ridges in case he should deem it wise to do so.

Constitution adopted by the Cherokee Nation.—A convention summoned by Ross and composed of his followers, together with such members of the Treaty and Old Settler parties as could be induced to participate, convened and remained in session at Tahlequah from the 6th to the 10th of September, 1839. This body adopted a constitution for the Cherokee Nation, which was subsequently accepted and adopted by the Old Settlers or Western Cherokees in council at Fort Gibson on the 26th of the following June, and an act of union was entered into between the two parties on that date.

Division of Cherokee territory proposed.—A proposition had been previously[4] submitted by the representatives of the Treaty and Old Settler parties, urging as the only method of securing peace the division of the Cherokee domain and annuities. They recommended that General Arbuckle and Captain Armstrong be designated to assign to them and to the Ross party each their proportionate share according to their numbers, but the adoption of this act of union avoided any necessity for the further consideration of the proposal. As a means also of relieving the Cherokees from further internal strife, General Arbuckle had,[5] pursuant to the direction of the Secretary of War, notified them that, in consequence of his public acts, John Ross would not be allowed to hold office in the nation, and that a similar penalty was denounced against William S. Coody for offensive opinions expressed in the presence of the Secretary of War.[6] Little practical effect was however produced upon the standing or influence of these men with their people.

Skeptical of the sincerity of the promises of peace and good feeling held out by the act of unification, John Brown, a noted leader and chief of the Old Settler Cherokees, in conjunction with many of his followers, among whom were a number of wandering Delawares, asked and obtained permission from the Mexican Government to settle within the jurisdiction of that power, and they were only persuaded to remain by

---

[1] August 21, 1839.

[2] September 4, 1839, *et seq.*

[3] November 9, 1839.

[4] January 22, 1840.

[5] April 21, 1840.

[6] Coody, in an interview with the Secretary of War, persisted in considering the murders of Boudinot and the Ridges as justifiable. General Arbuckle's letter of notification bore date April 21, 1840.

the earnest assurances of the Secretary of War that the United States could and would fully protect their interests.[1]

CHEROKEES CHARGE THE UNITED STATES WITH BAD FAITH.

No sooner had the removal of the Cherokees been effectually accomplished than the latter began to manifest much dissatisfaction at what they characterized a lack of good faith on the part of the Government in carrying out the stipulations of the treaty of 1835. The default charged had reference to the matter of payment of their claims for spoliations, improvements, annuities, etc. Each winter at least one delegation from the nation maintained a residence in Washington and urged upon the Executive and Congress with untiring persistency an adjudication of all disputed matters arising under the treaty.

At length the term of President Van Buren expired and was succeeded by a Whig administration. Then as now, the official acts of an outgoing political party were considered to be the legitimate subject of criticism and investigation by its political enemies. President Harrison lived but a month after assuming the duties of his office, but Vice-President Tyler as his successor considered that the treatment to which the Cherokees had been subjected during Jackson's and Van Buren's administrations would afford a field for investigation fraught with a rich harvest of results in political capital for the Whig party.

President Tyler promises a new treaty.—Accordingly, therefore, in the fall of 1841, just previous to the departure of the Cherokee delegation from Washington to their homes, the President agreed to take proper measures for the settlement of all their difficulties, expressing a determination to open the whole subject of their complaints and to bring their affairs to a satisfactory conclusion through the medium of a new treaty. In conformity with this determination the Commissioner of Indian Affairs[2] instructed the agent for the Cherokees to procure all the information possible to be obtained upon every subject connected with Cherokee affairs having a tendency to throw any light upon the wrongs and injustice they might have sustained to the end that full amends could so far as possible be made therefor. Before much information was collected under the terms of these instructions a change seems to have taken place in the views of the President, and the order for investigation was revoked. The draft of the new treaty was, however, in the mean time prepared under direction of the Secretary of War. It contained provisions regulating the licensing of traders in the Cherokee country, the jurisdiction over crimes committed by citizens of the United States resident in that country, the allotment of their lands in severalty by the Cherokee authorities, and the establishment of post-offices and post-routes within their limits. It further contemplated the appointment of two commissioners, whenever Congress should make provision

---

[1] Commissioner of Indian Affairs to Maj. William Armstrong, August 26, 1840.
[2] September 22, 1841.

therefor, whose duty it should be to examine into and make a report to that body upon the character, validity, and equity of all claims of whatsoever kind presented by Cherokees against the United States, and also to afford the Cherokees pecuniary aid in the purchase of a printing press and type as well as in the erection of a national council-house. This treaty, however, was never consummated.

President Jackson's method for compelling Cherokee removal.—In connection with this subject of an investigation into the affairs of the Cherokees, a confidential letter is to be found on file in the office of the Commissioner of Indian Affairs, from Hon. P. M. Butler, of South Carolina, who had a few months previous to its date[1] been appointed United States agent for the Cherokees, interesting as throwing light on the negotiation and conclusion of the treaty of 1835. Mr. Butler says it is alleged, and claimed to be susceptible of proof, that Mr. Merriweather, of Georgia, in an interview with President Jackson, a considerable time before the treaty was negotiated, said to the President, "We want the Cherokee lands in Georgia, but the Cherokees will not consent to cede them," to which the President emphatically replied, "You must get clear of them [the Cherokees] by legislation. Take judicial jurisdiction over their country; build fires around them, and do indirectly what you cannot effect directly."

PER CAPITA PAYMENTS UNDER THE TREATY.

In the same letter Mr. Butler, in alluding to the existing difficulties in the Cherokee Nation, observes that prior to the preceding October the Ross party had been largely in the ascendency in the nation, but that at their last preceding election the question hinged upon whether the "per capita" money due them under the treaty of 1835 should be immediately paid over to the people. The result was in favor of the Ridge party, who assumed the affirmative of the question, the opposition of Ross and his party being predicated on the theory that an acceptance of this money would be an acknowledgment of the validity of the treaty of 1835. This, it was feared, would have an unfavorable effect on their efforts to secure the conclusion of a new treaty on more satisfactory terms. On the settlement of this per capita tax, Mr. Butler remarks, will depend the peace and safety of the Cherokee Nation, adding that should the rumors afloat prove true, to the effect that the per capita money was nearly exhausted, neither the national funds in the hands of the treasurer nor the life of Mr. Ross would be safe for an hour from the infuriated members of the tribe.

POLITICAL MURDERS IN CHEROKEE NATION.

In the spring of 1842 an event occurred which again threw the whole nation into a state of the wildest excitement. The friends of the mur-

---
[1] March 4, 1842.

dered Ridges and Boudinot had never forgiven the act, nor had time served to soften the measure of their resentment against the perpetrators and their supposed abettors. Stand Watie had long been a leader among the Ridge party and had been marked for assassination at the time of the murders just alluded to. He was a brother of John Ridge, one of the murdered men, and he now, in virtue of his mission as an avenger, killed James Foreman, a member of the Ross party and one of the culprits in the murder of the Ridges. Although Stand Watie excused his conduct on the score of having come to a knowledge of certain threats against his life made by Foreman, no event could at that time have been more demoralizing and destructive of the earnestly desired era of peace and good feeling among the Cherokee people. From that time forward all hope of a sincere unification of the several tribal factions was at an end.

ADJUDICATION COMMISSIONERS APPOINTED.

In the autumn of 1842[1] the President appointed John H. Eaton and James Iredell as commissioners to adjudicate and settle claims under the treaty of 1835. Mr. Iredell declined, and Edward B. Hubley was appointed[2] to fill his place. This tribunal was created to continue the uncompleted work of the board appointed in 1836 under the provisions of the same article, the labors of which had terminated in March, 1839, having been in session more than two years.

TREATY CONCLUDED AUGUST 6, 1846; PROCLAIMED AUGUST 17, 1846.[3]

Held at Washington, D. C., between Edmund Burke, William Armstrong, and Albion K. Parris, commissioners on behalf of the United States, and delegates representing each of the three factions of the Cherokee Nation, known, respectively, as the " Government party," the " Treaty party," and the " Old Settler party."

MATERIAL PROVISIONS.

The preamble recites the difficulties that have long existed between the different factions of the nation, and because of the desire to heal those differences and to adjust certain claims against the United States growing out of the treaty of 1835 this treaty is concluded, and provides:

1. The lands now occupied by the Cherokee Nation shall be secured to the whole Cherokee people for their common use and benefit. The United States will issue a patent therefor to include the 800,000-acre tract and the western outlet. If the Cherokees become extinct or abandon the land it shall revert to the United States.

---

[1] September 9, 1842.
[2] November 8, 1842.
[3] United States Statute at Large, Vol. IX, p. 871.

2. All difficulties and differences heretofore existing between the several parties of the Cherokee Nation are declared to be settled and adjusted. A general amnesty for all offenses is declared and fugitives may return without fear of prosecution. Laws shall be passed for the equal protection of all. All armed police or military organizations shall be disbanded and the laws executed by civil process. Trial by jury is guaranteed.

3. The United States agree to reimburse to the Cherokee Nation all sums unjustly deducted for claims, reservations, expenses, etc., from the consideration of $5,000,000 agreed to be paid under the treaty of 1835 to the Cherokees for their lands, and to distribute the same as provided in the ninth article of that treaty.

4. The board of commissioners recently appointed by the President have declared that under the provisions of the treaty of 1828 the "Old Settlers," or Western Cherokees, had no exclusive title to the lands ceded by that treaty as against the Eastern Cherokees, and that by the equitable operation of that treaty the former acquired a common interest in the Cherokee lands east of the Mississippi. This interest of the "Old Settlers" was unprovided for by the treaty of 1835. It is therefore agreed that a sum equal to one-third of the residuum of per capita fund left after a proper adjustment of the account for distribution under the treaty of 1835 shall be paid to said "Old Settlers," and that in so doing, in estimating the cost of removal and subsistence, it shall be based upon the rate fixed therefor in the eighth article of the treaty of 1835. In consideration of the foregoing the "Old Settlers" release to the United States all interest in the Cherokee lands east of the Mississippi and all claim to exclusive ownership in the Cherokee lands west of the Mississippi.

5. The per capita allowance to the "Western Cherokees," or "Old Settlers," upon the principle above stated, shall be held in trust by the United States and paid out to each individual or head of family or his representative entitled thereto in person. The President of the United States shall appoint five persons as a committee from the "Old Settlers" to determine who are entitled to the per capita allowance.

6. The United States agree to pay the "Treaty party" the sum of $115,000 for losses and expenses incurred in connection with the treaty of 1835, of which $5,000 shall be paid to the legal representatives or heirs of Major Ridge, $5,000 to those of John Ridge, and $5,000 to those of Elias Boudinot. The remainder shall be distributed among those who shall be certified by a committee of the "Treaty party" as entitled, provided that the present delegation of the party may deduct $25,000, to be by them applied to the payment of claims and expenses. And if the said sum of $100,000 should be insufficient to pay all claims for losses and damages, then the claimants to be paid pro rata in full satisfaction of said claims.

7. All individuals of the "Western Cherokees" who have been dis-

possessed of salines, the same being their private property, shall be compensated therefor by the Cherokee Nation, upon an award to be made by the United States agent and a Cherokee commissioner, or the salines shall be returned to the respective owners.

8. The United States agree to pay the Cherokee Nation $2,000 for a printing press, etc., destroyed; $5,000 to be equally divided among all whose arms were taken from them previous to their removal West by order of an officer of the United States, and $20,000 in lieu of all claims of the Cherokee Nation, as a nation, prior to the treaty of 1835, except lands reserved for school funds.

9. The United States agree to make a fair and just settlement of all moneys due to the Cherokees and subject to the per capita division under the treaty of December 29, 1835. This settlement to embrace all sums properly expended or charged to the Cherokees under the provisions of said treaty, and which sums shall be deducted from the sum of $6,647,067. The balance found due to be distributed per capita among those entitled to receive the same under the treaty of 1835 and supplement of 1836, being those residing east of the Mississippi River at that date.

10. Nothing herein shall abridge or take away any rights or claims which the Cherokees *now* residing in States east of the Mississippi River had or may have under the treaty of 1835 and supplement of 1836.

11. It is agreed that the Senate of the United States shall determine whether the amount expended for one year's subsistence of the Cherokees, after their removal under the treaty of 1835 and supplement of 1836, is properly chargeable to the United States or to the Cherokee funds, and, if to the latter, whether such subsistence shall be charged at a sum greater than $33⅓ per head; also, whether the Cherokees shall be allowed interest upon the sums found to be due them; and, if so, from what date and at what rate.

12. (The twelfth article was struck out by the Senate.)

13. This treaty to be obligatory after ratification by the Senate and President of the United States.

HISTORICAL DATA.

CHEROKEES DESIRE A NEW TREATY.

In the spring of 1844 a delegation headed by John Ross arrived in Washington. In a communication[1] to the Secretary of War they inclosed a copy of a letter addressed to them by President Tyler on the 20th of September, 1841, previously alluded to, promising them a new treaty to settle all disputes arising under the treaty of 1835. They advised the Secretary of their readiness to enter upon the negotiation of the promised treaty, and submitted[2] a statement of the salient points of

---

[1] May 6, 1844.
[2] May 30, 1844.

difference to be adjudicated, involving (1) a fair and just indemnity to be paid to the Cherokee Nation for the country east of the Mississippi from which they were forced to remove; (2) indemnity for all improvements, ferries, turnpike roads, bridges, etc., belonging to the Cherokees; (3) indemnity for spoliations committed upon all other Cherokee property by troops and citizens of the United States prior and subsequent to the treaty of 1835; (4) that a title in absolute fee-simple to the country west of the Mississippi be conveyed to the Cherokee Nation by the United States; (5) that the political relations between the Cherokee Nation and the United States be specifically defined; (6) that stocks now invested by the President for the Cherokee Nation be guaranteed to yield a specified annual income, and (7) that provision be made for those Cherokees residing east of the Mississippi who should evince a desire to emigrate to the Cherokee country west of that river.

FEUDS BETWEEN THE ROSS, TREATY, AND OLD SETTLER PARTIES.

At this period delegations representing the anti-Ross parties were also in Washington, and their animosities, coupled with the frequent and unsavory reports of the events happening in the Cherokee country, determined the President to conclude no new treaty until the true cause was ascertained and the responsibility fixed for all this turbulence and crime.[1] The Old Settler and the Treaty parties alleged that grievous oppressions were practiced upon them by the Ross party, insomuch that they were unable to enjoy their liberty, property, or lives in safety, or to live in peace in the same community. The Old Settler delegation alleged that the act of union, by virtue of which their government was superseded and they were subjected to the constitution and laws of the Ross party, was never authorized or sanctioned by the legal representatives of their people. *Per contra*, the Ross delegation alleged that the Old Settler and the Treaty parties enjoyed the same degree of security and the same fullness of rights that any other portion of the nation enjoyed, and that the alleged dissatisfaction was confined to a few restless and ambitious spirits whose motto was "rule or ruin."

Commissioners appointed to inquire into Cherokee feuds.—In consequence of his determination, as above stated, the President appointed General R. Jones, Col. R. B. Mason, and P. M. Butler commissioners, with instructions[2] to proceed to the Cherokee country and ascertain if any considerable portion of the Cherokee people were arrayed in hostile feeling toward those who ruled the nation; whether a corresponding disposition and feeling prevailed among the majority who administered the government toward the minority; the lengths of oppression, resistance, and violence to which the excitement of each against the other had

---

[1] Letter of Secretary of War to Commissioners Jones and Butler, October 18, 1844.
[2] October 18, 1844.

severally led the opposing parties, and whether the discontent was of such extent and intensity among the great mass of the Old Settler and Treaty parties as to forbid their living peaceably together under the same government with the Ross party. This commission convened at Fort Gibson on the 16th of November,[1] but their labors resulted in nothing of practical benefit to the sorely distressed Cherokees.

DEATH OF SEQUOYAH OR GEORGE GUESS.

Sequoyah or George Guess, the inventor of the Cherokee alphabet, removed to the country west of the Mississippi long anterior to the treaty of 1835,[2] and was for several years one of the national council of the Western Cherokees.

In the year 1843 he left his home for Mexico in quest of several scattered bands of Cherokees who had wandered off to that distant region, and whom it was his intention to collect together with a view to inducing them to return and become again united with their friends and kindred.

He did not meet with the success anticipated. Being quite aged, and becoming worn out and destitute, he was unable without assistance to make the return trip to his home. Agent Butler, learning of his condition, reported the fact to the Indian Department[3] and asked that sufficient funds be placed at his disposal for the purpose of sending messengers to bring the old man back. Two hundred dollars were authorized[4] to be expended for the purpose, and Oo-no-leh, a Cherokee, was sent on the errand of mercy, but upon reaching Red River he encountered a party of Cherokees from Mexico who advised him that Guess had died in the preceding July, and that his remains were interred at San Fernando.[5]

OLD SETTLER AND TREATY PARTIES PROPOSE TO REMOVE TO MEXICO.

In the fall of 1845 the bulk of the Old Settler and Treaty parties, having become satisfied that it would be impossible for them to maintain a peaceful and happy residence in the country of their adoption while the influence of John Ross continued potent in their national

---

[1] Letter of General Jones to Commissioner of Indian Affairs, November 17, 1844.

[2] He was one of the chiefs of the Arkansas delegation who signed the treaty of May 6, 1828. (See United States Statutes at Large, Vol. VII, p. 314.)

[3] Letters of September 12 and November 23, 1844, from Agent Butler to Commissioner of Indian Affairs.

[4] Letter of Commissioner Indian Affairs to Agent Butler, January 17, 1845.

[5] Letter of Oo-no-leh to Agent Butler, May 15, 1845. Guess left a widow, a son, and two daughters. Hon. T. L. McKenny, in a letter to the Secretary of War, December 13, 1825, says: "His name is Guess, and he is a native and unlettered Cherokee. Like Cadmus, he has given to the people the alphabet of their language. It is composed of eighty-six characters, by which in a few days the older Indians who had despaired of deriving an education by means of the schools * * * may read and correspond." Agent Butler, in his annual report for 1845, says: "The Cherokees who cannot speak English acquire their own alphabet in twenty-four hours."

government, resolved to seek for themselves a new home on the borders of Mexico. A council was therefore held at which a delegation (consisting of forty-three members of the Treaty and eleven of the Old Settler party) was chosen to explore the country to the south and west for a future abode. They rendezvoused[1] at the forks of the Canadian and Arkansas Rivers, and, after electing a captain, proceeded via Fort Washita, crossing the Red River at Coffee's trading house, and following the ridge dividing the waters of Trinity and Brazos to the latter river, which they crossed at Basky Creek. Here they found a small settlement of sixty-three Cherokees, who had moved in the preceding June from a place called by them Mount Clover, in Mexico.

Among their number was found Tessee Guess, the son of George Guess. Leaving Brazos[2] the explorers traveled westward to the Colorado, reaching it at the mouth of Stone Fort Creek,[3] beyond which they proceeded in a southwesterly direction to the San Sabba Creek, at a point about 40 or 50 miles above its mouth. They returned on a line some 60 miles south of their outgoing trip,[4] and with their friends held a council at Dragoon Barracks in the Cherokee Nation.[5] At this meeting it was decided to ask the United States to provide them a home in the Texas country upon their relinquishment of all interest in the Cherokee Nation, or in case of a refusal of this request that the territory of the nation be divided into two parts, and a moiety thereof be assigned to them with the privilege of adopting their own form of government and living under it.

The governor of Arkansas[6] and General Arbuckle[7] both concurred in the conclusions reached by this council, and urged upon the authorities at Washington the necessary legislation to carry the same into effect.

MORE POLITICAL MURDERS.

Shortly after the delegation selected by the foregoing council had proceeded to Washington in the interest of the adoption of the scheme proposed, another epidemic of murder and outrage broke out in the nation. On the 23d of March, Agent McKissick reported to the Indian Department the murder of Stand, a prominent member of the Ross party, by Wheeler Faught, at the instigation of the "Starr boys," who were somewhat noted leaders of the Treaty party. This murder was committed in revenge for the killing of James Starr and others during the outbreak of the preceding November. It was followed[8] by the

---

[1] September 1, 1845.
[2] October 22, 1845.
[3] November 12, 1845. They explored up the valley of Stone Fort Creek a distance of 30 miles.
[4] Report of the exploring party to their council.
[5] January 19, 1846.
[6] Letter to the President, February 10, 1846.
[7] Letter to the Secretary of War, February 12, 1846.
[8] April 2, 1846.

murder of Cornsilk, another of Ross's adherents, by these same "Starr boys," and six days later the spirit of retaliation led to the killing of Turner, a member of the Treaty party. On the 25th of the same month [1] Ellis, Dick, and Billy Starr were wounded by a band of Ross's Cherokee police, who chased them across the line of Arkansas in the attempt to arrest them for trial before the Cherokee tribunals for the murder of Too-noo-wee two days before. General Arbuckle took them under his protection, and refused to deliver them up for trial to the Cherokee authorities until the latter should take proper steps to punish the murderers of James Starr. Subsequently Baldridge and Sides, of the Ross party, were murdered by Jim and Tom Starr, in revenge for which the light horse police company of the Ross government murdered Billy Ryder, of the Treaty party.[2]

In this manner the excitement was maintained and the outrages multiplied until, on the 28th of August, Agent McKissick reported that since the 1st of November preceding there had been an aggregate of thirty-three murders committed in the Cherokee Nation, nearly all of which were of a political character. The feeling of alarm became so widespread that General Arbuckle was constrained to increase the military force on the frontier by two companies.

NEGOTIATION OF TREATY OF 1846.

While these unhappy events were in progress Major Armstrong, superintendent of Indian affairs, who was in Washington, submitted to the Commissioner of Indian Affairs, at the suggestion of the several Cherokee delegations, a proposition for the appointment of a commissioner clothed with full powers to adjust all difficulties between the various factions of their people.

The Commissioner replied that as the matter was before Congress and would likely receive the speedy attention of that body, no action would be justified by the executive authorities without first being assured that the proposition was founded in good faith and would result in some certain and satisfactory arrangement. He must also have assurance that there existed a firm determination on the part of the Department and of Congress to bring these troubles to a close before the adjournment of the latter body. The Commissioner, however, drew up a memorandum agreement for the signature of the several delegations of Cherokees representing the different factions of the tribe. It provided for the appointment of three commissioners, whose duty it should be to examine into all matters in controversy and adjust the same, and that all parties should abide absolutely by their decision, agreeing to execute and sign such treaty or other instrument of agreement as should be considered necessary to insure the execution of the award of the com-

---

[1] Letter of Agent McKissick to Commissioner Indian Affairs, May 12, 1846, and General Arbuckle to Adjutant-General, April 28, 1846.

[2] Report of Agent McKissick July 4, 1846.

missioners.¹ This agreement was duly signed by the members of the several delegations present in Washington, and in pursuance of its provisions President Polk appointed ² Edmund Burke, William Armstrong, and Albion K. Parris commissioners with the powers and for the purposes above indicated. These commissioners at once entered into communication and negotiation with the three delegations representing the different factions of the Cherokee Nation, which were then in Washington, and the result was the conclusion of the treaty of August 6, 1846,³ in thirteen articles, making detailed provision for the adjustment of all questions of dispute between the Cherokees themselves and also for the settlement of all claims by the Cherokees against the United States.⁴ This treaty, with some slight amendments, was ratified and proclaimed by the President on the 17th of the same month; an abstract of its provisions has already been presented. It was not until this treaty that the Ross party ever consented in any manner to recognize or be bound by the treaty of 1835.⁵

Objects of the treaty.—The main principle involved in the negotiation of the treaty of 1846 had been the disposition on the part of the United States to reimburse to the Cherokee fund sundry sums which, although not justly chargeable upon it, had been improperly paid out of that fund.⁶ In the treaty of 1835 the United States had agreed to pay to the Cherokees $5,000,000 for their lands and $600,000 for spoliations, claims, expenses of removal, etc.⁷ By the act of June 12, 1838,⁸ Congress appropriated the further sum of $1,047,067 for expenses of removal. As all these sums were for objects expressed in the treaty of 1835, the commissioners who negotiated the treaty of 1846 regarded them as one aggregate sum given by the United States for the lands of the Cherokees, subject to the charges, expenditures, and investments provided for in the treaty. This aggregate sum was appropriated and placed in the Treasury of the United States, to be disposed of according to the stipulations of the treaty. The United States thereby became the trustee of this fund for the benefit of the Cherokee people, and were bound to manage it in accordance with the well known principles of law and equity which regulate the relation of trustee and *cestui que trust*.

Adjudication of the treaty of 1835.—In order, therefore, to carry out the principle thus established by the treaty of 1846, Congress, by joint

---

¹ Commissioner Indian Affairs to Maj. William Armstrong, June 24, 1846.

² July 6, 1846.

³ United States Statutes at Large, Vol. IX, p. 871.

⁴ The subject of the North Carolina Cherokee interests was also referred to this commission July 13, 1846.

⁵ Report of Commissioner Indian Affairs to Secretary Interior, January 20, 1855.

⁶ Second Comptroller of the Treasury to Commissioner of Indian Affairs, February 6, 1849.

⁷ United States Statutes at Large, Vol. VII, p. 478.

⁸ United States Statutes at Large, Vol. V, p. 241.

resolution of August 7, 1848,[1] required the proper accounting officers of the Treasury to make a just and fair statement of account with the Cherokee Nation upon that basis. The joint report of the Second Comptroller and Second Auditor was submitted to Congress[2] after a full and thorough examination of all the accounts and vouchers of the several officers and agents of the United States who had disbursed funds appropriated to carry into effect the treaty of 1835, and also of all claims that had been admitted at the Treasury.

The result of this examination showed that there had been paid—

For improvements	$1,540,572 27
For ferries	159,572 12
For spoliations	264,894 09
For removal and subsistence and commutation therefor, including $2,765.84 expended for goods for the poorer Cherokees under the fifteenth article of treaty of 1835, and including also necessary incidental expenses of enrolling agents, conductors, commissioners, medical attendance, and supplies, etc	2,952,196 26
For debts and claims upon the Cherokee Nation	101,348 31
For the additional quantity of land ceded to the nation	500,000 00
For amount invested as the general fund of the nation	500,880 00
The aggregate of which sums is	6,019,463 05
which, being deducted from the sum of	6,647,067 00
agreeably to the directions of the ninth article of the treaty of 1846, left a balance due the Cherokee Nation of	627,603 95

They also reported that there was a further sum of $96,999.31, charged to the general treaty fund, which had been paid to the various agents of the Government connected with the removal of the Indians and which the Cherokees contended was an improper charge upon their fund. The facts as to this item were submitted by the Auditor and Comptroller without recommendation for the decision of the question by Congress, and Congress, admitting the justice of the Cherokee claim, included this sum in the subsequent appropriation of February 27, 1851.[3]

It was also resolved[4] by the United States Senate (as umpire under the treaty of 1846) that the Cherokee Nation was entitled to the sum of $189,422.76 for subsistence, being the difference between the amount allowed by act of June 12, 1838, and the amount actually paid and expended by the United States, and which excess was improperly charged to the treaty fund in the report of the accounting officers of the Treasury just recited. It was further resolved that interest at 5 per cent. should be allowed upon the sums found due the Eastern and Western Cherokees respectively from June 12, 1838. The amount of this award was made

---

[1] United States Statutes at Large, Vol. IX, p. 339.
[2] December 3, 1849.
[3] United States Statutes at Large, Vol. IX, p. 572.
[4] September 5, 1850.

available to the Cherokees by Congressional appropriation of September 30, 1850.[1]

Settlement of claims of " Old Settler" party.—By the fourth and fifth articles of the treaty of 1846,[2] provision is made and a basis fixed for the settlement with that part of the Cherokee Nation known as " Old Settlers " or " Western Cherokees," or, in other words, those who had emigrated under the treaties of 1817,[3] 1819,[4] and 1828,[5] and who were, at the date of the treaty of 1835,[6] an organized and separate nation of Indians, whom the United States had recognized as such by the treaties of 1828 and 1833[7] made with them. In making the treaty of 1835 with the Cherokees east, which provided for their final and complete transfer to the country west, then occupied by the " Western Cherokees," and guaranteed in perpetuity by two treaties, upon considerations alone connected with them, the rights of the latter seem to have been forgotten. The consequences of the influx of the Eastern Cherokees were such that upon their arrival the " Old Settlers " were thrown into a hopeless minority; their government was subverted, and a new one, imported with the emigrants coerced under the treaty of 1835, substituted in its place.

To allay the discontent thus caused in the minds of the "Old Settlers," and to provide compensation to them for the undivided interest which the United States regarded them as owning in the country east of the Mississippi, under the equitable operation of the treaty of 1828, was one of the avowed objects of the treaty of 1846. To ascertain their interest it was assumed that they constituted one-third of the entire nation, and should therefore be entitled to an amount equal to one-third of the treaty fund of 1835, after all just charges were deducted. This residuum of the treaty fund, contemplated by the fourth article of the treaty of 1846, amounted, as first calculated, to $1,571,346.55, which would make the proportionate share of the " Old Settlers" amount to the sum of $523,782.18. The act of September 30, 1850,[8] made provision for the payment to the " Old Settlers," in full of all demands under the provisions and according to the principles established in the fourth article of the treaty of 1846, of the sum of $532,896.96 with interest at 5 per cent. per annum. This was coupled with the proviso that the Indians who should receive the money should first respectively sign a receipt or release acknowledging the same to be in full of all demands under the terms of such article.

---

[1] United States Statutes at Large, Vol. IX, p. 556.
[2] Ibid., p. 871.
[3] United States Statutes at Large, Vol. VII, p. 156.
[4] Ibid., p. 195.
[5] Ibid., p. 311.
[6] Ibid., p. 478.
[7] Ibid., p. 414.
[8] United States Statutes at Large, Vol. IX, p. 556.

A year later,[1] when the "Old Settlers" were assembled for the purpose of receiving this per capita money, although their necessities were such as to compel compliance with the conditions of payment, they entered a written protest against the sum paid being considered in full of all their demands, and appealed to the United States for justice, indicating at the same time in detail wherein they were entitled to receive large additional sums.

For many years this additional claim of the "Old Settlers" practically lay dormant. But toward the close[2] of the year 1875 they held a convention or council at Tahlequah, the capital of the Cherokee Nation, and resolved to prosecute their claim to a "speedy, just, and final settlement." To that end three of their people were appointed commissioners with full power to prosecute the claim, employ counsel, and to do all other necessary and proper things in the premises. The council set apart and appropriated 35 per centum of whatever should be collected to defray all the necessary expenses attendant upon such prosecution and collection. Several subsequent councils have been held about the subject,[3] and the matter continued to be pressed upon the attention of Congress until, by the terms of an act approved August 7, 1882,[4] that body directed the Secretary of the Interior to investigate this and other matters relating to the Cherokees and to report thereon to Congress. Pursuant to the purpose of this enactment, Mr. C. C. Clements was appointed a special agent of the Interior Department with instructions to make the required investigation. He submitted three reports on the subject, the latter two being supplemental to and corrective of the first. From this last report[5] it appears that he finds the sum of $421,653.68 to be due to the "Old Settler" Cherokees, together with interest at 5 per cent. per annum from September 22, 1851. In brief his findings are—

1. That they received credit, under the settlement made under the treaty of 1846, for one-third of the fund, and were chargeable with one-third of the items properly taxable thereto.

2. Independent of article four of the treaty of 1846, the "Old Settlers" were not chargeable with removal out of the $5,000,000 fund.

3. Independent of that article, they should not be charged out of the $5,000,000 fund with the removal of the Eastern Cherokees, for three reasons: (a) The "Old Settlers" removed themselves at their own expense; (b) the Eastern Cherokees were not required to reimburse the "Old Settlers" under the treaty of 1835; and (c) the Government was required to remove the Eastern Cherokees.

4. They were not properly chargeable with the removal of the Ross

---

[1] September 22, 1851.

[2] November 22, 1875.

[3] April 28, 1877, November 20, 1880, November 17, 1881, and October 13, 1882.

[4] United States Statutes at Large, Vol. XXII, p. 328.

[5] January 31, 1883.

party of 13,148, because (a) the United States were to remove them, and (b) an appropriation of $1,047,067 was made for that purpose, for which the "Old Settlers" received no credit in the settlement under the treaty of 1846.

5. Having received credit for their proportion of the $600,000, under article three of the treaty of 1836, they were chargeable with their proportion of that fund used for removal, etc., *i. e.*, 2,495 Indians at $53.33 per head, amounting to $133,058.35.

6. The Eastern Cherokees were properly chargeable with the removal of the Ross party, and therefore they received credit for the $1,047,067 appropriated by the act of June 12, 1838.

7. In the settlement, the $5,600,000 fund was charged with the removal and subsistence of 18,026 Indians at $53.33⅓ per head, amounting to $961,386.66.[1]

This report, with accompanying letters of the Commissioner of Indian Affairs and the Secretary of the Interior, was transmitted to Congress by the President, with a special message, on the 17th of December, 1883.

Other questions under the treaty of 1835.—There were two other questions about which the parties could not agree, and upon which, by the eleventh article of the treaty of 1846, the Senate of the United States was designated as the umpire. The first of these was whether the amount expended for the one year's subsistence of the Eastern Cherokees, after their arrival in the West, should be borne by the United States or by the Cherokee funds, and, if by the latter, then whether subsistence should be charged at a greater rate than $33⅓ per head.

The Senate committee to whom the subject was referred for report to that body found much difficulty, as shown by their report, in reaching a just conclusion. They observed that the faulty manner in which the treaty of 1835 was drawn, its ambiguity of terms, and the variety of constructions placed upon it, had led to a great embarrassment in arriving at the real intention of the parties, but that upon the whole the opinion seemed to be justified that the charge should be borne by the United States. By a strict construction of the treaty of 1835, the expense of a year's subsistence of the Indians was no doubt a proper charge upon the treaty fund and was so understood by the Government at the time. In the original scheme of the treaty furnished the commissioners empowered to treat with the Indians this item was enumerated among the expenditures, etc., to be provided for in its several articles, and which made up the aggregate sum of $5,000,000 to be paid for the Cherokee country. The Secretary of War, in a letter addressed to John Ross and others in 1836, had said that the United States, having allowed the full consideration for their country, nothing further would be conceded for expenses of removal and subsistence. The whole history of the negotiation of the treaty shows that the $5,000,000 was the maximum sum which the United States were willing to pay, and that

---

[1] See Senate Executive Document No. 14, Forty-Eighth Congress, 1st session.

this was not so much a consideration for the lands and possessions of the Indians as an indemnity to cover the necessary sacrifices and losses in the surrender of one country and their removal to another.

On the other hand, among the circumstances establishing the propriety of a contrary construction may be mentioned the language of the eighth article of the treaty, that "the United States also agree and stipulate to remove the Cherokees to their new homes and to subsist them one year after their arrival there." This language imports pecuniary responsibility rather than a simple disbursement of a trust fund. In the "talk" also which was sent[1] by President Jackson to the Indians to explain the advantages of the proposed treaty, he mentioned that the stipulations offered "provide for the removal at the expense of the United States of your whole people, and for their subsistence a year after their arrival in their new country."

It was also the common practice of the United States in removing the Indian tribes from one locality to another to defray the expense of such removal, and this was done in the cases of their neighbors, the Chickasaws, Choctaws, Creeks, and Seminoles. It is a matter of but little surprise, therefore, that a conflicting interpretation of this treaty through a series of years should have produced grave embarrassments.

Independent, however, of the literal provisions of the treaty of 1835, there existed other grounds upon which to base a judgment favorable to the claims of the Cherokees. The treaty with the supplementary article was finally ratified on the 23d of May, 1836, and by its provisions the Cherokees were required to remove within two years. It had been concluded (in the face of a protest from a large majority) with a small minority of the nation. Within the two years those who had favored the treaty had mostly emigrated to the West under its provisions.[2] The large majority of the nation, adopting the counsels of John Ross had obstinately withstood all the efforts of the Government to induce them to adopt the treaty or emigrate. They had repudiated its obligation and denounced it as a fraud upon the nation. In the mean time the United States had appointed its agents under the treaty and collected a large military force to compel its execution. The State of Georgia had adopted a system of hostile legislation intended to drive them from the country. She had surveyed their territory and disposed of their homes and firesides by lottery. She had dispossessed them of a portion of their lands, subjected them to her laws, and at the same time disqualified them from the enjoyment of any political or civil rights. In this posture of affairs, the Cherokees who had never abandoned the vain hope of remaining in the country of their birth or of obtaining better terms from the United States made new proposals to the United States through John Ross and others for the sale of their country and emigration to the West. Still pursuing the idea that

---

[1] March 16, 1835.
[2] Letter of John Mason, jr. to Secretary of War, September 25, 1837.

they were aliens to the treaty of 1835 and unfettered by its provisions, they proposed to release all claim to their country and emigrate for a named sum of money in connection with other conditions, among which was the stipulation that they should be allowed to take charge of their own emigration and that the United States should pay the expenses thereof. To avoid the necessity of enforcing the treaty at the point of the bayonet and to obtain relief from counter obligations to Georgia by the compact of 1802 and to the Cherokees by the treaties of 1817 and 1819, the proposal was readily acceded to by the United States authorities.

On the 18th of May, 1838, the Secretary of War addressed a reply to the proposals of the Cherokee delegation, in which he said:

If it be desired by the Cherokee Nation that their own agents should have charge of their emigration, their wishes will be complied with and instructions be given to the commanding general in the Cherokee country to enter into arrangements with them to that effect. With regard to the expense of this operation, which you ask may be defrayed by the United States, in the opinion of the undersigned the request ought to be granted, and an application for such further sum as may be required for this purpose shall be made to Congress.

A recommendation was made to Congress in compliance with this promise. Based upon an estimate of the probable cost thereof, Congress by act of June 12, 1838,[1] appropriated the sum of $1,047,067 in full for all objects specified in the third article of the treaty and the further object of aiding in the subsistence of the Indians for one year after their removal, with the proviso that no part thereof should be deducted from the $5,000,000 purchase money of their lands.

Here was a clear legislative affirmation of the terms offered by the Indians and acceded to by the Secretary of War. It was a new contract with the Ross party, outside of the treaty, or rather a new consideration offered to abide by its terms, by which the Secretary of War agreed that the expenses of removal and subsistence, as provided for by the treaty of 1835, should be borne by the United States, and Congress affirmed his act by providing that no part of the sum appropriated should be charged to the treaty fund. The appropriation thus made proved wholly inadequate for the purposes of removal and subsistence, the expense of which aggregated $2,952,196.26,[2] of which the sum of $972,844.78 was expended for subsistence. Of this last amount, however, $172,316.47 was furnished to the Indians when in great destitution upon their own urgent application, after the expiration of the "one year," upon the understanding that it was to be deducted from the moneys due them under the treaty. This left the net sum of $800,528.31 paid for subsistence and charged to the aggregate fund. Of this sum the United States provided by the act of June 12, 1838, for $611,105.55, leaving unprovided for, the sum of $189,422.76. This,

---

[1] United States Statutes at Large, Vol. V, p. 241.
[2] See report of Second Auditor and Second Comptroller to Congress, December 3, 1849.

added to the balance of $724,603.37 found due in pursuance of the report of the accounting officers of the Treasury,[1] amounted in the aggregate to $914,626.13.

The item of $189,422.76 was appropriated, as previously stated, by the act of September 30, 1850, and that of $724,603.37 by the act of February 27, 1851. Interest was allowed on each sum at the rate of 5 per cent. per annum from the date of the act of June 12, 1838, with the understanding that it should be in full satisfaction and a final settlement of all claims and demands whatsoever of the Cherokee Nation against the United States under any treaty theretofore made with them. Instructions were issued[2] in the fall of 1851 to John Drennan, superintendent of Indian affairs, to proceed without delay to make the payment. For this purpose a remittance was made to him at New Orleans of the sums of $1,032,182.33 and $276,179.84. The first of these sums, he was advised by his instructions, was intended for the per capita payment, principal and interest, to the Eastern Cherokees, or Ross party, in pursuance of the act of February 27, 1851. The latter was for a similar payment to the same parties in compliance with the terms of the act of September 30, 1850, previously mentioned. These sums were to be distributed, according to the census roll, among 14,098 Cherokees within his superintendency, and were exclusive of the pro rata share to which those Cherokees east of the Mississippi living within the States of North Carolina, Georgia, Tennessee, and Alabama were entitled. For the payment of the latter a clerk was detailed from duty in the Office of Indian Affairs to act in the capacity of a special disbursing agent.

The payments made by Superintendent Drennan, coupled with the conditions prescribed by the act of Congress, were very unsatisfactory to the Government or Ross party of Cherokees. Therefore their national council addressed[3] to the United States a solemn and formal protest against the injustice they had suffered through the treaties of 1835 and 1846, and the statement of account rendered by the United States under the provisions of those treaties.[4] After thus placing

---

[1] See report of Second Auditor and Second Comptroller to Congress, December 3, 1849.

[2] November 17, 1851.

[3] November 29, 1851.

[4] After reciting in detail the "forced" circumstances through which those treaties were brought about, they declared —

1. That no adequate allowance had been made for the sums taken from the treaty fund of 1835 for removal; that though an appropriation had been made, the estimates upon which it was based were too small, and the balance was taken out of the Indian fund.

2. That if allowable in any sense, the Government had no right to take from the Cherokee fund an expense for removal greater than the limit fixed by the eighth article of the treaty of 1835.

3. That the alternative of receiving for subsistence $33.33, as provided for in the

themselves on record, the Cherokees accepted the money and complied with the conditions prescribed in the act of Congress.

AFFAIRS OF THE NORTH CAROLINA CHEROKEES.

As has been already remarked, at the time of the general removal of the Cherokee Nation in 1838 many individuals fled to the mountains of Tennessee and North Carolina and refused to emigrate. They always maintained their right to an equal participation in the personal benefits provided in the treaty of 1835, which, though not denied, was held by the executive authorities of the United States to be conditional upon their removal west. At length by an act of Congress approved July 29, 1848,[1] provision was made for causing a census to be taken of all those Cherokees who remained in the State of North Carolina after the ratification of the treaty of 1835 and who had not since removed west. An appropriation was made equal to $53.33⅓ for each of such individuals or his or her representative, with interest at 6 per cent per annum from the 23d of May, 1836. Furthermore, whenever any of such individuals should manifest a desire to remove and join the tribe west of the Mississippi, the Secretary of War was authorized to expend their pro rata share of the foregoing fund, or so much thereof as should be necessary, toward defraying the expense of such removal and subsistence for one year thereafter, the balance, if any, to be paid to the individual entitled. The amount of this appropriation, it was stipulated, should be refunded to the United States Treasury from the general fund of the Cherokee Nation under the treaty of 1835. The census mentioned was taken by J. C. Mullay in 1849, and the number found to be entitled to the benefits of the appropriation was 1,517,[2] which by additions was increased to 2,133. Under the appropriation acts of Septem-

---

treaty of 1835, was refused to be complied with and their people forced to receive rations in kind at double the cost.

4. That the cost of the rations issued by the commandant at Fort Gibson to "indigent Cherokees" was improperly charged to the treaty fund, without legal authority.

5. That the United States was bound to reimburse the amount paid to some two or three hundred Cherokees who emigrated prior to 1835, but who were refused a participation in the "Old Settler" fund.

6. That the Cherokees who remained in the States of Georgia, North Carolina, and Tennessee were not entitled to any share in the per capita fund, inasmuch as they complied with neither of two conditions of their remaining East; and also because the census of those Cherokees was believed to be enormously exaggerated.

7. That the sum of $103,000 had been charged upon the treaty fund for expenses of Cherokees in Georgia during three months they were all assembled and had reported themselves to General Scott as ready to take up their emigration march.

8. That interest should be paid on the balance found due them from April 15, 1851, until paid, Congress having no power to abrogate the stipulations of a treaty.

9. That $20,000 of the funds of the emigrant Cherokees were taken to pay the counsel and agents of the Old Settler party without authority.

[1] United States Statutes at Large, Vol. IX, p. 264.
[2] Commissioner of Indian Affairs to Secretary of Interior, February 10, 1874.

ber 30, 1850, and February 27, 1851, these Cherokees remaining east of the Mississippi were entitled to their pro rata share of the amounts thus appropriated. Alfred Chapman was accordingly detailed[1] from the Interior Department to make the per capita payment, and was furnished with the amounts of $41,367.31 and $156,167.19 under those respective acts. He was directed to base his payments upon the census roll furnished him, which showed 2,133 Indians to be entitled. By section 3 of an act approved March 3, 1855,[2] provision was made for the distribution per capita among the North Carolina Cherokees on the Mullay roll[3] of the fund established by the act of July 29, 1848, provided that each Indian so receiving such payment in full should assent thereto. As a further condition to the execution of this act it was stipulated that satisfactory assurance should be given by the State of North Carolina, before such payment, that the Cherokees in question should be permitted to remain permanently in that State. The desired legislative assurance was not given by North Carolina until February 19, 1866, and the money was not, therefore, distributed, but carried to the surplus fund in the Treasury. Afterwards, by act of March 3, 1875,[4] it was made applicable to the purchase and payment of lands, expenses in quieting titles, etc.

In order to determine who were the legal heirs and representatives of those enrolled in 1849, but since deceased, the Secretary of the Interior was directed by an act of Congress, approved July 27, 1868,[5] to cause another census to be taken, to serve as a guide in future payments. It was further provided by the same act that the Secretary of the Interior should cause the Commissioner of Indian Affairs to take the same supervisory charge of this as of any other tribe of Indians.

This second census was taken by S. H. Sweatland in 1869, and he was instructed to make payment of interest then due to the Indians, guided by his roll, but on the same principle on which previous payments had been effected, that is, to those individuals only whose names appeared on the Mullay census roll, or their legal heirs or representatives, as ascertained by census taken by himself. As remarked by the Commissioner of Indian Affairs, the difficulty of tracing Indian genealogy through its various complications, in order to determine who are legal representatives of deceased Indians, without any rules by which hereditary descent among them may be clearly established, was fully demonstrated in the payment made by Mr. Sweatland, which was the occasion of many complaints and even of litigation.

---

[1] November 20, 1851.

[2] United States Statutes at Large, Vol. X, p. 700.

[3] The fourth section of this same act made provision that the eighth section of the act of July 31, 1854 (United States Statutes at Large, Vol. X, pp. 315), authorizing the payment of per capita allowance to Cherokees east of the Mississippi, be so amended as to authorize the payment of all such Cherokees as, being properly entitled, were omitted from the roll of D. W. Siler from any cause whatever.

[4] United States Statutes at Large, Vol. XVIII, p. 447.

[5] United States Statutes at Large, Vol. XV, p. 228.

The landed interests of these North Carolina Cherokees had also since the treaty of 1835 become much complicated, and through their confidence in others, coupled with their own ignorance of proper business methods, they were likely to lose the title to their homes. At this juncture Congress, by an act approved July 15, 1870,[1] authorized suit in equity to be brought in the name of the Eastern Band of Cherokee Indians in the district or circuit courts of the United States for the recovery of their interest in certain lands in North Carolina. This suit was instituted in the circuit court of the United States for the western district of North Carolina in May, 1873, against William H. Thomas and William Johnston. Thomas, as the agent and trustee of the Indians, it was alleged had received (between 1836 and 1861) from them and for their benefit large sums of money, which had or ought to have been invested by him, in pursuance of various contracts with the Indians, in certain boundaries of land as well as in a number of detached tracts. The legal title to all these lands was taken by Thomas, and was still held in his own name, he having in the mean time become *non compos mentis*. It was alleged against the other defendant, Johnston, that in the year 1869 he had procured sales to be made of all these lands to satisfy judgments obtained by him against Thomas, and that he had bought in the lands at these sales and taken sheriff's deeds therefor, although having himself a knowledge of the existing equities of the Indians. In fact, that after the purchase of the lands he had entered into a contract with the Indians to release to them all the rights he had acquired by such purchase for the sum of $30,000, payable within eighteen months. Under this contract, and at the time of its execution, the Indians paid him $6,500.

A suit in law was also instituted, at the same time with the foregoing, against James W. Terrell, their former agent (from 1853 to 1861), and his sureties, the above named Thomas and Johnston, to recover a balance of Cherokee funds which he had received for their use from the United States and which it was alleged he had not properly accounted for.

At the May term, 1874, of the circuit court the matters in dispute were by agreement submitted to a board of arbitrators. The arbitrators made their report and award, which were confirmed by the court at the November term, 1874.

The award finds that Thomas purchased for the Indians as a tribe and with their funds a large tract of land on Soco Creek and Oconalufty River and their tributaries, known as the Qualla boundary, and estimated by the arbitrators to contain 50,000 acres. It declares that such tract belongs to and shall be held by the Eastern Band of Cherokees as a tribe.

The award also determines the titles of a large number of individual Indians to tracts of land outside of the Qualla boundary. It further finds that the Indians owe Thomas a balance toward the purchase-

---

[1] United States Statutes at Large, Vol. XVI, p. 362.

money of the Qualla boundary of $18,250, from which should be deducted the sum of $6,500 paid by the Indians to Johnston, with interest thereon to the date of the award, amounting in the aggregate to $8,486.

The award also finds that Terrell and his bondsmen are responsible to the Cherokees for an unaccounted-for balance of $2,697.89, which should also be deducted from the amount due Thomas, leaving a net balance due from the Indians on the purchase money of the Qualla boundary of $7,066. Upon the payment of this sum the award declares they should be entitled to a conveyance from Johnston of the legal title to all the lands embraced within that boundary.[1]

To enable the Indians to clear off this lien upon their lands, Congress, upon the recommendation of the Indian Department, provided by the terms of an act approved March 3, 1875,[2] that the funds set apart by the act of July 29, 1848, should be applied under the direction of the Secretary of the Interior for the use and benefit of the Eastern Band of Cherokees. Specifically these funds were to be used in perfecting the titles to the lands awarded to them and to pay the costs, expenses, and liabilities attending their recent litigations, also to purchase and extinguish the titles of any white persons to lands within the general boundaries allotted to them by the court and for the education, improvement, and civilization of their people. This was done and the Indians have now possession of their rightful domain.[3]

---

[1] This balance, amounting in the aggregate (with interest) to $7,242.76, was paid April 3, 1875.

[2] United States Statutes at Large Vol. XVIII, p. 447.

[3] A short time prior (September 11, 1874) to the filing of the award of the arbitrators in the case of the Indians *vs.* Thomas, an agreement was made between the parties in interest to refer certain matters of dispute between Thomas and Johnston to the consideration and determination of the same arbitrators. As the result of this reference an award was made which showed that there was due from Thomas to Johnston upon three several judgments the sum of $33,887.11. Upon this sum, however, credits to the amount of $15,552.11 (including the $6,500 with interest paid to Johnston by the Cherokees under contract of September, 1869) were allowed, leaving the net amount due to Johnston $18,335, which sum he was entitled to collect with interest until paid, together with the costs taxed in the three judgments aforesaid. The arbitrators further found that Johnson held sheriff's deeds for considerable tracts of land which had been sold as the property of Thomas and which were not included among the lands held by him in trust for the Indians. These tracts Johnston had bought in by reason of clouds upon the title and "forbiddals" of the sales at a merely nominal figure. It was therefore declared that these sheriffs' deeds should be held by Johnston only as security for the payment of the balance due him on the judgments in question and for the costs taxed on each. It was further directed that Terrell and Johnston should make sale of so much of the lands embraced in the sheriff's deeds alluded to (excluding those awarded to the Cherokee Indians either as a tribe or as individuals) as would produce a sum sufficient to satisfy the above balance of $18,335 with interest and costs.

Following this award of the arbitrators Mr. Johnston submitted a proposition for the transfer and assignment of these judgments to the Eastern Band of Cherokees. Based upon this offer, the Commissioner of Indian Affairs reported to the Secretary of the Interior June 2, 1875, that the interests of the Indians required the acceptance of

PROPOSED REMOVAL OF THE CATAWBA INDIANS TO THE CHEROKEE COUNTRY.

It is perhaps pertinent to remark before proceeding further that by the terms of an act of Congress approved July 29, 1848 (United States Statutes at Large, Vol. IX, p. 264), an appropriation of $5,000 was made to defray the expenses of removing the Catawba Indians from Carolina to the country west of the Mississippi River, provided their assent should be obtained, and also conditioned upon success in securing a home for them among some other congenial tribe in that region without cost to the Government.

These Catawbas were but a miserable remnant of what a century and a half earlier had been one of the most powerful and warlike of the Southern tribes. They once occupied and controlled a large region of country in the two Carolinas, though principally in the Southern province. Their generally accepted western limit was the Catawba River and its tributaries, the region between this river and Broad River being usually denominated a neutral hunting ground for both the Catawbas and the Cherokees. An enmity of long standing had existed between the Catawbas and the Six Nations, and war parties of both nations for many years were wont to make long and devastating forays into each other's territory. The casualties of war and the ravages of infectious diseases had long prior to the beginning of the present century rendered the Catawbas insignificant in numbers and importance.

Johnston's proposition. This recommendation was confirmed by William Stickney, of the President's board of Indian commissioners, in a report to that body. Mr. J. W. Terrell, on behalf of the Eastern Cherokees, as well as their agent, W. C. McCarthy, joined in urging the acceptance of the proposal.

Supported by these opinions and recommendations, the Secretary of the Interior, on the 3d of June, 1875, authorized the purchase of the Johnston judgments, and two days later a requisition was issued for the money, and instructions were given to Agent McCarthy to make the purchase.

Under these instructions as subsequently modified (June 9, 1875), Agent McCarthy reported (July 27, 1875) the purchase of the judgments, amounting in the aggregate, including interest and costs, to $19,245.53, and an assignment of them was taken in the name of the Commissioner of Indian Affairs in trust for the Eastern Band of Cherokee Indians of North Carolina.

From investigations and reports afterward made by Inspectors Watkins and Vandever, it appears that there was much uncertainty and confusion as to the actual status of these lands. The latter gentleman reported (April 10, 1876) that the second award made by the arbitrators was a private affair between Thomas and Johnston and was entirely separate and distinct from the first award in the case of the Indians. He also reported that, despite the purchase of the Johnston judgments by the Indian Department in trust for the Indians, the two commissioners named in the second award proceeded to sell the lands upon which these judgments were a lien, and at the November, 1875, term of the court made a report of their proceedings, which was affirmed by the court.

Taking into consideration all these complications, it was recommended by Inspector Vandever that an agent or commission be appointed, if the same could be done by consent of all parties, who should assume the duty of appraising the lands affected by the Johnston judgments, and that such quantity of the lands be selected for the Chero-

Their territorial possessions had been curtailed to a tract of some fifteen miles square on the Catawba River, on the northern border of South Carolina, and the whites of the surrounding region were generally desirous of seeing them removed from the State.

In pursuance therefore of the provisions of the act of 1848 an effort was made by the authorities of the United States to find a home for them west of the Mississippi River. Correspondence was opened with the Cherokee authorities on the subject during the summer of that year, but the Cherokees being unwilling to devote any portion of their domain to the use and occupation of any other tribe without being fully compensated therefor, the subject was dropped.

FINANCIAL DIFFICULTIES OF THE CHEROKEES.

Unusual expenditures are always incident to the removal and establishment of a people in an entirely new country. Domestic dissensions and violence of a widespread character have a tendency to destroy the security of life and property usually felt in a well governed community, and insecurity in this manner becomes the parent of idleness and the destroyer of ambition.

Thus from a combination of adverse circumstances the Cherokees since their removal had been subjected to many losses of both an in-

---

kees as would at such appraisal equal in value the amount of the judgments, interest, and costs, after which the remainder of the lands, if any, should be released to Mr. Thomas. The representatives of Thomas and Johnston also submitted a proposition for adjustment to the Indians, who by resolution of their council (March, 1876) agreed to accept it. In the light of this action and of the recommendation of Inspector Vandever, Congress passed an act (August 14, 1876) authorizing the Commissioner of Indian Affairs to receive in payment of the amount due to the Indians on the Johnston judgments owned by them a sufficient quantity of the Thomas lands to satisfy, at the appraised value, the amount of such judgments, and to deed the lands thus accepted to the Eastern Band of Cherokees in fee simple.

The commissoner of appraisal appointed and acting under this act of Congress, and under the supervision of Inspector Watkins, selected 15,211.2 acres, the appraised value of which was $20,561.35, being the exact amount, including interest and costs, due upon the judgments up to October 7, 1876, the date of appraisal.

Thereupon a deed (known as the Watkins deed) was executed by the parties representing the Johnston and Thomas interests, conveying the lands so selected to the Commissioner of Indian Affairs in the manner directed by the act of Congress, which deed it was agreed should be supplemented by a new one so soon as a more definite description could be given of the lands after survey. The surveys were made by M. S. Temple, who also surveyed the Qualla boundary tract, a deed for which latter tract (known as the Brooks deed) was executed direct to the Eastern Band of North Carolina Cherokee Indians, and the supplemental deed spoken of above was also executed. Sundry difficulties and complications have continued from time to time to arise in connection with the affairs of these Indians, and as the most effective measure of protection to their interests the Commissioner of Indian Affairs has suggested (April 26, 1882) to Congress the advisability of placing the persons and property of these people under the jurisdiction of the United States district court for the western district of North Carolina.

dividual and a national character. Their debts had come to be very oppressive, and they were anxiously devising methods of relief.

Proposed cession of the "neutral land."—At length in the fall of 1852 they began to discuss the propriety of retroceding to the United States the tract of 800,000 acres of additional land purchased by them from the Government under the provisions of the treaty of 1835. This tract was commonly known as the "neutral land," and occupied the southeast corner of what is now the State of Kansas.

It was segregated from the main portion of their territory, and had never been occupied by any considerable number of their people. After a full discussion of the subject in their national council it was decided to ask the United States to purchase it, and a delegation was appointed to enter into negotiations on the subject. They submitted their proposition in two communications,[1] but after due consideration it was decided by the Secretary of the Interior[2] to be inexpedient for the Government to entertain the idea of purchase at that time. Thereupon, under instructions from their national council, they withdrew the proposition.

As soon as the Cherokees resident in North Carolina and the neighboring States learned of this proposed disposition of the "neutral land" they filed a protest[3] against any sale of it that did not make full provision for securing to them a proportional share of the proceeds.

MURDER OF THE ADAIRS AND OTHERS.

In September of this year occurred another of those sudden acts of violence which had too frequently marked the history of the Cherokee people during the preceding fifteen years. Superintendent Drew first reported[4] to the Indian Office that a mob of one hundred armed men had murdered two unoffending citizens, Andrew and Washington Adair; that not less than two hundred men were in armed resistance to the authorities of the nation, who were unable or disinclined to suppress the insurrection, and that from sixty to one hundred of the best-known friends of the Adairs had been threatened with a fate similar to theirs. The presence and protection of an additional force of United States troops was therefore asked to preserve order in the Cherokee country and to allay the fears of the settlers along the border of Arkansas.

An additional United States force was accordingly dispatched, but the Cherokee authorities found little difficulty in controlling and allaying the excitement and disorder without their aid. In truth, the first report had been in large measure sensational, the facts as reported by

---

[1] February 17 and March 17, 1853.

[2] March 26, 1853.

[3] This protest bore date of November 9, 1853, and was filed by Edwin Follin, as their attorney or representative.

[4] September 21, 1853.

Agent Butler some two months later[1] being that the murder was occasioned by a purely personal difficulty and had no connection with any of the bitter political animosities that had cursed the nation for so many years. It seems that several years previous to the murder a Cherokee by the name of Proctor and one of the Adairs had a difficulty. Adair's friends took Proctor a prisoner through false pretenses and murdered him while in their hands. Proctor's friends in consequence were much enraged and made violent threats of retaliation. In fact during the period immediately following Proctor's death several other persons had been killed in consequence of the existing feud. The murder of the Adairs was the culmination of their enemies' revenge. The murderers were arrested, tried, and acquitted by the Cherokee courts.[2]

FINANCIAL DISTRESSES — NEW TREATY PROPOSED.

The year 1854 was in an unusual degree a period of quiet and comparative freedom from internal dissensions among the Cherokees. Their government was, however, still in an embarrassed financial condition. Their national debt was constantly increasing, and they possessed no revenue aside from the small income derived from the interest on their invested funds in the hands of the United States.

For a while, following the payment of their per capita money, they were in the enjoyment of plenty, but with the natural improvidence of a somewhat primitive people, their substance was wasted and no lasting benefits were derived therefrom. To add to their embarrassments, a severe drought throughout the summer resulted in an almost total failure of their crops. Distress and starvation seemed to be staring them in the face. Their schools, in which they had taken much commendable pride, were languishing for want of the funds necessary to their support, and the general outlook was anything but cheerful.[3]

In this dilemma a delegation was sent to Washington with authority and instructions to negotiate, if possible, another treaty with the United States, based upon the following conditions:[4]

1. The Cherokees to retrocede to the United States the 800,000 acre tract of "neutral land" at the price of $1.25 per acre, as a measure of relief from their public debt burdens and to replenish their exhausted school fund.

2. To cede to the United States the unsold portion of the 12-mile-square school fund tract in Alabama, set apart by the treaty of 1819, also at $1.25 per acre, together with the other small reserves in Tennessee set apart for the same purpose and by the same treaty, for which latter tracts they should receive $20,000.

---

[1] November 22, 1853.

[2] Letter of Agent Butler, dated November 30, 1853.

[3] Annual report of Agent Butler for 1854.

[4] The delegation submitted these propositions in a communication to the Commissioner of Indian Affairs, dated December 28, 1854.

HISTORICAL DATA 199

3. The United States to compensate the Cherokees living on the 800,000 acre tract for the value of their improvements.

4. The United States to rectify the injustice done to many individual Cherokees in regard to their claims under the treaty of 1835.

5. The United States to compensate the Cherokees for damages sustained through the action of citizens of the former in driving and pasturing stock in the Cherokee country, and to provide effectual measures for the prevention of such losses in the future.

6. The United States to cause a careful investigation to e made as to the status of the Cherokee invested fund and to render an account of the accrued and unpaid interest thereon.

7. The Cherokees to be reimbursed for money expended out of their funds for subsistence after the expiration of the period of " one year " provided by the treaty of 1835, but before their people had opportunity to become settled in their new homes

8. A just compensation to be made to the Cherokees for the heavy losses sustained in their sudden and forced removal from their Eastern home.

9. An absolute and speedy removal of the garrison at Fort Gibson.

10. That the treaty should contain a clear and specific definition of the rights and status of the Cherokee Nation in its political attitude toward and relations with the United States.

The proposed treaty formed the subject of much careful consideration, and negotiations were conducted throughout a large portion of the winter, without, however, reaching satisfactory results.

The failure of the delegation to secure definite action on these matters caused a great degree of dissatisfaction among all classes of their people.[1] They were anxious to sell their surplus detached land, and by that means free themselves from financial embarrassment. They were fully conscious that, so long as their financial affairs continued in such a crippled condition, there was little ground for a hopeful advancement in their morals or civilization. A traditional prejudice against the policy of parting with any of their public domain was deep seated and well nigh universal among the Cherokees, but so grinding and irksome had the burdens of their pecuniary responsibilities become and so anxious were they to discharge in good faith their duty to their creditors that this feeling of aversion was subordinated to what was believed to be a national necessity.

SLAVERY IN THE CHEROKEE NATION.

The reports of the Cherokee agent during the year 1855 devote considerable space to the discussion of the slavery question in its relations to and among that nation, from which it appears that considerable local excitement, as well as a general feeling of irritation and insecurity among the holders of slave property, had been superinduced by the

---
[1] Annual report of Agent Butler for 1855.

antislavery teachings of the Northern missionaries and emissaries of the various free soil organizations throughout the North. Three years later the agent reported that the amicable relations which existed between the Cherokees and the General Government certainly merited the latter's fostering care and protection, for already they were evincing much interest in all questions that concerned its welfare; that the majority of them were strongly national or democratic in political sympathy, though it was with regret he was obliged to report the existence of a few black republicans, who were the particular foundlings of the abolition missionaries. This same agent the following year (1859), after commending their enterprise and thrift, remarks: "I am clearly of the opinion that the rapid advancement of the Cherokees is owing in part to the fact of their being slaveholders, which has operated as an incentive to all industrial pursuits, and I believe if every family of the wild roving tribes of Indians were to own a negro man and woman, who would teach them to cultivate the soil and to properly prepare and cook their food, and could have a schoolmaster appointed for every district, it would tend more to civilize them than any plan that could be adopted." The latter part of this proposition perhaps no one would be willing to dispute, but in the light of twenty-five years of eventful history made since its promulgation, the author himself, if still living, would scarcely be so "clearly of opinion" concerning the soundness of his first assumption.

REMOVAL OF WHITE SETTLERS ON CHEROKEE LAND.

The year 1856 was characterized by no event in the official history of the Cherokees of special importance, except, perhaps, the expulsion of white settlers who had intruded upon the "neutral lands," in which the aid of the military forces of the United States was invoked.

FORT GIBSON ABANDONED BY THE UNITED STATES.

The long and urgent demands of the Cherokees for the withdrawal of the garrison of United States troops at Fort Gibson was at length complied with in the year 1857,[1] and under the terms of the third article of the treaty of 1835 the fort and the military reserve surrounding it reverted to and became a part of the Cherokee national domain. In his annual message of that year to the Cherokee council John Ross, their principal chief, recommended the passage of a law which should authorize the site of the post to be laid off into town lots and sold to citizens for the benefit of the nation, reserving such lots and buildings as seemed desirable for future disposition, and providing for the suitable preservation of the burying-grounds in which, among others, reposed the remains of several officers of the United States Army. This recommendation was favorably acted upon by the council, and town

---

[1] Annual report of Agent Butler for 1857.

lots sold exclusively to the citizens of the nation brought the sum of $20,000.[1]

REMOVAL OF TRESPASSERS ON "NEUTRAL LAND."

White settlers having for several years preceding, in defiance of the notification and authority of the General Government, continued their encroachments and settlement on the "Cherokee neutral land," and the Cherokee authorities having made repeated complaints of these unauthorized intrusions, measures were taken to remove the cause of complaint. Notice was therefore given to these settlers in the winter of 1859, requiring them to abandon the lands by the 1st of April following. No attention was paid to the notice, but the settlers went on and planted their crops as usual. The newly appointed Cherokee agent, having failed to reach his agency until late in the spring, proceeded to the neutral land in August, and again notified the trespassers to remove within thirty-five days. To this they paid no more heed than to the first notification. Some two months later,[2] therefore, the agent, accompanied by a detachment of United States dragoons, under command of Captain Stanley, marched into the midst of the settlers and again commanded their immediate removal. Upon their refusal to comply he adopted the plan of firing their cabins, which soon brought them to terms. They proposed that if he would desist in his forcible measures and withdraw the troops, they would quietly remove on or before the 25th of November, unless in the mean time they should receive the permission of the Government to remain during the winter. This the agent agreed to, and subsequently the permission was granted them to so remain.

In connection with this subject it appears from the records of the Department that owing to an error in protracting the northern boundary of the "neutral land," the line was made to run 8 or 9 miles south of the true boundary, leaving outside of the reserve as it was marked on the map, a strip known as the "dry woods," which should have been included in it; it was generally believed that the "dry woods" was a part of the New York Indian reservation, on which settlements were permitted, and as the settlers on that particular portion had gone there in good faith the agent did not molest them.[3] The Secretary of the Interior himself expressed the opinion that the "dry woods" settlers were law abiding citizens and had settled there under a misapprehension of the facts, and that as they had expended large sums in opening and improving their farms it would be a great hardship if they should be compelled to remove. He therefore suspended the execution of the law as to them until the approaching session of Congress, in order that

---

[1] Annual report of Agent Butler for 1858.

[2] October 10, 1860.

[3] See reports of Agent Cowart in November, 1860, in Indian Office report of 1860, pp. 224, 225.

they might have an opportunity of applying to that body for relief. The Cherokees it was well known were anxious to dispose of the land, and the Secretary declared his intention of recommending the passage of a law with their consent, providing for the survey and sale of the "neutral lands," after the manner of disposing of the public lands, the proceeds to be applied to the benefit of the Cherokees. The outbreak of the great rebellion so soon thereafter, however, precluded the consummation of this proposed legislation.

JOHN ROSS OPPOSES SURVEY AND ALLOTMENT OF CHEROKEE DOMAIN.

During the winter of 1859-'60, the Commissioner of Indian Affairs, believing that a survey and subdivision of the Cherokee national domain, and its allotment in severalty among the members of the tribe, would produce an effect favorable to their progress in the cultivation of the soil, submitted the suggestion for the consideration of their lawfully constituted authorities. John Ross, as principal chief of the nation, in replying to this suggestion,[1] declined on behalf of the nation to give it favorable consideration, (1) because it conflicted with the general policy of the Government through which the Cherokees were removed from their homes east of the Mississippi River; (2) because it was inconsistent with existing treaties between the United States and the Cherokee Nation; (3) because it could not be done without a change in the constitution of the nation; and, finally, that it would not be beneficial to the Cherokee people.

POLITICAL EXCITEMENT IN 1860.

The year 1860 was characterized by great excitement and local disturbances. Many affrays occurred and numerous murders were perpetrated. The excitement and bitterness of feeling involved in the issues at stake between the great political parties of the country in the pending Presidential election extended to and pervaded the entire population of the civilized tribes of Indian Territory.

They were many of them slaveholders, especially the half-breeds and mixed bloods. They therefore vehemently resented the introduction and dissemination of any doctrines at variance with the dogma of the divine origin of slavery or that should set up any denial of the moral and legal right of the owner to the continued possession of his slave property. The missionaries and many of the school teachers among the Cherokees were persons of strong anti-slavery convictions, and the former especially were zealous in their dissemination of doctrines fatal alike to the peace and endurance of a slave community. In September John B. Jones, a Baptist missionary, who had devoted much of his life to Christian work among the Indians, was notified by the agent to leave the country within three weeks, because of the publication of an article from his pen in a Northern paper, wherein he stated that he

---

[1] January 1, 1860.

was engaged in promulgating anti-slavery sentiments among his flock.¹ Others were in like manner compelled to leave, and the excitement continued to increase daily until the outbreak of hostilities precipitated by the attack on Fort Sumter.

Before the actual outbreak of hostilities, in the winter of 1860, adherents of the Southern cause, among the most effectual and influential of whom were the official agents of the United States accredited to the Indian tribes, were active in propagating the doctrines of secession among the Cherokees, as well as among other tribes of the Indian Territory. Secret societies were organized, especially among the Cherokees, and Stand Watie, the recognized leader of the old Ridge or Treaty party, was the leader of an organization of Southern predilections known as the Knights of the Golden Circle. A counter organization was formed from among the loyally inclined portion of the nation, most, if not all, of whom were members of the Government or Ross party. The membership of this latter society was composed principally of full blood Cherokees, and they termed themselves the "Ki-tu-wha," a name by which the Cherokees were said to have been known in their ancient confederations with other Indian tribes.² The distinguishing badge of membership in this association was a pin worn in a certain position on the coat, vest, or hunting shirt, from whence members were given the designation in common parlance of "Pin" Indians. According to the statement of General Albert Pike, however (and I think he gives the correct version), this "Pin" society was organized and in full operation long before the beginning of the secession difficulties, and was really established for the purpose of depriving the half-breeds of all political power.³ Be this as it may, however, the society was made to represent in the incipient stages of the great American conflict the element of opposition to an association with the Southern Confederacy and on one occasion it prevented the distinctively Southern element under the leadership of Stand Watie from raising a Confederate flag at Tahlequah.⁴ It was also alleged to have been established by the Rev. Evan Jones, a missionary of more than forty years' standing among the Cherokees, as an instrument for the dissemination of anti-slavery doctrines.⁵

---

¹ Letter of Agent R. J. Cowart to Commissioner Indian Affairs, September 8, 1860.

² Letter of S. W. Butler, published in Philadelphia North American, January 24, 1863.

³ Letter of General Albert Pike to Commissioner of Indian Affairs, February 17, 1866, published in pamphlet report of Commissioner of Indian Affairs to the President, bearing date June 15, 1866.

⁴ Letter of S. W. Butler, in Philadelphia North American, January 24, 1863, and letter of General Albert Pike to Commissioner of Indian Affairs, February 17, 1866.

⁵ Letter of Albert Pike, February 17, 1866. The delegates representing the "Southern Cherokees," in their statement to the United States commissioners at the Fort Smith conference, September 16, 1865, say : "Years before the war one portion of the Cherokees was arrayed in deadly hostility against the other; a secret organized society called the 'Pins,' led by John Ross and Rev. Jones, had sworn destruction to the half-bloods and white men of the nation outside this organization," etc.

CHEROKEES AND THE SOUTHERN CONFEDERACY.

In May, 1861, General Albert Pike, of Arkansas, was requested by Hon. Robert Toombs, secretary of state of the Confederate States, to visit the Indian Territory as a commissioner, and to assure the Indians of the friendship of those States. He proceeded to Fort Smith,[1] where, in company with General Benjamin McCulloch, he was waited on by a delegation of Cherokees representing the element of that people who were enthusiastically loyal to the Confederacy and who were desirous of ascertaining whether in case they would organize and take up arms for the South the latter would engage to protect them from the hostility of John Ross and the association of "Pin" Indians who were controlled by him.[2] Assurances were given of the desired protection, and messengers were sent to a number of the prominent leaders of the anti-Ross party to meet General Pike at the Creek Agency, two days after he should have held an interview with Ross, then contemplated, at Park Hill. General Pike, as he alleges, had no idea of concluding any terms with Ross, and his intention was to treat with the leaders of the Southern party at the Creek Agency. At the meeting held with Ross at Park Hill, the latter refused to enter into any arrangement with the Confederate Government, and obstinately insisted on maintaining an attitude of strict neutrality. After vainly endeavoring to shake the old man's purpose, General McCulloch at length agreed to respect his neutrality so long as the Federal forces should refrain from entering the Cherokee country.[3]

General McCulloch having been ordered by the Confederate authorities to take command of the district of country embracing the Indian Territory, with headquarters at Fort Smith, addressed[4] a communication to John Ross again assuring him of his intention to respect the neutrality of the Cherokee people, except that all those members of the tribe who should so desire must be permitted to enlist in the Confederate army, without interference or molestation, for purposes of defense in case of an invasion from the North. To this Ross replied,[5] reasserting the determination of the Cherokees to maintain a strict neutrality between the contending parties. He refused his consent to any organization or enlistment of Cherokee troops into the Confederate service, for the reason, first, it would be a palpable violation of the Cherokee position of neutrality, and, second, it would place in their midst organized companies not authorized by the Cherokee laws, but in violation of treaty, and which would soon become effective instruments in stirring up domestic strife and creating internal difficulties among the Cherokee people. General McCulloch in his letter had assumed that his proposi-

---

[1] Early in June, 1861.
[2] Letter of General Albert Pike to Commissioner of Indian Affairs, February 17, 1866.
[3] Ibid.
[4] June 12, 1861.
[5] June 17, 1861.

tion for permitting enlistments of Cherokees of Confederate sympathies was in accordance with the views expressed to him by Ross in an interview occurring some eight or ten days previous, wherein the latter had observed that in case of an invasion from the North he himself would lead the Cherokees to repel it. Ross, in his reply above alluded to, takes occasion to assure McCulloch that the latter had misapprehended his language. It was only in case of a foreign invasion that he had offered to lead his men in repelling it. He had not signified any purpose as to an invasion by either the Northern or Southern forces, because he had not apprehended and could not give his consent to any.

Some time in August[1] a convention was assembled at Tahlequah upon the call of John Ross, to take into consideration the question of the difficulties and dangers surrounding the Cherokee Nation and to determine the most advisable method of procedure. At this convention a number of speeches were made, all of which were bitterly hostile in tone to the United States and favorable to an open alliance with the Southern Confederacy. Ross, among others, gave free expression to his views, and according to the published version of his remarks gave it as his opinion that an understanding with the Confederacy was the best thing for the Cherokees and all other Indians to secure and that without delay; that, as for himself, he was and always had been a Southern man, a State rights man; born in the South, and a slaveholder; that the South was fighting for its rights against the oppressions of the North, and that the true position of the Indians was with the Southern people. After this speech the convention, which was attended by four thousand male Cherokees, adopted without a dissenting voice a resolution to abandon their relations with the United States and to form an alliance with the Confederacy.

Treaties between Confederate States and various Southern tribes.—General Pike did not see Ross again until September.[2] In the meantime, the latter had secured the attendance of a large number of representatives of both Northern and Southern tribes, at a convocation held at Antelope Hills, where a unanimous agreement was reached to maintain a strict neutrality in the existing hostilities between their white neighbors. The alleged purpose of this assembly, as stated by General Pike, was to take advantage of the war between the States, and form a great independent Indian confederation, but he defeated its purpose by concluding a treaty with the Creeks on behalf of the Confederate States, while their delegates were actually engaged in council at the Antelope Hills. Following his negotiations with the Creeks, he concluded treaties in quick succession with the Choctaws and Chickasaws, the Seminoles, the Wichitas, and affiliated tribes, including the absentee Shawnees and Dela-

---

[1] According to the message of John Ross, as principal chief to the Cherokee national council, October 9, 1861, this convention was held on the 21st of August, 1861.

[2] Pike's letter to Commissioner of Indian Affairs, February 17, 1866.

wares, and the Comanches.[1] On returning from his treaty with the Comanches, he was met before reaching Fort Arbuckle by a messenger bearing a letter from Ross and his council, accompanied by a copy of the resolutions of the council and a pressing personal invitation to repair to the Cherokee country and enter into a treaty with that tribe. He consented and named a day when he would meet Ross, at the same time writing the latter to notify the Osages, Quapaws, Senecas, and the confederated Senecas and Shawnees, to meet him at the same time. At the time fixed he proceeded to Park Hill (Ross's residence), where he concluded treaties with these various tribes[2] during the first week in October, reserving the negotiations with the Cherokees to the last, the treaty with whom was concluded on the 7th of the month at Tahlequah. This instrument was very lengthy, being comprised in fifty-five articles.[3] The preamble set forth that—

> The Congress of the Confederate States of America having, by an "Act for the protection of certain Indian tribes," approved the 21st day of May, in the year of our Lord one thousand eight hundred and sixty-one, offered to assume and accept the protectorate of the several nations and tribes of Indians occupying the country west of Arkansas and Missouri, and to recognize them as their wards, subject to all the rights, privileges, immunities, titles and guarantees with each of said nations and tribes under treaties made with them by the United States of America; and the Cherokee Nation of Indians having assented thereto upon certain terms and conditions: Now, therefore, the said Confederate States of America, by Albert Pike, their commissioner, constituted by the President, under authority of the act of Congress in that behalf, with plenary powers for these purposes, and the Cherokee Nation by the principal chief, executive council, and commissioners aforesaid, has agreed to the following articles, etc.

With some slight amendments to the instrument as originally concluded it was duly ratified by the Confederate States.

CHEROKEE TROOPS FOR THE CONFEDERATE ARMY.

Long before[4] the conclusion of this treaty, authority was given by General McCulloch to raise a battalion of Cherokees for the service of the Confederate States. Under this authority a regiment was raised in December, 1861, and commanded by Stand Watie, the leader of the anti-Ross party. A regiment had also been previously raised, ostensibly as home guards, the officers of which had been appointed by Chief

---

[1] Pike's letter to Commissioner of Indian Affairs, February 17, 1866. These treaties were concluded on the following dates respectively: Creek, July 10; Choctaw and Chickasaw, July 12; Seminole, August 1; Shawnees, Delawares, Wichitas, and affiliated tribes resident in leased territory, and Comanches, August 12, 1861.

[2] The treaty with the Osages was concluded October 2, that with the Senecas and Shawnees on the same day, and also that with the Quapaws. (See Report Commissioner of Indian Affairs for 1865, p. 318.)

[3] The text of this treaty was reprinted for the use of the United States treaty commissioners in 1866.

[4] August, 1861. See letter of Commissioner of Indian Affairs to the President, June 15, 1866.

HISTORICAL DATA 207

Ross and the command assigned to Colonel Drew.[1] After the conclusion of the treaty this regiment was also placed at the service of the Confederate States, and in December[2] following, in an address to them, Ross remarked that he had raised the regiment "to act in concert with the troops of the Southern Confederacy."

These two regiments actively participated and co-operated in the military operations of the Confederates until after the battle of Pea Ridge, in which they were engaged.[3] In the summer of 1862,[4] following this battle, Colonel Weir, of the United States Army, commanding a force partly composed of loyal Indians on the northern border of the Cherokee country, sent a proposition to John Ross urging that the Cherokees should repudiate their treaty with the Confederacy and return to their former relations with the United States, offering at the same time a safe conduct to Ross and such of his leading counselors as he should designate through the Union lines to Washington, where they could negotiate a new treaty with the authorities of the United States. This proposition was declined peremptorily by Ross, who declared that the Cherokees disdained an alliance with a people who had authorized and practiced the most monstrous barbarities in violation of the laws of war; that the Cherokees were bound to the Confederate States by the faith of treaty obligations and by a community of sentiment and interest; that they were born upon the soil of the South and would stand or fall with the States of the South.[5]

A CHEROKEE CONFEDERATE REGIMENT DESERTS TO THE UNITED STATES.

Colonel Drew's regiment of Cherokees had now been in the Confederate service about ten months. During that period they had remained unpaid, were scantily clothed, and were generally uncared for, unthanked, and their services unrecognized.[6] When, therefore, Colonel Weir invaded the Cherokee country in July, 1862, and the power and

---

[1] General Albert Pike in his letter of February 17, 1866, speaks of being escorted from Fort Gibson to Park Hill on his way to conclude the treaty of October 7, 1861, by eight or nine companies of Colonel Drew's regiment, which had been previously raised as a home guard by order of the national council.

[2] This address (printed as document No. 7, accompanying the letter of Commissioner of Indian Affairs to the President, June 15, 1866) bears date of December 19, 1862. This is an evident typographical error for 1861, because the address was in the nature of a censure upon the regiment for its defection on the eve of a battle with the forces of O-poth-le-yo-ho-lo, the loyal Creek leader. This battle occurred at Bushy or Bird Creek, December 9, 1861, and before the expiration of another year Ross had left the Cherokee country under the escort of Colonel Weir.

[3] Greeley's American Conflict, Vol. II, p. 32; also, Report of Commissioner of Indian Affairs, June 15, 1866, and numerous other official documents.

[4] Report of Commissioner of Indian Affairs to the President, June 15, 1866, p. 10.

[5] Letter of General Albert Pike, February 17, 1866; also letter of T. J. Mackey, June 4, 1866.

[6] Letter of General Albert Pike, February 17, 1866.

prestige of the Confederacy seemed, for the time being, to have become less potent in that region, their troops having been withdrawn to other localities, these discontented and unfed Cherokee soldiers found themselves in a condition ripe for revolt. Almost *en masse*, they abandoned the Confederate service and enlisted in that of the United States.

Conduct of John Ross.—Ross, finding that he had been abandoned by Drew's regiment, concluded to make a virtue of necessity and become a loyal man too, with the shrewd assertion that such had always been the true impulse of his heart; he had been overborne, however, by the authority and power of the Confederate Government and felt constrained to save his people and their material interests from total destruction by dissembling before the officials of that Government, seeking only the first opportunity, which he had now embraced, to return with his people to the fealty they so delighted to bear to the Federal Government.[1] He was escorted out of the Cherokee country by Colonel Weir's regiment and did not soon return. The burden of proof seems to be almost, if not quite, conclusive against his pretensions to loyalty up to this period, and now that the opportunity he had so long desired of placing himself and his people within the protection of the United States had arrived, instead of manifesting any of that activity which had characterized his conduct in behalf of the Confederate States, he retired to Philadelphia, and did not return to his people for three years.[2]

O-poth-le-yo-ho-lo and his loyal followers.—General Pike, in his letter to the Commissioner of Indian Affairs pending the negotiation of the treaty of 1866, seeks to convey the impression that there were no actively loyal Indians among the Southern tribes during the incipient stages of the rebellion, and perhaps this is in large measure correct as to most of those tribes.

Their situation was such as would have worked confusion in the ideas of a less primitive and simple minded people. For years before the outbreak of the rebellion their superintendents, agents, and agency employés had been, almost without exception, Southern men or men of Southern sympathies. They were a slaveholding people, and the idea was constantly pressed upon them that the pending difficulties between the North and the South were solely the result of a determination on the part of the latter to protect her slave property from the aggressions and rapacity of the former. When at last hostilities commenced, they saw the magnitude of the preparation and the strength of the Confederate forces in their vicinity. The weakness of the Federal forces was equally striking. Within the scope of their limited horizon there was naught that seemed to shed a ray of hope upon the rapidly darkening sky of Federal supremacy. Those who were naturally inclined to sympathize with, and who retained a feeling of friendship and reverence for,

---

[1] Commissioner of Indian Affairs to the President, June 15, 1866.
[2] Ibid.

the old Government were awed into silence. A sense of fear and helplessness for the time being compelled them to accept and apparently acquiesce in a state of affairs for which many of them had no heart.

After the Cherokee convention at Tahlequah, in August, 1861, at which it was decided with such unanimity to renounce their treaty relations with the United States and to enter into diplomatic alliance with the Confederacy, O-poth-le-yo-ho-lo, an old and prominent Creek chief, whom Ross had notified by letter of the action taken, and upon whom he urged the wisdom of securing similar action by the Creeks,[1] refused to lend himself to any such measure. He called a council of the Creeks, however, representing to them the action of the Cherokees, alleging that their chiefs had been bought, and reminded the Creeks of the duties and obligations by which they were bound to the Government of the United States.

The majority of the Creeks, notwithstanding, were for active co-operation with the Confederacy, and an internecine war was at once inaugurated. The loyal portion of the Seminoles, Wichitas, Kickapoos, and Delawares joined O-poth-le-yo-ho-lo and his loyal Creeks, who after two or three engagements with the disloyal Indians, backed by a force of Texas troops, was compelled to retreat to the north, which he did in December, 1861.[2] The weather was extremely inclement; the loyal Indians were burdened with all their household goods, their women and children, and at the same time exposed to the assaults of their enemies. Their baggage was captured, leaving many of them without shoes or comfortable clothing. Hundreds perished on the route, and at last, after a journey of 300 miles, they reached Humboldt, Kansas, racked with disease, almost frozen, and with starvation staring them in the face. Immediately upon learning of the condition of these sufferers, Indian Superintendent Coffin promptly inaugurated measures for their relief. Having inconsiderable funds at his command for the purpose, application was made to General Hunter, commanding the Department of Kansas, who promptly responded with all the supplies at his disposal. The Indians in their retreat had become scattered over an area of territory 200 miles in extent, between the Verdigris and Fall River, Walnut Creek and the Arkansas. As they became aware of the efforts of the Government for their relief, they began to pour into the camp of rendezvous on the Verdigris, but were later removed to Le Roy, Kansas. Authority was given to enlist the able bodied males in the service of the United States, and two regiments were at once organized and placed under command of Colonel Weir for an expedition against the Indian Territory, mention of which has been previously made. A census taken of these refugees by Superintendent Coffin,

---

[1] Letter of John Ross to O-poth-le-yo-ho-lo, September 19, 1861.
[2] Report of Agent Cutler and Superintendent Coffin for 1862. See pages 135 and 138 of the Report of the Commissioner of Indian Affairs for 1862.

in August, 1862, showed that there were in camp, exclusive of the 2,000 who had enlisted in the service of the United States, 3,619 Creeks, 919 Seminoles, 165 Chickasaws, 223 Cherokees, 400 Kickapoos, 89 Delawares, 19 Ionies, and 53 Keechies, in all 5,487, consisting of 864 men, 2,040 women, and 2,583 children. In addition to these at least 15 per cent. had died since their arrival from hardships encountered in the course of their retreat. They were subsequently removed to the Sac and Fox reservation in Kansas.

Until after Colonel Weir's expedition to the Indian Territory not exceeding three hundred Cherokees had taken refuge within the Union lines; but in the autumn of 1862, after Weir's retreat, a body of refugees, mostly women and children, claiming the protection of the United States, made their way to a point on the Cherokee neutral lands some 12 miles south of Fort Scott, Kansas.

Like all the other refugees, they were in a most destitute and suffering condition. In need of food, clothing, and supplies of all kinds, these sufferers, to the number of two thousand, appealed for relief, and were for a time supplied by the Superintendent of Indian Affairs, but afterwards, on being taken under charge of the military authorities, were transferred to Neosho, Missouri.

Relations with the Southern Confederacy renounced.—During the month of February, 1863 (as reported[1] by John Ross from Philadelphia), a special meeting of the Cherokee national council was convened at Cowskin Prairie, and the following legislation was enacted:

1. Abrogating the treaty with the Confederate States, and calling a general convention of the people to approve the act.

2. The appointment of a delegation with suitable powers and instructions to represent the Cherokee Nation before the United States Government, consisting of John Ross, principal chief, Lieutenant-Colonel Downing, Capt. James McDaniel, and Rev. Evan Jones.

3. Authorizing a general Indian council to be held at such time and place as the principal chief may designate.

4. Deposing all officers of the nation disloyal to the Government.

5. Approving the purchase of supplies made by the treasurer and directing their distribution.

6. Providing for the abolition of slavery in the Cherokee Nation.

RAVAGES OF WAR IN THE CHEROKEE NATION.

In the latter part of the winter of 1862 and early spring of 1863 the military authorities conceived the propriety of returning the refugee Cherokees to their homes in time to enable them to plant their spring crops. Two military expeditions were organized, one to move from Springfield, Mo., under the command of General Blunt, and the other from Scott's

---

[1] April 2, 1863.

Mills, in charge of Colonel Phillips.[1] The Indians were furnished with the necessary agricultural implements, seeds, etc., and were promised complete protection from the incursions of their enemies. The refugees, in charge of Indian Agent Harlan, set out for their homes a week after the army had marched, reaching Tahlequah in safety, and immediately scattering themselves throughout the country engaged busily in planting their crops. Their labors had only fairly commenced when they were alarmed by the reported approach of Stand Watie and his regiment of Confederate Cherokees. The Indians immediately suspended their labors, and, together with the troops under Colonel Phillips, were compelled to take refuge in Fort Gibson. Their numbers were, as reported by the superintendent, now increased to upwards of six thousand, by the addition of many who, up to this time, had remained at their homes. The troops of Stand Watie, alleged to number some seven hundred, scoured the country at their pleasure, and not only everything of value that had previously escaped confiscation in the nation, but everything that had been brought back with them by the refugees to aid in their proposed labors, was either carried off or destroyed. The failure of these expeditions in accomplishing the objects for which they were organized rendered it necessary that the refugees should be fed and maintained at Fort Gibson, some 200 miles distant from the base of supplies. This situation of affairs remained practically unchanged until the close of the war, except that the number of destitute Indians requiring subsistence from the Government increased to sixteen or seventeen thousand. The United States forces continued to occupy Forts Smith and Gibson, and the Indians were thus enabled to cultivate, to a limited extent, the lands within the immediate protection of those posts, but their country was infested and overrun by guerrillas, who preyed upon and destroyed everything of a destructible character. There was no portion of country within the limits of the United States, perhaps, that was better suited to the demands of stock-raising, and the Cherokees had, prior to the war, entered largely into this pursuit. Many of them were wealthy and numbered their herds by hundreds and even thousands of head. Almost the entire nation was surrounded by all the comforts and many of the luxuries of a civilized people. When they were overwhelmed by the disasters of war, and saw the labors and accumulations of more than twenty years' residence in that pleasant and fruitful country swept away in a few weeks, the sullen bitterness of despair settled down upon them. Their losses in stock alone aggregated, according to the best estimates, more than 300,000 head. Is it any wonder that the springs of hope should dry up within their breasts?

---

[1] Report of Commissioner of Indian Affairs for 1863, p. 24.

TREATY CONCLUDED JULY 19, 1866; PROCLAIMED AUGUST 11, 1866.

Held at Washington, D. C., between Dennis N. Cooley, Commissioner of Indian Affairs, and Elijah Sells, superintendent of Indian Affairs for the southern superintendency, on behalf of the United States, and the Cherokee Nation of Indians, represented by its delegates, James McDaniel, Smith Christie, White Catcher, S. H. Benge, J. B. Jones, and Daniel H. Ross, John Ross, principal chief, being too unwell to join in these negotiations.[1]

MATERIAL PROVISIONS.

Whereas existing treaties between the United States and the Cherokee Nation are deemed to be insufficient, the contracting parties agree as follows, viz:

1. The pretended treaty of October 7, 1861, with the so-called Confederate States, repudiated by the Cherokee National Council February 18, 1863, is declared to be void.

2. Amnesty is declared for all offenses committed by one Cherokee against the person or property of another or against a citizen of the United States prior to July 4, 1866. No right of action arising out of acts committed for or against the rebellion shall be maintained in either the United States or the Cherokee courts, and the Cherokee Nation agree to deliver to the United States all public property in their control which belonged to the United States or the so-called Confederate States.

3. The confiscation laws of the Cherokee Nation shall be repealed, and all sales of farms and improvements are declared void. The former owners shall have the right to repossess themselves of the property so sold. The purchaser under the confiscation laws shall receive from the treasurer of the nation the money paid and the value of the permanent improvements made by him. The value of these improvements shall be fixed by a commission, composed of one person appointed by the United States and one appointed by the Cherokee Nation, who in case of disagreement may appoint a third. The value of these improvements so fixed shall be returned to the Cherokee treasurer by returning Cherokees within three years.

4. All Cherokees and freed persons who were formerly slaves to any Cherokee, and all free negroes, not having been such slaves, who resided in the Cherokee Nation prior to June 1, 1861, who may within two years elect not to reside northeast of the Arkansas River and southeast of Grand River, shall have the right to settle in and occupy the Canadian district southwest of the Arkansas River; and also the country northwest of Grand River, and bounded southeast by Grand River and west by the Creek country, to the northeast corner thereof; from thence west on north line of Creek country to 96° west longitude; thence north with

---

[1] United States Statutes at Large, Vol. XIV, p. 799.

said 96° so far that a line due east to Grand River will include a quantity of land equal to 160 acres for each person who may so elect to reside therein, provided that the part of said district north of Arkansas River shall not be set apart until the Canadian district shall be found insufficient to allow 160 acres to each person desiring to settle under the terms of this article.

5. The inhabitants electing to reside in the district described in the preceding article shall have the right to elect all their local officers and judges, also their proportionate share of delegates in any general council that may be established under the twelfth article of this treaty; to control all their local affairs in a manner not inconsistent with the constitution of the Cherokee Nation or the laws of the United States, provided the Cherokees residing in said district shall enjoy all the rights and privileges of other Cherokees who may elect to settle in said district as herein before provided, and shall hold the same rights and privileges and be subject to the same liabilities as those who elect to settle in said district under the provisions of this treaty; provided, also, that if any rules be adopted which, in the opinion of the President, bear oppressively on any citizen of the nation he may suspend the same. And all rules or regulations discriminating against the citizens of other districts are prohibited and shall be void.

6. The inhabitants of the aforesaid district shall be entitled to representation in the national council in proportion to their numbers. All laws shall be uniform throughout the nation. The President of the United States is empowered to correct any evil arising from the unjust or unequal operation of any Cherokee law and to secure an equitable expenditure of the national funds.

7. A United States court shall be created in the Indian Territory; until created, the United States district court nearest the Cherokee Nation shall have exclusive original jurisdiction of all causes, civil and criminal, between the inhabitants of the aforesaid district and other citizens of the Cherokee Nation. All process issued in said district against a Cherokee outside of said district shall be void unless indorsed by the judge of the district in which the process is to be served. A like rule shall govern the service of process issued by Cherokee officers against persons residing in the aforesaid district. Persons so arrested shall be held in custody until delivered to the United States marshal or until they shall consent to be tried by the Cherokee court. All provisions of this treaty creating distinctions between citizens of any district and the remainder of the Cherokee Nation shall be abrogated by the President whenever a majority of the voters of such district shall so declare at an election duly ordered by him. No future law or regulation enacted in the Cherokee Nation shall take effect until ninety days after promulgation in the newspapers or by written posted notices in both the English and Cherokee languages.

8. No license to trade in the Cherokee Nation shall be granted by the

United States unless approved by the Cherokee national council, except in the districts mentioned in article 4.

9. The Cherokee Nation covenant and agree that slavery shall never hereafter exist in the nation. All freedmen, as well as all free colored persons resident in the nation at the outbreak of the rebellion and now resident therein or who shall return within six months and their descendants, shall have all the rights of native Cherokees. Owners of emancipated slaves shall never receive any compensation therefor.

10. All Cherokees shall have the right to sell their farm produce, live stock, merchandise, or manufactures, and to ship and drive the same to market without restraint, subject to any tax now or hereafter levied by the United States on the quantity sold outside of the Indian Territory.

11. The Cherokee Nation grant a right of way 200 feet in width through their country to any company authorized by Congress to construct a railroad from north to south and from east to west through the Cherokee Nation. The officers, employés, and laborers of such company shall be protected in the discharge of their duties while building or operating said road through the nation and at all times shall be subject to the Indian intercourse laws.

12. The Cherokees agree to the organization of a general council, to be composed of delegates elected to represent all the tribes in the Indian Territory, and to be organized as follows:

I. A census shall be taken of each tribe in the Indian Territory.

II. The first general council shall consist of one member for each tribe, and an additional member for each one thousand population or fraction thereof over five hundred. Any tribe failing to elect such members of council shall be represented by its chief or chiefs and headmen in the above proportion. The council shall meet at such time and place as the Superintendent of Indian Affairs shall approve. No session shall exceed thirty days in any one year. The sessions shall be annual; special sessions may be called by the Secretary of the Interior in his discretion.

III. The council shall have power to legislate upon matters pertaining to intercourse and relations of the tribes and freedmen resident in Indian Territory; the arrest and extradition of criminals and offenders escaping from one tribe or community to another; the administration of justice between members of different tribes and persons other than Indians and members of said tribes or nations; and the common defense and safety. All laws enacted by the council shall take effect as therein provided, unless suspended by the President of the United States. No law shall be enacted inconsistent with the Constitution or laws of the United States or with existing treaty stipulations. The council shall not legislate upon matters other than above indicated, unless jurisdiction shall be enlarged by consent of the national council of each nation or tribe, with the assent of the President of the United States.

IV. Said council shall be presided over by such person as may be designated by the Secretary of the Interior.

V. The council shall elect a secretary, who shall receive from the United States an annual salary of $500. He shall transmit a certified copy of the council proceedings to the Secretary of the Interior and to each tribe or nation in the council.

VI. Members of the council shall be paid by the United States $4 a day during actual attendance on its meetings and $4 for every 20 miles of necessary travel in going to and returning therefrom.

13. The United States may establish a court or courts in the Indian Territory, with such organization and jurisdiction as may be established by law, provided that the judicial tribunals of the Cherokee Nation shall retain exclusive jurisdiction in all civil and criminal cases arising within their country in which members of the nation shall be the only parties, or where the cause of action shall arise in the Cherokee Nation, except as otherwise provided in this treaty.

14. Every society or denomination erecting or desiring to erect buildings for missionary or educational purposes shall be entitled to select and occupy for those purposes 160 acres of vacant land in one body.

15. The United States may settle any civilized Indians, friendly with the Cherokees, within the latter's country on unoccupied lands east of 96°, on terms agreed upon between such Indians and the Cherokees, subject to the approval of the President of the United States. If any tribe so settling shall abandon its tribal organization and pay into the Cherokee national fund a sum bearing the same proportion to such fund as said tribe shall in numbers bear to the population of the Cherokee Nation such tribe shall be incorporated into and ever after remain a part of that nation on equal terms with native citizens thereof.

If any tribe so settling shall decide to preserve its tribal organization, laws, customs, and usages not inconsistent with the constitution and laws of the Cherokee Nation, it shall have set apart in compact form for use and occupancy a tract equal to 160 acres for each member of the tribe. Such tribe shall pay for this land a price agreed upon with the Cherokees, subject to the approval of the President of the United States, and in case of disagreement the price to be fixed by the President.

Such tribe shall also pay into the national fund a sum to be agreed upon by the respective parties, not greater in proportion to the whole existing national fund and the probable proceeds of the lands herein ceded or authorized to be ceded or sold than their numbers bear to the whole number of Cherokees, and thereafter they shall enjoy all the rights of native Cherokees.

No Indians without tribal organization, or who having one shall have determined to abandon the same, shall be permitted to settle in the Cherokee country east of 96° without the permission of the proper Cherokee authorities. And no Indians determining to preserve their tribal organization shall so settle without such consent, unless the President, after a full hearing of the Cherokee objections thereto, shall deem them insufficient and authorize such settlement.

16. The United States may settle friendly Indians on any Cherokee lands west of 96°; such lands to be selected in compact form and to equal in quantity 160 acres for each member of the tribe so settled. Such tribe shall pay therefor a price to be agreed upon with the Cherokees, or, in the event of failure to agree, the price to be fixed by the President. The tract purchased shall be conveyed in fee simple to the tribe so purchasing, to be held in common or allotted in severalty as the United States may decide.

The right of possession and jurisdiction over the Cherokee country west of 96° to abide with the Cherokees until thus sold and occupied.

17. The Cherokee Nation cedes to the United States, in trust to be surveyed, appraised, and sold for the benefit of that nation, the tract of 800,000 acres sold to them by the United States by article 2, treaty of 1835, and the strip of land ceded to the nation by article 4, treaty of 1835, lying within the State of Kansas, and consents that said lands may be included in the limits and jurisdiction of said State. The appraisement shall not average less than $1.25 per acre, exclusive of improvements.

The Secretary of the Interior shall, after due advertisement for sealed bids, sell such lands to the highest bidders for cash in tracts of not exceeding 160 acres each at not less than the appraised value. Settlers having improvements to the value of $50 or more on any of the lands not mineral and occupied for agricultural purposes at the date of the signing of this treaty, shall, after due proof under rules to be prescribed by the Secretary of the Interior, be allowed to purchase at the appraised value the smallest quantity of land to include their improvements, not exceeding 160 acres each.

The expenses of survey and appraisement shall be paid out of the proceeds of the sale of the lands, and nothing herein shall prevent the Secretary of the Interior from selling to any responsible party for cash all of the unoccupied portion of these lands in a body, for not less than $800,000.

18. Any lands owned by the Cherokees in Arkansas or in States east of the Mississippi River may be sold by their national council, upon the approval of the Secretary of the Interior.

19. All Cherokees residing on the ceded lands desiring to remove to the Cherokee country proper shall be paid by the purchasers the appraised value of their improvements. Such Cherokees desiring to remain on the lands so occupied by them shall be entitled to a patent in fee simple for 320 acres each, to include their improvements, and shall thereupon cease to be members of the nation.

20. Whenever the Cherokee national council shall so request, the Secretary of the Interior shall cause the country reserved for the

Cherokees to be surveyed and allotted among them at the expense of the United States.

21. The United States shall at its own expense cause to be run and marked the boundary line between the Cherokee Nation and the States of Arkansas, Missouri, and Kansas as far west as the Arkansas River, by two commissioners, one of whom shall be designated by the Cherokee national council.

22. The Cherokee national council shall have the privilege of appointing an agent to examine the accounts of the nation with the United States, who shall have free access to all the accounts and books in the Executive Departments relating to the business of the Cherokees.

23. All funds due the nation or accruing from the sale of their lands shall be invested in United States registered stocks and the interest paid semi-annually on the order of the Cherokee Nation, and applied to the following purposes : 35 per cent. for the support of the common schools of the nation and educational purposes; 15 per cent. for the orphan fund, and 50 per cent. for general purposes, including salaries of district officers. The Secretary of the Interior, with the approval of the President, may pay out of the funds due the nation, on the order of the national council, an amount necessary to meet outstanding obligations of the Cherokee Nation, not exceeding $150,000.

24. Three thousand dollars shall be paid out of the Cherokee funds to the Rev. Evan Jones, now in poverty and crippled, as a reward for forty years' faithful missionary labors in the nation.

25. All bounty and pay of deceased Cherokee soldiers remaining unclaimed at the expiration of two years shall be paid as the national council may direct, to be applied to the foundation and support of an orphan asylum.

26. The United States guarantee to the Cherokees the quiet and peaceable possession of their country and protection against domestic feuds and insurrection as well as hostilities of other tribes. They shall also be protected from intrusion by all unauthorized citizens of the United States attempting to settle on their lands or reside in their territory. Damages resulting from hostilities among the Indian tribes shall be charged to the tribe beginning the same.

27. The United States shall have the right to establish one or more military posts in the Cherokee Nation. No sutler or other person, except the medical department proper, shall have the right to introduce spirituous, vinous, or malt liquors into the country, and then only for strictly medical purposes. All unauthorized persons are prohibited from coming into or remaining in the Cherokee Nation, and it is the duty of the United States agent to have such persons removed as required by the Indian intercourse laws of the United States.

28. The United States agree to pay for provisions and clothing furnished the army of Appotholehala in the winter of 1861 and 1862 a sum not exceeding $10,000.

29. The United States agree to pay out of the proceeds of sale of Cherokee lands $10,000, or so much thereof as may be necessary, to defray the expenses of the Cherokee delegates and representatives invited to Washington by the United States to conclude this treaty, and also to pay the reasonable costs and expenses of the delegates of the Southern Cherokees.

30. The United States agree to pay not exceeding $20,000 to cover losses sustained by missionaries or missionary societies, in being driven from the Cherokee country by United States agents and on account of property taken and destroyed by United States troops.

31. All provisions of former treaties not inconsistent with this treaty shall continue in force; and nothing herein shall be construed as an acknowledgment by the United States or as a relinquishment by the Cherokee Nation of any claims or demands under the guarantees of former treaties, except as herein expressly provided.

TREATY CONCLUDED APRIL 27, 1868; PROCLAIMED JUNE 10, 1868.[1]

Held at Washington, D. C., between Nathaniel G. Taylor, commissioner on the part of the United States, and the duly authorized delegates of the Cherokee Nation.

MATERIAL PROVISIONS.

This treaty is concluded as a supplemental article to the treaty of July 19, 1866.

After reciting that a contract was entered into August 30, 1866, for the sale of the Cherokee neutral land, between James Harlan, Secretary of the Interior, and the American Emigrant Company; that such contract had been annulled as illegal by O. H. Browning, as Secretary of the Interior, who in turn entered into a contract of sale October 9, 1867, with James F. Joy, for the same lands, it is agreed by this treaty, in order to prevent litigation and to harmonize conflicting interests, as follows, viz: An assignment of the contract of August 30, 1866, with the American Emigrant Company shall be made to James F. Joy. Said contract as hereinafter modified is reaffirmed and declared valid. The contract with James F. Joy of October 9, 1867, shall be relinquished and canceled by said Joy or his attorney. The said first contract, as hereinafter modified, and the assignment thereof, together with the relinquishment of the second contract, are hereby ratified and confirmed whenever such assignment and relinquishment shall be entered of record in the Department of the Interior, and when said Joy shall have accepted such assignment and entered into contract to perform all the obligations of the American Emigrant Company under said first contract as hereinafter modified.

The modifications of said contract are declared to be:

1. Within ten days from the ratification of this treaty, $75,000 shall

---

[1] United States Statutes at Large, Vol. XVI, p. 727.

be paid to the Secretary of the Interior, as trustee for the Cherokee Nation.

2. The other deferred payments shall be paid when they fall due, with interest only from the ratification hereof.

It is distinctly understood that said Joy shall take only the residue of said lands after securing to "actual settlers" the lands to which they are entitled under the amended seventeenth article of the treaty of July 19, 1866. The proceeds of the sales of such lands so occupied by settlers shall inure to the benefit of the Cherokee Nation.

HISTORICAL DATA.

UNITED STATES DESIRE TO REMOVE INDIANS FROM KANSAS TO INDIAN TERRITORY.

It had for several years been the hope of the Government that so soon as the war was ended arrangements could be perfected whereby concessions of territory could be obtained from the principal Southern tribes. To territory thus acquired it was proposed, after obtaining their consent, to remove the several tribes possessing reservations in Kansas, or at least such of them as were not prepared or willing to dissolve their tribal relations and become citizens of the United States. The fertile and agreeable prairies of that State were being rapidly absorbed by an ever increasing stream of immigration, which gave promise as soon as the war should close and the armies be disbanded of an indefinite increase. The numerous Indian reservations dotting the face of the State in all directions afforded most desirable farming and grazing lands that would soon be needed for this rapidly multiplying white population.

COUNCIL OF SOUTHERN TRIBES AT CAMP NAPOLEON.

It was, therefore, with much gratification that the Secretary of the Interior learned during the month of June, 1865,[1] of the holding of a council at Camp Napoleon, Chattatomha, on the 24th of May preceding, which was attended by representatives of all the southern and southwestern tribes, as well as by the Osages. At this council delegates representing each tribe had been appointed to visit Washington, authorized to enter into treaty negotiations. Before these delegations were ready to start, however, it had been determined by the President to appoint special commissioners, who should proceed to the Indian country and meet them at Fort Smith.

GENERAL COUNCIL AT FORT SMITH.

This commission as constituted consisted of D. N. Cooley, Commissioner of Indian Affairs; Elijah Sells, superintendent of Indian affairs; Thomas Wistar, a leading Quaker; General W. S. Harney, of the United States Army; and Col. E. S. Parker, of General Grant's

---
[1] Letter of General J. J. Reynolds to Secretary of the Interior, June 28, 1865; printed in report of Commissioner of Indian Affairs for 1865, p. 295.

staff.[1] Proceeding to Fort Smith, the council was convened on the 8th day of September, and was attended by delegates representing the Creeks, Choctaws, Chickasaws, Cherokees, Seminoles, Osages, Senecas, Shawnees, Quapaws, Wyandots, Wichitas, and Comanches. In opening the council the Indians were informed that the commissioners had been sent to ascertain their disposition and feeling toward the United States; that most of them had violated their treaty obligations to the Government and, by entering into diplomatic relations with the so-called Confederate States, had forfeited all right to the protection of the United States and subjected their property to the penalty of confiscation.

They were assured, however, that the Government had no disposition to deal harshly with them. On the contrary, it was desirous of undertaking such measures as would conduce to their happiness, and was especially determined to grant handsome recognition to those of them whose loyalty had been so firmly and consistently manifested in the face of the most cruelly adverse conditions. The council continued in session for thirteen days. On the second day the Indians were informed that the commissioners were empowered to enter into treaties with the several tribes upon the basis of the following propositions:

1. That opposing factions of each tribe must enter into a treaty for permanent peace and amity among themselves; also between each other as tribes, and with the United States.

2. The tribes settled in the "Indian country" should bind themselves at the call of the United States authorities to assist in compelling the wild tribes of the plains to keep the peace.

3. Slavery should be abolished and measures should be taken to incorporate the slaves into the several tribes, with their rights guaranteed.

4. A general stipulation as to the final abolition of slavery.

5. A part of the Indian country should be set apart to be purchased for the use of such Indians from Kansas or elsewhere as the Government should desire to colonize therein.

6. That the policy of the Government to unite all the Indian tribes of this region into one consolidated government should be accepted.

7. That no white persons, except Government employés or officers or employés of internal improvement companies authorized by Government, should be permitted to reside in the country unless incorporated with the several nations.

Reasons for Cherokee disloyalty.—The subsequent sessions of the council were largely taken up in the discussion of these propositions by the representatives of the various tribes. It is only with the conduct of the Cherokees, however, that the present history is concerned. The address of the representatives of the "loyal" portion of this tribe is especially noteworthy in this, that they charged the cause of their alliance with the rebel authorities upon the United States, by reason of the

---

[1] Report of D. N. Cooley, president of the commission, dated October 30, 1865.

latter having violated its treaty obligations in failing to give them protection, whereby they were *compelled* to enter into treaty relations with the Confederacy. This statement the president of the commission took occasion to traverse, and to assure them of the existence of abundant evidence that their alliance with the Confederacy was voluntary and unnecessary.

Before the close of the council it was ascertained that no final and definite treaties could be made with the tribes represented, for the reason that until the differences between the loyal and disloyal portions could be healed no truly representative delegations of both factions could be assembled in council. Preliminary articles of peace and amity with the different factions of each tribe were prepared and signed as a basis for future negotiations.

Factional hostility among the Cherokees.—The only tribe with whom the commissioners were unsuccessful in re-establishing friendly relations between these factions was the Cherokees.[1]

The ancient feuds between the Ross and Ridge parties were still remembered. Many of the latter who had remained under Stand Watie in the service of the Confederacy until the close of the war were yet debarred from returning to their old homes, and were living in great destitution on the banks of the Red River.[2] When the Ross party had returned to their allegiance, in 1863, their national council had passed an act of confiscation[2] against the Watie faction, which had been enforced with the utmost rigor, so that some five or six thousand members of the tribe had been rendered houseless, homeless, and vagabonds upon the face of the earth. All prospect of securing a reconciliation between these parties was for the time being abandoned by the commissioners, and the proposition was seriously considered of securing a home for Watie and his followers among the Choctaws or Chickasaws.[3]

John Ross not recognized as principal chief.—On the day[4] on which the draft of the proposed preliminary treaty was presented to the council by the commissioners John Ross arrived in the camp of the Cherokees. It had already been determined by the commissioners among themselves that his record had been such as to preclude his recognition by them as principal chief of that nation, and it was believed that his influence was being used to prevent the loyal Cherokees from coming to any amicable arrangement with their Southern brethren.

The chairman therefore read to the council[5] a paper signed by the several commissioners, reciting the machinations and deceptions of John Ross. It was alleged that he did not represent the will and wishes of the loyal Cherokees, and was not the choice of any considerable por-

---

[1] Report of D. N. Cooley, president of the commission, dated October 30, 1865.

[2] Report of Commissioner of Indian Affairs for 1865, p. 36.

[3] Report of Elijah Sells, superintendent of Indian Affairs, October 16, 1865.

[4] September 13, 1865.

[5] September 15, 1865.

tion of the nation for the office claimed by him, an office which by the Cherokee law the commissioners believed he did not in fact hold. They therefore refused, as commissioners representing the interests of the United States, to recognize Ross in any manner as the chief of the Cherokee Nation.

Loyal Cherokees will sign treaty conditionally.—At the same sitting of the council, Colonel Reese, of the loyal Cherokee delegation, declared that they were willing to sign the proposed treaty, but in so doing would not acknowledge that they had forfeited their rights and privileges to annuities and lands as set forth in the preamble, but that their signatures must be made under the following statement, viz: "We, the loyal delegation, acknowledge the execution of the treaty of October 7, 1861, but we solemnly declare that the execution was procured by the coercion of the rebel army."

Southern Cherokees will sign treaty conditionally.—On the following day[1] the credentials of the Southern Cherokees were presented by E. C. Boudinot, accompanied by the statement that they cordially acceded to the 1st, 2d, 4th, 5th, and 7th propositions of the commissioners without qualification; that they accepted the abolition of slavery as an accomplished fact, and were willing to give such fact legal significance by appropriate acts of council. They insisted, however, that it would neither be for the benefit of the emancipated negro nor for that of the Indian to incorporate the former into the tribe on an equal footing with its original members. They were also opposed to the policy of consolidating all the tribes in the Indian Territory under one government, because of the many incongruous and irreconcilable elements which no power could bring into a semblance of assimilation.[2]

Southern Cherokees want a division of territory.—They had already proffered and were willing again to proffer the olive-branch of peace and reconciliation to their brethren of the so called loyal portion of the nation, but respectfully urged that after all the blood that had been shed and the intense bitterness that seemed to fill the bosoms of their brethren they ought not to be expected to live in an undivided country. They wished peace, and they believed they could have it in no other way than by an equitable division of the Cherokee country in such manner as should seem most appropriate to the United States.

Statement by John Ross.—The delegation of loyal Cherokees at the next session of the council[3] presented their exceptions to the action of the commissioners in declining to recognize John Ross and that gentleman was permitted to make a statement in his own behalf. The constantly accumulating evidence against him was such, however, as to more fully confirm the commissioners in the propriety of their previous action.

---

[1] September 16, 1865.

[2] This objection to consolidation was afterwards withdrawn, and, based upon fuller information of the proposed plan, was most fully concurred in.

[3] September 18, 1865.

On the 21st of September the council adjourned, to meet again at the call of the Secretary of the Interior.

CONFERENCE AT WASHINGTON, D. C.

Early in 1866, in accordance with the understanding had at the adjournment of the Fort Smith council, delegations representing both factions of the Cherokees proceeded to Washington for the purpose of concluding some definite articles of agreement with the United States. They were represented by eminent counsel in the persons of General Thomas Ewing for the loyal and Hon. D. W. Voorhees for the Southern element. Many joint interviews and discussions were held in the presence of Commissioners Cooley, Parker, and Sells, but without any hopeful results. The bitterness exhibited in these discussions upon both sides gave but little promise that enmities of more than twenty years' standing could be subordinated to the demands of a peaceful and harmonious government. The Southern element, which numbered about sixty-five hundred, constituted but a minority of the whole nation. These, with the exception of perhaps two hundred, were still living in banishment among the Choctaws and Chickasaws, and felt it would be unsafe to return to their old homes with the Ross party in full possession of the machinery of government and ready to apply with severest rigor the enginery of their confiscation law. Their representatives were therefore instructed to demand, as the only hope for their future peace and happiness, a division of the Cherokee lands and funds in proportion to their numbers between the two contending parties.[1] On the other hand, the representatives of the Ross or loyal party insisted that there was no good reason existing why the Southern element should be unable to dwell harmoniously with them in the same country and under the same laws, which they asserted always had been and always would be impartially and justly administered, so far as they were concerned.

A just feeling of national pride would always forbid their consent to any scheme against the integrity and unity of the whole Cherokee Nation. But, while they were thus on principle compelled to antagonize the demand of the Southern faction, yet if that element felt the impossibility of living comfortably in the midst of their loyal brethren the latter were willing that the portion of their national domain known as the Canadian district should be devoted to their sole occupation and settlement for a period of two years or until the President of the United States should deem it inadvisable to longer continue such exclusiveness.[2] To this again the Southern Cherokees refused assent,

---

[1] Statement of Southern delegation at an interview held with Commissioners Cooley and Sells, March 30, 1866. They also proposed that a census be taken and each man be allowed to decide whether or not he would live under the jurisdiction of the Ross party.

[2] Statement of loyal delegation at interview held with Commissioners Cooley and Sells, March 30, 1866.

because of the insufficient area of the Canadian district, and because they were unwilling to trust themselves under the jurisdiction of their enemies' laws and courts.

Factious conduct of both parties.—Each faction was desirous of making a treaty with the Government, and each was fearful lest the United States should recognize the other as the proper party with which to conclude that treaty. The United States officials were convinced that the Ross party represented the rightfully constituted authorities of the nation, and their delegates were thus the only really authorized persons with whom a treaty could with strict propriety be made. But they were also convinced that it would be highly improper to conclude any treaty which should leave the Southern Cherokees in any degree subject to the malice and revengeful disposition of their enemies. It was the desire of the United States to secure from the Cherokees a cession of sufficient land upon which to colonize the Indian tribes then resident in Kansas. The Southern party therefore agreed to cede for that purpose all of the Cherokee domain west of 96° west longitude, and to sell the "neutral land" for the sum of $500,000, provided the Government would treat with them. The loyal party, however, refused to cede any territory for purposes of colonization east of 97° west longitude, and demanded $1,000,000 for the "neutral land," at the same time assuming that the United States had no right or authority to entertain any proposition from any other source whatever involving the disposition of the domain or funds of the Cherokee Nation.[1]

Interviews, consultations, and discussions followed each other in rapid succession, covering a period of several months, with no apparent approach toward a final agreement.

Treaty concluded with Southern Cherokees.—At length the United States commissioners despairing of success with the loyal element, concluded a treaty with the Southern party.[2]

Among other things, this treaty provided that a quantity of land equal to 160 acres for every man, woman, and child, including the freedmen belonging to the Southern party, and also for each North Carolina Cherokee who should, within one year, remove and join them, should be set apart in that portion of their territory known as the Canadian district, for their sole use and occupancy. In case this district should afford an insufficient area of land, there should be added a further tract extending northward and lying between Grand River and the Creek boundary, and still further northward and westward between that river and the line of 95° 30' west longitude, or a line as far west if necessary as 96° west longitude, until the necessary complement of land, based upon a census of their people, should be secured. It was further agreed that the Southern Cherokees should have exclusive

---

[1] Sundry interviews between Commissioners Cooley and Sells and the loyal and Southern delegations, from March to June, 1866.

[2] June 13, 1865.

jurisdiction and control in the Canadian district, southwest of the Arkansas River, and of all that tract of country lying northeast of the Arkansas River and bounded on the east by Grand River, north by the line of 36° 30′ north latitude, and west by 96° of west longitude and the Creek reservation. In consideration of these things, the Southern Cherokees ceded absolutely to the United States all other Cherokee lands owned by them, at such price as should be agreed upon by the respective parties, whenever the Northern or loyal Cherokees should agree with the United States to sell the same. The sale of the "neutral land" was provided for at a sum per acre to be fixed by the President, which should amount in the aggregate to not less than $500,000. In all future negotiations with the United States, as in the past, but one Cherokee Nation should be recognized, but each of the two parties or divisions should be represented by delegates in proportion to their respective numbers. All moneys due the nation should be divided between the parties in the same proportion, and whenever the state of feeling throughout the nation should become such as by their own desire to render a complete and harmonious reunion of the two factions practicable, the United States would consent to the accomplishment of such a measure.

This treaty was duly signed, witnessed, and transmitted through the Secretary of the Interior to the President for submission to the Senate of the United States. The President retained it for more than a month, when, upon the conclusion of a treaty under date of July 19, 1866,[1] with the loyal Cherokees, he returned the former to the commissioners at the time he transmitted the latter instrument to the Senate for the advice and consent of that body to its ratification.

Treaty concluded with loyal Cherokees.—The treaty of July 19, though not filling the full measure of desire on the part of the United States, and though not thoroughly satisfactory in its terms to either of the discordant Cherokee elements, was the best compromise that could be effected under the circumstances, and was ratified and proclaimed August 11, 1866. It is unnecessary to recite its provisions here, as a full abstract of them has been given in the preceding pages. Nine days prior to its conclusion the Secretary of the Interior addressed a communication to Commissioner Cooley, who was president of the board of treaty commissioners, reminding him of their action the preceding fall at Fort Smith in suspending John Ross from his functions as principal chief, suggesting that the reasons rendering that action necessary at the time no longer existed, and giving his consent, in case the commissioners should feel so inclined, to the immediate recognition of Ross in that capacity.

Death of John Ross.—The old man was at this time unable, by reason of illness, to participate in the deliberations concerning the new treaty,[2]

---

[1] United States Statutes at Large, Vol. XIV, p. 799.
[2] See preamble to treaty of July 19, 1866.

and within a few days thereafter he died. He was in many respects a remarkable man. Though of Scotch-Indian parentage he was the champion of the full-blood as against the mixed-blood members of the nation, and for nearly half a century had been a prominent figure in all the important affairs of the Cherokee Nation. Notwithstanding his many opportunities for immense gains he seems to have died a poor man and his family were left without the necessaries of life. His sixty slaves, and everything he possessed in the way of houses, stock, and other like property, were swept away during the war.[1]

CESSION AND SALE OF CHEROKEE STRIP AND NEUTRAL LANDS.

The seventeenth article of the treaty of July 19, 1866, ceded to the United States, in trust to be disposed of for the benefit of the Cherokees, both the tract known as the "neutral land," previously alluded to, and that known as the "Cherokee strip." The latter was a narrow strip, extending from the Neosho River west to the western limit of the Cherokee lands. The Cherokee domain, as described in the treaty of 1835, extended northward to the south line of the Osage lands. When the State of Kansas was admitted to the Union its south boundary was made coincident with the thirty-seventh degree of north latitude, which was found to run a short distance to the southward of the southern Osage boundary, thus leaving the narrow "strip" of Cherokee lands within the boundaries of that State.

The proviso of the seventeenth article just mentioned required that the lands therein ceded should be surveyed, after the manner of surveying the public lands of the United States, and should be appraised by two commissioners, one of whom should be appointed by the United States and the other by the Cherokee Nation, such appraisement not to average less than $1.25 per acre. After such appraisement, the lands were to be sold under the direction of the Secretary of the Interior on sealed bids, in tracts of not exceeding 160 acres each, for cash, with the proviso that nothing should forbid the sale, if deemed for the best interests of the Indians, of the entire tract of "neutral land" (except the por-

---

[1] John Ross, or Kooeskoowe, was of mixed Scotch and Indian blood on both father's and mother's side. His maternal grandfather was John Stuart, who for many years prior to the Revolutionary war was British superintendent of Indian affairs for the southern tribes and who married a Cherokee woman. He was born about 1790 in that portion of the Cherokee Nation within the present limits of Georgia, and died in Washington, D. C., August 1, 1866. As early as 1813 Ross made a trip to the Cherokee country west of the Mississippi, ascending the Arkansas River to the present limits of Indian Territory, and wrote a detailed account of the situation and prospects of his brethren, the character of the country, etc. In 1820 (and perhaps earlier) he had become president of the Cherokee national committee, and continued so until the adoption of a constitution by the Cherokee Nation, July 26, 1827. Of this constitutional convention Mr. Ross was the president, and under its operation he was elected principal chief, a position which he continued to hold until his death.

tion occupied by actual settlers) in one body to any responsible party for cash for a sum not less than $800,000. An exception was made as to the lands which were occupied by bona fide white settlers at the date of the signing of the treaty, who were allowed the privilege of purchasing at the appraised value, exclusive of their improvements, in quantities of not exceeding 160 acres each, to include such improvements.

The language of this seventeenth article being somewhat obscure and subject to different interpretations as to the actual intent concerning the method of disposing of the "Cherokee strip," no action was taken toward its survey and sale until the year 1872, when by an act of Congress[1] provision was made for the appraisal of that portion of it lying east of Arkansas River at not less than $2 per acre, and the portion west of that river at not less than $1.50 per acre. Further provision was also made, by the same act, for its disposal on certain conditions to actual settlers, and any portion not being rendered amenable to these conditions was to be sold on sealed bids at not less than the minimum price fixed by the act. A considerable quantity of the most fertile portion of the tract was thus disposed of to actual settlers, though, as an encouragement to the sale, Congress was induced to pass an act[2] extending the limit of payment required of settlers to January 1, 1875. The price fixed by the act of 1872 being so high as to render the remainder of the land unattractive to settlers, a subsequent act of Congress[3] directed that all unsold portions of the said tract should be offered through the General Land Office to settlers at $1.25 per acre, for the period of one year, and that all land remaining unsold at the expiration of that period should be sold for cash at not less than $1 per acre. This act was conditional upon the approval of the Cherokee national council, which assent was promptly given, and the lands were disposed of under its provisions.

Shortly after the ratification of the treaty of 1866 steps were taken toward a disposition of the "neutral lands." Under date of August 30 of that year Hon. James Harlan, Secretary of the Interior, entered into a contract with a corporation known as the American Emigrant Company, whereby that company became the purchaser, subject to the limitations and restrictions set forth in the seventeenth article of the treaty, of the whole tract of neutral land at the price of $1 per acre, payable in installments, running through a period of several years. This contract was subsequently declared invalid[4] by Hon. O. H. Browning, the successor of Secretary Harlan, on the score that the proviso "for cash," contained in the treaty of 1866, in the common business acceptation of the term, meant a payment of the purchase price in full by the

---

[1] May 11, 1872. United States Statutes at Large, Vol. XVII, p. 98.
[2] April 29, 1874. United States Statutes at Large, Vol. XVIII, p. 41.
[3] February 28, 1877. United States Statutes at Large, Vol. XIX, p. 265.
[4] See treaty of April 27, 1868. United States Statutes at Large, Vol. XVI, p. 727.

purchaser at the time of the sale, and was intended to forbid any sale on deferred payments.

In the following spring[1] an agreement was entered into between the Cherokee authorities and the Atlantic and Pacific Railway Company, which involved a modification of the seventeenth article of the treaty of 1866, and engaged to sell the "neutral lands" to that company on credit. This agreement was submitted by the Commissioner of Indian Affairs to the Secretary of the Interior for transmission through the President to the Senate for ratification as an amended article to the treaty of July 19, 1866, but did not meet with favorable action. Subsequently[2] the Secretary of the Interior entered into an agreement with James F. Joy, of Detroit, Mich., whereby the latter became the purchaser of all that portion of the "neutral land" not subject to the rights of actual settlers, at the price of $1 per acre in cash. Difficulties having arisen by reason of the conflicting claims of the different would-be purchasers, it was finally deemed judicious to obviate them by concluding a supplemental article to the treaty of 1866. This was accordingly done, at Washington, on the 27th of April, 1868, and the same was ratified and proclaimed on the 10th of June following.[3] This supplemental treaty provided for the assignment by the American Emigrant Company to James F. Joy of its contract of August 30, 1866. It was further stipulated that that contract, in a modified form, should be reaffirmed and declared valid, and that the contract entered into with James F. Joy on the 9th of October, 1867, should be relinquished and canceled. Furthermore, it was agreed that the first contract, as modified, and the assignment to Joy, together with the relinquishment of the second contract, should be considered ratified and confirmed whenever such assignment and relinquishment should be entered of record in the Department of the Interior and when James F. Joy should have accepted such assignment and entered into a contract with the Secretary of the Interior to assume and perform all the obligations of the American Emigrant Company under the first mentioned contract as modified.

The assignment of their contract with Secretary Harlan by the American Emigrant Company to James F. Joy was made on the 6th of June, 1868. The contract of October 9, 1867, between Secretary Browning and James F. Joy was relinquished by the latter June 8, 1868, and on the same day a new contract was entered into with Joy accepting the assignment of the American Emigrant Company and undertaking to assume and perform all the obligations of the original contractor thereunder, subject to the modifications prescribed in the supplemental treaty of April 27, 1868.[4]

---

[1] See report of Commissioner of Indian Affairs to Secretary of Interior, March 1, 1867, transmitting the agreement.
[2] October 9, 1867.
[3] United States Statutes at Large, Vol. XVI, p. 727.
[4] See Indian Office records.

HISTORICAL DATA 229

The requirement of the treaty of 1866 as to the appraisal of the neutral lands was carried into effect by the appointment of John T. Cox, on behalf of the United States, and of William A. Phillips, on behalf of the Cherokees, as commissioners of appraisal. From their report as corrected it is ascertained that the quantity awarded to settlers was 154,395.12[1] acres; quantity purchased by Joy under his contract, 640,199.69 acres. A portion of the lands awarded to settlers, but upon which default was made in payment, and amounting to 3,231.21[2] acres, was advertised and sold on sealed bids to the highest bidders.[3] A small portion[4] of the tract was also absorbed by the claims of Cherokees who were settled thereon. The entire area of the neutral lands, as shown by the plats of survey, was 799,614.72 acres.

APPRAISAL OF CONFISCATED PROPERTY—CENSUS.

In pursuance of the third article of the treaty of 1866, and in accordance with the terms of an act of Congress approved July 27, 1868,[5] H. R. Kretschmar, on behalf of the United States, and —— Stephens, on behalf of the Cherokee Nation, were appointed, in the summer of 1868,[6] commissioners to appraise the cost of property and improvements on farms confiscated and sold by the Cherokee Nation from acts growing out of the Southern rebellion. J. J. Humphreys had been appointed May 21 of the preceding year to perform the same duties, but had not fulfilled the object of his instructions. The commission reported[7] the value of the improvements of the character referred to as $4,657.

Mr. H. Tompkins was designated in the summer of 1867[8] to take the census of Cherokees in the Indian Territory contemplated by the twelfth article of the treaty of 1866. From his returns it appears that the nation then numbered 13,566 souls.

NEW TREATY CONCLUDED BUT NEVER RATIFIED.

During the two years following the conclusion of the treaty of 1866 peace and quietude prevailed among the Cherokees. They were blessed with abundant crops and the bitter animosities of the past years became greatly softened, insomuch that the Secretary of the Interior, in the spring of 1868,[9] under the authority of the President, directed that negotiations be opened with them for a new treaty in compliance with their request.[10] Articles of agreement were accordingly entered into

---

[1] See report of Commissioner Indian Affairs for 1870, p. 376.
[2] See report of Commissioner Indian Affairs for 1871, p. 671.
[3] August 11, 1871.
[4] 5,019.91 acres.
[5] United States Statutes at Large, Vol. XV, p. 222.
[6] August 27, 1868.
[7] December 23, 1868.
[8] July 6, 1867.
[9] March 3, 1868.
[10] February 26, 1868.

on the 9th of July, 1868,[1] between N. G. Taylor, commissioner on behalf of the United States, and the principal chiefs and delegates representing the Cherokee Nation. The reasons rendering this treaty both desirable and necessary are thus set forth in the preamble, viz:

Whereas the feuds and dissensions which for many years divided the Cherokees and retarded their progress and civilization have ceased to exist, and there remains no longer any cause for maintaining the political divisions and distinctions contemplated by the treaty of 19th July, 1866; and whereas the whole Cherokee people are now united in peace and friendship, and are earnestly desirous of preserving and perpetuating the harmony and unity prevailing among them; and whereas many of the provisions of said treaty of July 19, 1866, are so obscure and ambiguous as to render their true intent and meaning on important points difficult to define and impossible to execute and may become a fruitful source of conflict not only amongst the Cherokees themselves but between the authorities of the United States and the Cherokee Nation and citizens; and whereas important interests remain unsettled between the Government of the United States and the Cherokee Nation and its citizens, which in justice to all concerned ought to be speedily adjusted: Therefore, with a view to the preservation of that harmony which now so happily subsists among the Cherokees, and to the adjustment of all unsettled business growing out of treaty stipulations between the Cherokee Nation and the Government of the United States, it is mutually agreed by the parties to this treaty as follows, etc.

Among the more important objects sought to be accomplished, and for which provision was made in the treaty, were:

1. The abolition of all party distinctions among the Cherokees and the abrogation of all laws or treaty provisions tending to preserve such distinctions.

2. The boundaries of the Cherokee country are defined in detail and as extending as far west as the northeast corner of New Mexico.

3. The United States reaffirm all obligations to the Cherokees arising out of treaty stipulations or legislative acts of the Government.

4. The United States having by article 2 of the treaty with the Comanches and Kiowas of October 18, 1865, set apart for their use and occupation and that of other friendly tribes that portion of the Cherokee domain lying west of 98° W. longitude and south of 37° N. latitude; and having further, by article 16 of Cherokee treaty of July 19, 1866, set apart in effect for the like purpose of settling friendly Indians thereon all the remaining Cherokee domain west of 96° W. longitude, agree to pay to the Cherokees therefor, including the tract known as the "Cherokee strip," in the State of Kansas, and estimated to contain in the aggregate the quantity of 13,768,000 acres, the sum of $3,500,000. This agreement was accompanied with the proviso that the Cherokees should further relinquish to the United States all right and interest in and to that portion of the Cherokee "outlet" embraced within the Pan Handle of Texas, containing about 3,000,000 acres, as well as that portion within New Mexico and Colorado, excepting and reserving, however, all salines west of 99° to the Cherokees.

5. The United States agree to refund to the Cherokees the sum of

---

[1] See document "Fortieth Congress, second session — confidential — Executive 3 P."

$500,000 paid by the latter for the tract of "neutral land," under the treaty of 1835, together with 5 per cent. interest from the date of that treaty, and to apply for the use and benefit of the former all moneys accruing from the sale of that tract.

6. The United States agree to ascertain the number of acres of land reserved and owned by the Cherokee Nation in the State of Arkansas, and in States east of the Mississippi River, and to pay to the Cherokees the appraised value thereof.

7. The United States agree to pay all arrears of Cherokee annuities accruing during the war and remaining unpaid.

8. Citizens of the United States having become citizens of the Cherokee Nation, shall not be held to answer before any court of the United States any further than if they were native-born Cherokees. All Cherokees shall be held to answer for any offense committed among themselves within the Cherokee Nation only to the courts of that nation, and for any offense committed without the limits of the nation shall be answerable only in the courts of the United States.

9. The post and reservation of Fort Gibson having been reoccupied by the United States, it is agreed that all Cherokees who purchased lots at the former sale of the military reserve by the Cherokee authorities, after its abandonment by the United States, shall be reimbursed for all losses occasioned by such military reoccupation.

10. The United States shall continue to appoint a superintendent of Indian affairs for the Indian Territory and an agent for the Cherokees.

11. A commission of three persons (two citizens of the United States and one Cherokee) shall be appointed to pass upon and adjudicate all claims of the Cherokee Nation, or its citizens, against the United States, or any of the several States.

12. The powers of the agent provided for by the twenty-second article of the treaty of 1866 to examine the accounts of the Cherokee Nation with the United States are enlarged to include the accounts of individual Cherokees with the United States.

13. All claims against the United States for Cherokee losses through the action of the military authorities of the United States, or from the neglect of the latter to afford the protection to the Cherokees guaranteed by treaty stipulation, are to be examined and reported on by the commission appointed under the eleventh article of this treaty.

14. Full faith and credit shall be given by the United States to the public acts, records, and judicial proceedings of the Cherokee Nation when properly authenticated.

15. Cherokees east of the Mississippi River, who remove within three years to the Cherokee Nation, shall be entitled to all the privileges of citizens thereof. After that date they can only be admitted to citizenship by act of the Cherokee national council.

16. Every Cherokee shall have the free right to sell, ship, or drive to market any of his produce, wares, or live stock without taxation by the

United States, or any State, and no license to trade in the Cherokee Nation shall be granted unless approved by the Cherokee council.

17. Fifty thousand dollars shall be allowed for the expenses of the Cherokee delegation in negotiating this treaty, one half to be paid out of their national fund.

18. Executors and administrators of the owners of confiscated property shall have the right, under the third article of the treaty of 1866, to take possession of such property.

19. Twenty-four thousand dollars shall be paid by the Cherokee Nation to the heir of Bluford West, as the value of a saline and improvements of which he was dispossessed.

20. Abrogation is declared of so much of article 7, treaty of 1866, as vests in United States courts jurisdiction of causes arising between citizens of the Cherokee Nation, and transfers such jurisdiction to the Cherokee courts.

21. Provision of the treaty of 1866 relative to freedmen is reaffirmed; the United States guarantee the Cherokees in the possession of their lands and protection from domestic strife, hostile invasions, and aggressions by other Indian tribes or lawless whites.

BOUNDARIES OF THE CHEROKEE DOMAIN.

During the proceedings incident to the negotiation of this treaty the question arose as to what constituted the proper western limit of the Cherokee country.

The Cherokees themselves claimed that their territory extended at least as far west as 103° west longitude, being the northeast corner of New Mexico. Their claim was based in part upon the second article of the treaty of 1828,[1] the first article of the treaty of 1833,[2] the second article of the treaty of 1835,[3] and the first article of the treaty of 1846.[4]

The treaty of 1828 guaranteed to the Cherokees seven millions of acres of land, and then declared in the following words: "In addition to the seven millions of acres thus provided for, and bounded, the United States further guarantee to the Cherokee Nation a perpetual outlet west, and a free and unmolested use of all the country lying west of the western boundary of the above described limits, and as far west as the sovereignty of the United States and their right of soil extend."

This guarantee was reaffirmed in similar language by the treaties of 1833 and 1835, and the guaranty contained in the treaty of 1835 was reaffirmed by the treaty of 1846. The question, therefore, to be determined was what constituted the extreme western limit of the sovereignty of the United States in that vicinity.

The colony or province of Louisiana had originally belonged to France.

---

[1] United States Statutes at Large, Vol. VII, p. 311.
[2] Ibid., p. 414.
[3] Ibid., p. 478.
[4] United States Statutes at Large, Vol. IX, p. 871.

In 1762 it was transferred to Spain, but was by Spain retroceded to France by the treaty of 1800. In 1803 the Emperor Napoleon, fearing a war with England and the consequent occupation of the territory by that power, ceded it to the United States, but the boundaries of the cession were very indefinite and, according to Chief Justice Marshall, were couched in terms of "studied ambiguity."

It seems to have been consistently claimed by the United States up to the treaty of 1819 with Spain that the western boundary of the Louisiana purchase extended to the Rio Grande River. The better opinion seemed also to be that it followed up the Rio Grande from the mouth to the mouth of the Pecos, and thence north. By that treaty, however, all dispute concerning boundaries was adjusted and the undefined boundary between Louisiana and Mexico was settled as following up the course of the Sabine River to the Red River; thence by the course of that river to the one hundredth meridian, thence north to the Arkansas River and following the course of that river to the forty-second parallel, and thence west to the Pacific Ocean. By many the position was taken that this treaty was a *nudum pactum,* and Henry Clay, when it was under consideration in the Senate, introduced a resolution into the House of Representatives declaring that Texas, being a part of the territory of the United States, could not be ceded by the treaty making power to a foreign country, and that the act was not only unauthorized by the Constitution but was void for another reason, viz, that this cession to Spain was in direct conflict with clear and positive stipulations made by us in the treaty with France as to the disposition of the whole territory. Under this theory of the invalidity of the treaty of 1819 the Cherokees claimed the extension of their boundary west of the one hundredth meridian. But, assuming the insufficiency of this claim, they still fortified their title upon another proposition. Mexico succeeded, by the consummation of her independence, to all the territorial rights of Spain in this region. Texas in turn achieved her independence of Mexico in 1836. In March, 1845, Texas became one of the United States, and thus, according to the Cherokee assumption, " the United States again came into possession of that portion of the outlet west of 100°, if indeed it had ever been a part of the territory claimed by Mexico and which by Texan independence she was forced to relinquish. The United States, more than a year after she had come into possession of the country now claimed by the Cherokees, reaffirmed the grant to them, that is to say, by the treaty of August 17, 1846."

The "portion of the outlet west of 100°" here alluded to is the strip of country lying between Kansas and Texas from north to south and between the 100° and New Mexico from east to west. By act of Congress of September 9, 1850,[1] the east boundary of New Mexico was fixed at 103° west longitude and the north boundary of Texas at 36°

---

[1] United States Statutes at Large, Vol. IX, p. 446.

30′ north latitude, and by act of May 30, 1854,[1] the south boundary of Kansas was established at 37° north latitude, thus leaving this strip of country outside the limits of any organized State or Territory, and so it still remains. This claim of the Cherokees was admitted by the Commissioner of Indian Affairs at the time of the conclusion of the treaty of July 9, 1868, to be a valid one, and was inserted in the boundaries defined by that treaty. The treaty, however, failed of ratification, and it was afterwards determined by the executive authorities of the United States that at the date of the treaty of 1835 with the Cherokees the sovereignty of the United States extended only to the one hundredth meridian, and that the reaffirmation of the treaty guarantee of 1835 by subsequent treaties was not intended to enlarge the area of their territory, but simply as an assurance that the United States were fully conscious of their obligation to maintain the integrity of such guarantee. Consequently the Cherokee outlet was limited in its western protraction to that meridian.

DELAWARES, MUNSEES, AND SHAWNEES JOIN THE CHEROKEES.

By the fifteenth article of the treaty of 1866 provision was made that, upon certain conditions, the United States should have the right to settle civilized Indians upon any unoccupied Cherokee territory east of 96° west longitude. The material conditions limiting this right were that terms of settlement should be agreed upon between the Cherokees and the Indians so desiring to settle, subject to the approval of the President of the United States; also that, in case the immigrants desired to abandon their tribal relations and become citizens of the Cherokee Nation, they should first pay into the Cherokee national fund a sum of money which should sustain the same proportion to that fund that the number of immigrant Indians should sustain to the whole Cherokee population. If, on the other hand, the immigrants should decide to preserve their tribal relations, laws, customs, and usages not inconsistent with the constitution and laws of the Cherokee Nation, a tract of land was to be set apart for them by metes and bounds which should contain, if they so desired, a quantity equal to 160 acres for each soul. For this land they were to pay into the Cherokee national fund a sum to be agreed upon between themselves and the Cherokees, subject to the approval of the President, and also a sum bearing a ratio to the Cherokee national fund not greater than their numbers bore to the Cherokees. It was also stipulated that, if the Cherokees should refuse their assent to the location of any civilized tribe (in a tribal capacity) east of 96°, the President of the United States might, after a full hearing of the case, overrule their objections and permit the settlement to be made.

The Delawares were the first tribe to avail themselves of the benefits of the foregoing treaty provisions. Terms of agreement were entered

---

[1] United States Statutes at Large, Vol. X, p. 283.

into between them and the Cherokees, which were ratified by the President on the 11th of April, 1867. Under the conditions of this instrument the Delawares selected a tract of land equal to 160 acres for each member of their tribe who should remove to the Cherokee country. For this tract they agreed to and did pay one dollar per acre. They also paid their required proportional sum into the Cherokee national fund. The number of Delawares who elected to remove under this agreement was 985. The sums they were required to pay were: for land, $157,600; and as their proportion of the national fund, $121,834.65, the latter amount having been calculated on the basis of an existing Cherokee national fund of $1,678,000 and a population of 13,566.[1]

For a time after their removal the Delawares were much dissatisfied with what they characterized as the unequal operation of the Cherokee laws, and because much of the tract of land to which they were assigned was of an inferior character. At one time some two hundred of them left the Cherokee country, but after an absence of two years returned, since which a feeling of better contentment has prevailed. Following the Delawares, the Munsee or Christian Indians, a small fragmentary band who under the treaty of July 16, 1859, had become confederated with the Chippewas of Saginaw, Swan Creek, and Black River, residing in Kansas, perfected arrangements for their removal and assimilation with the Cherokees.

An agreement was entered into[2] at Tahlequah, Cherokee Nation, having this end in view, and which was duly filed with the Commissioner of Indian Affairs.[3] The condition of this agreement was that, after the complete dissolution of their relations with the Chippewas, the Munsees should pay into the Cherokee national fund all moneys that should be found due them in pursuance of such separation. In the spring of 1868 an effort was made by the Commissioner of Indian Affairs, under the authority of this same article of the treaty of 1866, to secure a tract of 900,000 acres for the location of the Navajoes. This tract, it was desired, should be so far east of 96° that sufficient room should be left between the Navajoes and that meridian to admit of the accommodation of a settlement of Cherokees thereon. This proposition, however, the Cherokees refused to entertain, asserting that the Navajoes were not civilized Indians within the meaning of the treaty of 1866.[4]

The next Indians to avail themselves of the privileges of Cherokee citizenship were the Shawnees. By the treaty of 1825[5] a reserve had been granted them covering an area in the richest portion of what is now

---
[1] Indian Office records.
[2] December 6, 1867.
[3] July 31, 1868.
[4] Letter of Cherokee delegation to Commissioner of Indian Affairs, April 23, 1868.
[5] Treaty of November 7, 1825, in United States Statutes at Large, Vol. VII, p. 284.

the State of Kansas 50 by 120 miles in extent. By a subsequent treaty in 1854,[1] they ceded, in deference to the demands of encroaching civilization, all of this immense tract except 200,000 acres. Among those who so elected, the greater portion of this diminished reserve was divided into individual allotments of 200 acres each. Patents were issued to the head of each family for the quantity thus allotted to the members of his or her family, with the power of alienation, subject to such restrictions as the Secretary of the Interior might prescribe. In course of time alienation was made by these allottees of the greater portion of their land; the money thus received was squandered with the thriftless prodigality that characterizes barbarous or semi-civilized tribes the world over, and their impoverished condition was rendered still more uncomfortable by the seeming determination of the rapidly increasing white settlers to take possession of their few remaining lands. In this unfortunate condition of affairs they turned their eyes for relief toward the country of the Cherokees. Negotiations were entered into which resulted in the conclusion of an agreement, under date of June 7, 1869, and which received the approval of President Grant two days later. By the terms of this compact, the Shawnees then residing in Kansas, as well as their absentee brethren in the Indian Territory and elsewhere, who should enroll themselves and permanently remove within two years to the Cherokee country, upon unoccupied lands east of 96°, should be incorporated into, and ever after remain a part of the Cherokee Nation, with the same standing in every respect as native Cherokees. In consideration of these benefits the Shawnees agreed to transfer to the Cherokee national fund a permanent annuity of $5,000 held by them under previous treaties, in addition to the sum of $50,000 to be derived from the sale of the absentee Shawnee lands provided for by the resolution of Congress approved April 7, 1869.[2] Under the provisions of this agreement, seven hundred and seventy Shawnees removed to and settled in the Cherokee country, as shown by the census roll filed[3] with the Commissioner of Indian Affairs.

FRIENDLY TRIBES TO BE LOCATED ON CHEROKEE LANDS WEST OF 96°.

In addition to the provision contained in the treaty of 1866 concerning the location of *civilized* Indians east of 96°, the sixteenth article of that treaty made further provison enabling the United States to locate *friendly* tribes on Cherokee lands west of that meridian. The conditions of this concession were that any tracts selected for such location should be in compact form and in quantity not exceeding 160 acres for each member of the tribe so located, and that the boundaries of the tracts should be surveyed and marked and should be conveyed in fee simple to the tribes respectively located thereon. It was further

---

[1] Treaty of May 10, 1854, in United States Statutes at Large, Vol. X, p. 1053.
[2] United States Statutes at Large, Vol. XVI, p. 53.
[3] August 14, 1871.

stipulated that the price to be paid for the lands so set apart should be such as might be agreed upon between the Cherokees and the immigrant tribes, subject to the approval of the President of the United States, who, in case of a disagreement between the parties in interest, was authorized to fix the value.

Osages.—The treaty of September 29, 1865,[1] with the Osages, having in view the possibility of some early arrangement whereby the Kansas tribes might be removed to Indian Territory, made provision that in case such a removal of the Osages should take place their remaining lands in Kansas should be disposed of and 50 per cent. of the proceeds might be applied to the purchase of their new home. Nothing was done in the line of carrying out this idea until the spring of 1868, when, in reply[2] to a communication from the Commissioner of Indian Affairs on the subject, the Cherokee delegation asserted the willingness of their nation to dispose of a tract for the future home of the Osages not exceeding 600,000 acres in extent and lying west of 96°, provided a reasonable price could be agreed upon for the same. A few weeks later[3] a treaty was concluded between the United States and the Osages, which made provision for setting apart a tract for their occupation in the district of country in question, but the treaty failed of ratification. The necessity for their removal from Kansas, however, increased in correspondence with the demands of advancing settlements, and Congress, by an act approved July 15, 1870,[4] provided that, whenever the Osages should give their assent, a tract should be set apart for their permanent occupancy in the Indian Territory equal in extent to 160 acres for each member of the tribe who should remove there. For this tract they were to pay a price not exceeding that paid by the United States, the cost to be defrayed out of the proceeds arising from the sale of their Kansas lands. The assent of the Osages to the provisions of this act was promptly secured through the medium of a commission consisting of J. V. Farwell, J. D. Lang, and Vincent Colyer, of the President's Board of Indian Commissioners. A tract was selected in the Cherokee country immediately west of 96°, as was supposed, and the Osages were removed to it. Their condition was for a time, however, most unsatisfactory. Many trespassers were found to be upon the lands selected for them. To crown this trouble, a new survey located the line of the 96th meridian a considerable distance to the west of what had previously been presumed its proper location. This survey deprived the Osages of the greater part of the tillable land upon which they had settled and included the most valuable of their improvements. To a proposition allowing the Osages to retain the lands thus found to be east of 96°, the Cherokees returned an emphatic refusal, on the ground that the

---

[1] United States Statutes at Large, Vol. XIV, p. 687.
[2] April 10, 1868.
[3] May 27, 1868.
[4] United States Statutes at Large, Vol. XVI, p. 362.

former were not "civilized Indians."[1] Another subject of annoyance was the inability of the Osages and Cherokees to agree upon a price for the lands selected by the former. The matter was therefore laid before the President, who, by executive order,[2] fixed the price to be paid at 50 cents per acre. To this action the Cherokees strenuously objected, urging that not only was the price too low, but that a uniform valuation ought to be fixed for all the Cherokee lands west of 96°.[3] To remedy the evils arising from these complications, legislation was asked of Congress approving a new selection for the Osages, and, by act approved June 5, 1872,[4] such selection was affirmed (the previous consent of the Cherokees having been obtained),[5] to include the tract of country "bounded on the east by the 96th meridian, on the south and west by the north line of the Creek country and the main channel of the Arkansas River, and on the north by the south line of the State of Kansas."

Kansas or Kaws.—This act contained a proviso that the Osages should permit the settlement within the limits of this tract of the Kansas or Kaw tribe of Indians, and a reservation was accordingly set off for them in the northwest corner, bounded on the west by the Arkansas River. The area of the country thus assigned to the Kaws was 100,137 acres, and of that portion intended for the occupation of the Osages 1,470,059 acres.[6]

The question of the future location of these Indians having been definitely settled, it only remained for an agreement to be reached concerning the price to be paid to the Cherokees for the tract so purchased. The value fixed by the President on the tract originally selected was considered as having no application to the lands set apart by the act of 1872. As in the first instance no agreement was reached between the Osages and Cherokees, and the President was again called on to establish the price. This he did, after much discussion of the subject, on the 14th of February, 1873. The price fixed was 70 cents per acre, and applied to the "Kaw reserve" as well as to that of the Osages.

Pawnees.—In further pursuance of the privilege accorded by the treaty of 1866, the Pawnee tribe has also been located on Cherokee lands west of 96°. The Pawnees are natives of Nebraska, and possessed as the remnant of their original domain a reservation on the Platte River, in that State. Their principal reliance as a food supply had been the buffalo, though to a very limited extent they cultivated corn and vegetables.

For two years prior to 1874, however, their efforts in the chase were almost wholly unrewarded, and during the summer of that year their

---

[1] Letter of Cherokee delegation to Commissioner of Indian Affairs, February 15, 1871.
[2] May 27, 1871.
[3] Letter of Cherokee delegation to Commissioner of Indian Affairs, June 10, 1871.
[4] United States Statutes at Large, Vol. XVII, p. 228.
[5] April 8, 1872.
[6] See surveyors' plats on file in Indian Office.

small crops were entirely destroyed by the ravages of the grasshoppers. The winter and spring of 1874–'75 found them, to the number of about three thousand, in a starving condition. In this dilemma they held a council and voted to remove to Indian Territory, asking permission at the same time to send the male portion of the tribe in advance to select a home and to break the necessary ground for planting crops. They also voted a request that the United States should proceed to sell their reserve in Nebraska, and thus secure funds for their proper establishment in the Indian Territory. Permission was granted them in accordance with their request, and legislation was asked of Congress to enable the desired arrangement to be carried into effect. Congress failed to take any action in relation to the subject during the session ending March 3, 1875. It therefore became necessary to feed the Pawnees during the ensuing season.[1]

The following year, by an act approved April 10,[2] Congress provided for the sale of the Pawnee lands in Nebraska, as a means of securing funds for their relief and establishment in their new home, the boundaries of which are therein described. It consists of a tract of country in the forks of the Arkansas and Cimarron Rivers comprising an area of 283,020 acres. Of this tract, 230,014 acres were originally a portion of the Cherokee domain west of 96° and were paid for at the rate of 70 cents per acre. The remainder was ceded to the United States by the Creek treaty of 1866.

Appraisal of the lands west of 96°.—By the 5th section of the Indian appropriation act of May 29, 1872,[3] the President of the United States was authorized to cause an appraisement to be made of that portion of the Cherokee lands lying west of 96° west longitude and west of the Osage lands, or, in other words, all of the Cherokee lands lying west of the Arkansas River and south of Kansas mentioned in the 16th article of the Cherokee treaty of July 19, 1866. No appropriation, however, was made to defray the expense of such an appraisal, and in consequence no steps were taken toward a compliance with the terms of the act. This legislation was had in deference to the long continued complaints of the Cherokees that the United States had, without their consent, appropriated to the use of other tribes a large portion of these lands, for which they (the Cherokees) had received no compensation. The history of these alleged unlawful appropriations of the Cherokee domain may be thus briefly summarized:

1. By treaty of October 18, 1865,[4] with the Kiowas and Comanches, the United States set apart for their use and occupancy an immense tract of country, which in part included all of the Cherokee country

---

[1] See report of Commissioner of Indian Affairs to Secretary of the Interior, March 6, 1875.
[2] United States Statutes at Large, Vol. XIX, p. 28.
[3] United States Statutes at Large, Vol. XVII, p. 190.
[4] United States Statutes at Large, Vol. XIV, p. 717.

west of the Cimarron River. No practical effect, however, was given to the treaty, because the United States had not at this time acquired any legal right to settle other tribes on the lands of the Cherokees and because of the fact that two years later[1] a new reservation was by treaty provided for the Kiowas and Comanches, no portion of which was within the Cherokee limits.

2. By the treaty of October 28, 1867,[2] with the Southern Cheyennes and Arapahoes the United States undertook to set apart as a reservation for their benefit all the country between the State of Kansas and the Arkansas and Cimarron Rivers. The bulk of this tract was within Cherokee limits west of 96°. As a matter of fact, however, the Cheyennes and Arapahoes could not be prevailed upon to take possession of this tract, and were finally, by Executive order,[3] located on territory to the southwest and entirely outside the Cherokee limits.

Pursuant to the act of May 29, 1872,[4] the Commissioner of Indian Affairs negotiated an agreement with the Southern Cheyennes and Arapahoes in the following autumn[5] by which they ceded to the United States all interest in the country set apart by the treaty of 1867, and accepted in lieu thereof a reserve which included within its limits a portion of the Cherokee domain lying between the Cimarron River and the North Fork of the Canadian.

This agreement with the Southern Cheyennes and Arapahoes not having been ratified by Congress, an agreement was concluded late in the following year[6] by the Commissioner of Indian Affairs with both the Cheyennes and the Arapahoes, whereby they jointly ceded the tract assigned them by the treaty of 1867, as well as all other lands to which they had any claim in Indian Territory, in consideration of which the United States agreed to set apart other lands in that Territory for their future home.

Like its predecessor, this agreement also failed of ratification by Congress, and the Indians affected by it still occupy the tract set apart by Executive order of 1869.

In the light of these facts it appears that although the United States made several attempts, without the knowledge or concurrence of the Cherokees, to appropriate portions of the latter's domain to the use of other tribes, yet as a matter of fact these tribes never availed or attempted to avail themselves of the benefits thus sought to be secured to them, and the Cherokees were not deprived at any time of an opportunity to sell any portion of their surplus domain for the location of other friendly tribes.

---

[1] Treaty of October 21, 1867, United States Statutes at Large, Vol. XV, p. 581.
[2] United States Statutes at Large, Vol. XV, p. 593.
[3] August 10, 1869.
[4] United States Statutes at Large, Vol. XVII, p. 190.
[5] October 24, 1872.
[6] November 18, 1873.

By a clause contained in the sundry civil appropriation act of July 31, 1876,[1] provision was made for defraying the expenses of the commission of appraisal contemplated by the act of 1872, and the Secretary of the Interior appointed[2] such a commission, consisting of Thomas V. Kennard, Enoch H. Topping, and Thomas E. Smith. Before the completion of the duties assigned them, Mr. Kennard resigned and William N. Wilkerson was appointed[3] to succeed him. The commission convened at Lawrence, Kansas, and proceeded thence to the Cherokee country, where they began the work of examination and appraisal. Their final report was submitted to the Commissioner of Indian Affairs under date of December 12, 1877. From this report it appears that the commissioners in fixing their valuations adopted as the standard of their appraisal one-half the actual value of the lands, on the theory that being for Indian occupancy and settlement only they were worth only about half as much as they would have been if open to entry and settlement by the white people.

The entire tract, including the Pawnee reserve, contains 6,574,576.05 acres, and was appraised at an average valuation of $41\frac{1}{4}$ cents per acre. The average valuation placed upon the Pawnee reserve separately was 59 cents per acre, leaving the average of the remaining 6,344,562.01 acres 40.47 cents per acre.

To this standard of appraisal the Cherokees strenuously objected as being most unfair and unjust to them, claiming that the same measure of value used by the United States in rating its lands of a similar character in the adjoining State of Kansas, and from which they were separated only by an imaginary line, should prevail in determining the price to be paid for the Cherokee lands.

The Secretary of the Interior, after a careful examination of the whole subject, was of the opinion[4] that the restriction placed upon the use of these lands (being limited to Indian occupancy only) did not warrant a reduction of 50 per cent. in an appraisal of their value.

The price paid by the Osages for their reserve was 70 cents per acre. The Pawnee tract was of about the same general character as that of the Osages, and there seemed to be no good reason why the same price should not be allowed to the Cherokees therefor. This Pawnee tract was appraised by the commissioners at 59 cents per acre. As the appraisal of the whole unoccupied country west of 96° was made by the same appraisers and upon the same basis, if an increase was determined upon in the case of the Pawnee tract from 59 to 70 cents per acre, it was only just that a proportionate increase above the appraised value of the remainder of the lands should also be allowed.

---

[1] United States Statutes at Large, Vol. XIX, p. 120.
[2] January 30, 1877.
[3] September 8, 1877.
[4] Letter of the Secretary of the Interior to the President, June 21, 1879.

This would give an increase for the latter from 40.47 cents to 47.49 per acre. The adoption of this standard was therefore recommended to the President and was by him approved and ratified.[1]

In addition to the Osages, Kansas, and Pawnees there have been removed to the Cherokee lands west of 96° the Poncas, a portion of the Nez Percés, and the Otoes and Missourias.

Poncas.—An appropriation of $25,000 was made by act of Congress approved August 15, 1876,[2] for the removal of the Poncas, whenever their assent should be obtained. After much trouble and a threatened resort to military force, their assent to remove to the Indian Territory was secured in the beginning of 1877.[3] They came overland from Nebraska in two different parties and encountered great hardships, but finally reached the Territory, where they were temporarily located on the northeast portion of the Quapaw reserve, a few miles from Baxter Springs, Kansas.[4]

They were not satisfied with the location, which was in many respects unsuitable, especially in view of its proximity to the white settlements. They were, therefore, permitted to make another selection, which they did in the Cherokee country, on the west bank of the Arkansas, including both banks of the Salt Fork at its junction with the parent stream. To this new home they removed in 1878,[5] but it was not until 1881[6] that Congress made an appropriation out of which to pay the Cherokees for the land so occupied. This tract embraces 101,894.31 acres, for which the price of 47.49 cents per acre, fixed by the President, was paid.

Nez Percés.—The Nez Percés, previously alluded to, are the remnant of Chief Joseph's band, who surrendered to General Miles in 1877. They were at first removed from the place of their surrender to Fort Leavenworth, Kansas, where they arrived in November of that year as prisoners of war, to the number of 431. Congress having made provision[7] for their settlement in the Indian Territory, a reservation was selected for them on both sides of the Salt Fork of the Arkansas. To this tract, which adjoined the Poncas on the west, they removed in the summer of 1879,[8] having in the mean time lost a large number by death, the mortality being occasioned in great measure by their unsanitary location while at Fort Leavenworth. The reserve selected for them contains 90,735 acres and was paid for at the same price as that of the Poncas.

Otoes and Missourias.—By act of March 3, 1881,[6] provision was also

---

[1] June 23, 1879.
[2] United States Statutes at Large, Vol. XIX, p. 187.
[3] January 27, 1877.
[4] Report of Commissioner of Indian Affairs for 1877, pp. 21-23.
[5] Report of Commissioner of Indian Affairs for 1878, p. xxxvi.
[6] United States Statutes at Large, Vol. XXI, p. 380.
[7] Act of May 27, 1878, United States Statutes at Large, Vol. XX, p. 63.
[8] Report of Commissioner of Indian Affairs for 1879, p. xl.

made for the removal of the Otoes and Missourias to the Indian Territory and for the sale of their lands in Nebraska.

A reservation was accordingly selected for them west of the Arkansas River and south of the Ponca Reserve, to which they were removed in the autumn of the same year.[1] It contains 129,113.20 acres and was paid for at the same rate as that of the Poncas and Nez Percés.[2]

EAST AND NORTH BOUNDARIES OF CHEROKEE COUNTRY.

For many years there had been much doubt and dispute concerning the correctness of the boundary line between the Cherokee Nation and the adjacent States. Especially had this been the cause of much controversy with the citizens of Arkansas. In the interest of a final adjustment of the matter, it was stipulated in the twenty-first article of the Cherokee treaty of July 19, 1866, that the United States should, at its own expense, cause such boundary to be resurveyed between the Cherokee Nation and the States of Arkansas, Missouri, and of Kansas as far west as the Arkansas River, and the same should be marked by permanent and conspicuous monuments by two commissioners, one of whom should be designated by the Cherokee national council.

Nothing definite was done in pursuance of this provision until the year 1871, when W. D. Gallagher was[3] appointed a commissioner on behalf of the United States to co-operate with the commissioner on the part of the Cherokees. Mr. Gallagher declined and R. G. Corwin was substituted in his stead,[4] but he having also refused to serve, the place was finally filled by the appointment[5] of James M. Ashley. The Cherokee national council on their part selected John Lynch Adair. The commission advertised for proposals for the surveying, and, as a result, entered into contract with D. P. Mitchell, who completed the survey to the satisfaction of the commissioners.[6] The new line from Fort Smith, Ark., to the southwest corner of Missouri ran north 7° 50′ west, 77 miles 39.08 chains; thence to the southeast corner of the Seneca lands it ran north 0° 02′ west 8 miles 53.68 chains. The north boundary between the nation and the State of Kansas, extending from the Neosho to the Arkansas River, was protracted due west on the 37° of north latitude and was found to be 105 miles 60 chains and 75 links in length. The report of the commissioners was approved by the Secretary of the

---

[1] Report of Commissioner of Indian Affairs for 1881, p. lxiii. The removal was accomplished between October 5 and October 23.

[2] Deeds were executed June 14, 1883, by the Cherokee Nation to the United States in trust for each of the tribes located upon Cherokee country west of 96°, such deeds being in each case for the quantity of land comprised within the tracts respectively selected by or for them for their future use and occupation. See Report of Commissioner of Indian Affairs, for 1883, p. lii.

[3] February 27, 1871.
[4] April 14, 1871.
[5] May 4, 1871.
[6] The survey was approved by the commissioners December 11, 1871.

Interior, and although some distress for the time being was occasioned to individual settlers, whose improvements were by the resurvey of the line thrown within the limits of the Indian Territory, the boundary has been so plainly marked that "he who runs may read."

RAILROADS THROUGH INDIAN TERRITORY.

The series of treaties concluded in 1866 with the five principal tribes in Indian Territory all contained limited concessions of right of way for railroads through their country to the State of Texas. The eleventh article of the Cherokee treaty contained a grant of right of way 200 feet in width to a contemplated railroad through their domain from north to south and also from east to west. In pursuance of these treaty concessions, as essentially a part of the same scheme, Congress, by appropriate legislation,[1] granted public lands and privileges to the Kansas and Neosho, the southern branch of the Union Pacific, and the Atlantic and Pacific Railroad Companies, respectively, for the construction of their roads. The Leavenworth, Lawrence and Fort Gibson Railroad was also conceded like privileges. The stipulated point of entering the Indian Territory was in each case the west bank of Neosho River, where it crosses the Kansas line. As there seemed to be some question whether more than one line of road would be permitted to traverse the Territory in each direction a race was inaugurated between all the north and south lines, each in the effort to outstrip the other in reaching the prescribed point for entering the Indian country. The Union Pacific Southern Branch (subsequently known as the Missouri, Kansas, and Texas) Railway Company, in the fervency of their desire to reach the line first, omitted the construction of a portion of their route, and began operations within the limits of the Cherokee country without having received the previous permission of either the United States or the Cherokee authorities so to do. To this conduct the Cherokees made vigorous objection, and appealed to the Secretary of the Interior. That officer notified[2] the railroad officials that the Cherokees did not recognize their right to so intrude upon the Territory, and that no work of the kind referred to could be permitted therein until the Executive should be satisfied, by evidence submitted in proper manner, that such entry and occupation were in accordance with law. Thereupon the officers and attorneys of the several companies interested appeared and submitted arguments before the Secretary of the Interior on behalf of their respective interests. The point submitted for the consideration of the Secretary and for the determination of the President was, what rights had been given to railroad companies to construct railroads through the Indian Territory and what railroads, if any, were entitled to such privileges and right of way.

On the part of the Indians it was claimed that the whole scheme of

---

[1] Acts of July 25, 26, and 27, 1866.
[2] May 13, 1870.

treaties and of legislation looked to the construction of but a single trunk road through the Territory from north to south, and, as far as the Cherokee Nation was concerned, for the like construction of but a single road through its territory from east to west. This interpretation of the treaties and the laws was admitted to be the correct one by all the companies but the Missouri, Kansas, and Texas. This company insisted that the meaning of the legislation and of the treaties was to give the right of way to as many roads as might in any manner be authorized by Congress to enter the Territory.

The Secretary of the Interior in his opinion[1] expressed an emphatic concurrence in the interpretation insisted upon by the Cherokee delegation. He was further of the opinion that neither of the roads had so far earned a right to enter the Indian country by the construction of a continuous line of road to the legal point of entrance, but that as it might soon be necessary to decide which company should first completely fulfill the conditions of the law, an executive order ought to be issued declaring that no railroad company should be permitted to enter the Territory for the purpose of grading or constructing a railroad until a report should be received from a commission composed of the superintendents of Indian affairs for the central and southern superintendencies designating which company had first reached the line. These views and findings of the Secretary of the Interior were approved by the President and directed to be carried into effect.[2]

This commission reported[3] that the Union Pacific Railway, southern branch — otherwise the Missouri, Kansas, and Texas Railway — reached the northern boundary of the Indian Territory, in the valley of the Neosho River on the west side, and about one mile therefrom, at noon on the 6th day of June, 1870, and that at that time there was no other railroad nearer than 16 miles of that point.

Predicated upon this report, supplemented by the certificate of the governor of Kansas that it was a first class completed railway up to that point, permission was given the Missouri, Kansas, and Texas Railway Company by the President, under certain stipulations and restrictions as to the methods and character of construction, to proceed with the work of building a trunk road through the Indian Territory to a point at or near Preston, in the State of Texas, and the road was rapidly constructed under this authority.

The Atlantic and Pacific road, having no competitor, experienced no difficulty in securing the right of construction of its east and west line through the Cherokee country.

REMOVAL OF INTRUDERS — CHEROKEE CITIZENSHIP.

On various pretexts, both white and colored men had from time to time established themselves among the Cherokees and taken up their

---

[1] May 21, 1870.
[2] May 23, 1870.
[3] June 13, 1870.

residence as permanent citizens of the nation. The increase of their numbers at length became so formidable and their influence upon the national polity and legislation of the Cherokees so great as to excite the apprehension and jealousy of the latter.

The policy of their removal therefore became a subject of serious consideration with the national council. This involved a question as to what were the essential prerequisites of Cherokee citizenship, and who of the objectionable class were entitled, on any score, to the privileges of such citizenship, as well as who were mere naked intruders. Upon these points the national council assumed to exercise absolute control, and proceeded to enact laws for the removal of all persons, both white and colored, whom the council should declare not entitled to remain in the Cherokee country.[1] The action of the council in this respect was communicated to the Indian Department in the fall of 1874, through the United States agent for that tribe, coupled with a demand for the removal by the military force of the United States of all who had thus been declared to be intruders. The Department not being fully satisfied of the justice of this demand, detailed an inspector to proceed to the Indian country and make a thorough investigation of the subject. His report[2] revealed the fact that there were large numbers of people in that country who had been declared intruders by the national authorities, but who had presented to him strong *ex parte* evidence of their right to Cherokee citizenship, either by blood, by adoption, or under the terms of the 9th article of the treaty of 1866 defining the status of colored people. Affidavits in large numbers corroborative of the inspector's report continued to be filed in the Indian Department during the succeeding summer, from which it appeared that many persons belonging to each of the classes alluded to had applied to the courts or to the council of the nation for an affirmative ruling upon their claim to citizenship, but that in many instances such applications had been entirely ignored. In other cases, where the courts had actually affirmed the right of applicants, the council had arbitrarily and without notice placed their names upon the list of intruders and called upon the United States for their removal. In this situation of affairs the Indian Department advised[3] the principal chief of the Cherokees that the Department would neither remove these alleged intruders nor permit their removal until the Cherokee council had devised a system of rules by which authority should be vested in the Cherokee courts to hear and determine all cases involving the citizenship of any person. These rules should be subject to the approval of the Secretary of the

---

[1] The persons affected by this action were comprised within four classes, viz:
1. White persons who had married into the tribe.
2. Persons with an admixture of Indian blood, through either father or mother.
3. Adopted persons.
4. Persons of African descent who claimed rights under the treaty of 1866.

[2] February 15, 1876.

[3] October —, 1876.

Interior, to whom an appeal should also lie from any adverse decision of those courts. As there were a number of these intruders, however, who made no claim to the right of Cherokee citizenship, it was directed by the Interior Department, in the spring of 1877, that all who should not present *prima facie* evidence of such right should be summarily removed from the Territory. The main cause of difficulty, however, continuing unadjusted, the principal chief of the Cherokees asked the submission of the subject, from the Cherokee standpoint, to the Attorney-General of the United States for his opinion. This was done in the spring of 1879,[1] by the Commissioner of Indian Affairs through the Secretary of the Interior, wherein the former, alleging that the question submitted by the Cherokee authorities did not fully meet the subject in dispute, and being desirous that a complete statement of the case should be presented to the Attorney-General, suggested three additional inquiries for the consideration of that officer. These inquiries were, first, Have the Cherokee national authorities such original right of sovereignty over their country and their people as to vest in them the exclusive jurisdiction of all questions of citizenship in that nation without reference to the paramount authority of the United States? Second, If not, do they derive any such power or right by the provisions of any of the treaties beween the United States and the Cherokees? Third, Can they exclude from citizenship any of the Cherokees who did not remove under the provisions of the treaty of 1835 upon their removal to the Cherokee country as now defined by law? The reply[2] of the Attorney-General was to the effect that it seemed quite plain in executing such treaties as those with the Cherokees, the United States were not bound to regard simply the Cherokee law and its construction by the council of that nation, but that any Department required to remove alleged intruders must determine for itself, under the general law of the land, the existence and extent of the exigency upon which such requisition was founded.

One class of these so-called intruders, as previously suggested, was composed of colored people who resided in the Cherokee country prior to the war, either as slaves or freemen, and their descendants.

The fourth article of the treaty of July 19, 1866, contained a provision setting apart a tract within the Cherokee country known as the Canadian district, for the settlement and occupancy of "all the Cherokees and freed persons who were formerly slaves of any Cherokee, and all free negroes not having been such slaves who resided in the Cherokee Nation prior to June 1, 1861, who may within two years elect not to reside northeast of the Arkansas River and southeast of Grand River."

The fifth article of the same treaty guaranteed to such persons as should determine to reside in the district thus set apart the right to select their own local officers, judges, etc., and to manage and control

---

[1] April 4, 1879.
[2] December 12, 1879.

their local affairs in such manner as seemed most satisfactory to them not inconsistent with the constitution and laws of the Cherokee Nation or of the United States. Again it was provided by the ninth article of the treaty that all freedmen who had been liberated by voluntary act of their former owners or by law, as well as all free colored persons who were in the country at the commencement of the rebellion and were still residents therein or who should return within six months and their descendants, should have all the rights of native Cherokees.

Congressional legislation was sought in 1879, having in view the enforcement of this ninth article, but it failed of consummation.[1] The Cherokee council, in the mean time had passed[2] an act urging upon the United States the adoption of some measures calculated to reach a satisfactory adjustment of the status of the colored people within their jurisdiction, and requested the attendance of some properly authorized representative of the Government at their ensuing council for consultation as to the most satisfactory method of settling the vexed question. United States Indian Agent Tufts was accordingly instructed[3] to attend the council, which he did. It resulted in the passage[4] of an act by that body authorizing the principal chief to appoint a commission of three Cherokees to confer with the United States agent and draft articles of agreement, which should, after receiving the approval of the council and of Congress, be considered as permanently fixing the status of the colored people. The agent, however, soon discovered that no action looking to the full recognition of the rights to which they were entitled was likely to receive favorable consideration. It seems from his report[5] that it was still very unpopular in the Cherokee Nation to advocate any measure conceding to the colored people the same rights enjoyed by the Cherokees themselves, and that until a radical revolution of public sentiment should take place among them it was useless to expect any favorable action from the national council. Agent Tufts concluded his report with a recommendation that a commission be appointed by the Interior Department and instructed to hold sessions in the Cherokee country, hear evidence, and determine the status of each disputed claimant to citizenship, subject to the final revision and approval of the Department. Inspector Ward and Special Agent Beede were, therefore, instructed[6] to consult with Agent Tufts, and, after familiarizing themselves with the question in all its details, to visit the executive officers of the Cherokee Nation and see if some satisfactory solution of the troublesome problem could be brought about. This conference, like all

---

[1] A bill to this effect was introduced into the Senate by Senator Ingalls, of Kansas, June 3, 1879, and reported from the Committee on Indian Affairs, with amendments, June 4, 1880, by Senator Williams, of Kentucky.

[2] December 6, 1879.

[3] October 16, 1880.

[4] November 23, 1880.

[5] January 26, 1882.

[6] May 9, 1883.

previous efforts, failed of accomplishing the desired end. Thus the question still stands, and all those persons who have been able to make out a *prima facie* showing of Cherokee citizenship, under the ruling of the Department, are allowed to remain in the Territory unmolested.

GENERAL REMARKS.

With the exception of these questions and complications arising out of the construction of the various articles of the treaty of July 19, 1866, nothing of an important character has occurred in connection with the official relations between the Cherokee Nation and the Federal Government since the date of that treaty.

Their history has been an eventful one. For two hundred years a contest involving their very existence as a people has been maintained against the unscrupulous rapacity of Anglo-Saxon civilization. By degrees they were driven from their ancestral domain to an unknown and inhospitable region. The country of their fathers was peculiarly dear to them. It embraced the head springs of many of the most important streams of the country. From the summit of their own Blue Ridge they could watch the tiny rivulets on either side of them dashing and bounding over their rocky beds in their eagerness to join and swell the ever increasing volume of waters rolling toward the Atlantic Ocean or the Gulf of Mexico: the Tennessee and the Cumberland, the Kanawha and the Kentucky, the Peedee and the Santee, the Savannah and the Altamaha, the Chattahoochee and the Alabama, all found their beginnings within the Cherokee domain. The bracing and invigorating atmosphere of their mountains was wafted to the valleys and low lands of their more distant borders, tempering the heat and destroying the malaria. Much of their country was a succession of grand mountains, clothed with dense forests; of beautiful but narrow valleys, and extensive well watered plains. Every nook and corner of this vast territory was endeared to them by some incident of hunter, warrior, or domestic life. Over these hills and through the recesses of the dark forests the Cherokee hunter had from time immemorial pursued the deer, elk, and buffalo. Through and over them he had passed on his long and vengeful journeys against the hated Iroquois and Shawnee.

The blood of his ancestors, as well as of his enemies, could be trailed from the Hiwassee to the Ohio. The trophies of his skill and valor adorned the sides of his wigwam and furnished the theme for his boastful oratory and song around the council fire and at the dance. His wants were few and purely of a physical nature. His life was devoted to the work of securing a sufficiency of food and the punishment of his enemies. His reputation among his fellow men was proportioned to the skill with which he could draw the bow, his cleverness and agility in their simple athletic sports, or the keen and tireless manner that characterized his pursuit of an enemy's trail. His life was simple, his wants were easily supplied; and, in consequence, the largest measure of his existence was spent in indolence and frivolous amusements. Such proportion of the family food as the chase did not supply was found in the cultivation of Indian corn. The pride of a warrior scorned the performance of menial labor, and to the squaw was this drudgery, as well as that of the household, assigned. His general character has been much misunderstood and misrepresented. He was in fact possessed of great ingenuity, keen wit, and rare cunning. In the consideration of matters of public importance, his conduct was characterized by a grave dignity that was frequently almost ludicrous. The studied stolidity of his countenance gave the spectator no clew to the inward bent of his feelings or determination. The anxious prisoner, from a watchful study of his face and actions, could read nothing of his probable fate. He was physically brave, and would without hesitancy attack the most dangerous beasts of the forests or his still more ferocious human enemies. In the hands of those enemies he would endure, with the most unflinching nerve, the cruelest tortures their ingenuity could devise, and at the same time chant his death song in the recital of his numerous personal acts of triumph over them.

His methods of warfare were, however, very different from those which meet the approval of civilized nations. He could not understand that there was anything of merit in meeting his antagonist in the open field, where the chances of victory were nearly equal. It was a useless risk of his life, even though his numbers exceeded those of his enemy, to allow them to become advised of his approach. His movements were stealthy, and his blows fell at an unexpected moment from the hidden ambush or in the dead hours of the night. His nature was cruel, and in the excitement of battle that cruelty was clothed in the most terrible forms. He was in the highest degree vindictive, and his memory never lost sight of a personal injury. He was inclined to be credulous until once deceived, after which nothing could remove his jealous distrust.

His confidence once fully secured, however, the unselfishness of his friendship as a rule would put to shame that of his more civilized Anglo-Saxon brother. His scrupulous honor in the payment of a just debt was of a character not always emulated among commercial nations. His noble qualities have not been granted the general recognition they deserve, and his ignoble traits have oftentimes been glossed over with the varnish of an unhealthy sentimentality.[1]

For many years following his first contact with the whites the daily

---

[1] William Bartram, who traveled through their country in 1776, says (Travels in North America, p. 483): "The Cherokees in their dispositions and manners are grave and steady, dignified and circumspect in their deportment; rather slow and reserved in conversation, yet frank, cheerful, and humane; tenacious of the liberties and natural rights of man; secret, deliberate, and determined in their councils; honest, just, and liberal, and always ready to sacrifice every pleasure and gratification, even their blood and life itself, to defend their territory and maintain their rights."

life of the Cherokee underwent but little change. The remoteness of his villages from the coast settlements and the intervening territory of other tribes limited in large degree any frequency of association with his white neighbors. In spite of this restricted intercourse, however, the superior comforts and luxuries of civilization were early apparent to him. His new-found desires met with a ready supply through the enterprising cupidity of the fur traders. At the same time and through the same means he was brought to a knowledge of the uses and comforts of calico and blankets, and the devastating though seductive influence of spirituous liquors. Yet nothing occurred to mar the peace hitherto existing with his white neighbors until their continued spread and seemingly insatiate demand for more territory aroused a feeling of jealous fear in his bosom. This awakening to the perils of his situation was, unfortunately for him, too late. The strength of the invaders already surpassed his own, and henceforth it was but a struggle against fate. Prior to the close of the Revolutionary war but little, if anything, had been done toward encouraging the Cherokee to adopt the customs and pursuits of civilized life. His native forests and streams had afforded him a sufficiency of flesh, fish, and skins to supply all his reasonable wants. Immediately upon the establishment of American Independence the policy to be pursued by the Government in its relations with the Indian tribes became the subject of grave consideration. The necessity began to be apparent of teaching the proximate tribes to cultivate the soil as a substitute for the livelihood hitherto gained through the now rapidly diminishing supplies of game. In the report of the commissioners appointed to negotiate the treaty of 1785, being the first treaty concluded between the Cherokees and the United States, they remark that some compensation should be made to the Indians for certain of their lands unlawfully taken possession of by the whites, and that the sum so raised should be appropriated to the purpose of teaching them useful branches of mechanics. Furthermore, that some of their women had lately learned to spin, and many others were "very desirous that some method should be fallen on to teach them to raise flax, cotton, and wool, as well as to spin and weave it."

Six years later, in the conclusion of the second treaty with them, it was agreed, in order "that the Cherokee Nation may be led to a greater degree of civilization, and to become herdsmen and cultivators instead of remaining in a state of hunters, the United States will from time to time furnish gratuitously the said nation with useful implements of husbandry." From this time forward the progress of the Cherokees in civilization and enlightenment was rapid and continuous.[1] They had

---

[1] Hon. J. C. Calhoun, Secretary of War, under date of March 29, 1824, in a communication addressed to the President to be laid before the United States Senate, alludes to the provision contained in the treaty of 1791 and says: "In conformity to the provisions of this article the various utensils of husbandry have been abundantly and constantly distributed to the Cherokee Nation, which has resulted in creating a taste for farming and the comforts of civilized life."

made such advancement that, nearly thirty years later,[1] Return J. Meigs, their long time agent and friend, represented to the Secretary of War that such Government assistance was no longer necessary or desirable; that the Cherokees were perfectly competent to take care of themselves, and that further contributions to their support only had a tendency to encourage idleness and dependence upon the Government.

Their country was especially adapted to stock raising and their flocks and herds increased in proportion to the zeal and industry of their owners. The proceeds of their surplus cotton placed within reach most of the comforts and many of the luxuries of life. The unselfish devotion of the missionary societies had furnished them with religious and school instruction, of which they had in large numbers eagerly availed themselves.[2] From the crude tribal government of the eighteenth century they had gradually progressed until in the month of July, 1827, a convention of duly elected delegates from the eight several districts into which their country was divided[3] assembled at New Echota, and announced that "We, the representatives of the people of the Cherokee Nation, in convention assembled, in order to establish justice, insure tranquillity, promote our common welfare, and secure to ourselves and our posterity the blessings of liberty, acknowledging with humility and gratitude the goodness of the sovereign Ruler of the Universe in offering us an opportunity so favorable to the design and imploring His aid and direction in its accomplishment, do ordain and establish this constitution for the government of the Cherokee Nation." By the constitution thus adopted the power of the nation was divided into legislative, executive, and judicial departments. The legislative power was vested in a committee and a council, each to have a negative on the other, and together to be called the "General Council of the Cherokee Nation." This committee consisted of two and the council of three members from each district, and were to be elected biennially by the suffrages of all free male citizens (excepting negroes and descendants of white and Indian men by negro women who may have been set free) who had attained the age of eighteen years. Their sessions were annual, beginning on the second Monday in October. Persons of negro or mulatto blood were declared ineligible to official honors or emoluments.

The executive power of the nation was confided to a principal chief,

---

[1] May 30, 1820.

[2] Letter of Hon. J. C. Calhoun Secretary of War, March 29, 1824. In this letter Mr. Calhoun says: "Certain benevolent societies in the year 1816 applied for permission to make establishments among the Cherokees and other southern tribes, for the purpose of educating and instructing them in the arts of civilized life. Their application was favorably received. The experiment proved so favorable, that Congress, by act of March 3, 1819, appropriated $10,000 annually as a civilization fund, which has been applied in such a manner as very considerably to increase the extent and usefulness of the efforts of benevolent individuals and to advance the work of Indian civilization."

[3] The eight districts into which the nation was at this time divided were, Chickamauga, Chatooga, Coosawatee, Amohee, Hickory Log, Etowah, Taquoe, and Aquohee.

elected by the general council for a term of four years, and none but native born citizens were eligible to the office. The chief was required to visit each district of the nation at least once in two years, to keep himself familiarized with the condition and necessities of the country. His approval was also required to all laws, and, as in the case of our own Government, the exercise of the veto power could be overcome only by a two-thirds majority in both houses of the national legislature. An executive council of three members besides the assistant principal chief was also to be elected by the joint vote of the two houses for the period of one year.

The judicial functions were vested in a supreme court of three judges and such circuit and inferior courts as the general council should from time to time prescribe, such judges to be elected by joint vote of the general council.

Ministers of the gospel who by their profession were dedicated to the service of God and the care of souls, and who ought not therefore to be diverted from the great duty of their function, were, while engaged in such work, declared ineligible to the office of principal chief or to a seat in either house of the general council. Any person denying the existence of a God or a future state of rewards and punishments was declared ineligible to hold any office in the civil department of the nation, and it was also set forth that (religion, morality, and knowledge being necessary to good government, the preservation of liberty, and the happiness of mankind) schools and the means of education should forever be encouraged in the nation.

Under this constitution elections were regularly held and the functions of government administered until the year 1830, when the hostile legislation of Georgia practically paralyzed and suspended its further operation. Although forbidden to hold any more elections, the Cherokees maintained a semblance of their republican form of government by tacitly permitting their last elected officers to hold over and recognizing the authority and validity of their official actions. This embarrassing condition of affairs continued until their removal west of the Mississippi River, when, on the 6th of September, 1839, they, in conjunction with the "Old Settlers," adopted a new constitution, which in substance was a duplicate of its predecessor.

This removal turned the Cherokees back in the calendar of progress and civilization at least a quarter of a century. The hardships and exposures of the journey, coupled with the fevers and malaria of a radically different climate, cost the lives of perhaps 10 per cent. of their total population. The animosities and turbulence born of the treaty of 1835 not only occasioned the loss of many lives, but rendered property insecure, and in consequence diminished the zeal and industry of the entire community in its accumulation. A brief period of comparative quiet, however, was again characterized by an advance toward a higher civilization. Five years after their removal we find from the report of their agent that they are again on the increase in population; that their houses, farms, and fixtures have greatly improved in the comforts of life; that in general they are living in double cabins and evincing an increasing disposition to provide for the future; that they have in operation eleven common schools, superintended by a native Cherokee, in which are taught reading, writing, arithmetic, bookkeeping, grammar, geography, and history, which are entirely supported at the expense of their own national funds, and which are attended by upwards of five hundred scholars; that the churches are largely attended and liberally supported, the Methodists having 1,400 communicants, the Baptists 750, and other denominations a smaller number; that a national temperance society boasts of 1,752 members; that they maintain a printing press, from which publications are issued in both the English and Cherokee tongues; that some of them manifest a decided taste for general literature and a few have full and well selected libraries; that thousands of them can speak and write the English language with fluency and comparative accuracy; that hundreds can draw up contracts, deeds, and other instruments for the transfer of property, and that in the ordinary transactions of life, especially in making bargains, they are shrewd and intelligent, frequently evincing a remarkable degree of craft and combination; that their treatment of their women had undergone a radical change; that the countenance and encouragement given to her cultivation disclosed a more exalted estimate of female character, and that instead of being regarded as a slave and a beast of burden she was now recognized as a friend and companion.

Thus, with the exception of occasional drawbacks—the result of civil feuds—the progress of the nation in education, industry, and civilization continued until the outbreak of the rebellion. At this period, from the best attainable information, the Cherokees numbered twenty-one thousand souls. The events of the war brought to them more of desolation and ruin than perhaps to any other community.

Raided and sacked alternately, not only by the Confederate and Union forces, but by the vindictive ferocity and hate of their own factional divisions, their country became a blackened and desolate waste. Driven from comfortable homes, exposed to want, misery, and the elements, they perished like sheep in a snow storm. Their houses, fences, and other improvements were burned, their orchards destroyed, their flocks and herds slaughtered or driven off, their schools broken up, and their school-houses given to the flames, their churches and public buildings subjected to a similar fate, and that entire portion of their country which had been occupied by their settlements was distinguishable from the virgin prairie only by the scorched and blackened chimneys and the plowed but now neglected fields.

The war over and the work of reconstruction commenced, found them numbering fourteen thousand impoverished, heart broken, and revengeful people. But they must work or starve, and in almost sullen despair they set about rebuilding their waste places. The situation was one calculated to discourage men enjoying a higher degree of civilization than they had yet reached, but they bent to the task with a determination and perseverance that could not fail to be the parent of success.

To-day their country is more prosperous than ever. They number twenty-two thousand, a greater population than they have had at any previous period, except perhaps just prior to the date of the treaty of 1835, when those east added to those west of the Mississippi are stated to have aggregated nearly twenty-five thousand people.[1] To-day they have twenty-three hundred scholars attending seventy-five schools, established and supported by themselves at an annual expense to the nation of nearly $100,000. To-day thirteen thousand of their people can read and eighteen thousand can speak the English language. To-day five thousand brick, frame, and log houses are occupied by them, and they have sixty-four churches with a membership of several thousand. They cultivate a hundred thousand acres of land and have an additional one hundred and fifty thousand fenced. They raise annually 100,000 bushels of wheat, 800,000 of corn, 100,000 of oats and barley, 27,500 of vegetables, 1,000,000 pounds of cotton, 500,000 pounds of butter, 12,000 tons of hay, and saw a million feet of lumber. They own 20,000 horses, 15,000 mules, 200,000 cattle, 100,000 swine, and 12,000 sheep.

They have a constitutional form of government predicated upon that of the United States. As a rule, their laws are wise and beneficent and are enforced with strictness and justice. Political and social prejudice has deprived the former slaves in some instances of the full measure of rights guaranteed to them by the treaty of 1866 and the amended constitution of the nation, but time is rapidly softening these asperities and will solve all difficulties of the situation.

The present Cherokee population is of a composite character. Remnants of other nations or tribes have from time to time been absorbed and admitted to full participation in the benefits of Cherokee citizenship. The various classes may be thus enumerated:

1. The full blood Cherokees.
2. The mixed blood Cherokees.
3. The Delawares.
4. The Shawnees.
5. White men and women intermarried with the foregoing.
6. A few Creeks who broke away from their own tribe and have been citizens of the Cherokee Nation for many years.

[1] The census of the nation east of the Mississippi, taken in 1835, exhibited the following facts:

	Cherokees.	Slaves.	Whites intermarried with Cherokees.	Total.
In Georgia	8,946	776	68	9,790
In North Carolina	3,644	37	22	3,703
In Tennessee	2,528	480	79	3,087
In Alabama	1,424	299	32	1,755
Aggregate	16,542	1,592	201	18,335

7. A few Creeks who are not citizens, but have taken up their abode in the Cherokee country, without any rights.

8. A remnant of the Natchez tribe, who are citizens.

9. The freedmen adopted under the treaty of 1866.

10. Freedmen not adopted, but not removed as intruders, owing to an order from the Indian Department forbidding such removal pending a decision upon their claims to citizenship.

If the Government of the United States shall in this last resort of the Cherokees prove faithful to its obligations and maintain their country inviolate from the intrusions of white trespassers, the future of the nation will surely prove the capability of the American Indian under favorable conditions to realize in a high degree the possibilities of Anglo-Saxon civilization.

Table showing approximately the area in square miles and acres ceded to the United States by the various treaties with the Cherokee Nation.

Date of treaty.	State where ceded lands are located.	Area in square miles.	Area in acres.
1721	South Carolina	2,623	1,678,720
November 24, 1755	do	8,635	5,526,400
October 14, 1768	Virginia	850	544,000
	do	4,500	2,880,000
October 18, 1770	West Virginia	4,300	2,752,000
	Tennessee	150	96,000
	Kentucky	250	160,000
	do	10,135	6,486,400
1772	West Virginia	437	279,680
	Virginia	345	220,800
June 1, 1773	Georgia	1,050	672,000
	Kentucky	22,600	14,464,000
March 17, 1775	Virginia	1,800	1,152,000
	Tennessee	2,650	1,696,000
May 20, 1777	South Carolina	2,051	1,312,640
July 20, 1777	North Carolina	4,414	2,824,960
	Tennessee	1,760	1,126,400
May 31, 1783	Georgia	1,650	1,056,000
	North Carolina	550	352,000
November 28, 1785	Tennessee	4,914	3,144,960
	Kentucky	917	586,880
July 2, 1791	Tennessee	3,435	2,198,400
	North Carolina	722	462,080
October 2, 1798	Tennessee	952	609,280
	North Carolina	587	375,680
October 24, 1804	Georgia	135	86,400
October 25, 1805	Kentucky	1,086	695,040
	Tennessee	7,032	4,500,480
October 27, 1805	do	1¼	800
	do	5,269	3,372,160
January 7, 1806	Alabama	1,602	1,025,280
March 22, 1816	South Carolina	148	94,720
September 14, 1816	Alabama	3,429	2,194,560
	Mississippi	4	2,560
July 8, 1817	Georgia	583	373,120
	Tennessee	435	278,400
	Georgia	837	535,680
February 27, 1819	Alabama	1,154	738,560
	Tennessee	2,408	1,541,120
	North Carolina	1,542	986,880
May 6, 1828	Arkansas	4,720	3,020,800
	Tennessee	1,484	949,760
December 29, 1835	Georgia	7,202	4,609,280
	Alabama	2,518	1,611,520
	North Carolina	1,112	711,680
July 19, 1866 a	Kansas	b1,928	1,233,920
Total		126,906¼	81,220,374

a In addition there was ceded by this treaty for the location of other Indian tribes all the Cherokee domain in Indian Territory lying west of 96°, containing by actual survey 8,144,772.35 acres or 12,726 square miles.

b And a fractional square mile comprising 374 acres.

BIOGRAPHICAL NOTES

Although Charles C. Royce made two very valuable contributions to the literature on the American Indian—this monograph on the Cherokee and his monumental *Indian Land Cessions in the United States* (another Bureau of Ethnology publication)—he is an obscure figure. He was born December 22, 1845, in Defiance, Ohio, and he married Isabella Harter in 1871. They had no children. Three months short of his nineteenth birthday, Royce enlisted in the U.S. Navy and spent the last months of the Civil War as Acting Master's Mate aboard the monitor U.S.S. *Neosho*. Following his honorable discharge, he went to Washington, D.C., where he became a clerk in the Office of Indian Affairs. His work on Indian land cessions was brought to the attention of John Wesley Powell, the first head of the Bureau of Ethnology, who helped Royce pursue his studies by borrowing books for him from the of Library Congress and providing him with funds for research trips. Although he was appointed an ethnologist on the staff of the Bureau in February 1883, Royce returned to Ohio a year later to work as an accountant at the Miami County Bank. Before leaving, Royce submitted this monograph to the Bureau for publication. Originally scheduled for inclusion in the Fourth Annual Report, it had to be held back a year, to the great disappointment of the aspiring author. "The thing has been on my mind and hands so long already that I was anxious to get rid of it," he wrote in August 1885. "Of course I never had any conceit that in a strict sense of the term it belonged among scientific papers. It is purely historical and yet I am constrained to believe that the 'popularity' of a work such as the report of the Bureau of Ethnology, would not be abridged in the mind of the average reader by having a little politico-Indian History sandwiched between their 'myths' and 'stone implements' on the one side and their 'sign language' and 'mortuary customs' on the other. But of course that is a question entirely for the determination of the Bureau authorities and I shall have no complaint to offer, whatever may be their decision."

In 1888 Royce became manager of Rancho Chico, a California fruit ranch. Upon his retirement in 1912, he returned to Washington where he suffered ill health until his death on February 11, 1923.

Richard Mack Bettis was born in Spiro, Oklahoma, in 1934. He is currently employed in Tulsa as a Personnel Management Specialist and Labor Relations Officer for the Southwestern Power Administration of the U.S. Interior Department. Mr. Bettis received his B.A. in Sociology from Northeastern State College in Tahlequah, Oklahoma, and his law degree from Oklahoma City University. He practices law part-time and teaches political science at Tulsa Junior College. Both his parents are of Cherokee extraction, and he is involved in many tribal activities. He is president of the Tulsa Tsa-La-Gi-Ya Cherokee Community and a member of the Medicine Springs Tribal Town near Gore, Oklahoma. The goal of both groups is the preservation of the Cherokee heritage for future generations. Mr. Bettis dedicates his remarks in this book to his daughters, Tiffany and Dandre.

MAPS

Numerical and Chronological Schedule of Cherokee Cessions

No.	Date and Designation of Treaty
	Colonial Period
1	Treaty of 1721 with Gov. Nicholson of South Carolina.
2	Treaty of Nov. 24, 1755, with Gov. Glenn of South Carolina.
3	Treaty of Oct. 14, 1768, with J. Stuart, British Supt. Indian Affairs.
4	Treaty of Oct. 18, 1770, at Lochaber, South Carolina.
5	Treaty of 1772 with Governor of Virginia.
6	Treaty of June 1, 1773, with J. Stuart, British Supt. Indian Affairs.
7	Treaty of March 17, 1775, with Richard Henderson *et al.*
8	Treaty of May 20, 1777, with South Carolina and Georgia.
9	Treaty of July 20, 1777, with Virginia and North Carolina.
10	Treaty of May 31, 1783, with Georgia.
	Federal Period
10A–10B	Treaty of Nov. 28, 1785, with the United States.
11	Treaty of July 2, 1791, with the United States.
12–14	Treaty of Oct. 2, 1798, with the United States.
15	Treaty of Oct. 24, 1804, with the United States.
16	Treaty of Oct. 25, 1805, with the United States.
17–18	Treaty of Oct. 27, 1805, with the United States.
19–20	Treaty of Jan. 7, 1806, with the United States.
21	Treaty of March 22, 1816, with the United States.
22	Treaty of Sept. 14, 1816, with the United States.
23–26	Treaty of July 8, 1817, with the United States.
27–35	Treaty of Feb. 27, 1819, with the United States.
36	Treaty of Dec. 29, 1835, with the United States.
37	Treaty of May 6, 1828, with the United States. [Only those Cherokee living west of the Mississippi River were parties to this treaty.]
38–47	Treaty of July 19, 1866, with the United States.

Note: In order to reduce the maps to page size, some information had to be omitted. Readers interested in the locations of rivers, towns, Indian agencies, trails, and other features not shown on the simplified maps should consult the originals.

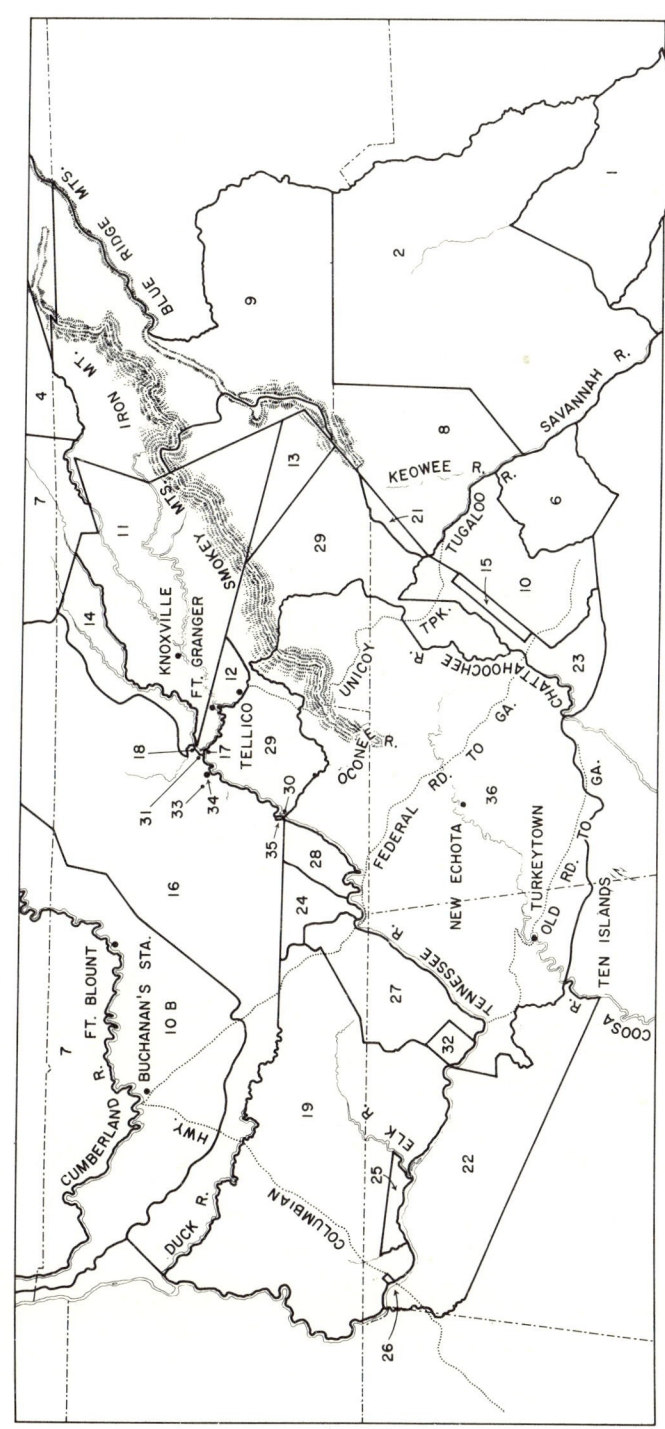

Map 1. Principal geographical features, settlements, and routes of communication in the territory originally claimed by the Cherokee, taken from the map compiled by C. C. Royce in 1884. Numbers identify tracts covered by treaties; for specific information see Map 2 and page 260. Redrawn from Pl. VIII.

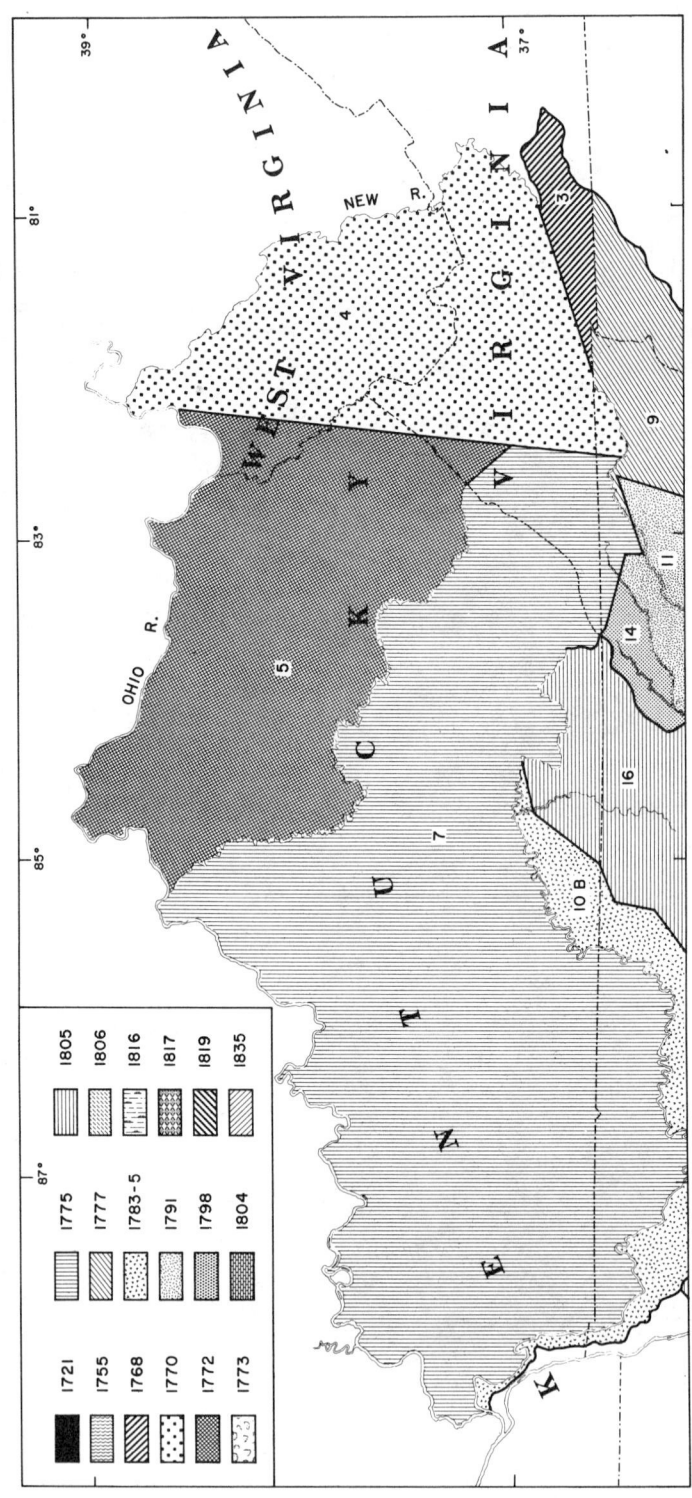

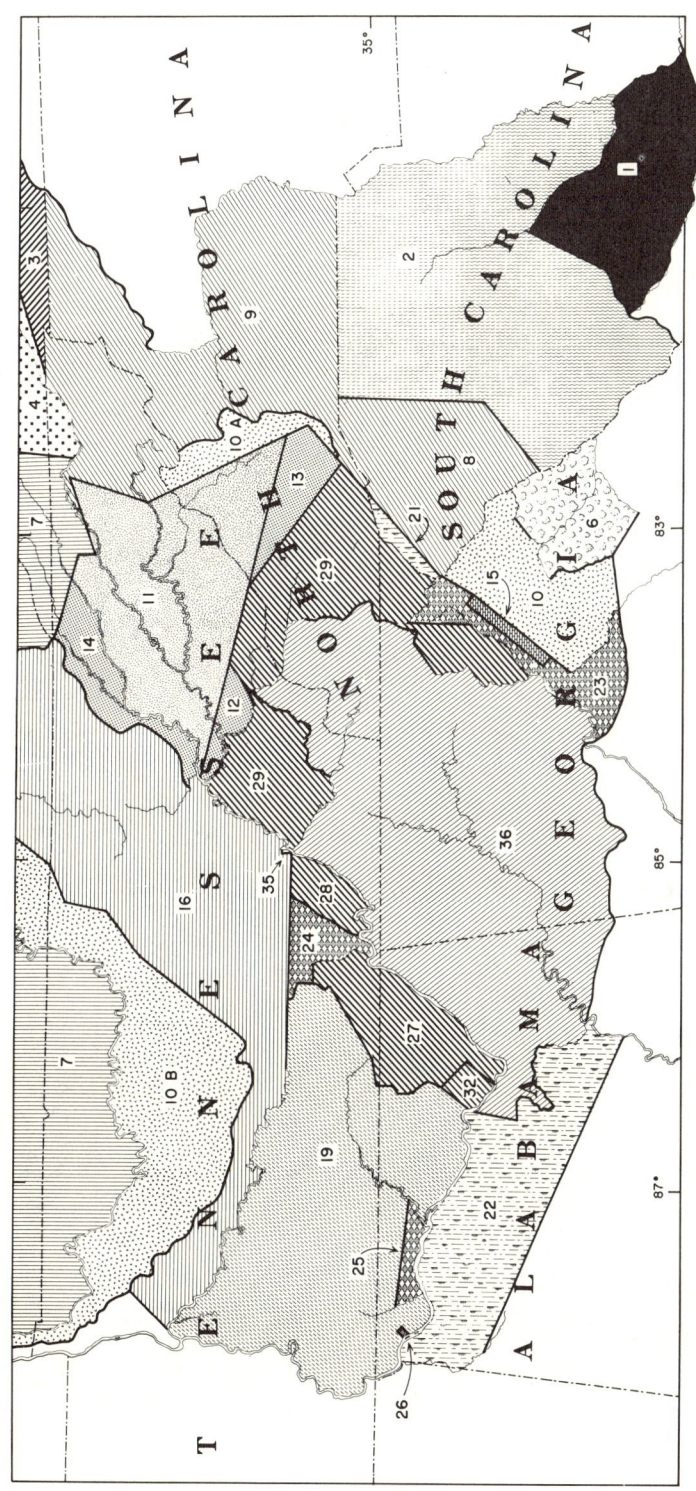

Map 2. The former territorial limits of the Cherokee Nation of Indians exhibiting the boundaries of the various cessions to the colonies and the United States by treaty stipulations, from the beginning of their relations with the whites to the date of their removal west of the Mississippi River. The numbers identify tracts covered by each treaty; for specific information see page 260. Redrawn from Pl. VIII.

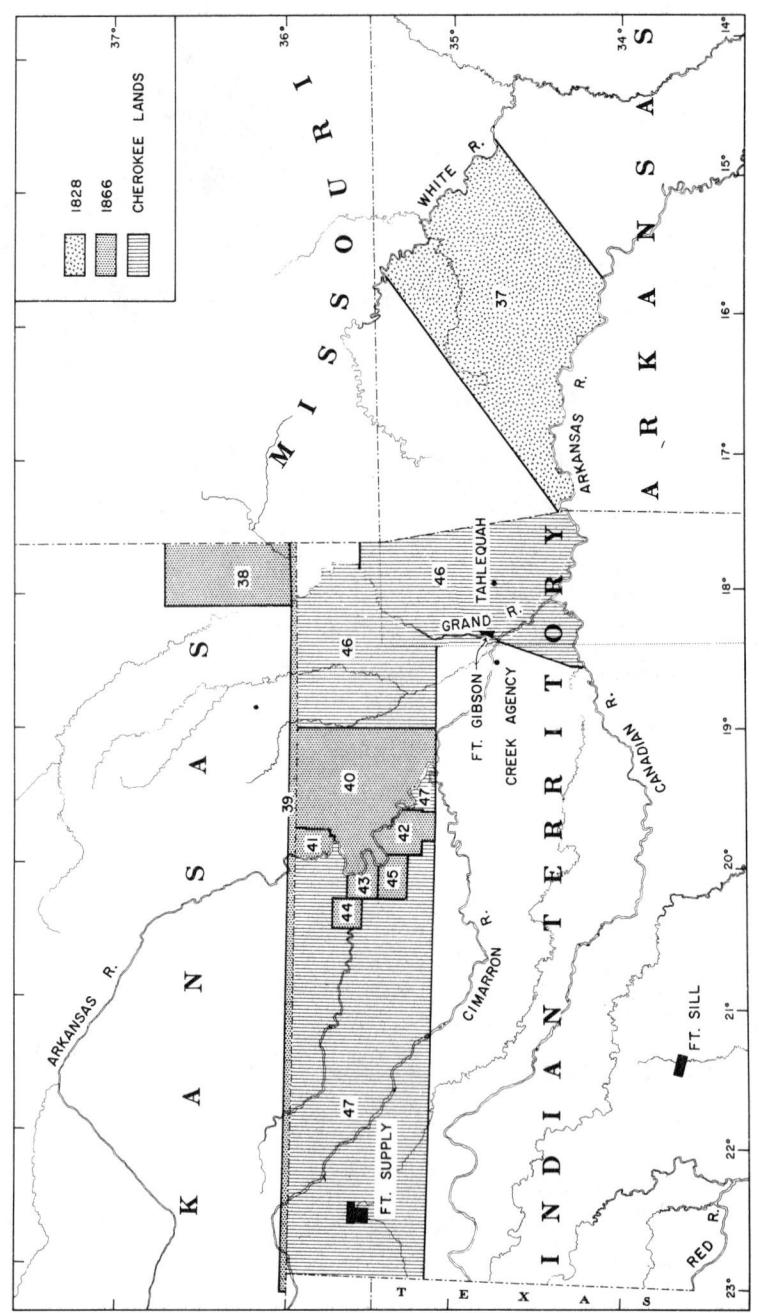

Map 3. The territory originally assigned to the Cherokee Nation of Indians west of the Mississippi, and the boundaries of the territory occupied or owned by them. Redrawn from Pl. IX.

INDEX

Adair, Andrew, murder of, 197
Adair, James, on Cherokee boundaries, 13
Adair, John Lynch, commissioner for Cherokee boundary, 243
Adair, Washington, murder of, 197
Adams, Captain, aid acknowledged, 2
Adams, John Quincy, on relations of Georgia and Cherokee, 111
Alabama, alleges error in survey of Cherokee boundary, 83
Allegan or Allegwi identical with Cherokee, 9
American Emigrant Company negotiates for neutral lands, 227
Armstrong, F. W., commissioner to extinguish Cherokee title, 113
Armstrong, R. H., aid acknowledged, 2
Armstrong, William, commissioner to treat with Cherokee, 80, 177
    plan of, for adjusting Cherokee differences, 192
Ashley, James M., commissioner for Cherokee boundary, 243

Barbour, James, authorized to treat with Cherokee, 101
Barnett, William, Cherokee boundary commissioner, 79, 80
Bartram, William, remarks on the Cherokee, 7, 250
    list of Cherokee towns, 15
Batt, Capt. Henry, exploring party under, 10
Berkeley, William, exploring expedition by, 10
Blair, James, Georgia commissioner in treating with Cherokee, 108
Blount, William, protest against Hopewell treaty, 27
    treaty with Cherokee, 30
    instructed to treat with Cherokee, 34
Boudinot, E. C., address on condition of Cherokee, 163
    murder of, 171
    compensation to heirs of, 177
    on Cherokee treaty of April 27, 1868, 222
Bridges, J. S., commissioner to appraise Cherokee property, 130
Brodie, Paul, aid acknowledged, 2
Brown, David, report on Cherokee, with census by, 112
Brown, Jacob, purchase from Cherokee, 19
Browning, O. H., annuls sale of Cherokee neutral land by Secretary Harlan, 227
Burke, Edmund, commissioner to treat with Cherokee, 176, 183

265

Butler, P. M., Cherokee agent, 175
  commissioner to examine Cherokee feuds, 179
Butler, Thomas, commissioner for Cherokee treaty, 46

Calhoun, John C., treats with Cherokee, 91
  on Cherokee civilization, 251, 252
Campbell, David, surveyor of Cherokee boundary line, 37
Campbell, Duncan G., commissioner to extinguish Indian title in Georgia, 105
Campbell, William, surveyed line between Virginia and Cherokee lands, 28
Carroll, William, commissioner for making and executing Cherokee treaty, 125, 161
  report on the Cherokee, 131
Cass, Lewis, holds Cherokee council at Wapakoneta, Ohio, 93
Catawba Indians, treaty of 1736 with, 17
  proposed removal of, to Cherokee country, 195
Census, Cherokee, in 1825, 112
  in 1835, 167, 255
  in 1867, 229
  in North Carolina in 1849, 191
  in North Carolina in 1869, 192
Census, refugee Indians, in 1862, 209, 210
Chelague identical with Cherokee, 13
Cherokee and Creek boundary disputes, 144
Cherokee boundary of 1785, dissatisfaction with, 32
Cherokee census, in 1825, 112
  in 1835, 167, 255
  in 1867, 229
Cherokee cessions to the United States, area of, 256
Cherokee citizenship, 245
Cherokee Confederate regiment, desertion of, 207
Cherokee constitution, 77, 232, 243, 252, 253
Cherokee country, boundaries of, 77, 232, 243

Cherokee hostilities, 42, 45
Cherokee lands, purchase of, 82
  removal of white settlers from, 200, 201
  cession and sale of, 226
  appraisal of, west of 96°, 239
Cherokee migration, 8
Cherokee Nation, political murders in, 175, 181
Cherokee population, 14, 255, 256
Cherokee western outlet, 118, 120
Cherokee, the cessions of land by, 2, 3
  known by North Carolina and Virginia settlers, 10, 11
  treaty relations of, with the United States, 24
  war with, 42,
  proposed removal of, 74
  removals of, 86–90, 94, 98, 126, 128, 170, 219
  situation of, west of the Mississippi, 93, 170, 171
  progress in civilization of, 112
  adoption of constitution by, 113, 173
  material prosperity among, 132
  protests against claims of Georgia, 150
  proposition of, to become citizens, 152
  memorials of, in Congress, 153, 155, 167
  unification of Eastern and Western, 172
  charge United States with bad faith, 174
  financial difficulties of, 196, 198
  new treaty proposed in 1854 by, 198
  political excitement in 1860 among, 202
  the Southern Confederacy and, 204, 210, 211, 220
  treaty of 1868 concluded with Southern, 224
  treaty of 1866 with loyal, 225
  jurisdiction of, 247
Cherokee and Osage, difficulties between, 114
Chester, E. W., instructed as to treaty with Cherokee, 135
Chickamauga band, emigration of, 22, 23

Chickasaw, Choctaw, Creek, and Cherokee, boundary between, 77
Chisholm, John D., deputized by Cherokee to treat, 84
Choctaw, Chickasaw, Cherokee and Creek, boundary between, 77
Clark, William, instructed to end Cherokee hostilities, 93, 94
Clay, Henry, sympathy with Cherokee, 165
   resolution by, regarding title to Texas, 233
Clements, C. C., special agent on Cherokee claims, 186
Cocke, John, commissioner to extinguish Cherokee title, 113
Coffee, John, objection to survey by, 79, 80
   appointed to assist in Cherokee removal, 132
   appointed to report on line between Cherokee and Georgia, 148
Columbia River, Cherokee contemplate removal to, 136
Confederacy, relation of Cherokee to Southern, 254
Cooley, Dennis N., commissioner to treat with Cherokee, 212, 219
Corwin, R. G., commissioner for Cherokee boundary, 243
Cox, John T., commissioner to appraise neutral lands, 229
Creek and Cherokee boundary disputes, 138
Crockett, David, denounces policy toward Cherokee, 166
Cumming, Alexander, treaty with Cherokee, 16, 17
Curry, Benjamin F., to appraise Cherokee improvements, 161
Cutifachiqui, visit of De Soto to, 7

Davidson, G. L., commissioner to extinguish Cherokee title, 113
Davie, William R., commissioner for Cherokee treaty, 56
Davis, William M., report on state of feeling among Cherokee in Georgia, 162
Dearborn, Henry, treats with Cherokee, 65, 67

Delaware Indians, cession of land in Indiana by, 9
   join Cherokee, 234–236
De Soto, visit of, to Cherokee, 6
   visit of, to Cutifachiqui, 7
Dobbs, Arthur, grant by, 17
Doublehead, Cherokee chief, secret agreement with, 63, 64, 65
   grant for, 64, 65
Doublehead tract, controversy respecting, 64
Drennan, John, authorized to pay Cherokee claims, 190
Drew, Colonel of Cherokee Confederate regiment, 207
Dunlap, R. G., speech on Cherokee affairs, 163

Earle, Elias, negotiates for iron ore tract of Cherokee Nation, 71, 72
Eaton, John H., appointed to negotiate treaty with Cherokee, 153
   commissioner to settle Cherokee claims, 176
Ellicott, Andrew, survey of Cherokee boundary by, 35–37
Ellsworth, Henry L., commissioner to treat with Cherokee, 121
   commissioner to report on country assigned to the Indians of the West, 123
Everett, Edward, denounces policy toward Cherokee, 166
Ewing, Thomas, counsel for Cherokee, 223

Franklin, treaties with the State of, 23, 24

Gallagher, W. D., commissioner for Cherokee boundary, 243
Georgia, protests of, against Hopewell treaty, 27
   United States agree to extinguish Indian title in, 105
   action by, regarding Cherokee, 106, 108
Georgia, view of, as to Indian title, 113
   Supreme Court decision in Cherokee Nation vs. Georgia, 134

INDEX

Georgia—cont.
   Supreme Court decision in Worcester vs. Georgia, 136
   refusal of, to submit to decision of Supreme Court respecting Cherokee, 138
   hostility of, to Van Buren's compromise in Cherokee affairs, 168
Georgia and United States, measures of to remove Indians, 132
Glassock, Thomas, and John King protest against treaty of 1785, 27
"Government" or "Ross" party of Cherokee, 171, 176, 177
Graham, George, commissioner to treat with Cherokee, 69, 70, 77
Grey, Alexander, commissioner to extinguish Cherokee title, 113
Guess, George, inventor of Cherokee alphabet, 102
   death of, 180
Gwin, James W., commissioner to treat with Cherokee, 166

Hardin, Joseph, survey of Cherokee boundary by, 28
Harlan, James, contracts for sale of Cherokee neutral land, 218, 227
Harney, W. S., commissioner to treat with Indians, 219
Hawkins, Benjamin, commissioner to treat with Cherokee, 5, 56
   journal of, 43–47
Haywood, John, on origin and habitat of Cherokee, 8
Henderson, Richard, purchase of land from Cherokee by, 20
Hood, Robert N., aid acknowledged, 2
Hopewell, proceedings at treaty of, 24, 25, 27 30
Houston, Robert, surveyor of Cherokee line in Tennessee, 99, 104
Hubley, Edward B., commissioner to settle Cherokee claims, 176
Hunter, A. R. S., commissioner to appraise Cherokee property, 130

Indians, removal of, west of the Mississippi River, 86
Intercourse act of 1796, 45

Jack, Patrick, grant to, 17
Jackson, Andrew, protests against Cherokee boundary of 1816, 78
   commissioner for Cherokee treaty, 81, 84, 87, 88
   refuses to approve Cherokee treaty of 1834, 124
   advice to Cherokee, 130
   on decision in Worcester vs. Georgia, 138
   urges Cherokee to remove, 151
   method of, for compelling Cherokee removal, 125
Jefferson, Thomas, on removal of Cherokee, 74, 75
Jones, Evan, alleged founder of Pin Society, 203
   appropriation for, 217
Jones, John B., warned to leave Cherokee, 202
Jones, R., commissioner to examine Cherokee feuds, 179
Johnson, Robert, Indian census in South Carolina in 1715 by, 14
Johnston, William, financial relations to Cherokee Indians, 193
Joy, James F., contract for Cherokee neutral lands by, 219, 228

Kansa or Kaw, removal to Indian Territory, 238
Kennard, Thomas V., commissioner to appraise Indian lands, 241
Kennedy, John, commissioner to treat with Cherokee, 160
Keowee Old Town on map by Bowen, 13, 14
Kilpatrick, John Clark, surveyor of Cherokee boundary line, 37, 40
King, John, and Thomas Glasscock protest against treaty of 1785, 27
Knox, Henry, on violation of treaty of Hopewell, 32, 33
   treaty with Cherokee executed by, 43
Kretschmar, H. R., commissioner to appraise confiscated property of Cherokee, 229

Lea, John M., aid acknowledged, 2
Liddell, James, commissioner to treat with Cherokee, 166

INDEX

Lovely's purchase, 117
Lowry, John, commissioner to urge Cherokee to remove, 134
Lumpkin, Wilson, surveyor of Cherokee line, 99
  commissioner to execute Cherokee treaty, 161

McCulloch, Benjamin, Confederate commander in Cherokee country, 204
McIntosh, Lachlane, agent of Tennessee with Cherokee, 51
  commissioner to treat with Cherokee, 5
McMinn, Joseph, commissioner for Cherokee treaty, 84, 88
  on Cherokee migration, 90, 95–97
  appointed Cherokee agent, 108
Martin, Joseph, commissioner to treat with Cherokee, 5
Mason, John, jr. report on Cherokee affairs, 158
Mason, R. B., commissioner to examine Cherokee feuds, 179
Maxwell, C. A., aid acknowledged, 2
Meigs, Return J., commissioner of survey of Cherokee boundary, 53–55, 59, 60, 61, 62, 63, 64, 66, 68, 72, 73, 75, 81, 82, 89–103, 105, 252
  relations of, to the Cherokee, 103, 105
  death of, 109
Merriwether, David, commissioner for Cherokee treaty, 81, 84, 88, 108
Merriwether, James, commissioner to extinguish Indian title in Georgia, 106, 108
Missouria removed to Indian Territory, 242
Mitchell, D. P., surveys Cherokee boundary, 243
Monroe, James, on relations of Cherokee and Georgia, 110, 111
Moore, Alfred, commissioner to treat with Cherokee, 48
Mouzon's map, 1771, Cherokee towns on, 15
Mullay, J. C., census of Cherokee in North Carolina in 1849 by, 191
Munsee join Cherokee, 234–236

Munson, Spencer, aid acknowledged, 2

New Echota, Cherokee council at, 158
  adoption of Cherokee constitution at, 252
Neutral land, proposed cession of, by Cherokee, 197, 198
Nez Percé removed to Indian Territory, 242
North Carolina, protests against Hopewell treaty, 27
  Cherokee refuse to cede lands in, 132

Old Settler Cherokee party, 171, 253
  payments to, 177
  propose to remove to Mexico, 180
  claims of, settled, 185
O-poth-le-yo-ho-lo loyal to the United States, 208, 209
Osage half breed reserves, purchase of, 124
Osage and Cherokee, treaty between, 94
  difficulties between, 114
Osage removed to Indian Territory, 237
Otoe removed to Indian Territory, 242

Parker, E. S., commissioner to treat with Indians, 239
Parris, Albion K., commissioner to treat wtih Cherokee, 176, 183
Pawnee removed to Indian Territory, 238
Phillips, Wm. A., Cherokee commissioner to appraise neutral lands, 229
Pickens, Andrew, commissioner to treat with Cherokee as to boundary, 5, 37, 58
Pike, Albert, as to Pin Society, 203
  Cherokee commissioner for Confederate States, 204, 205, 206, 207
Pin Society of Cherokee, 203
Ponca removed to Indian Territory, 242
Price, Hiram, aid acknowledged, 2

Rector, William, surveyed Cherokee line in Arkansas, 94

Ridge, John, with Cherokee delegation at Washington, 156, 157
  murder of, 171
  compensation to heirs of, 177
"Ridge" party of Cherokee, 171
Ridge Treaty rejected by Cherokee, 158
Rogers, James, deputized by Cherokee to treat, 84
Ross, Andrew, proposition for Cherokee treaty, 152, 153
  and others, preliminary treaty concluded with, 153
Ross, John, applies for injunction against Georgia, 134, 150
  alleged attempt to bribe, 151
  protests against the removal of Cherokee, 151, 153
  opposition to Andrew Ross's proposition, 153
  heads Cherokee delegation to Washington in 1835, 156, 157
  arrest of, 159
  opposition to treaty, 160
  refusal of, to acquiesce in treaty, 161
  proposes new Cherokee treaty, 169
  heads delegation to Washington in 1844, 178
  advises sale of Fort Gibson in town lots, 200
  opposes survey and allotment of Cherokee domain, 202
  relations of, to Southern Confederacy, 204–210
  not recognized as principal chief of Cherokee, 221, 222
  death of, 225
"Ross" or "Government" party of Cherokee, 171
Robertson, Charles, deed to, on the Watauga, 19
Robertson, General, agent of Tennessee with Cherokee, 51
Rutherford, Griffith, march against Cherokee, 29

Saline or salt plains, treaty provisions regarding, 122, 178
Schermerhorn, John F., commissioner to treat with Cherokee, 123, 127, 131, 160
  commissioner to report on country assigned to Indians of the West, 123
  appointed to treat with Ridge Cherokee delegation, 156, 157
Schoolcraft, H. R., on identity of the Allegan with the Cherokee, 9
Scott, Winfield, ordered to command troops in Cherokee country, 169
Sells, Elijah, commissioner to treat with Cherokee, 212, 219
Sequoyah, or George Guess, death of, 180
Shawnee, expelled by Cherokee and Chickasaw, 16
  join Cherokee, 234–236
Smith, Daniel, commissioner for treaty with Cherokee, 55, 59, 62
Smith, Thomas E., commissioner to appraise Indian lands, 241
South Carolina, endeavors of, to extinguish Cherokee title, 76, 77
Southern Confederacy and the Cherokee, 204–211, 220
Sprague, Peleg, denounces policy toward Cherokee, 166
Steele, John, commissioner to treat with Cherokee, 48
Stevens, E. L., aid acknowledged, 2
Stokes, Montfort, commissioner to treat with Cherokee, 121
  commissioner to report on country assigned to Indians of the West, 123
Storrs, Henry R., denounces policy toward Cherokee, 166
Strum, G. P., aid acknowledged, 2
Stuart, James, agent of Tennessee to treat with Cherokee, 51
Supreme Court decision, in Cherokee Nation vs. Georgia, 134
  in Worcester vs. Georgia, 136
Sweatland, S. H., census of Cherokee in North Carolina in 1869 by, 192

Talootiske, Cherokee, grant of, 65
Tatnall, E. F., appointed to assist in Cherokee removal, 138
Taylor, Nathaniel G., commissioner to treat with Cherokee, 218, 230

INDEX

Tennessee, commissioners from, to treat council of Cherokee, 51
  endeavor of, to treat with Cherokee, 73
  on validity of Cherokee reservations, 104
Tennessee Company, purchase of Cherokee land by, 34
Thomas, William H., agent for Cherokee, 193
Thompson, R. F., aid acknowledged, 2
Tompkins, H., census of Cherokee in 1867 by, 229
Topping, Enoch H., commissioner to appraise Indian lands, 241
Treaties and purchases of 1777, 21
Treaties between the State of Franklin and the Cherokee, 23, 24
Treaties of March 22, 1816, 69, 70
Treaty and purchase of 1721, 16
Treaty and purchase of 1755, 17
Treaty and purchase of 1768, 18
Treaty and purchase of 1770, 18
Treaty and purchase of 1772, 18
Treaty and purchase of 1773, 20
Treaty and purchase of 1783, 23
Treaty between Confederate States and Cherokee, 206
Treaty Cherokee propose to remove to Mexico, 180
Treaty of Hopewell, proceedings at, 24
Treaty of 1756, 17
Treaty of 1760, 17
Treaty of 1761, 18
Treaty of 1775, 20
Treaty of November 28, 1785, 5, 30
Treaty of July 2, 1791, 30
Treaty of February 17, 1792, 41
Treaty of June 26, 1794, 43
Treaty of October 2, 1798, 46
Treaty of October 24, 1804, 55
Treaty of October 25, 1805, 61
Treaty of October 27, 1805, 62
Treaty of January 7, 1806, 65
Treaty of September 11, 1807, 66
Treaty of September 14, 1816, 81
Treaty of July 8, 1817, 84
Treaty of February 27, 1819, 91
Treaty of May 6, 1828, 101
Treaty of February 14, 1833, 112
Treaty of December 29, 1835, 125
Treaty of 1835, adjudication of, 183
Treaty of 1835, declared void by Cherokee, 172
Treaty of March 1, 1836, supplementary, 135
Treaty of August 6, 1846, 176
Treaty of July 19, 1866, 212
Treaty of April 27, 1808, 218
"Treaty" or "Ridge" party of Cherokee, 171
  payments to, 177
  feud of, 179, 180
Troup, Governor, on relations of Cherokee to Georgia, 109
Tyler, John M., promises settlement of difficulties with Cherokee, 174

Van Buren, Martin, offers a compromise in Cherokee affairs, 168
Vashon, George, negotiates a treaty with Cherokee, 124
Voorhees, D. W., counsel for Cherokee, 223

Waddell, Hugh, negotiates treaty of 1756 with Cherokee and Catawba, 17
Wafford's settlement, 58, 59
Wales, Samuel A., instructed by Governor Forsyth to establish Cherokee boundary line, 147
Walton, George, commissioner to treat with Cherokee, 46, 48
Washington, George, in relation to Cherokee, 33, 45
Watie, Stand, a Confederate leader in the Civil War, 176, 203, 206, 211
  confiscation act against adherents of, 221
Webster, Daniel, denounces policy toward Cherokee, 166, 168
Wellborn, Johnson, Georgia commissioner in treating with Cherokee, 108
Whitner, Joseph, surveyor of Cherokee boundary line, 37, 40
Wilkerson, William N., commissioner to appraise Indian lands, 241
Wilkinson, James, commissioner for Cherokee treaty, 56
Winchester, James, survey of Cherokee boundary line by, 26

Winchester, James—*cont.*
    commissioner for Cherokee boundary, 37
Wise, Henry A., denounce policy toward Cherokee, 167, 168
Wistar, Thomas, commissioner to treat with Indians, 219
Wool, John E., in command of troops in Cherokee Nation, 162
    report on Cherokee affairs, 165
    relieved, 168
Worcester vs. Georgia, Supreme Court decision in, 136

Yellow Creek settlement, 55